Interactive Web Applications
With Tcl/Tk

Interactive Web Applications
With Tcl/Tk

Hattie Schroeder

Michael Doyle

Eólas Technologies, Inc.
Chicago, IL

AP PROFESSIONAL
AP PROFESSIONAL is a Division of Academic Press

Boston   San Diego   New York
London   Sydney   Tokyo   Toronto

AP Professional
1300 Boylston St., Chestnut Hill, MA 02167, USA
An Imprint of Academic Press
A Division of Harcourt Brace & Company
http://www.apnet.com

United Kingdom Edition published by
ACADEMIC PRESS LIMITED
24–28 Oval Road, London NW1 7DX, GB
http://www.hbuk.cc.uk/ap/

Library of Congress Cataloging-In-Publication Data

Schroeder, Hattie.
  Interactive web applications with Tcl/Tk / Hattie Schroeder,
Michael Doyle.
      p.   cm.
    Includes index.
    ISBN 0-12-221540-0 (alk. paper). — ISBN 0-12-221541-9 (CD-ROM)
    1. TK toolkit.   2. Web sites—Design.   3. Tcl (Computer program
language) I. Doyle, Michael.   II. Title
TK5105.8885.T54S37   1997
005.2'762—dc21   97-38645
                                                          CIP

Printed in the United States of America

98   99   00   01   02   IP   9   8   7   6   5   4   3   2   1

Contents

Acknowledgements

The authors wish to acknowledge all the people who made this effort possible: Peg Doyle for doing all of the design, typography and layout for the pages of the book, and for putting up with many late nights and bleary-eyed mornings during the writing and coding phases; Roy Cantu for his encouragement and support; Clif Flynt for doing the technical review, for making many valuable coding suggestions, and for providing the clever HTML-page-parsing code for the stock ticker applications; Hengbing Duan, for helping to convert the rolodex program into a client/server application, and for doing the C coding for the gifto64 image conversion utility; Steve Wahl, for crafting many of the building blocks of the Spynergy Toolkit; Dave Roseman, for helping to test the various example applications and for providing many useful application-design suggestions; Jason Singer, Mark Swords, Paul Doyle and Maury Pescitelli, for agreeing to be our "guinea pigs" by using the book to learn Tcl/Tk from scratch; everyone at AP Professional, especially Tom Stone and Ken Morton for the acceptance of this project and for the constant encouragement, Samantha Libby for her helpful assistance, Diane Grossman and Abby Heim for their design skills and accommodating attitudes, and Thomas Park for his contributions; and, finally, the Tcl Group at Sun, especially John Ousterhout, Jacob Levy, Brent Welch and Steve Uhler, for various code examples, for providing the platform, and for doing more for the future of cross-platform interactive application development than all of the purveyors of caffeine-metaphor programming tools combined.

Introduction

If you have spent any time on the World Wide Web, you know that it is a communication medium that is not only rapidly growing, but is also developing into a multimedia showcase. Web sites with colorful graphics, animation, and embedded applications, called applets, are now expected rather than exceptional. But the Web is not just a place for interactive applets; it has also enabled the development of an entire new generation of powerful client-server Internet applications that can fetch and send data across a network for many different purposes.

Whether you use it for your business or for your hobby, this book and its CD resources can help you create interactive Web page applets and powerful server-side Internet applications with only a small amount of time and effort. Even if you don't have the experience that you think you should have, or you don't have time to learn Java® or other complex languages, you will learn how to create interactive and secure Web applications that range in capabilities from animated text to client-server applications. You don't need to be an experienced programmer. We will teach you step-by-step all you need to know to create and adapt for your own use all the applications presented in this book.

About This Book

The Web applications presented in this book are developed in Tcl/Tk. Tcl (pronounced "tickle"), the Tool Command Language, and its associated Toolkit, Tk, are widely considered to be the fastest, most powerful, and easiest way to develop cross-platform graphical user interfaces. Developers worldwide already use Tcl/Tk to create user-friendly and sophisticated applications. The characteristics of Tcl/Tk make it a natural language for the World Wide Web. With this book and the resources available on its CD, you will be able to immediately start creating powerful and secure Web applications.

In the first part of this book, "Basic Web Applets," you will learn the fundamentals of Tcl/Tk to create applets that you can incorporate immediately into your Web pages using the Tcl Plug-in from Sun Microsystems. You learn how to work with the Plug-in and how to create applets with digital signatures using Pretty Good Privacy®, a powerful encryption technology. Each chapter provides you with enough information to build the applications presented in that chapter, and also teaches you Tcl/Tk as you go, to prepare you for more advanced applications.

In the second part of this book, "Advanced Server-Based Applications," we introduce Web applications that run on servers and communicate with one or more clients. You will learn how to build a Tcl Web server and how to work with a Tcl database, using the Spynergy Toolkit, to build a client-server application and an application that pushes files over a network.

In the third part of this book, "Integrating with the Web," we cover several applications that can exist independently or as application add-ons written in Tcl/Tk. You will learn how to work with a data stream, how to parse HTML data, and how to build a Tcl/Tk Web browser using the Spynergy Toolkit that lets you display Web content in your applications. In this section we cover several examples of browser-pull applications.

The first appendix of this book, "Ed, the Tcl Code Editor," includes information on how to construct a text editor and Tcl code tester. This section gives you more information on building graphical applications in Tcl/Tk, and how to use the Spynergy Toolkit to enable your Tcl/Tk applications to connect to the Web.

This book will also introduce you to a feature included in the latest release of the Tcl Plug-in: the use of *security policies*. A security policy is a list of things that an applet can and can't do. Sun Microsystems includes a number of security policies with the release of the Tcl Plug-in 2.0. This book includes several demos using security policies.

Who can use this book

Anyone who is interested in building Web applets or client-server Web applications or learning more about Tcl/Tk and the Internet can use this book. You may be a developer interested in building Internet applications for your organization's network, or you may be interested in putting some animation on your personal Web page.

This book assumes that you have basic computer skills and some familiarity with fundamental programming, but not necessarily knowledge of Tcl/Tk. You don't have to be an experienced programmer. We will teach you the fundamentals of Tcl/Tk and get you started immediately creating interactive applets and Internet applications.

How you can use this book

We suggest that you use this book at your computer, experimenting with the examples as you read. If you don't already have Tcl/Tk, then you can install it from the CD included with this book. Chapter 2 tells you how to get started using Tcl/Tk.

If you have never worked with Tcl/Tk before, then be sure to read Chapter 2 and Chapter 3 thoroughly. Try out the examples on your computer and access the examples on the CD. There is a full directory of demo Tcl/Tk applications from the book included on the CD that you can study and manipulate.

If you are an expert at Tcl/Tk, then Chapters 4-11 that cover specific applications will get you started immediately. The first chapters cover simple applets; the final chapters focus on advanced applications that use the Spynergy Toolkit (available on the CD).

Included on the CD is the Ed Tcl Code Editor, an editing and testing application written entirely in Tcl/Tk that runs on Windows® and UNIX®. This text editor and testing environment lets you enter, search, cut, and paste Tcl/Tk script that you can test simply by clicking a button. With a connection to the Internet, you can also run applets from any location on the Web simply by entering a URL, a Uniform Resource Locater that specifies the location of a file on the Web. You can use this editor to learn Tcl/Tk and to build Tcl/Tk applications. Chapter 3 gives you more information on how to work with the Ed Tcl Editor. Appendix A shows you how the Editor is constructed, in order to give you an example for creating your own Tcl/Tk graphical applications.

Chapter Outline

Part I: Basic Web Applets

This section covers the basics of Tcl/Tk and creating simple and interactive Web applets that you can incorporate into your Web pages immediately.

Chapter 1: Introduction to Tcl/Tk Applets

Explanation of Tcl/Tk applets, Pretty Good Privacy (PGP), the benefits of Tcl/Tk. Explanation of the Tcl Plug-in and the Spynergy Plug-in. Learn how to incorporate Spynergy into your Web browser and use PGP to sign a Spynergy application.

Chapter 2: Basic Tcl

The fundamentals of Tcl/Tk, including how to install and set up Tcl/Tk on your computer. Concepts of Tcl, basic syntax, data structures, commands, variables, and how to write procedures.

Chapter 3: Tk Commands

Introduction to Tcl's Toolkit. How to build and manipulate widgets to create an interface, how to tie widgets together with procedures, bindings, and variables.

Chapter 4: Text Applications

The text widget and the canvas widget and their capacities to tag and manipulate text to create several Tcl/Tk applications. Building a ticker tape, a typewriter, sliding text, and animated text and graphics.

Chapter 5: Interactive Applications

Creating interactive animations and games with the canvas widget and text widget. How to work with images in Tcl/Tk applications.

Chapter 6: Publishing Tcl/Tk Applications

Publishing a Tcl/Tk applet on a Web page. Basic HTML and concepts of Web page development.

Part II: Advanced Server-Based Applications

This section focuses on creating graphical TCL/Tk applications that use the Internet.

Chapter 7: Building a Client-Server Database

Basic database concepts and how to use the Spynergy's Web Fusion database library. Build your own Tcl database and online Rolodex application. Learn how to use the Spynergy Remote Call Procedures to build a client-server Rolodex.

Chapter 8: The Tcl Web Server

Elements of a Web server and how you can build one with Spynergy Tcl/Tk. Learn about HTTP (Hypertext Transfer Protocol), MIME types, socket communications, and server event loops.

Chapter 9: Building a Server-Push Application

Create a server-push application that can serve files to multiple clients using the Tcl Web server and the Spynergy remote procedure calls.

Part III: Integrating with the Web

This section shows you how to design application add-ons including a stockticker that sends you e-mail, a Web browser, and an animated image map.

Chapter 10: Automated Data Retrieval and Agent Technology

Create a stockticker that retrieves, parses, and displays data as an applet or an enhancement to an application. Create a stockticker that send e-mail notofications based on the contents of the downloaded data.

Chapter 11: Building a Browser-Pull Application

The basic elements of a Web browser, and using the Spynergy HTML procedures to create a Web browser in Tcl/Tk for use as an applet, an application, or as an enhancement to an existing application. Create several browser-pull applications, including an animated image map.

Appendices:

A. Ed, the Tcl Code Editor

Create a text editor in Tcl/Tk that lets you search, copy, cut, and paste text; access files from any place on the Internet; and test Tcl code with a click of a button. Learn the basics of creating independent graphical applications in Tcl/Tk.

B. About the Spynergy Web Developer

Use the Spynergy Web Developer (a drag-and-drop GUI builder and sophisticated testing environment) from Eòlas Technologies to build your applets. Free copy of the Spynergy Web Developer available (an $80 value) with the coupon included at the end of this book. More information about the Spynergy Web Developer.

C. Pretty Good Privacy and Tcl/Tk resources

Internet shareware and professional versions of Pretty Good Privacy. Information on how to obtain PGP and references to resources, as well as references to Tcl/Tk resources.

D. CD Resources

Complete index to all the tools and programs included on the CD-Rom.

About the CD Resources

You will find a complete index of the CD in the last appendix to this book. The CD also has an HTML interface. Just access the directory of your CD-Rom and load the file `index.htm` in your Web browser.

Tcl/Tk and extensions

The CD included with this book has the most recent versions of Tcl/Tk: Tcl 7.5, 7.6, and 8.0 in source and binary code and Tk 4.2 and 8.0 in source and binary code. The CD also includes ODBC extensions for Tcl 7.5 and 7.6.

Spynergy Toolkit and Spynergy Plug-in

Also included is the Spynergy Toolkit with pure Tcl procedures for remote procedure calls, a complete database engine, and Web browsing and HTML rendering functions. The Spynergy Plug-in includes an enhanced version of Tcl/Tk that lets you create PGP-signed applets and powerful server-side applications.

The Ed Tcl Editor

The Ed Tcl Editor is written entirely in Tcl/Tk and will run on Windows® and UNIX® platforms. It is a text editor and testing environment to build Tcl/Tk applications. You will learn how to work with the Ed Tcl Editor in Chapter 3, and Appendix A shows you how it is constructed from pure Tcl code.

Image conversion tool

The Spynergy image conversion tool enables you to create inline image code from image files that you can use in Tcl/Tk graphic applications. Chapter 5 shows you how to create inline images and how to work with images in Tcl/Tk applications.

Tcl Tutor

The Tcl Tutor, developed by Clif Flynt, is available on the CD for Windows and UNIX. The Tcl Tutor is a full tutorial application that teaches Tcl step-by-step. You can set the level of detail for each Tcl lesson, and you can learn by either going through lessons sequentially or accessing lessons of your choice.

Tcl Web browser and Web server

The CD also includes a complete Tcl-based Web browser and Web server. You will learn to build and modify both of these applications for your own use in this book.

Full reference documentation

The CD also gives you full reference documentation for Tcl/Tk and Spynergy Toolkit in HTML. You can view this documentation with either the Tcl/Tk Web browser included on the CD or a Web browser of your choice. The Spynergy Tcl/Tk reference documentation is also available in a Windows help file.

Tcl/Tk applications and games

The CD includes a full directory of Tcl/Tk applications and games that are described and built in this book.

Conventions Used in This Book

We use two conventions in this book to help organize and present information.

Tcl/Tk code and file names are presented in `this font`.

 A **note** is an important bit of information that you shouldn't miss.

One Last Note About Our Approach

Even if you do not know Tcl/Tk when you first pick up this book, you will be able to learn it by studying Chapters 2 and 3, following examples and instructions. Also, you will learn more with each of the succeeding chapters, beginning with the simple text-based applets and ending with advanced, server-side applications. Each chapter is detailed and full of examples.

However, this book is not primarily a book on Tcl/Tk. We do not focus entirely on the language itself but also on how to apply it to create Web and graphical applications. We give you all the information you need to develop the applications presented in this book. You will not need to look elsewhere for information, but if you are interested in continuing your study of Tcl/Tk, there are several excellent Tcl/Tk books available, as well as online mailing groups and Web sites that support the Tcl/Tk community. See Appendix C for more details on these resources.

Finally, we would like to point out that, after developing an application that is presented in this book, you may find ways to improve on it, or you may even find that you can develop the same application more efficiently than we present it. If this happens to you, then congratulations! The best thing about Tcl/Tk is the community that supports it, a community that encourages change, freedom, and communication. It is for the Tcl/Tk community that we write this book.

Part I

Basic Web Applets

The first section of this book introduces Tcl/Tk Web applets, with information on the various Tcl Plug-ins available and how you can sign an applet with a digital signature. Chapters 1, 2, and 3 provide an overview of Tcl and a tutorial on the basic widgets of Tk. Chapters 4 and 5 cover the text widget and canvas widget in depth, developing applets that you can incorporate into your Web pages immediately. Chapter 5 also includes information on how to work with images in Tcl/Tk applications. Chapter 6 covers basic HTML to help you get started writing your own Web pages. The applications that you will learn to build include animated and moving text, a Tcl/Tk crossword and wordsearch puzzle, a Tcl/Tk calculator, a complex canvas animation using inline image data, and an applet that uses the outside security policy and the HTTP package, a feature of Tcl 8.0.

1

Introduction to Tcl/Tk Applets

What Is a Tcl/Tk Applet?

An applet is an application that is embedded within a Web page. It can have capabilities ranging from animating text and graphics to interacting with a remote server. When you visit a Web page that includes an embedded application, the Web page references the source of the applet, which means that it indicates to your Web browser where to find the applet on the remote server. It also specifies the height and width of the interface of an applet and where to place it on the page.

When you request a Web page from a remote server to view in your Web browser, you download the source of the applet as well as the source of the Web page. The applet will execute within your Web browser (assuming you have the proper plug-ins installed). The Web page and applet may look like they are together, but they are actually two separate entities. They may even be located on separate Web servers.

Most people are familiar with applets written in the Java® programming language that run using the Java Virtual Machine (a preinstalled plug-in) under Netscape Navigator™ or Microsoft Internet Explorer™. Applets can also be written in Tcl/Tk and run under the Tcl Plug-in available from Sun Microsystems, or the Spynergy Plug-in from Eòlas Technologies, which adds security through the use of digital signatures. You can use either plug-in with Netscape Navigator or the Microsoft Internet Explorer.

Tcl/Tk applets with the ".tcl" extension are sometimes called tclets. They run under the Tcl Plug-in from Sun Microsystems available from http://sunscript.sun.com. These applets run in a safe environment similar to Java applets. Tclets cannot modify your computer system and, like Java applets, do not notify the user when they are running. All the basic applets in the first section of this book are tclets and can be run using Sun's Tcl Plug-in.

About signed Tcl/Tk applets

Signed Tcl/Tk applets are applets written in Tcl/Tk that include digital signatures. To run a signed Tcl/Tk applet within a Web page, you need either the Spynergy Tcl/Tk Plug-in available on the CD, or you can use the Spynergy security policy with Sun's Tcl Plug-in version 2.0 that allows flexible security policies. You can find the Spynergy security policy on the Eòlas Technologies Tcl Web site at http://www.eolas.com/tcl.

Signed applets that run under the Spynergy Plug-in have an ".app" extension and are sometimes called *Weblets*™. Signed applets use a digital signature to enable you to confirm the source of the applet before you allow it to execute on your computer. Signed applets that use the Spynergy security policy and run under the Tcl Plug-in version 2.0 have a ".tcl" extension.

The Rouser applet that we develop in Chapter 11 of this book is an example of a Weblet. It is a powerful HTML rendering engine that enables you to embed a complete Web browser within your Web page.

Why the Spynergy Plug-in?

The Spynergy Plug-in was developed by Eòlas Technologies in late 1995 for UNIX and early 1996 for Windows. It enabled, for the first time, the use of the Tcl/Tk language for the development of interactive Web applets. The UNIX version was based upon

Tcl/Tk 7.4/4.0 and included the Tcl-DP extension in order to provide socket communications capabilities, which didn't exist at the time in the standard Tcl interpreter. We realized then that a security mechanism would need to be included that would let trusted applets tap the full power of the Tcl/Tk platform. We therefore introduced the idea of using PGP and public-key digital signatures as a mechanism for applet authentication.

The Windows version of the Spynergy Plug-in was based upon an early beta version of the 7.6/4.2 interpreter and added support for inline image data to the interpreter's capabilities. Since the socket protocol in this interpreter was incompatible with that of Tcl-DP, we built a pure-Tcl replacement that could run on top of the socket facilities in Tcl 7.5 and 7.6. This set of procedures became the "seed crystal" for the Spynergy Toolkit, which was further developed as time went on.

When the Sun Tcl Plug-in was released in the summer of 1996, Eòlas determined that having multiple versions of plug-ins would just confuse users, so further development on the Spynergy Plug-in was stopped. We intended to use the security policy capabilities of the Sun Plug-in to provide the PGP authentication capabilities that we believed to be crucial to acceptance of the Tcl applet technology as a serious contender on the Web. It is only with the recent 2.0b1 version of the Sun Plug-in, however, that the needed capabilities were added to allow the development of a Spynergy (PGP) security policy. For this reason, we decided to provide the readers of this book with the capability to use either the Spynergy Plug-in or the Sun-Plug-in-with-Spynergy-security-policy combination to allow the use of PGP digital signatures on applets. As time goes on, the advantages of the Tcl/Tk 8.0 support in the Sun Plug-in will make it preferable to use the security-policy approach for new application development.

Using Digital Signatures in Tcl/Tk Applets

A digital signature is a unique identifying code that you use to sign electronic messages and applets. With the aid of Pretty Good Privacy®, your digital signature assures the user of your message or applet that you are the creator. Pretty Good Privacy, or PGP, was created by Phil Zimmerman at the Massachusetts Institute of Technology. It is an extremely powerful encryption technology that any citizen of the United States or Canada can use. See Appendix C of this book for a list of PGP resources for obtaining and learning more about PGP.

You can use your Pretty Good Privacy private key to sign the source code of applets in the same way that you sign electronic mail messages. A PGP signature is an identifying code encrypted by your private key that can only be recognized by your public key. Public and private key pairs are encryption codes generated by PGP software. You use your private key to decrypt messages sent to you or to sign messages or applets. The companion to your private key is your public key that others use to encrypt messages to you or to recognize your digital signature. When you place a signed applet on your Web page, then a person who visits your Web page uses your public key to recognize your PGP signature.

When you view (download) a Web page that points to a Spynergy Tcl/Tk applet, the Spynergy security policy (or the Spynergy Plug-in) will look for a PGP signature. If the applet includes a PGP signature, it searches the public keyring of the user for a matching public key that will recognize the signature. If the applet is not signed or the signature is not recognized, the plug-in will ask for permission to run the applet. If the signature is recognized, the plug-in will automatically run the applet within the Web page without needing any additional permission.

Why use digital signatures?

The issue of security on the Internet is one that everyone is concerned about. As Web-based applications become more powerful and more interactive, we search for reassurance that Web pages we visit will not include applets that may damage our computer systems or internal networks.

Unsigned applets (applets that do not include digital signatures) are applications that you may normally encounter on Web pages, such as animation and simple applications. If you download a Web page containing a common Tcl/Tk applet that doesn't require a signature, then it runs immediately without asking for permission. It does not need to ask you if it can run on your system, because it is not allowed to do anything that could possibly be harmful. The Tcl Plug-in restricts unsigned applets to a "safe" version of Tcl/Tk with potentially dangerous commands removed.

However, the restrictions that protect your computer from sinister applets also limit the potential power of a Web application. If there was a way that you could verify that an applet was from a source that you trust, and if you had the opportunity to give or to withhold permission for it to run, then you could use Web-based applications that are less restricted and more powerful. Pretty Good Privacy enables you to do all these things. PGP lets a person who visits your Web page verify that an applet is really from you. If the applet's PGP signature is not recognized, then the visitor can decide whether or not to allow the applet to run. The digital signature enables you to create applets that perform powerful tasks that unsigned applets may not be allowed to perform. Applets with PGP signatures require the Spynergy Plug-in, available on the CD, or the Spynergy security policy.

There is an element of trust in the use of signed applets. You are assured of an applet's creator and the fact that the applet has not been modified by someone else, but you still must trust the person who created the applet. This functionality is not practical for simple applications like animations that you create to enhance your Web pages, but it is an absolute necessity for practical, powerful applications in networked environments.

Signing a Tcl/Tk applet

To sign a Tcl/Tk applet with a digital signature, all you need to do is sign the source code of the applet using your digital signature generated by Pretty Good Privacy software. You can then embed the application in your Web page like you would any other applet.

The source code of a signed Tcl/Tk applet begins with the line that indicates that it is signed with a PGP digital signature. This line is not preceded with the pound symbol (#) that you use to place comments in your Tcl/Tk code. The end of the file includes the digital signature.

```
-----BEGIN PGP SIGNED MESSAGE-----

#
# The complete source code for the applet is located
# here
#

-----BEGIN PGP SIGNATURE-----
Version: 2.6.2

ePFbhsiRM1FDc1E3uONiC1XGFOTi3uTUEPuniNxoCuLXnxVD4wRGP
vfusdNylwgr+aCBTSFTdKF29WnaB7RatFaM5ORtwco3smOTA3LwKh
hf9NcFP3u3wUj7cWn2QZ6mXwxsFKn7zJecf2s==s1pP

-----END PGP SIGNATURE-----
```

The version of Pretty Good Privacy that you must use to sign Tcl/Tk applets is Version 2.6.2. The Spynergy Plug-in and Spynergy security policy for the Sun Microsystems' Tcl Plug-in do not support Version 5.0 of Pretty Good Privacy.

If you run the applet under the Spynergy Plug-in, you must rename the file extension from ".tcl" to ".app". For example, an applet with the filename `sample.tcl` would be renamed to `sample.app` to run under the Spynergy Plug-in. But if you use the Spynergy security policy, you can run the applet under Sun Microsystems' Tcl Plug-in using the original file extension of ".tcl".

For more information on PGP and creating digital signatures, see Appendix C on PGP, or go to the Massachusetts Institute of Technology's PGP Web site at `http://web.mit.edu/net-work/pgp.html`.

Embedding Tcl/Tk Applets in Web Pages

To embed Tcl/Tk applications into your Web page, you simply use the HTML tag <EMBED> with arguments that specify the source, height, and width of the applet. You must specify the height and width of an applet so the Web page knows how much space it should use to display it.

The format of the EMBED tag is:

```
<EMBED SRC=filename HEIGHT=pixels WIDTH=pixels>
```

You can design Spynergy Tcl/Tk applets to run under the Spynergy Plug-in with additional arguments in the <EMBED> tag. For example, when embedding the Rouser applet (described in Chapter 11), you can specify the URL that the applet automatically displays.

Here is the source code for a simple Web page with an embedded applet. The HTML file starts and ends with the <HTML> tag, the head of the file is specified with the <HEAD> tag, and the body of the page is specified with the <BODY> tag. If these tags are unfamiliar to you, see Chapter 6 of this book for more information on basic HTML.

```
<HTML>
<HEAD>
<TITLE>
Tcl/Tk Crossword
</TITLE>
</HEAD>
<BODY BGCOLOR=#FFFFFF>
        <CENTER>

<H2> Tcl/Tk Crossword </H2>
<EMBED
SRC="http://www.eolas.com/tcl/examples/cword.tcl"
HEIGHT=299 WIDTH=222>
        </CENTER>

        </BODY>
</HTML>
```

Figure 1.1 The Tcl/Tk Crossword applet embedded in a Web page

If your Web page includes an applet needing a plug-in such as the Tcl Plug-in or the Spynergy Plug-in, you can place a link on your Web page for users to find and download the plug-in if they don't have it.

What You Need to Develop and Use Tcl/Tk Applets

When you develop applets on your own system, you need only the Tcl *wish* interpreter to run and test the applets. See the next chapter for more information on how to install and work with the wish interpreter.

You can also use the Ed Tcl Editor to write and test your Tcl/Tk code. This application, included on the CD, is written entirely in Tcl/Tk. It is a text editor and testing environment that enable you to test Tcl script simply by pressing a button. Chapter 3 tells you more about how to work with Ed. Appendix A shows you how it is constructed.

To publish Tcl/Tk applets on a Web page, you need either the Tcl Plug-in from Sun Microsystems, freely available at `http://sunscript.sun.com`, or the Spynergy Plug-in included on the CD and also available at `http://www.eolas.com/tcl/`. Sun Microsystems' Tcl Plug-in supports Tcl/Tk applets with the ".tcl" extension, while the Spynergy Plug-in supports applets with the ".app" extension. Everyone who uses your applet needs one of these two Web browser plug-ins. Both plug-ins can be installed on one Web browser without interfering with each other. The plug-ins work with both Netscape Navigator and Microsoft Internet Explorer.

You can create applets that use some of the more powerful Tcl/Tk commands and will run under the Tcl Plug-in from Sun Microsystems with an appropriate security policy. A security policy is a list of things that an applet can do. These applets still need a ".tcl" extension to be recognized by the Tcl Plug-in. This book includes a number of demos that use security policies.

To develop signed Tcl/Tk applets, you need Pretty Good Privacy 2.6.2. You can publish signed Tcl/Tk applets using either the Spynergy Plug-in or the Spynergy security policy, available at `http://www.eolas.com/tcl`, with Sun's Tcl Plug-in. To authenticate a signed Tcl/Tk applet, each user must also have Pretty Good Privacy. See Appendix C of this book on where to get PGP.

Why Use Tcl/Tk?

You may be wondering why you should use Tcl/Tk to build applets instead of using another language, such as Java. There are many characteristics of Tcl/Tk that make it a natural tool for building secure interactive Web applications quickly and easily. Tcl/Tk is easy to learn and extend and is very flexible.

One of the best things about Tcl/Tk is the community that supports it. There are over 300,000 Tcl developers worldwide. Tcl/Tk is constantly growing and changing, influenced both by John Ousterhout, the creator of Tcl/Tk, and the online Tcl/Tk community.

Other features of Tcl/Tk include:

- **Rapid development**
  Tcl is an interpreted unstructured language, which means that it has a rapid development cycle and a short learning curve. You can develop Tcl applications in one tenth the time that it would take using systems programming languages such as Java, C, and C++. Unlike Java, Tcl/Tk programs don't have to be compiled before use, so applications can be quickly debugged.

- **Cross-platform**
  Tcl applications are truly cross-platform. The same Tcl script can run on Windows®, UNIX® and Macintosh® platforms with identical functionality. With Tcl/Tk, you can create applications for the *Web platform*, with little or no concern for the differences between various operating systems.

- **Tk widgets**
  Tk (Toolkit) refers to the powerful and convenient facility in Tcl/Tk for graphical user interface development. Tk widgets provide standard high-level interface elements, such as menus, buttons, listboxes, and scrollbars, as well as megawidgets such as the text widget, the image widget, and the canvas widget. These widgets provide rich functionality for WYSIWYG text handling and powerful graphics operations. Since the Tk widget set is implemented in native code, Tcl/Tk GUI-based applications routinely display higher performance than similar programs developed with the Java programming language.

- **Application integration**
  You can easily adapt existing legacy applications to Tcl/Tk through a powerful C/C++ application programming interface (API). This enables you to create Tcl/Tk extensions that applets and server scripts load at runtime. In this way, Tcl/Tk becomes the glue that binds many heterogeneous application components into large, stable, well-integrated network applications.

About the Spynergy Toolkit

The Spynergy Toolkit is a set of Tcl/Tk procedures that can run under Sun's Tcl interpreter and the Spynergy Plug-in. These procedures add a large number of functions to Tcl that allow you to build powerful features into your Tcl/Tk applications, including:

- **Socket communications and distributed processing**
  The Spynergy Toolkit provides powerful network communications tools. The support of full socket communications enables you to develop new generations of Internet applications rapidly. Remote procedure calls (RPCs) allow applets to access transparently powerful remote server scripts. Server-side scripts can coordinate the actions of many types of servers to cooperate and process large computations. Combining Spynergy's RPC facility with dynamically loaded legacy-data-access extensions allows the rapid development of powerful, secure, and stable enterprise-wide applications.

- **Web browsing and HTML rendering**
  The Spynergy Toolkit has powerful HTML libraries and Web browsing capabilities. Documents in HTML format can be easily rendered for viewing, in fully browserable form, enabling you to embed Web-browsing capabilities in any Tcl/Tk application interface.

- **Integrated server-side application code database and repository**
  Spynergy's very easy-to-use, flexible, yet powerful database engine can be called from within any applet or servlet application. A new database and data table can be created, opened, accessed, modified, and closed in fewer than 10 lines of code.

Tcl/Tk versus Java

After reading about all that Tcl/Tk and Spynergy Tcl/Tk has to offer Web developers, you may still be thinking, "But what about

Java?" Java is the best-known Internet programming language. Like Tcl/Tk applets, Java applets are portable across platforms, making Java an excellent candidate for the Web's standard systems programming language.

But there are several reasons to choose Tcl/Tk over Java to develop your Web applications. Some of these reasons are:

- **Power and flexibility**

  Applets developed in Tcl/Tk can be as powerful as Java applets. Plus, Tcl/Tk applets are not compiled, but commands are executed at runtime. This lets you develop applications that can modify how they operate at runtime, depending, for example, on the current value of some rapidly-changing data available over the Web. This gives you more flexibility than many Java applications.

- **PGP Signatures**

  Java does not currently support signed applets, while the Spynergy Plug-in does. You are therefore able to provide additional security and privacy to your Web applications.

- **Easy to learn and use**

  Similar to C++, Java is a difficult language for the lay programmer to learn. Tcl/Tk is simple to understand and much easier to use.

- **Short development cycle**

  Applets created in Java typically have a much longer development cycle than those built with Tcl/Tk. Tcl/Tk applets do not need to be compiled before running, and Tcl script is therefore easier to debug than Java code.

Tcl/Tk's ease of use and flexibility, combined with the functionality of the Spynergy Toolkit and Spynergy Plug-in, will enable you to develop Web applets and Internet applications that are secure, reliable, and powerful enough to meet any of your needs.

Conclusion

We have introduced Tcl/Tk applets, including the tools you need to create them, how to embed them into Web pages, and how to sign them using Pretty Good Privacy digital signatures. We hope that we have also convinced you of the value of using Tcl/Tk to develop Web applets and Internet applications.

The next four chapters of this book introduce Tcl and help you get started creating Web applets in Tcl/Tk.

2

Basic Tcl

Introducing Tcl/Tk

Tcl stands for Tool Command Language, Tk for the associated Toolkit. Tcl/Tk was created and designed by Professor John Ousterhout of the University of California, Berkeley in 1989. First imagined as an extension language to configure applications and perform other high-level tasks, Tcl's reputation has since grown because of its portability and strength. You can write complete applications in this easy-to-use scripting language. The Spynergy Web Developer from Eòlas Technologies is an example of an entire application written in Tcl/Tk, as well as the Ed Tcl Editor included on the CD with this book.

Tcl/Tk is free and readily available. The latest versions of Tcl/Tk are on the CD packaged with this book. Tcl/Tk is also available on the World Wide Web for all platforms on Sun's Tcl Web site at `http://sunscript.sun.com/`.

Getting Tcl/Tk and getting started

Before you get started developing Web applications, you need to install Tcl/Tk and the *wish* interpreter, if it is not already a part of your system.

You can install Tcl/Tk 8.0 or Tcl 7.6/Tk 4.2. There are several differences between these two versions. One of the most noticeable differences is that graphical applications developed in Tcl/Tk 8.0 adopt a native "look and feel" when running on a particular platform. This means that when a Tcl/Tk graphical application runs on a Windows operating system, it adopts native colors to appear as a Windows application, while on a Macintosh platform it will appear as a typical application designed for the Macintosh. You may or may not want to use this feature in your applications. If you want your application to appear consistent across all platforms, then you should develop in Tcl 7.6/Tk 4.2.

Tcl/Tk 8.0 also supports inline images, like the current Tcl Plug-in. This means that you can specify image data within the source of your Tcl code for your graphical applications; you do not need to refer to an image file. Chapter 5 explains more about inline images and how to work with them.

Most of the other applications developed in this book operate similarly for both versions of Tcl/Tk, except when noted. There are other differences between the two versions that may have impact on other applications you develop. You can find a complete list of all the differences between these two versions and other versions on Sun's Tcl Web site at `http://sunscript.sun.com/`.

On the CD included with this book, locate the Tcl file appropriate for your platform.

Windows 3.1, Windows 95, and Windows NT
> **win80.exe** - Installs Tcl/Tk 8.0
> **win76.exe** - Installs Tcl 7.6/Tk 4.2

1. Run this self-extracting executable on your system. To run the executable, you can double-click on its name, or you can run it from the command line. (If you are using Windows 95, select the Run option from the Start menu)
2. The installation program will install the Tcl and Tk libraries, the wish and tclsh programs, and reference documentation.

Macintosh (both 68K and PowerPC):
mactk8.0.sea.hqx Installs Tcl/Tk 8.0
mactk4.2.sea.hqx Installs Tcl 7.6/Tk 4.2

1. Double-click on the name of this file. It is a self-installing executable. The file is in binhex format, which is understood by Fetch, StuffIt, and many other Mac utilities.
2. The installation program will create a folder containing the Tcl and Tk libraries, the wish and tclsh programs, and reference documentation.

UNIX (Solaris, Sun, Linux)
tcl8.0.tar.z - Installs Tcl 8.0
tk8.0.tar.z - Installs Tk 8.0
tcl7.6.tar.z - Installs Tcl 7.6
tk4.2.tar.z - Installs Tk 4.2

Decompress and untar the pair of files for the desired version. The software will be unpacked into a directory.

Working with the wish interpreter

To open a live Tcl console, run the wish interpreter. *Wish* stands for "Window Shell." It is a Tcl interpreter that has Tk already loaded into it, so it understands both Tcl and Tk commands. The *tclsh* interpreter understands only Tcl commands. You should work with the wish interpreter to use the Tk commands to build graphical interfaces.

Finding the wish interpreter

You can find the wish interpreter executable in the `bin` subdirectory of the directory on your computer where Tcl is located. The name of your Tcl directory will be Tcl or Tcl76 for Tcl 7.6.

The name of the executable that runs the wish interpreter is `wish42.exe` or `wish80.exe`. The last two digits are the version number of the interpreter.

For example, if you are working on the Windows 95 operating system, then you may find the wish interpreter executable under C: /Program Files/Tcl76/bin/. You will also find the Tcl folder on your Program menu.

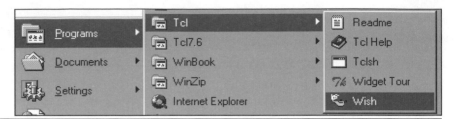

Figure 2.1 Finding the wish interpreter on Windows 95

Running the program

To run the wish interpreter, you can double-click on the name `wish80.exe` if your platform is Windows or Macintosh, or you can run the program from your command line. If your platform is Windows 95, you can run the interpreter from your Program menu.

When you run the wish interpreter, two windows appear. One is a console window, where you will type your commands after the prompt %. The other window is a "toplevel" window, where any graphical elements of your Tcl/Tk commands, such as a button or listbox, will appear. The toplevel shows the various Tk widgets that make up the GUI (Graphical User Interface) portion of the Tcl/Tk script that you type in the console.

Figure 2.2 The console and toplevel window on Windows 95

After you run the wish interpreter, you can start typing commands in the console and see their results immediately. For this chapter, we will use the wish interpreter for examples of Tcl commands. In the next chapter, we will work with the Ed Tcl Editor to build Tcl/Tk widgets and to show you how you can use this editing and testing environment to develop your Tcl/Tk applications.

Syntax

Tcl/Tk is a text-oriented command language. It treats all commands and arguments as text. To write a Tcl/Tk program, you simply write one command after another. A command is either a built-in Tcl or Tk command, or a user-defined procedure. Commands are executed in the order given and according to *grouping* and *substitution* rules. You will learn more about the benefits and specifics of grouping and substitution rules later in this chapter.

The basic syntax of Tcl/Tk is a command followed by arguments:

```
command arg1 arg2 arg3....
```

Here is a simple example:

Type in the wish interpreter after the prompt:

```
% puts stdout "Hello World"
==> Hello World
```

 Note: Don't type the "%." That is the console prompt, indicating that the console is waiting for a command. The "==>" is the notation we use to show what is returned by the interpreter.

The Tcl command puts that is used in this example has the form:

```
puts channel string
```

It writes the string ("Hello World") to a channel, stdout (standard output). Here, the standard output is the next line in the interpreter. The standard output may be defined differently in a particular application.

Notice the double quotes around the string argument, "Hello World." The double quotes group the string into one argument. If you don't include the double quotes, the interpreter assumes that each word is a separate argument. (Try the command again without the quotes and see what happens.)

The arguments of a command may be required, or they may be optional. Usually, optional arguments begin with a single dash "-". These optional arguments are sometimes called switches.

Creating a button

This next example creates a Tk widget, a button. It uses the two Tk commands button and pack.

Example:

Type into the wish interpreter:

```
% button .b -text "Push me"
==> .b
% pack .b
```

When you type this example into the Tcl/Tk interpreter, a button will appear in the toplevel window.

These two commands look different from the first example that used the command puts, but they actually have the same syntax as puts. The Tk command button has the form:

```
button name options?
```

The command is button, and the arguments are name and various options. In this example, the name of the widget is .b, and the -text option specifies what text will appear on the button.

The name argument is required. But the `-text` option is not required. You can create a button that has no text, but not a button that has no name.

The second command in this example, `pack`, specifies how the button will be placed in the main window. The pack command has the form:

```
pack name options?
```

The command is `pack`, and the arguments are `name` and various `options`. The `name` argument is required, but additional options that we didn't use in this example, such as `-anchor` (the corner of the widget that anchors it), are optional and have default values.

In Tk commands, the name of the widget is always a required argument. You will learn more about `button` and `pack` in the next chapter on Tk commands.

You can enhance the basic syntax of Tcl/Tk by using substitution and grouping rules that are discussed in the following sections. Once you master these rules, you will be able to understand and eventually write any Tcl program.

Special symbols in Tcl: Line continuation and comments

Tcl supports several symbols to help you create readable and manageable code.

The backslash "\" lets you break up a line of code. In general, a Tcl or Tk command and its arguments must be on the same line, except when an argument is enclosed by curly braces. For example, the Tk command button can have up to 27 arguments. All of these arguments must be on the same line. But you can use the backslash to join arguments on different lines.

This one long line:

```
button  .b   -relief raised -activebackground
lightblue -activeforeground red -disabledfore-
ground grey -text "Push me" -state normal -back-
ground white -foreground black -command {.b con-
fig -background green}
```

can be converted to:

```
button   .b    -relief raised \
  -activebackground lightblue \
  -activeforeground red        \
  -disabledforeground grey     \
  -text "Push me"              \
  -state normal                \
  -background white            \
  -foreground black            \
  -command {.b config -background green}
```

Using this symbol creates readable code that is easy to modify.

The backslash also lets you quote special characters. For example, if you want to place a dollar sign "$" in your script, but you don't want the Tcl interpreter to try to perform variable substitution, then you precede the dollar sign with the backslash. It causes the Tcl interpreter to read the dollar sign as a character. Typing "\$" results in "$".

Another convention is to put comments in your code using the pound sign "#". The Tcl interpreter ignores anything after a pound sign.

```
#   This is a button

button .b1 -foreground black -background white

#   This is another button

button .b2 -foreground blue -background white

# These are the buttons packed

pack .b1 .b2
```

You will see the use of comments in the examples throughout this book.

Variables

This section will introduce you to variables and the commands that you use to manage them.

Like most programming languages, Tcl uses *variables* to manage information. A variable is a string that stores a value. A variable can store a value or list of values.

 Note: Remember that variables are stored and treated as strings, whatever their values may be.

You determine a name of a variable as well as its value. The name of a variable is case-sensitive, can be any length, and can contain any alphanumeric character. You can use some symbols as well, such as an underscore "_". However, many symbols have special meaning for Tcl, such as the backslash "\", the dollar sign "$", and the pound sign "#". You should not use these symbols in your variable names.

To declare and assign a value to a variable, you use the command set.

set

The Tcl command set assigns a value to a variable:

```
% set var1 3
==> 3
```

This command declares a variable as well as assigns a value to it. Unlike many other programming languages, Tcl does not require you to declare a variable as a separate step before you use it.

Variable substitution

Once a variable has a value, you can obtain that value with the use of a dollar sign.

This example uses the command puts that we saw before, and returns the value of the variable.

```
% puts $var1
==> 3
```

Obtaining the value of a variable with a dollar sign is an example of *variable substitution*. Variable substitution gives you a lot of flexibility and you will use it again and again as you learn Tcl.

The next example shows that you can assign the value of one variable to the value of another using variable substitution:

```
% set var2 $var1
==> 3
```

unset

The command unset removes a variable's value, causing it to be unrecognized by the interpreter.

Type into your interpreter:

```
% unset var1
```

After you unset a variable, it is "forgotten" by the interpreter, but the results from any commands that previously used the variable remain. For example, the second variable still retains the value that it received from the first variable in the example on variable substitution, but the first variable is now not recognized.

```
% puts $var1
==> can't read "var1": no such variable

% puts $var2
==> 3
```

append

The command append sets a variable to the original value of the variable with other specified value or values appended to its end.

```
% append var2 5
==> 35
```

```
% append var2 6 1
==> 3561
```

 Note: This command does not add the values *mathematically*, but simply adds the values that you specify to the end of the original value of the variable.

You can use this command with alphabetical text as well.

```
% set text_string "Hello"
==> Hello
```

```
% append text_string " there"
==> Hello there
```

incr

The command `incr` adds a specified integer to the value of a variable.

For example, here the value is increased by 4.

```
% incr var2 4
==> 3565
```

If you do not specify an integer, then the default integer is 1.

```
% incr var2
==> 3566
```

You can also add a negative number:

```
% incr var2 -50
==> 3516
```

A number of Tcl's basic commands necessarily involve the use of variables and variable substitution, such as the looping commands that we discuss later in this chapter. You will find that they are

essential when you start writing your own Tcl procedures and
designing applications.

Tcl Commands

Introduction

Tcl supports built-in commands that make it possible, among
other things, to perform mathematical calculations, declare variables and procedures, manage Tcl files, control the flow of the program with loop and conditional commands, and work with lists
by adding, deleting, sorting, and scanning elements. See the end of
this chapter for a full list of built-in Tcl commands.

We will go into detail about several different types of commands, but touch lightly on others. For full reference information
on all Tcl commands, see the on-line Tcl reference documentation
included on the CD.

A careful study of Tcl commands will enable you to understand the more sophisticated examples presented later in this
book.

Command substitution

Before you get started learning about Tcl commands in depth, you
should know about command substitution. We have already seen
several examples of command subsitution.

Command substitution lets you substitute the results of a command as an argument for another command. When you place an
argument of a command in square brackets, everything inside
those square brackets is resolved before the rest of the command is
interpreted.

This example substitutes the value of an expression for an
argument of the command puts:

```
% set x 4
==>  4
```

```
%  puts [expr $x + 9]
==> 13
```

The command `expr` evaluates a mathematical expression and returns a value. It is often useful when working with arrays. We discuss arrays in the following sections.

List commands

The list is a primary data structure of Tcl/Tk. The list commands manage lists by adding, deleting, sorting, and scanning elements. Lists and list commands are easy to understand and very useful.

Indices

You can retrieve information from a list using the *indices* of the list elements. A list numbers its elements from 0 to the length of the list. The index of a list element specifies its place in the list. Several list commands including `lsearch`, `lrange`, and `lindex` use indices to give you information.

Creating a list: list, split, join, concat

You can create a list by specifying arguments, splitting a string, or joining two or more lists.

list

The command `list` creates a list out of its arguments. In this example, you assign a variable to a list. Using a variable to represent a list is a good idea when working with lists and list commands.

```
% set example_list [list  A B C DE]
==> A B C DE
```

split

The command `split` also creates a list. It takes a string and splits it at a specified character. It returns a proper Tcl list. The form of the split command is `split  string  char`, where char is the character at which it splits the string.

In this example, the command splits the string at the character ".".

```
% split "www.eolas.com"  .
==> www eolas com
```

In this example, the second argument of `split` is an empty string. It splits the string into a list with each character as a separate element.

```
% split "Hi, I'm a string." {}
==> H i , {} I ' m {} a {} s t r i n g .
```

join

The command `join` accomplishes the reverse of `split`. It creates a string from a list by joining the list elements together with a specified character.

```
% join $example_list 1
==> A1B1C1DE
```

```
% join $example_list .
==> A.B.C.DE
```

 Note: The original list, `example_list`, is unaffected by this command. It retains its original value.

concat

You can create a new list by joining two or more existing lists. The command `concat` creates a list by joining two or more existing lists together.

```
% concat $example_list {J K LMN}
==> A B C DE J K LMN
```

The example_list is unaffected. The list created by the command concat is a new list that you can assign to a new variable.

```
% puts $example_list
==> A B C DE
```

```
% set new_list [concat $example_list {J K LMN}]
==> A B C DE J K LMN
```

```
% puts $new_list
==> A B C DE J K LMN
```

Creating a new list by changing old lists: lreplace, linsert, lappend

You can change specific elements or insert new elements into a list. The commands lreplace and linsert will create new lists and leave intact the lists they use as arguments.

lreplace

The command lreplace replaces an element of a specified index with a new element. It has the form:

```
lreplace list first last element
```

The arguments first and last name the indices of the list that will be replaced by element.

In this example, you replace the elements between and including the indices 0 and 1, the first two elements.

```
% lreplace $example_list 0 1 F
==> F F C DE
```

If you want to replace only one element, then you specify the first and last indices with the same number.

```
% lreplace $example_list 0 0 F
==> F B C DE
```

If you do not specify an element to add to the list, then the elements at the specified indices will be deleted.

```
% lreplace $example_list 0 0
==> B  C  DE
```

Notice that the original list remains unchanged.

```
% puts $example_list
==> A  B  C  DE
```

You can retain the value of the new list by creating a variable and assigning its value to the results of this command.

```
% set new_list [lreplace $example_list 0 0 F]
==> F  B  C  DE
```

```
% puts $new_list
==> F  B  C  DE
```

linsert

The command `linsert` inserts a new element at a specified index.

```
% linsert $example_list 0 E
==> E  A  B  C  DE
```

This command increases the length of the list, and will move elements that follow the inserted character to new indices.

It also will not affect the original list, but will create a new list that you can assign to a variable.

```
% puts $example_list
==> A  B  C  DE
```

```
% set $new_longer_list [linsert $example_list 0 E]
==> E  A  B  C  DE
```

lappend

The command `lappend` adds any values that you specify to the
end of a list. Unlike `lreplace` and `linsert`, however, it changes
the value of the old list to the new list it creates.

```
% lappend example_list F G
==> A B C DE F G

% puts $example_list
==> A B C DE F G
```

Retrieving information from a list: llength, lsearch, lrange, lindex

These commands enable you to get information about a list, such
as its length, its range of values, or the index of a specific element.

llength

The command `llength` returns the number of elements in a list.

```
% puts $example_list
==> A B C DE F G

% llength $example_list
==> 6
```

Notice that the element "DE" of the `example_list` is one element. Elements are separated by spaces. You can include an empty
string as an element by placing quotes or braces around the space.

```
% set space_list [linsert $example_list 0 { }]
==> { } A B C DE F G
```

lsearch

The command `lsearch` will search a list for an element that
matches a specified pattern. This command uses glob-style pattern

matching. See the following section on the switch command for more information about glob-style pattern matching.

The command lsearch returns the index of the element that matches the specified pattern.

In this example, the -exact switch searches the list for an element that exactly matches the pattern.

```
% puts $example_list
==> A  B  C  DE  F  G
```

```
% lsearch -exact $example_list C
==> 2
```

In this example, the command using the -glob switch will return the indices of any element that matches the specified pattern.

```
% lsearch -glob $example_list [A-C]
==> 0  1  2
```

lrange

The command lrange returns the elements between and including the specified indices. It has the form:

```
lrange list ?first? ?last?
```

First and last are the indices between which it collects elements.

In this example, the command returns the element at index 0, at index 1, and at index 2.

```
lrange $example_list 0 2
==> A  B  C
```

lindex

The command lindex simply returns the element of the list at the specified index.

```
lindex $example_list 3
==> DE
```

If there is no element at the specified index, then it returns an empty string.

```
lindex $example_list 6
==>
```

Table 2.1 Summary of list commands

Command	Function
list	Create a list
concat	Join lists together
split	Split a string into a proper Tcl list
lappend	Append list elements onto a variable
lindex	Retrieve an element from a list
linsert	Insert elements into a list
llength	Count the number of elements in a list
lrange	Return one or more adjacent elements from a list
lreplace	Replace elements in a list with new elements
lsearch	Search a list for a particular element
lsort	Sort the elements of a list
join	Create a string by joining together list elements

String commands

In addition to list commands, Tcl also includes the string command with many options. Most options are similar to the list commands. With the string command, you can sort, manage, and manipulate strings much in the same way that you can sort, manage, and manipulate lists.

The string command has the form:

```
string operation name -options?
```

The following is a summary of the string command operations.

Comparing two strings: compare, first, last

```
string compare string1 string2
```

compares two strings, and returns -1, 0, or 1, depending on whether the first string is lexicographically less than, equal to, or greater than the second.

```
string first string1 string2
```

searches the second string for a sequence of characters that exactly match the characters in the first. If a match is found, it returns the index of the first character in the first match in string2. If it is not found, it returns -1.

```
string last string1 string2
```

searches the second string for a sequence of characters that exactly match the characters in the first. If a match is found, it returns the index of the first character in the last match in string2. If there is no match, then it returns -1.

Retrieving a character from a string: index, range

```
string index string char
```

returns the character with the index specified by char of the string.

```
string range string first last
```

returns a range of consecutive characters from string, between and including the first and last characters.

Retrieving the index of a character: wordend, wordstart

```
string wordend string index
```

returns the index of the character just after the last one in the word containing the specified index. A word is considered to be any contiguous range of alphanumeric or underscore characters, or any single character.

```
string wordstart string index
```

returns the index of the first character in the word containing the specified index. A word is considered to be any contiguous range of alphanumeric or underscore characters, or any single character other than these.

Retrieving information about the string: length, match

```
string length string
```

returns the number of characters in the specified string.

```
string match pattern string
```

determines if the specified pattern matches the string; returns 1 if it does, 0 if it doesn't. Uses glob-style pattern matching.

Modifying a string: tolower, toupper, trim, trimleft, trimright

```
string tolower string
```

returns the `string` with all uppercase letters converted to lower case.

```
string toupper string
```

returns the `string` with all lowercase letters converted to upper case.

```
string trim string ?chars?
```

returns the string with any beginning or ending characters from the set of chars removed. If chars is not specified then white space is removed (spaces, tabs, newlines, and carriage returns).

```
string trimleft string ?chars?
```

returns the string with any beginning characters from the set of chars removed. If chars is not specified then white space is removed (spaces, tabs, newlines, and carriage returns).

```
string trimright string ?chars?
```

returns the string with any trailing characters from the set of chars removed. If chars is not specified, then white space is removed (spaces, tabs, newlines, and carriage returns).

Arrays and the Array Command

One of the basic data structures in Tcl is the *associative* array. This is different from many other languages, so even if you have programming experience, you may have never worked with associative arrays.

A variable that holds a set of *variables* and *values* represents an associative array. Arrays make it possible to manage a large list of related variables. An associative array has one name that you use with array commands to get information and configure the array. Each element in the array has the form arrayname(variable), where arrayname is the name of the array. Each element of an array is represented by a different variable

You can treat an array variable as you would a standard variable for many commands. For example, you can set a single element of an array using the set command:

```
% set fruit(1) apple
==> apple
```

In this manner, you can set any number of elements of the same array:

```
% set fruit(2) banana
==> banana
% set fruit(3) orange
==> orange
% set fruit(4) grape
==> grape
% set fruit(5) cherry
==> cherry
```

The value of a single element of an array also be obtained by variable substitution using the dollar sign, as with standard variables:

```
% puts $fruit(4)
==> grape
```

In this example, you are dealing with only a single element. If you try to obtain the value of the entire array with variable substitution, you will generate an error:

```
% puts $fruit
==> can't read "fruit": variable is array
```

The more efficient way to create arrays is to use the command `array set`. With the command `array set`, you can create and set the values of an array using an organized list of values and variables. The list should be organized in the form `{ variable1 value1 variable2 value2 variable3 value3...}`.

For example:

```
% array set info {
      firstname Jane
      lastname  Doe
```

```
city        Chicago
zip   60614
        }
```

Now you have the entire array info. You can get the value of any element in the array info:

```
% puts $info(lastname)
==> Doe

% puts $info(city)
==> Chicago

% puts "$info(firstname) $info(lastname) lives \
    in  $info(city), $info(zip)."
==> Jane Doe lives in Chicago, 60614.
```

Arrays let you keep track of large numbers of variables easily. When working with arrays containing three or four elements like our example arrays, it may be just as easy to work with those variables independently. But think of arrays of database entries containing five hundred elements. You can easily manage a large group of related variables with array commands.

Another situation in which array variables are useful is when the variable of each element is an integer that you can treat as an *index*.

The index of an array can be the result of a *variable substitution* or *command substitution*.

Example:

First, declare an array and set a variable:

```
% array set color {
    1 black
    2 blue
    3 red
```

```
    4 purple
        }
```

```
% set v 1
==> 1
```

In the next example, the index of an array is the result of *variable substitution*:

```
% puts $color($v)
==> black
```

Here, the index of an array is the result of command substitution:

```
% puts $color([expr $v +1])
==> blue
```

The command `expr` evaluates a mathematical expression and returns its value.

Arrays can be a little confusing if you've never worked with them before, but these examples and the section later in this chapter that explains array commands will aid you.

Array commands

The array command is a powerful tool that enables you to manage arrays easily.

It has the form:

```
array operation name -options?
```

The command is `array`, and the `operation` is the operation to be performed on the array specified by `name`. The operation can be one of `set, get, exist, startsearch, nextelement, anymore, donesearch, names,` and `size`.

Setting and obtaining array elements: array set , array get, array names

You have already read about array variables, and seen an example of the array command, `array set`.

array set

This command uses a list containing pairs of elements. The first member in each pair is the variable or index of an array element, and the second member of each pair is the value of the same array element. It requires this list as an argument.

Creating an array:

```
% array set color {
        1 black
        2 blue
        3 red
        4 purple
        5 green
        6 white
            }
```

array get

The command `array get` returns a list of paired variables and values in the same form as the argument that you supply to `array set`.

```
%   array get color
==> 4 purple 5 green 1 black 6 white 2 blue 3
red
```

Notice that the list that `array get` returns is not in any obvious order.

Note: As we mentioned before, this is very different from other programming languages that have fixed arrays. Associated arrays have no order. An element of an associated array is only associated with its variable, not with its place in the array.

array names

You can obtain the list of array indices with the `array names` command. The command `array names` can search the indices of an array using glob-style pattern matching. For more information about glob-style pattern matching, see the following section on the `switch` command.

```
% array names color 4
==> 4
```

This command will seem more useful if you consider the case where the variables in your array are not integers.

For example, set the following array.

```
% array set personal {
     firstname "Joe"
     lastname "Smith"
     address "555 American Lane"
     city "Anywhere USA"
     companyname "US Systems"
     petname "Spot"
     }
```

If you are interested in an element of the array, but didn't know the exact name of the variable to look for, you could use array names to get all the variables that matched a specified pattern.

```
array names personal *name*
==> firstname lastname companyname petname
```

This command can be useful for very large arrays. You can use similar variables to group-related values within arrays.

Verifying arrays: array exist and array size

The command `array exist` returns True (1) if the array exists, meaning that it contains at least one element having a value, and False (0) if the array has no elements.

```
% array exist color
==> 1

% array exist no_array
==> 0
```

The command `array size` returns the number of elements in an array.

```
% array size color
==> 6
```

Searching through arrays: array startsearch, array nextelement, array anymore, array donesearch

You can search through arrays with the commands `array startsearch`, `array nextelement`, `array anymore`, and `array donesearch`.

These examples use the array created in the `color` example from our discussion of array variables.

array startsearch

The command `array startseach` initiates a search through an array. It returns a string that is a search ID. You can use the search ID with other array commands to progress and end the search.

```
% array startsearch color
==> s-1-color
```

The search ID the interpreter returned for this example is "s-1-color." Your interpreter may return something slightly different. The interpreter is simply using an identifier to use other array commands and to distinguish the search from other searches of the same array.

You can set the search ID to a variable for use with the other commands:

```
% set id [array startsearch color]
s-1-color
```

array nextelement

The command `array  nextelement` takes as arguments the name of the array and the search ID. It returns the first element of the array that has not been returned yet for this particular search.

```
% array nextelement color $id
==> 4
```

```
% array nextelement color $id
==> 1
```

```
% array nextelement color $id
==> 5
```

Notice that the elements are being returned in the same order as the organization of the list returned by `array  get` in the previous example.

array anymore

The command `array  anymore` returns true if there are any remaining elements of the array not yet returned by `array  nextelement`. Its arguments are the name of the array and the search ID.

```
% array anymore color $id
==> 1
```

Notice that it does not return the elements that have yet to be identified, but only indicates if these elements exist. This is useful when you are searching through large arrays. You don't need to keep count of how many elements are in the array at any point; you can use this command to check if there are any elements left to examine.

array donesearch

The command `array donesearch` will end a search, even if there are elements that remain unidentified:

```
% array donesearch color $id
```

This command also disposes of the search ID, so if you try to look for the next element of a search, it will not recognize it:

```
% array nextelement color $id
==> couldn't find search "s-1-color"
```

Arrays are useful data structures for a variety of applications. You will use them in Chapter 4, when creating text-based applications. They will be important in the latter half of this book as well when you learn how to design server-side applications, so it is a good idea to get the hang of them now if you've never worked with them before.

Summary of array commands (for more details, view the online reference documentation)

Creating arrays and retrieving information about arrays

`array set name list`	Sets the values of elements in name. The list must be an even number of elements, pairs of variables, and values
`array get name`	Returns a list containing pairs of elements. Each pair is a variable (index) and a value of an array element
`array names name ?pattern?`	Returns a list containing the names of all of the elements in the array that match a pattern, if given

| `array exists` *name* | Returns 1 if name is an array variable, 0 if there is no array by that name |
| `array size` *name* | Returns a decimal string giving the number of elements in the array. If name isn't the name of an array, then 0 is returned |

Searching through arrays

`array startsearch` name	Starts a search through the array *name*. This command returns a `search ID` to use with the other search commands
`array anymore name` *searchId*	Returns 1 if there are any more elements left to be processed in an arraysearch, 0 if all elements have already been returned
`array donesearch` name *searchId*	Terminates an array search and destroys all the states associated with that search
`array nextelement` *name searchId*	Returns the name of the next element in name, or an empty string if all elements of name have already been returned in this search

Flow Control Commands

In the previous section, you learned about commands that determine and manage the values of variables, lists, and arrays. This section will introduce you to commands that serve another purpose. They direct the flow of the script.

Flow control commands are essential to a Tcl/Tk application. As you will see in the next chapter on Tk commands, flow control commands enable you to tie widgets together to create interactive applications.

A flow control command is a command that executes another command when some criterion is met. Commands that appear within the body of flow control commands are grouped with curly braces.

For example, the conditional command if has the basic form:

```
if expression then body else body2
```

The if command tests the expression. If it is true, it executes body. If it is not true, it executes body2. You can find examples of the if command in the following sections.

Flow control commands include conditional commands (if, switch), looping commands (for, while, foreach), and specific control commands (continue, break, catch).

But before you look at each of these commands, you should understand *expressions*. Expressions set the criteria that determines which command gets executed in a flow control command.

Expressions

Commands that control the flow of the script rely upon *expressions*. Expressions return True or False, based on either a comparison of two values with an *operator*, or as the result of a command substitution. A flow control command will execute different commands as a result of an expression returning True or False.

When an expression returns True, it might return "1," "Y," "true," or some variant, such as "True" or "TRUE." All these options have the same meaning. Similarly, False may be expressed as "0," "N," "false," or a variant such as "False" or "FALSE."

Operators in expressions

An operator makes a direct comparison of two values. One value is usually the result of a variable substitution, the other value is usually (but not always) a fixed value. You can think of an expression as something that tests how the value of a certain variable compares with a fixed value.

Table 2.2 Operators that Tcl recognizes

Operator	Meaning
v1 == v2	True if v1 is equal to v2
v1 != v2	True if v1 is not equal to v2
v1 < v2	True if v1 is less than v2
v1 > v2	True if v1 is greater than v2
v1 <= v2	True if v1 is less than or equal to v2
v1 >=v2	True if v1 is greater than or equal to v2
!v1	True if v1 is 0
v1 && v2	True if both v1 and v2 are nonzero
v1 || v2	True if either v1 or v2 are nonzero

Usually you would use these operators to compare two numbers or integers. But the values being compared don't need to be numbers or integers; they can be text if the operator used in the expression is "==". Tcl treats both text and numbers as strings.

For example, all of the following are valid expressions:

```
{ $t == 1 }
{ $t =="Banana" }
{ $t <= [expr $v +3]}
```

The last expression listed above uses *command substitution.*

Command substitution in expressions

Expressions can also be the result of *command substitution* that uses no operator at all.

For example, the Tcl command regexp examines a string and compares it with a specified pattern. The string can be text or numbers, or a combination of both.

The following are valid expressions:

```
{[regexp 2|7 $t]}
{[regexp 2? $t]}
```

These expressions will return True(1) if the value of the variable *t* matches the pattern. Notice the square brackets around the command. The square brackets indicate that the result of the command must be substituted before the expression is evaluated.

See the following section on the `switch` command for more information about regular expression syntax.

We will see many more examples of expressions as we discuss flow control commands.

Conditional commands: if, switch

As we saw earlier, conditional commands evaluate an expression, and execute a command based on the outcome of that expression.

if

The `if` command is a common conditional construct that you will find in most programming languages.

The syntax of the command is:

```
if expression then body1 else body2
```

You can omit "then" and "else" if desired.

Here's a simple example:

```
if { $t == 1 } {
        set var "Apples"
        } else {
        set var "Oranges"
        }
```

This example tests the value of the variable *t* to determine the value of the variable `var`. If the value of *t* is equal to 1, then the value of var is set to "Apples." If the value of *t* is not equal to 1, then the value of var is set to "Oranges."

You can also test more than one expression within a single if command. For example, the form of the if command can be expanded to:

```
if expression body1 elseif expression body2 else
body3
```

Adding onto the example above,

```
if { $t == "Banana" } {
    set var "Apples"
    }  elseif  {$t =="Grapes"} {
    set var "Oranges"
    } else {
    set var "Bananas"
    }
```

These are very simple examples. When you start designing the applications in this book, you will work with more examples of the if command that are more complicated but still follow this basic structure.

switch

If you want to test for many different conditions, then you probably want to use the switch command instead of the if command. You would also use the switch command if you want to compare a string against a pattern or patterns.

You can use the switch command to test multiple conditions. The conditions can be based on pattern matching as well as direct comparisons.

The syntax of the switch command is:

```
switch flags string {pattern1 body1 pattern2
body2 pattern3 body3...}
```

The `string` is tested against each `pattern`. When the match is true, then the corresponding `body`, a Tcl script, is executed.

The `flags` of the switch command determine how the value is matched. There are four possible flags, shown in the table below.

Table 2.3 Flags of the switch command

Option	Meaning
—	No flag or end of flags
-exact	Matches the value exactly to the pattern
-glob	Uses "glob-style" pattern matching
-regexp	Matches a regular expression

The following sections will give you more details of these flags.

Exact matching

The flag -exact will match the pattern exactly to the string.

```
%set fruit apples
==> apples

%switch -exact $fruit   {
      apples    {puts "The choice is apples"}
      oranges   {puts "The choice is oranges"}
      }
==> The choice is apples.
```

You will achieve the same results if you use the `if` command and the "==" operator. However, you can match many different patterns without needing to write separate "else" statements. The above example would look like this if you used the `if` command:

```
if {$ fruit == apples} {
    puts "The choice is apples"
    } elseif {$fruit == oranges} {
    puts "The choice is oranges"
    }
```

This is a simple example, but you can see how the `switch` command is more economical than the `if` command, especially if you are matching many patterns against a single string.

Glob-style matching

The `switch` command also lets you use glob-style matching. Glob-style matching is a specific syntax that you will recognize if you have worked with the UNIX operating system.

Glob-style syntax lets you match any number of characters, a specific character, or one character out of a set of characters.

Table 2.4 Glob-style syntax

Character	Function
*	Matches any number of any characters
?	Matches any single character
\	Matches only the following character
[abc] [c-g]	Matches any one of a set of characters

In this example, the string "Name" and the string "name" both would match the pattern "[Nn]ame."

```
%   switch -glob "Name" {[Nn]ame} {puts "Any
case accepted"}
==> Any case accepted
```

In this example, the first option is chosen because the string "A1" contains two characters, one alphabetic and the other numeric. The other option "?" allows for only one character.

```
% switch -glob "A1" {
     {[A-Z][1-9]} { puts "Body 1 is executed" }
     {?} { puts "Body 2 is executed" }
     }
==> Body 1 is executed
```

Regular expression matching

The -regexp switch uses regular expression matching syntax that is used in the Tcl command regexp. We will look at the regexp command to get the feel of using regular expression syntax.

Examples of the regexp command

The regexp command is similar to the tag used for the switch command. It compares a pattern to a value and returns true if the pattern matches, false if it does not match. The summary of regexp syntax is in the table on the next page.

The following are a few examples of regular expression syntax.

Note: You must group the pattern in curly braces to avoid variable substitution.

In the following example, the pattern allows for any number "+" of lowercase alphabetic characters "[a-z]."

```
% regexp  {^([a-z]+)$}   value
==> 1
```

The following example returns false because the same pattern does not allow for numeric characters.

```
% regexp  {^([a-z]+)$} value1
==> 0
```

In this example, the pattern allows for any number "+" of lowercase alphabetic characters "[a-z]" followed by one capital alphabetic character or one numeric character "[A-Z0-9]." It does not allow for more than one character because it is not grouped with a "+" sign that indicates there can be more than one of a pattern.

```
% regexp {^([a-z]+)[A-Z0-9]$}   abc1
==> 1
```

The following example returns false because the pattern does not allow for one capital alphabetic character as well as a numeric character.

```
% regexp    {^([a-z]+)[A-Z0-9]$}   aA1
==> 0
```

The "+" sign refers to the [a-z] pattern only.

Table 2.5 Summary of regular expression syntax

Character	Function
.	Matches any character
*	Matches 0 or more instances of previous pattern item
+	Matches 1 or more instances of previous pattern item
?	Matches 0 or 1 instance of previous pattern item
( )	Groups a subpattern
|	Alternation
[ ]	Delimits a set of characters
^	Anchors a pattern to the beginning of a string
$	Anchors the pattern to the end of a string

Looping commands: for, foreach, while

Looping commands execute the same command using a variable whose value changes according to a pattern. Unlike conditional commands that choose between two separate body commands to execute, looping commands have one body command which they execute over and over again for different values of a variable. The value of the variable changes until it fails a test of a condition described in an expression. When the expression is no longer true, the looping command stops executing its body command.

for

The `for` command has the same structure as the `for` command of the C programming language. It starts with an initial value of a variable, executes a command that involves that variable, then changes the variable's value and executes the command again, and so on, until the value of the variable fails a test.

The syntax of the `for` command is:

```
for start test next body
```

Components of the `for` command:

`start`	Sets the initial value of the variable. It is in the form {set i 0}, where i is the variable and 0 is the initial value
`test`	Evaluates the value of a variable and returns true or false
`next`	Determines how the variable changes with each iteration of a loop. It may be in the form {incr i 10} where i is the variable
`body`	The command that is executed repeatedly

Example of the `for` command:

```
% for {set i 1} {$i<8} { incr i} {
          puts "The current value is $i."
          }

%     The current value is 1.
      The current value is 2.
      The current value is 3.
      The current value is 4.
      The current value is 5.
      The current value is 6.
      The current value is 7.
      The current value is 8.
```

You are not restricted to setting the value of *i* at 1 or to increasing it by 1.

```
% for {set i 15} {$i<120} { incr i 15} {
            puts "The current value is $i."
            }
```

```
==>   The current value is 15.
       The current value is 30.
       The current value is 45.
       The current value is 60.
       The current value is 75.
       The current value is 90.
       The current value is 105.
```

The `for` command uses a variable with a numeric variable. This is very useful, especially when working with arrays. To use a variable with an alphabetic value, you can use the `foreach` command.

foreach

The `for` command uses a variable that is numeric and changes its value according to a specific pattern. The `foreach` command executes a specified command for each member of a list that can be comprised of any type of element: alphabetic, numeric, string, or variable.

The form of the `foreach` command is:

```
foreach var list body
```

The component *var* is the variable that the `body` command uses. With each iteration, the value of *var* changes to the next element of the `list`, and the command is executed for that element.

Example of the `foreach` command:

```
% foreach var {apple, orange, banana} {
     puts "She ate the $var."
     }

==> "She ate the apple."
    "She ate the orange."
    "She ate the banana."
```

The foreach command can be useful in a procedure in which the number of arguments is undetermined. The argument variable args is taken by the foreach command as a list.

In this example, the procedure fruit takes an undetermined number of arguments.

```
% proc fruit { args }  {
     foreach var $args {
     puts "She ate the $var."
     }
```

Now you can run this procedure with any number of arguments.

Note: The name args is a special variable recognized by Tcl. It is a placeholder for an undetermined number of arguments.

To run this procedure, write the name of the procedure and the list of arguments, similar to built-in Tcl and Tk commands.

```
% fruit apple orange banana
==> She ate the apple.
    She ate the orange.
    She ate the banana.

% fruit orange kiwi grape strawberry
==> She ate the orange.
    She ate the kiwi.
    She ate the grape.
    She ate the strawberry.
```

```
% fruit lemon
==> She ate the lemon.
```

See the following section for more information about writing procedures.

while

The while command tests an expression and executes a command if the expression is true. In many cases, the body of the while command includes a command that changes the value of the variable that is tested in the expression. However, that is not a requirement; there are many situations where the value of the variable is changing outside the looping command.

The form of the while command is:

```
while test body
```

Example of the while command:

```
% set var 15
% while {$var<=120} {
        puts "We've looped [expr $var/15-1]
times."
        set var [expr $var+15]
             }
```

```
==>      We've looped 0 times.
      We've looped 1 times.
      We've looped 2 times.
      We've looped 3 times.
      We've looped 4 times.
      We've looped 5 times.
      We've looped 6 times.
      We've looped 7 times.
```

If you want to stop the flow of the script or skip a loop or two, you can use break and continue in the body of the command. See the next section for more information.

Other flow control commands: continue, break, catch

These commands enable you to direct the flow of the script in specific conditions. For example, if you want to stop a looping command when a variable is a certain value, but you also want to continue with the looping for values that follow after that value, you can use the command continue.

continue

The continue command skips to the next iteration of a loop. It does not require any arguments.

In this example, when the variable is 60, another command is executed and the looping begins again with the next value, skipping over the main body command.

```
% set var 0
% while {$var<=120} {
        set var [expr $var+15]
        if {$var==60} {
        puts "Now the value is $var."
        continue
        }
        puts "We've looped [expr $var/15-1] times."
            }

==>    We've looped 0 times.
       We've looped 1 times.
       We've looped 2 times.
       Now the value is 60.
       We've looped 4 times.
       We've looped 5 times.
       We've looped 6 times.
```

```
We've looped 7 times.
We've looped 8 times.
```

break

Like the command continue, the break command aborts a loop-ing command. It does not require any arguments. Unlike the con-tinue command, the break command does not continue to the next iteration of the loop.

Example of the break command:

```
% set var 0
% set var2 0
% while {$var<=10} {
    incr var
    while {$var2<=10} {
        incr var2
        if {$var2==7} {
            break
            } else {
            puts "The value is $var2."
        }}
    }

==>    The value is 1.
    The value is 2.
    The value is 3.
    The value is 4.
    The value is 5.
    The value is 6.
    The value is 8.
    The value is 9.
    The value is 10.
    The value is 11.
```

In this example, the inner `while` loop is keeping count with the outer `while` loop. When the variable is a certain value, the inner `while` loop is aborted for that iteration.

catch

The `catch` command captures errors from a Tcl script, but allows the script to continue. It can be in the body of a looping or conditional command, or it can stand alone.

The form of the `catch` command is

```
catch script var
```

The `catch` command returns 0 if the script is error free, and a return code if there is an error. The optional `var` stores the returned value.

We will use the `catch` and the `return` commands in many of the applications in this book. You can also get more details of the `catch` command and all other commands in the online reference documentation.

Mathematical Commands: expr

The math expressions that Tcl supports are listed in Table 2.6. The `expr` command that you have already seen in several examples evaluates a math expression and returns its value. The form of the `expr` command is

```
expr expression
```

Math expressions

The expression can be mathematical or logical. A logical comparison is the comparison of two values. You can find a description of the logical operators in the preceding section on expressions.

Table 2.6 Mathematical expressions

Expression	Definition
-v1	Negative of v1
v1*v2	Multiply v1 and v2
v1/v2	Divide v1 by v2
v1+v2	Add v1 and v2
v1-v2	Subtract v1 and v2

Procedures

Now that you know a few of the commands of Tcl/Tk, you can write your own in the form of *procedures*.

The Tcl command `proc` declares a procedure. The command `proc` has the form

```
proc name arguments body
```

Components of `proc`:

`name`	The name of the procedure, which you can use to run the procedure from another location in your Tcl program
`arguments`	Variables whose values you need to specify when you call the procedure, grouped with a pair of curly braces
`body`	The body of the procedure, which can consist of any number of commands, grouped with a pair of curly braces

In the following example, the name of the procedure is `one_pro-cedure`. It has one argument, *t*.

```
% proc one_procedure { t }  {
    if { $t == 1} {
    puts stdout "$t == 1"
    }  else {
    puts stdout "$t does not equal 1"
    } }
```

You can use a user-defined procedure when creating a new procedure, as you could any Tcl built-in command.

```
% proc post_value { t } {
    if { $t == 1}  {
    one_procedure 1
    } else {
     one_procedure 2
    }    }
```

Global scope

Procedures have *global scope*. This means that a procedure, like a built-in command, is recognized anywhere in the Tcl program in which it was defined.

Variables have a scope that is local to the procedure in which they appear.

If you want to use a variable in one procedure whose value was set in another procedure or another part of your Tcl script, you must use the Tcl command global.

Here is an example of global and local scope:

Type these two procedures into your interpreter:

```
% proc test_procedure { } {
        global test
        while {$test<=10} {
        puts "This is test number $test"
        set test [expr $test+1]
```

```
            }
        }
% proc second_test_procedure { } {
            while {$test<=20} {
            puts "This is test number $test"
            set test [expr $test+1]
            }
        }
```

Now call the two procedures:

```
%   test_procedure
==>    This is test number 1.
       This is test number 2.
       This is test number 3.
       This is test number 4.
       This is test number 5.
       This is test number 6.
       This is test number 7.
       This is test number 8.
       This is test number 9.
       This is test number 10.

% second_test_procedure
==> can't read "test": no such variable
```

The second procedure does not recognize the variable set in the first procedure. But you can rewrite the second procedure and declare the variable as global:

```
% proc second_test_procedure { } {
      global test
      while {$test<=10} {
      puts "This is test number $test"
      set test [expr $test+1]
      } }
```

When you call the two procedures, the output from the second procedure is what you would expect:

```
==>    The  is  test  number  11.
       The  is  test  number  12.
       The  is  test  number  13.
       The  is  test  number  14.
       The  is  test  number  15.
       The  is  test  number  16.
       The  is  test  number  17.
       The  is  test  number  18.
       The  is  test  number  19.
       The  is  test  number  20.
```

In this example, the value of the variable is affected by both procedures.

In the next chapter on Tcl/Tk, you will write procedures that tie Tk widgets together.

Conclusion

This introduction to Tcl included an overview of the basic data structures of Tcl: the string, the list, and the array; and examples of the most common Tcl commands. You should be prepared to work with Tk widgets. If you don't feel prepared, you should still try working with Tk widgets, because they can be a lot of fun and will help you learn more about Tcl/Tk syntax. For more details on any Tcl command, you can consult the online reference documentation included on the CD.

In this chapter we have touched on a number of substitution and grouping rules that affect the outcome of your Tcl script. You do not need to memorize these rules right now; you will come to know them naturally as you work with Tcl/Tk.

A dollar sign causes variable substitution. For example, the variable var is replaced by the value assigned to that variable when the variable name is preceded by the dollar sign: $var. Substitutions can occur anyplace, including the middle of a string or list.

Square brackets cause command substitution. You can nest command substitutions. For example, the valid command

```
[expr 5 + [expr 6 *2]]
```

results in the initial execution of the innermost command [expr 6 * 2], the result of which is substituted in the outer command

```
[expr 5 + 12]
==> 17
```

Grouping with braces prevents substitution, while grouping with quotes allows substitutions. A variable preceded by a dollar sign grouped in curly braces is interpreted literally with no variable substitution. When the variable is grouped using double quotes, variable substitution is performed.

```
set text "hello there"
==> hello there
set string1 {$text}
==>$text
set string1 "$text"
==> hello there
```

When the curly braces appear inside double quotes, then variable substitution is performed, and the curly braces group the resulting value.

```
set string1 "She said {$text}"
==>She said {hello there}
```

When curly braces group body arguments to looping commands, then variable and command substitution are performed inside those curly braces.

```
if { $text == "hello there" } {
    set num [llength $string1]
    }
==> 3
```

The value of the variable or command substitution do not affect grouping. Components are grouped before command substitution and variable substitution are performed.

Backslash is used to quote special characters. The backslash and the character immediately following it are replaced by one character. For example, "\$" is interpreted as the character $, rather than the symbol that indicates variable substitution.

3

Tk Commands

Introduction

This chapter will introduce you to the general characteristics of Tk widgets, how they work together, and how you might use them in your Web applications. This chapter is not a comprehensive description of all Tk commands, but only an introduction to help you get started working with widgets. You can find a complete description of Tcl and Tk commands in the reference documentation included on the CD-Rom.

The best way to familiarize yourself with the characteristics and abilities of widgets is to create sample widgets and experiment with them. You can get started by working through the examples included in this section using the Tcl interpreter, or by using the Ed Tcl Editor. Examples in this chapter build on each other to show you how widgets can work together. With the Ed Tcl Editor, you can simply add and test commands in a single Tcl file as you work through the examples. This chapter includes informaton on how to work with the Ed Tcl Editor.

About Widgets

Widgets are user interface elements, like buttons, radiobuttons, text boxes, and entry fields. Tk commands such as `button` and `frame` create widgets. Other Tk commands such as `pack` and `place` control the position of the widgets.

To display a widget, you use a minimum of two Tk commands. The first command creates the type and name of the widget, while the second command displays the widget.

Declaring a widget:

```
widget widgetname options
```

The second command, usually `pack` or `place`, causes the widget to appear on your screen in the main window or within another widget. A widget that contains another widget is called a *parent* of the widget.

Positioning a widget:

```
command widgetname options
```

We can see these two commands in an example that appeared in the previous chapter:

```
% button .b1    -text "Hello World"
==>  .b1
% pack .b1
```

The geometry managers of Tk are `pack`, `place`, and `grid`, of which the most common are `pack` and `place`. We will explain these geometry managers later in this chapter.

List of widgets

You can use the following widgets in your Tcl/Tk Web applets under the current Tcl Plug-in. Examples of each widget are presented later in this chapter.

Table 3.1 Widgets

Name	Function	Page
frame	Groups and positions widgets	98
label	Displays text	98
message	Displays multiline text	99
button	Calls a command when pushed	100
radiobutton	Set of mutually exclusive on-off choices	101
checkbutton	Set of on-off choices	101
listbox	Scrolled list of choices to select	102
scrollbar	Scrolls widgets	103
entry	Text-entry	104
text	Sophisticated text-entry	105
çanvas	Displays and accepts graphical data	110
scale	Displays a value from min to max	111

The following two widgets are currently not supported under the Sun Tcl Plug-in. But if you design Tcl/Tk applets for the Spynergy Plug-in or design graphical applications to run in stand-alone form, then you can incorporate these widgets into your application. You can also write a security policy to allow your applets to use these widgets under Sun's Tcl Plug-in.

toplevel	Application or dialog window
menu	Menu of choices, each of which sets an on-off choice or calls a command

See the end of this chapter for more information about restrictions on what you can do with Tcl/Tk applets.

Widget command

After you create a widget using a Tk command, you can then use the name of the widget as a command to change its attributes or to get information about it. The general form of the widget command is:

```
widgetname option -arg1 -arg2 ...
```

For example, to change the background color of the button you created in the earlier example, you can enter in the wish interpreter the name of the button with the configure option. The configure option lets you change any attributes of the widget.

```
% .b1 configure -background pink
```

You now have a pink button.

You can also get information about a widget with the get option. For example, create an entry widget in the interpreter:

```
% entry .e1 -width 5
==> .e1
% pack .e1
```

In the entry field, type "hello."

Now return to the wish interpreter and type:

```
% .e1 get
==> hello
```

The `get` option of the widget command returns the string of the entry.

In these two examples, the name of the widget is a Tk command. You can also use a widget command to flash a widget, get information about its configuration, or activate particular elements. For a list of all options available for a particular widget, see the online reference documentation for that widget.

Widget names

The widgets that comprise a graphical application are ordered in a hierarchy. In that hierarchy, a widget may be contained within another widget that is called a parent. Each widget has a unique name assigned by the programmer that reflects its place in this hierarchy and includes the name of its parent. The name of its parent includes the name of the parent's parent, and so on. As a result, all widget names start with the name of the main window, "." (a period).

In summary, widget names are in the form:

```
.parent.name
```

Each section of a name that describes an individual widget is separated by a period.

For example, a button contained in a frame may be named

```
.f1.f2.b1
```

This name indicates that `f1` is the name of a frame, `f2` is the name of a frame within the frame `f1`, and `b1` is the individual name of the button. Of course, you could have assigned any name to the individual widgets, such as `frame-one`, `frame-two`, or something more meaningful. You always refer to a widget using its full name such as `.f1.f2.b1` that includes the name of the parent, and never the individual name.

Widget attributes

The attributes of a widget determine the appearance and performance of a widget. You can define a widget's attributes when you create the widget. Attributes are listed after the widget's command in this form:

```
widget widgetname -attribute1 value1 -attribute2
value3
```

Example:

```
% button .b1 -background white -foreground black \
            -text "This is  black text"
==> .b1
% pack .b1
```

In this example, we specify the color of the background, the foreground, and the text on the button. If you don't specify any attributes when you create a widget, then some attributes will have default values, such as a default foreground and background color, and some attributes simply do not exist, such as the text attribute.

Note: Notice that the backslash character is used to continue the line. The widget's command and attributes must be declared on one line.

Example attributes

Table 3.2 contains a list of common attributes. It is not a complete list, nor does every widget use every attribute on this list. For a widget's specific attributes, see the online reference documentation.

Widget bindings

You can bind widgets to keyboard and mouse events using the Tk command bind. Keyboard and mouse events are user actions such as clicking the mouse button, typing a letter, or pressing the

Enter button on a keyboard. These actions can direct a widget to perform a function. To bind a widget to an event and action, the syntax of the command is:

```
bind widgetname <Event> script
```

The `<Event>` describes the user action such as a mouse click. Examples of events are `<Return>` (the Return key) and `<Button-1>` (the first button of the mouse). The script that follows in the command is the Tcl code that is called when the event occurs.

Table 3.2 Common widget attributes

Attribute	Function
`-background color`	Background color. Can be abbreviated to -bg. Attribute of most widgets
`-activebackground color`	Background color when activated by the mouse or other stimulus
`-foreground color`	Foreground color (usually the text color). Can be abbreviated to -fg
`-activeforeground color`	Foreground color when activated by the mouse or other stimulus
`-image imagefile`	Displays two-color or full-color image, GIF or PPM.* Used with labels and buttons
`-borderwidth width`	Border width in pixels
`-width width`	Width in pixels
`-height height`	Height in pixels
`-relief relief`	Sets relief to flat, groove, raised, ridge, sunken
`-text string`	Text to display
`-textvariable var`	Variable to use for text
`-justify justification`	Sets justification to left, center, or right for text

* You can create images for use in Tcl/Tk applications with most paint applications, like Paint Shop Pro from JASC, Inc. See Chapter 5 for more information on working with images in Tcl/Tk applications.

Most widgets already have default bindings. For example, you will notice that when your cursor enters the button widget that we created in the previous example, the widget turns its background color to the highlight color. The default highlight color is white.

You could bind the <Enter> event to the entry widget that we created in the previous example so it will also change its background color when the mouse enters the widget.

```
% bind .e2 <Enter> {.e2 configure -background \
     white}
```

You will notice that once it turns to that color, it stays that color. You need to bind another event to change it to its original color when the mouse leaves the widget.

```
% bind .e2 <Leave> {.e2 configure -background \
     gray}
```

You could also bind the Return key of the keyboard to a command that changes the background color of the widget.

```
% bind .e2 <Return> {.e2 configure -background \
     pink}
```

When you type a word and press Return in the entry widget, the widget changes its background color. Instead of changing color, it could call a command that uses the text you typed for a particular function, whatever the application required.

 Note: When you bind an event to a widget, all of its children (all widgets contained within that widget) are affected by the event.

List of events

Many of these events can be modified with keyboard or mouse buttons, such as the Shift key or the Control key. The syntax of a modified event is

```
bind widgetname <Mod-event> script
```

Table 3.3 Events that you can use to bind scripts to widgets

Event	Meaning
Button, ButtonPress	Mouse button pressed
ButtonRelease	Mouse button released
Key, Key Press	Keyboard key pressed
KeyRelease	Keyboard key released
Enter	Mouse enters widget
Leave	Mouse leaves widget
FocusIn	Received focus
FocusOut	Loses focus
Motion	Mouse moves while in widget
Expose	Widget is exposed
Map	Widget is mapped
Unmap	Widget is unmapped
Gravity	Widget moves because its parent has changed size
Circulate	The stacking order has changed
Colormap	The colormap has changed
Configure	Widget has changed size, position, border, or stacking order
Destroy	Widget is destroyed
Visibility	Widget changes visibility
Expose	Widget is exposed

Example:

```
% bind .e2 <Shift-b> {.e2 configure -background \
    blue}
```

Click on the entry widget that you have created, and press Shift-b on your keyboard to see the effect of this binding. Notice that the other bindings of .e2 remain in effect: When your mouse leaves the entry widget, the background will become grey again.

Note: Some keystrokes, such as Control-v and Control-x, will not work if you bind them to widgets. The Web browser will have priority regarding the use of these keystrokes.

Table 3.4 Event modifiers

Control	Control key
Shift	Shift key
Lock	Caps-lock key
Meta, M	Modifier that is mapped to M1
Alt	Modifier mapped to Alt_L and Alt_R
Button1, B1	Left mouse button
Button3, B3	Right mouse button
Double	Double press
Triple	Triple press
Any	Matches any combination of modifiers

Packing Widgets

Up until now we have been packing our example widgets with the simple pack widgetname command. But the pack command has a number of options that you can use to arrange your widgets.

Pack is the most common geometry manager, probably because it is easy to use and provides good results. It controls the position of a widget by specifying constraints. You can anchor a widget at a certain position, stretch or expand a widget to consume extra space in its parent, place a widget before or after another widget, or pad a widget by pixels.

Note: When you use pack for a Web application, you may want to make sure that the widgets are all a fixed size, or at least packed into a frame that is a fixed size. To embed a Tcl/Tk application in a Web page, you must specify the height and width of an application exactly. The height and width cannot change. Some widgets may resize spontaneously in your application, depending on their function. If this is the case, then you may need to use the `place` geometry manager for your Web applications, described in the next section. If you develop a Tcl/Tk graphical application that is not embedded in a Web page, then you will probably want to use `pack` and not `place`, because `pack` lets widgets resize and rearrange themselves gracefully.

The syntax of the `pack` command is:

```
pack widgetname -option1 -option2 -option3 \
      -option4
```

You can repack widgets at any time in your script.

Before beginning the next example, you should clear all examples from the wish interpreter by entering the command `destroy widgetname` for each of the widgets that you have created:

```
% destroy .b1 .e1
```

You can also close the interpreter and run it again, to destroy the widget.

After your main window is clear, create three buttons:

```
% button .b1 -text 1
% button .b2 -text 2
% button .b3 -text 3
% pack .b1 .b2 .b3
```

The three buttons will be located on top of each other.

Now you can repack the widgets to the side:

```
% pack .b1 .b2 .b3 -side left
```

The buttons line up in a horizontal row.

You can place a particular widget before or after another widget:

```
% pack .b1 -after .b2
```

You can also place a specific amount of padding around a widget.

```
% pack .b3 -padx 5
```

You can also expand widgets to fill up extra space.

```
% pack .b2 -side top -fill x
```

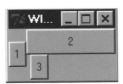

All buttons are stacked on top of each other, and the third button is expanded to fill the main window in the x direction.

Notice that the pack command modifies the existing status of the packing order. Packing options remain in effect until they are explicitly changed. As a result, the same pack command may have different effects depending on where it appears in your script and what packing restraints have already been placed on your widgets.

Table 3.5 Pack options

Option	Function
-after *widgetname*	Places widget after widgetname
-anchor *anchor*	Anchors at position such as n or sw
-before *widgetname*	Places widget before widgetname
-expand *boolean*	Specifies whether widget should be expanded to cover extra space in its parent. Defaults to 0 (no expansion)
-fill *style*	Stretches the widget according to style. Style can be none (no stretching), x (stretch horizontally), y(stretch vertically), or both (stretch horizontally and vertically)
-in *widgetname*	Inserts the widget at the end of the packing order in widgetname
-ipadx *amount*	Amount of horizontal internal padding on each side of the widget
-ipady *amount*	Amount of vertical internal padding on each side of the widget
-padx *amount*	Amount of horizontal external padding on each side of the widget
-pady *amount*	Amount of vertical external padding on each side of the widget
-side *side*	Specifies which side of the parent the widgets will be stacked against. Must be left, right, top, or bottom. Defaults to top

Placing Widgets

The place command is another Tk geometry manager. With place, you specify the coordinates of a widget in relationship to its parent. You can also specify the widget's exact location within its parent.

If your Web application includes a widget that may change size (because of the addition of text, for example) then you will probably want to use place rather than pack when arranging them to make sure that the overall height and width of the Web application does not change. If you would rather use pack than place, you can pack them into a frame that has a fixed size.

The general form of the place command is

```
% place widgetname -arg1 -arg2
```

To place a widget explicitly in the parent, use the -x and -y options.

```
% place .b1 -x 5 -y 5
```

You will notice that the other buttons cover a portion of another button. The two geometry managers are not necessarily compatible with each other.

To place a widget in the parent relative to the parent's dimensions, use the -relx, -rely, -relheight, and -relwidth options.

```
% place .b1 -relx 0.4 -rely 0.4
```

The values of the -relx and -rely options should not be above 1. If you specify the value as 1, then the widget is placed in the lower right hand corner of its parent. A value of 0 will place the widget in the upper right hand corner of its parent.

Table 3.6 Place options

Option	Function
-in *parent*	Places the widget in a particular widget
-x *location*	Places the widget at a specific x coordinate
-relx *location*	Places the widget at an x coordinate relative to its parent widget. The relative location is a per centage and must be between 1 and 0
-y *location*	Places the widget at a specific y coordinate
-rely *location*	Places the widget at an y coordinate relative to its parent widget. The relative location is a per centage and must be between 1 and 0
-anchor *where*	Places a particular point of the widget at its (x,y) location. The anchor point includes any border
-width *size*	The width of the widget, including any border
-relwidth *size*	Width of the widget relative to the width of its parent
-height *size*	The height of the widget, including any border
-relheight *size*	Height of the widget relative to the height of its parent
-bordermode *mode*	The degree to which borders within the parent are used in determining the placement of the widget. The default and most common mode is inside

Gridding Widgets

The grid geometry manager places widgets in a grid using columns and rows, resulting in a tabular layout. You can control

row and column sizes, as well as how a widget is positioned within a cell.

The syntax of the `grid` command is:

```
grid widgetname1 widgetname2 ...-option1 value1 /
                 option2 -value2....
```

You can grid your widgets relative to each other by using multiple
`grid` commands. Each `grid` command can be a separate row. You
list as many widgets as are in that row after a `grid` command.

```
% grid .b1 .b2
% grid .b3
```

You can also specify a row and column for a particular widget.
This lets you move widgets around from cell to cell. Rows and
columns are numbered starting from 0.

```
% grid .b1 -row 1 -column 1
```

Widgets can span two or more columns or rows as well, using the
`-columnspan` and `-rowspan` attributes.

```
% grid .b2 -row 0 -column 0 -columnspan 2
```

Table 3.7 contains a summary of options of the `grid` command. See the online documentation for more information about the `grid` command.

Table 3.7 A summary of the options of the grid command

Option	Function
`-sticky` *location*	Places widget next to n, s, e, or w, or any combination of directions, such as sw
`-row` *number*	Row to place widget
`-column` *number*	Column to place widget
`-rowspan` *number*	Number of rows that widget spans
`-column` *number*	Number of columns that widget spans
`-in` *widgetname*	Places widget inside of another named widget
`-ipadx` *pixels*	Pads widgets internally in X direction
`-ipady` *pixels*	Pads widgets internally in Y direction
`-padx` *pixels*	Pads widgets externally in X direction
`-pady` *pixels*	Pads widgets internally in Y direction

Using Widgets

This section will outline the specific widgets that you can use in your Web applets. We have designed this section as a tutorial to introduce you to the Tk widgets and the ways they might work together. Each example widget in this section builds on the examples that occur before it. You should go through these examples consecutively. When you reach the end of this chapter, you will have built a demo application that uses all the widgets described in this section.

You can use the Ed Tcl Editor to create this demo application. The Editor lets you build a Tcl/Tk application by simply adding and testing commands as you go. This is a better process than entering commands into the console, because the text editor lets you see all your work at once, and lets you undo mistakes and manipulate commands already written. You can then save your Tcl/Tk code to a file as a complete application.

Working with the Ed Tcl Editor

You can find the Tcl Editor on the CD included with this book with the filename `ed.tcl`.

The Ed Tcl Editor runs under all versions of Tcl/Tk, from 7.5/4.1 to 8.0.

To run the Editor, open a new Tcl/Tk console window, or clear your window by using the `destroy  widgetname` command. Then change to the directory of your CD drive. In this example, "D" is the name of the CD drive.

```
% cd D:
```

Change to the examples directory, and then source `ed.tcl`.

```
% cd examples
% source ed.tcl
```

You can also select "Source" from the File menu of the Console window, and then select the file from the appropriate directory.

The Ed Tcl Editor is a text editor that lets you edit, paste, cut, copy, and search through Tcl/Tk code. You can test code simply by clicking on the Test button.

The Row and Column field in the upper right-hand corner tells you where your cursor is located. The message bar at the bottom of the window tells you the status of the file and gives you help messages for working with the user interface.

The Get URL command under the Web menu lets you load any text file into the Ed Tcl Editor from any place on the Internet if you have an Internet connection.

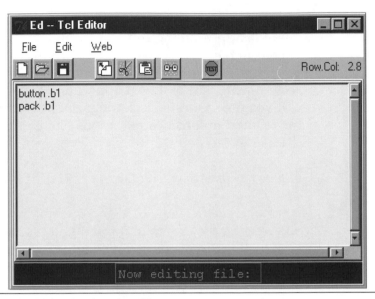

Figure 3.1 The Ed Tcl Code Editor

Note: After you have started the Ed Tcl Editor, you should mini-
mize the wish toplevel window that is running under the Tcl/Tk
console, but do not destroy it. When you test applications using
the Editor, a "slave" Tcl interpreter runs and opens another window for the application that is being tested. This will give you several windows on the screen and could be confusing. If you kill the
wish window that is running under the main Tcl/Tk console by
using its kill box, you will destroy all the applications that are running, including the Editor and the Tcl/Tk console.

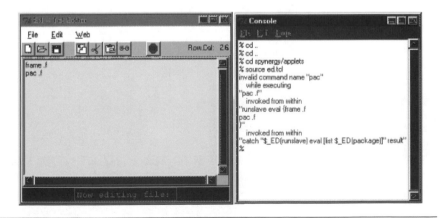

Figure 3.2 Ed and the Tcl console

As you test applications through the Ed Tcl Editor, error messages will appear in the Tcl/Tk console.

Look at the first few lines of the error message to find the error message within your Tcl/Tk code. The rest of the error message specifies what part of the Ed application caught the error.

If you are interested in finding out how the Editor works and how to build graphical applications like Ed, Chapter 7 covers the Ed Tcl Editor in depth.

Building an application with Ed

As we discuss Tk widgets in the remaining half of this chapter, you can enter the examples into Ed and periodically click on Test to run all the commands. If you want to use the standard Tcl interpreter and not Ed, then you can simply enter commands sequentially in the interpreter and see the results immediately. But if you work with the interpreter, you will not be able to manipulate commands already written and executed, whereas Ed lets you manage your Tcl code easily.

The frame widget

The frame widget is a container for other widgets. Frames are not interactive. Because of the limitations of the pack geometry manager, frames are useful to arrange and place widgets.

You can specify the color, the relief, width, height, and several other attributes.

Create three frames by typing these commands in the Editor window:

```
frame .f1
frame .f2
frame .f3
pack .f1 .f2 .f3
```

Presenting text: the label widget and the message widget

The label widget

The label widget displays one line of text. The label widget is the length of the text that it displays, unless you specify a width or wraplength of text.

Create a frame and a label widget within that frame:

```
frame .f1.f3 -width 50
pack .f1.f3 -side left -anchor nw

label .f1.f3.l1  -text "Other?"
pack .f1.f3.l1 -side top
```

Now click on the Test button to execute all the commands in the Editor window:

Figure 3.3 The label widget with text packed in a frame

The frame resizes to hold the widget.

The message widget

The message widget displays text like the label widget, but you can format the text by splitting it up into separate lines.

Create a message widget within the third frame by adding to your text in Ed:

```
message .f3.m1 -text "This is a line of text,\n
this is another line of text, \n this is a
third line of text."  \
                  -width 200

pack .f3.m1 -side left
```

Click on the Stop button to stop the previously running example, then click Test to run the application with the new code.

Note: Notice that you can use the newline character "\n" to split your lines. If you don't split your text up into lines, the message widget will do it for you, based on its width attribute.

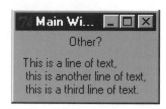

Figure 3.4 The label widget and message widget packed in separate frames

Button widgets: button, checkbutton, radiobutton, menubutton

The button widget

As seen in previous examples, the button widget has a command attribute. The button executes the command when pushed.

Create a frame and three buttons by adding to the text in Ed:

```
frame .f2.f3
pack .f2.f3 -side left -anchor nw -fill x

button .f2.f3.b1 -text "Select"
button .f2.f3.b2 -text "Clear"
button .f2.f3.b3 -text "Done"
pack .f2.f3.b1 .f2.f3.b2 .f2.f3.b3 -side top \
     -anchor nw  -fill x
```

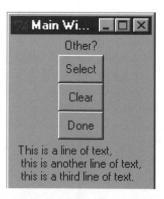

Figure 3.5 The three buttons are packed in a frame sandwiched between the two frames that hold the label and message widget

You will add commands to these buttons after creating more widgets in the following sections.

The radiobutton and checkbutton widgets

The checkbutton and radiobutton assign a value to a global Tcl variable. In a set of checkbuttons, each choice can assign a value to a different variable. A set of radiobuttons shares the same global variable.

Before creating a radiobutton, create a frame to contain the set. While not absolutely necessary, frames help to control the organization of widgets.

In Ed window, enter commands to create a frame and three radiobuttons with the global variable "food."

```
frame .f1.f2 -width 50
pack .f1.f2 -side left -anchor nw -before .f1.f3

radiobutton .f1.f2.r1 -text Pancakes -variable food    \
                            -value Pancakes

radiobutton .f1.f2.r2 -text "French Toast"        \
            -variable food  -value "French Toast"

radiobutton .f1.f2.r3 -text Waffles -variable food   \
                            -value Waffles

pack .f1.f2.r1 .f1.f2.r2 .f1.f2.r3 -side top \
            -anchor nw
```

Now place two checkbuttons in .f1.f3.

```
checkbutton .f1.f3.cb1 -text Coffee -variable coffee   \
            -onvalue "Coffee" -offvalue "No coffee"

checkbutton .f1.f3.cb2 -text Juice -variable juice     \
            -onvalue "Juice" -offvalue "No juice"

pack .f1.f3.cb1 .f1.f3.cb2 -side top -anchor nw        \
            -before .f1.f3.l1
```

Click on Stop to stop the running application, then Test to test the
entire application with these new additions:

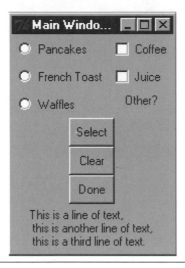

**Figure 3.6 Three radiobuttons are packed in a separate frame; the two check-
buttons are packed in the same frame as the label widget**

The menubutton widget

The menubutton creates a pulldown menu similar to those that
you would find in a graphical application. Menus are not currently supported under Sun's Tcl Plug-in for use in Tcl/Tk applications on the Web, but you can create them under the Spynergy
Plug-in. You could also use a security policy to allow use of
menubuttons under the latest release of the Tcl Plug-in. However,
because menubuttons create toplevel windows, you might consider using them only for independent graphical applications.

You can find more information about the menubutton and the
menu command in Chapter 7. You can also see the online reference
documentation for a full explanation of the menubutton widget.

The listbox widget

The listbox displays a set of text lines. A user will not typically
modify the text. The listbox is typically scrolled and accompanied
by the scrollbar widget.

You should put the listbox and scrollbar in a frame together so that the two widgets are aligned.

Example of the listbox:

```
frame .f1.f4
pack .f1.f4 -side left -padx 5

listbox .f1.f4.list1 -height 3 -width 10
pack .f1.f4.list1 -side left
```

An empty listbox will appear when you run this application. To add items in the listbox, you use the widget command widget-name insert end string. This command adds the string to the end of the list.

```
.f1.f4.list1 insert end "Fries"
.f1.f4.list1 insert end "Hashbrowns"
.f1.f4.list1 insert end "Eggs"
.f1.f4.list1 insert end "Muffins"
```

The scrollbar widget

You can now create a scrollbar to accompany the listbox widget. Scrollbars can also accompany text and canvas widgets.

Add to your list of commands:

```
scrollbar .f1.f4.s1 -command ".f1.f4.list1 yview"
pack .f1.f4.s1 -side left -fill y
```

When you create a scrollbar widget, you need to specify which widget it is controlling. You can do this with the -command option of the scrollbar widget, as in the above example. The yview option indicates that the scrollbar is scolling the listbox vertically.

Similarly, for the listbox widget, you specify the name of the scrollbar widget that is controlling it with the `yscrollcommand` option. (The `xscrollcommand` option assumes that the scrollbar is scrolling the listbox horizontally.)

```
.f1.f4.list1 configure \
    -yscrollcommand ".f1.f4.s1 set"
```

 Note: If you don't specify the relationship for both the listbox and scrollbar widgets using these options, then the scrollbar and the listbox will not be connected together.

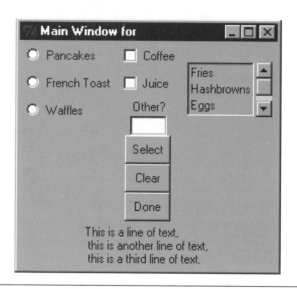

Figure 3.7 The listbox and scrollbar are packed in a separate frame. If you pack any other widgets in this frame, the listbox and scrollbar may become unaligned

User text input: the entry widget and the text widget

The entry widget

The entry widget is a one-line entry field for user input. Its default bindings allow a user to enter, select, and delete text. A common use for an entry widget would be to bind the <Return> key that a user typically presses after entering text to execute a command.

Example:

```
entry .f1.f3.e1 -width 5
pack .f1.f3.e1 -side top
```

Run the application by clicking on the Test button:

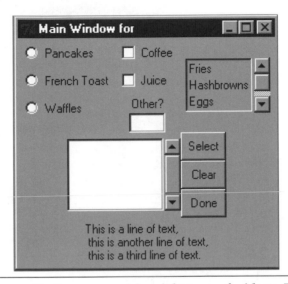

Figure 3.8 Your application now contains eight types of widgets. The entry widget has default bindings that enable you to enter and erase text

The text widget

The text widget is a sophisticated text entry widget with many attributes for manipulating text. Many of its options use indices as arguments. An index is a string that indicates a particular place in the text. In this example, we will insert a simple text widget. The text widget will let you delete and add text.

Chapters 4 and 5 cover the text widget in depth. Chapter 7 shows you how to create a text editor using the text widget.

```
frame .f2.f1
pack .f2.f1 -side left -before .f2.f3

text .f2.f1.t1 -width 15 -height 5
pack .f2.f1.t1 -side left
```

```
scrollbar .f2.f1.s1 -command ".f2.f1.t1 yview"
pack .f2.f1.s1 -side left -fill y

.f2.f1.t1 configure -yscrollcommand ".f2.f1.s1 \
set"
```

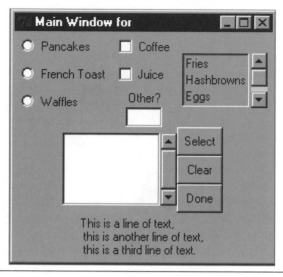

Figure 3.9 The text widget and its accompanying scrollbar widget are packed in the same frame so they are aligned with each other

You can now write a procedure to tie things together in this example application. The following procedure places the choices of the radiobuttons, checkbuttons, entry field, and listbox in the text widget.

```
proc post_selection { } {
      global food coffee juice
      .f2.f1.t1 delete 1.0 end
      .f2.f1.t1 insert end "$food\n"
      if {$coffee == "Coffee"} {
            .f2.f1.t1 insert end "$coffee\n"
            }
      if {$juice == "Juice"} {
            .f2.f1.t1 insert end "$juice"
            }
```

```
if {[.f1.f3.e1 get]== ""} { } else {
.f2.f1.t1 insert end "[.f1.f3.e1 get]\n"
}
if {[.f1.f4.list1 curselection] == ""} {
      return
      } else {
      set i [.f1.f4.list1 curselection]
      .f2.f1.t1 insert end "[.f1.f4.list1 \
      get $i] n"
} }
```

This procedure looks long and intimidating, but is actually straightforward. Here is what the procedure does when it is called, explained line by line:

```
proc post_selection { } {
```

declares the name of the procedure. Notice that the open bracket for the body of the procedure must be on the same line.

```
global food coffee juice
```

declares the variables that the procedure uses. The variables will take their values from the global scope.

```
.f2.f1.t1 delete 1.0 end
```

clears any information already in the text box.

```
.f2.f1.t1 insert end "$food\n"
```

inserts the value of the food variable which is determined by the selected radiobutton.

```
if {$coffee == "Coffee"} {
            .f2.f1.t1 insert end "$coffee\n"
            }
```

If the value of the coffee variable is "Coffee," this command inserts that value.

```
if {$juice == "Juice"} {
            .f2.f1.t1 insert end "$juice\n"
            }
```

If the value of the juice variable is "Juice," this command inserts that value.

```
if {[.f1.f3.e1.get]== ""} { } else {
        .f2.f1.t1 insert end "[.f1.f3.e1 get]\n"
        }
```

checks the entry field and inserts any string it finds.

```
if {[.f1.f4.list1 curselection] == ""} {
            return
            } else {
            set i [.f1.f4.list1 curselection]
            .f2.f1.t1 insert end "[.f1.f4.list1 \
            get $i] n"
    } }
```

checks if there are any choices selected in the listbox. If there are, it retrieves the index of that selection with the command `wid-getname curselection` and then inserts the string of the index in the text box with the command `widgetname get index`.

    Now all you need to do is configure the buttons to complete this application. Configure the Select button to call this procedure:

```
% .f2.f3.b1 configure -command post_selection
```

When you push the Select button, the choices that have been selected will appear in the text box. The text box allows for additional user input.

Configure the Clear button to erase the contents of the text widget.

```
.f2.f3.b2 configure -command {.f2.f1.t1 delete 1.0\
end}
```

Configure the Done button to call a command that will place the information in the text box to the message widget.

```
.f2.f3.b3 configure -command {.f3.m1 configure    \
                    -text [.f2.f1.t1 get 1.0 end]}
```

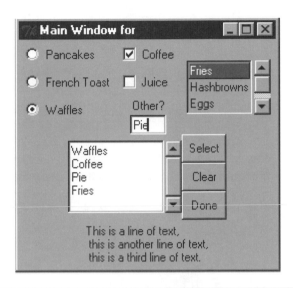

Figure 3.10 Enter a word in the entry widget and try out the Select button

Figure 3.11 Try different combinations, including adding to your list in the text box

You can add items to the textbox, and they will be included in the final list when you press Done.

Your basic application now includes nine types of widgets. It includes radiobuttons, checkbuttons, a label, an entry widget, a listbox widget, a text box, buttons, scrollbars, and a message widget.

The widgets interact with each other. The scrollbars control the text and listbox widgets. The radiobuttons, checkbuttons, entry widget, listbox, and text box enable the user to provide information by selecting choices or entering text. With buttons, the user has several choices of what to do with the information: select it, clear the selections, or finish the process. The message widget displays the result of the selections for the user to check.

We will now add two more widgets to the application: a canvas widget that displays graphical elements, and a scale widget that displays a list of values from a minimum to a maximum.

The canvas widget

The canvas widget is a versatile environment that can display objects such as lines, shapes, figures, and bitmaps. Objects placed on a canvas can respond to a user's input, such as the keyboard and mouse clicks.

To place an object on the canvas widget, the general form of the command is

```
widgetname create style x y x1 y1 -arg1 -arg2 ..
```

The style of an object can be a line, arc, oval, polygon, rectangle, text, image, bitmap, or window. The four coordinates specify the corners of the rectangle that binds the shape.

In this example, we add several shapes to our example application using a canvas widget.

First, pack the third main frame of the application to move it to the left:

```
% pack .f3 -side left
```

Now create a canvas in the right corner of the application:

```
canvas .c -height 100 -width 100
```

```
pack .c -side right
.c create oval 25 25 75 75 -fill yellow
.c create oval 40 40 45 50 -fill black
.c create oval 55 40 60 50 -fill black
.c create arc 35 35 65 65 -start 180 \
      -extent 180 -style arc -tag smile
```

The result of these commands:

See the online reference documentation for a full description of the attributes of the canvas widget. Chapters 4 and 5 also cover the canvas widget in depth, using it to create many different applications.

The scale widget

The scale widget displays a user-draggable scale across a range of values. It can execute a command based on its value.

Create a scale widget by entering these commands into the Editor:

```
scale .s -from 7 -to 12 -tickinterval 2    \
      -orient horizontal -length 300 -variable time  \
            -label "Brunch is at:"
pack .s
```

Notice that the scale widget uses a -label option, not a -text option. If you use a text option, you will generate an error.

Tying the widgets together

We can tie the canvas widget and the scale widget together by giving the scale widget a command that will change the objects on the canvas widget.

First, add two additional objects to the canvas widget:

```
% .c create line 35 55 65 55 -tag straight
% .c create arc 35 55 65 75 -start 0 -extent 180   \
                           -style arc -tag frown
```

Now you can write a procedure that changes the attributes of the objects on the canvas widgets based on the value of the scale widget variable. In this procedure, each object is colored yellow or black, based on the value of the scale.

Notice that you configure items on a canvas using their tags. You will learn more about working with the canvas widget in the next chapter.

```
proc change_face { time } {
    if {$time <= 9} {
            .c itemconfigure frown -outline yellow
            .c itemconfigure straight -fill yellow
            .c itemconfigure smile -outline black
            .c raise smile
    } elseif {$time == 10} {
            .c itemconfigure frown -outline yellow
            .c itemconfigure smile -outline yellow
            .c itemconfigure straight -fill black
            .c raise straight
    } else {
            .c itemconfigure smile -outline yellow
            .c itemconfigure straight -fill yellow
            .c itemconfigure frown -outline black
            .c raise frown
    }
}
```

Finally, configure the scale widget to call this procedure:

```
.s configure -command change_face
```

Notice that you do not need to include the argument of the procedure. When you assign a command to a scale widget, the command automatically takes the value of the scale variable as an argument.

Run the application by clicking on the Test button.

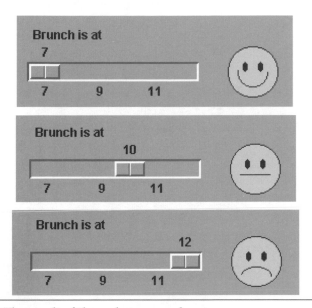

Figure 3.12 The result of the scale command

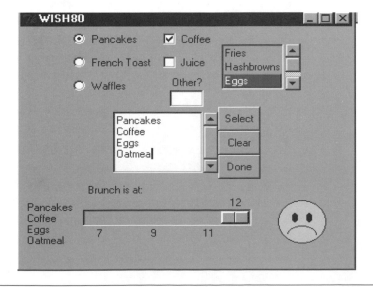

Figure 3.13 The completed application. Try dragging the scale and entering different combinations of choices

See the online reference documentation for a full description of the attributes of the scale widget.

This completed example application can be found on the CD with the name `tutorial.tcl`. Here is the complete code:

```
#————————————————————————————————————————————
frame .f1

frame .f2

frame .f3

pack .f1 .f2 .f3

frame .f1.f3 -width 50

pack .f1.f3 -side left -anchor nw

label .f1.f3.l1  -text "Other?"

pack .f1.f3.l1 -side top

message .f3.m1 -text "This is a line of text,\n
this is another line of text, \n this is a
third line of text."  \
-width 200

pack .f3.m1 -side left

frame .f2.f3

pack .f2.f3 -side left -anchor nw -fill x

button .f2.f3.b1 -text "Select"

button .f2.f3.b2 -text "Clear"

button .f2.f3.b3 -text "Done"

pack .f2.f3.b1 .f2.f3.b2 .f2.f3.b3 -side top \
      -anchor nw  \-fill x

frame .f1.f2 -width 50

pack .f1.f2 -side left -anchor nw -before .f1.f3

radiobutton .f1.f2.r1 -text Pancakes -variable food \
-value Pancakes

radiobutton .f1.f2.r2 -text "French Toast" \
-variable food \-value "French Toast"

radiobutton .f1.f2.r3 -text Waffles -variable food
-value Waffles

pack .f1.f2.r1 .f1.f2.r2 .f1.f2.r3 -side top -anchor
nw

checkbutton .f1.f3.cb1 -text Coffee -variable coffee \
-onvalue "Coffee" -offvalue "No coffee"
```

```
checkbutton .f1.f3.cb2 -text Juice -variable juice \
                    -onvalue "Juice" -offvalue
"No juice"
pack .f1.f3.cb1 .f1.f3.cb2 -side top -anchor nw \
                    -before .f1.f3.l1
frame .f1.f4
pack .f1.f4 -side left -padx 5
listbox .f1.f4.list1 -height 3 -width 10
pack .f1.f4.list1 -side left
.f1.f4.list1 insert end "Fries"
.f1.f4.list1 insert end "Hashbrowns"
.f1.f4.list1 insert end "Eggs"
.f1.f4.list1 insert end "Muffins"
scrollbar .f1.f4.s1 -command ".f1.f4.list1 yview"
pack .f1.f4.s1 -side left -fill y
.f1.f4.list1 configure  \
-yscrollcommand ".f1.f4.s1 set"
entry .f1.f3.e1 -width 5
pack .f1.f3.e1 -side top
frame .f2.f1
pack .f2.f1 -side left -before .f2.f3
text .f2.f1.t1 -width 15 -height 5
pack .f2.f1.t1 -side left
scrollbar .f2.f1.s1 -command ".f2.f1.t1 yview"
pack .f2.f1.s1 -side left -fill y
.f2.f1.t1 configure -yscrollcommand ".f2.f1.s1 set"
proc post_selection { } {
     global food coffee juice
     .f2.f1.t1 delete 1.0 end
     .f2.f1.t1 insert end "$food\n"
     if {$coffee == "Coffee"} {
          .f2.f1.t1 insert end "$coffee\n"
          }
     if {$juice == "Juice"} {
          .f2.f1.t1 insert end "$juice\n"
```

```
         }
       if {[.f1.f3.e1 get]== ""} { } else {
       .f2.f1.t1 insert end "[.f1.f3.e1 get]\n"
           }
       if {[.f1.f4.list1 curselection] == " "} {
           return
           } else {
           set i [.f1.f4.list1 curselection]
           .f2.f1.t1 insert end "[.f1.f4.list1 get \
           $i]\n"
       } }
.f2.f3.b1 configure -command post_selection
.f2.f3.b2 configure -command [.f2.f1.t1 delete \
1.0 end]
.f2.f3.b3 configure -command {.f3.m1 configure   \
                    -text [.f2.f1.t1 get 1.0 end]}
pack .f3 -side left
canvas .c -height 100 -width 100
pack .c -side right
.c create oval 25 25 75 75 -fill yellow
.c create oval 40 40 45 50 -fill black
.c create oval 55 40 60 50 -fill black
.c create arc 35 35 65 65 -start 180 -extent 180  \
                    -style arc -tag smile
scale .s -from 7 -to 12 -tickinterval 2   \
         -orient horizontal -length 300 \
         -variable time  \
         -label "Brunch is at:"
pack .s
 .c create line 35 55 65 55 -tag straight
 .c create arc 35 55 65 75 -start 0 -extent 180  \
                    -style arc -tag frown
proc change_face { time } {
       if {$time <= 9} {
```

```
                            .c itemconfigure frown -outline yellow
                            .c itemconfigure straight -fill yellow
                            .c itemconfigure smile -outline black
                            .c raise smile
                } elseif {$time == 10} {
                            .c itemconfigure frown -outline yellow
                            .c itemconfigure smile -outline yellow
                            .c itemconfigure straight -fill black
                            .c raise straight
                } else {
                            .c itemconfigure smile -outline yellow
                            .c itemconfigure straight -fill yellow
                            .c itemconfigure frown -outline black
                            .c raise frown
                }
        }
        .s configure -command change_face
        #————————————————————————————————
```

Tcl and Tk commands not available for applets

There are several Tcl/Tk commands that have been disabled under the current release Sun Tcl Plug-in. You cannot use these commands as part of your applet, because they are considered unsafe.

The following information was taken from the Sun Microsystem's Tcl/Tk Frequently Asked Questions list:

These commands have been removed from Tcl for use under the Sun Tcl Plug-in:

```
cd, exec, fconfigure, file, glob, pwd, socket
```

These commands have been removed from Tk for use under the Sun Tcl Plug-in:

```
bell, clipboard, grab, menu, send, tk, tkwait,
toplevel, wm
```

Table 3.8 Aliases provided by the safe.tcl security policy

Option	Function
exit	A safe version that only destroys the tclet
load	A safe version that only loads files from a pre-determined set of directories
source	A safe version that only sources from a predetermined set of directories
open	Only allows opening files (for reading only) in a predetermined list of directories. A tclet can only have a total of four channels open at any one time. This increments the count and fails if it would go over four
close	Removes temporary files and decrements the count of the number of files a tclet has open
maketmp	Makes a temporary file, limited in size to 1MB, opened for reading and writing. Returns the channel for the file. Also increments the count and fails if it would have gone over four
puts	Safe version that redirects stdout and stderr to Netscape's output mechanism
fconfigure	Only allows querying of options on channels, not setting them
dirname	Allows access to a safe subset of the subcommands available through dir

Safe.tcl is a *security policy*, a list of things that a Tcl/Tk applet can and can't do through your Web browser. The current release of the Tcl plug-in from Sun Microsystems also allows for different security policies. The alias command used by safe.tcl is used to alter built-in Tcl commands. You will learn more about the alias command and how to use it for your own purposes in the later chapters of this book.

The commands in Table 3.8 are considered unsafe not because they are inherently dangerous, but because they have the potential to harm, if someone intended to use them for that purpose.

Spynergy Tcl/Tk applets that may use more powerful versions of these commands are signed applets. They will not run unless you have the author's public key or unless you give them permission to run. Although this will give you enhanced functionality, you should understand what some of the dangers are and how to protect your internal systems.

Chapter 6 provides more information about security policies and using the Tcl Plug-in and Spynergy Plug-in.

Conclusion

This chapter introduced you to almost all of the basic widgets of Tcl's Toolkit. A complete specification of all their options is available in the reference documentation included on the CD and with your installation of Tcl/Tk.

We merely touched on the many capabilities of these widgets. The next two chapters cover the text widget and the canvas widget in greater depth with example applications.

4

Text Applications

Introduction

This chapter focuses on applications that enhance Web pages with animated text and graphics using the text widget and the canvas widget. It gives you an overview of these two widgets, and examples of how you can create text and graphics that move independently. With these applications, we intend to show you what is possible with the text and canvas widgets, and to give you ideas to to use when you build your own projects.

The text widget enables you to create and manipulate strings of text. You can color, move, and even link text to Tcl commands. In this chapter, we build several noninteractive applications with the text widget. Applications are noninteractive when they run without needing input from the user. These include the Tcl/Tk ticker tape, the Tcl/Tk typewriter, and the Tcl/Tk text slider. Chapter 5 will focus on working with the text widget in an interactive environment.

With the canvas widget, you can create objects such as arcs, shapes, and lines, as well as text objects. Using object tags and IDs, you can manipulate separate objects on the canvas widget independent of each other. Applications presented in this chapter that use the canvas widget are animated text and graphics, such as "nervous" and sliding text. In the next chapter we explore interactive applications of the canvas widget.

Working with Tcl/Tk files

We created a sample application in Chapter 3 by entering commands in the Ed Tcl Editor. With the applications presented in this chapter and the following chapters, you will want to test and save your Tcl code in complete files. You can do this easily with the Ed Tcl Editor, in the same manner as we described in Chapter 3. You can build a file in the Tcl Editor and test your Tcl code at any point during your development process, saving your changes whenever you choose.

If you cannot or do not want to use the Ed Tcl Editor, then you can create your Tcl files in any text editor that can save *plain text* files. To create, test, and save your applications, follow these steps:

1.   Write the commands in a plain text file. If you use a word processing application such as Microsoft Word, then be sure to save the file as plain text.
2.   Save the file with the extension `*.tcl`, such as `sample.tcl`.
3.   Test the application by entering `source sample.tcl` in the wish interpreter, where `sample.tcl` is the name of your file. If your interpreter is not referencing the directory where the file is located, then you also need to provide the pathname to the file, such as `/applets/sample.tcl`.

If you develop your Tcl/Tk applications in this manner, then each time that you want to change and test your code, you need to save the entire Tcl file. We designed the Ed Tcl Editor so that you can manipulate and test your code without having to save the entire file each time you want to test a modification.

 Note: When using Ed to develop applications, be sure to explicitly save your file to your hard disk before quitting the application. You can save your file by selecting Save from the File menu or by pressing the Save button.

A note about coding style

We present examples of applications in this chapter by first creating the graphical user interface, then by writing the procedures that will perform the actions that we want the application to do. Then we describe the inline code that usually starts up the application by invoking a procedure. "Inline code" describes commands that are not contained within a procedure, and that are executed immediately when the application is run. This is one approach that you could take while developing an application - creating a GUI and making it do what you want.

However, this is not the way that finished Tcl/Tk programs are typically organized. In the finished examples, we organize the code a little differently. Procedures that the application uses are defined first, and then all the inline code, which may include the Tcl and Tk commands that create the user interface. If we included code that was site-specific and needed to be modified for separate platforms, such as a font definition, then this code would go before the procedure definitions. As you get comfortable in the role of a Tcl programmer, you might consider using this organization for your own applications.

Another good practice is to use comments in your code, to explain what the procedures do and how everything works together. You can place a line of comments in your code by starting it with the pound sign (#). Anything following a pound sign is ignored by the Tcl interpreter.

The Text Widget

Possibilities of a text widget

You can create and manipulate text in a text widget with *indices*, *tags*, and *marks*.

We briefly introduced the text widget in the previous chapter on Tk commands. You saw how it can interact with other widgets:

It can be paired with a scrollbar widget, and other widgets such as the listbox and entry widget can contribute text to it. You also saw that you can enter and erase text with the keyboard and write Tcl procedures that erase or modify text.

The text widget has many more capabilities. You can build procedures to search through, copy, paste, select, and replace text. You could create a sophisticated text editor as part of a graphical user interface, like the Ed Tcl Editor which we will build in Appendix A. You can also modify existing text in a text widget, such as coloring or changing a string of text, or linking a string of text to Tcl code. The Spynergy Rouser, presented in Chapter 11, is a complete Web browser built on a text widget. It links strings of text to Tcl code that launches Web pages.

The text widget also does not need to be static, waiting for user input. You can build procedures that animate the text in a text box. The Tcl/Tk ticker tape presented in this chapter is an example of animated text. It displays text that seems to move across the page without any input from a user.

The text widget enables you to do these things because you can specify text in several different ways. You can identify a character with its *index*, its position with the text box. You can *tag* particular text with a certain description, or you can specify a particular place in a text box with a *mark*. These different pointers, with their associated Tcl commands, provide a lot of flexibility in how you can manipulate the text widget.

We begin the introduction to the text widget with an overview of these different pointers and the various Tcl commands associated with them.

Working with indices

Before learning about tags and applications with the text widget, it is important to understand how to work with indices.

An *index* specifies a position in the text widget. It is not associated with a specific character, but with a particular place. There are several ways of specifying an index. Some are *exact*, such as a specific x and y location. Some are *descriptive*, such as the index at the end of the text or the index of a tagged character. Descriptive indices can change their exact values.

When you add or delete text in a text widget, the characters at any particular index may change. For example, if you delete the first character of a text box, all the characters move over one character space. They are now located at the index that was previously to their left. Also, the actual location of a descriptive index might change. For example, the index end, which specifies the end of the text, will fluctuate every time you add or delete text from the text widget.

1.0	1.1	1.2	1.3	1.4	1.5	1.6	1.7	1.8	1.9	1.10	1.11	1.12
2.0	2.1	2.2	2.3	2.4	2.5	2.6	2.7	2.8	2.9	2.10	2.11	2.12
3.0	3.1	3.2	3.3	3.4	3.5	3.6	3.7	3.8	3.9	3.10	3.11	3.12
4.0	4.1	4.2	4.3	4.4	4.5	4.6	4.7	4.8	4.9	4.10	4.11	4.12

The above grid is one way to think of indices in a text widget. Each position of a widget has the form line.char. The lines of a text widget start with 1, and the character position starts with 0. For example, if you insert a character using this command: "text_box insert 3.9 H," the character "H" will appear on the third row at the ninth character place.

You can also specify an index by using modifiers to an index such as "chars" and "wordstart." For example, you can specify the index of the character located at three characters before the end of the text as "end -3 chars." The text widget recognizes words as separate entities, so you can also find the index at the beginnings and endings of words. For example, "1.0 wordend" is the index of the character at the end of the first word in the text widget.

There will be more examples of working with indices in the applications of this chapter. Table 4.1 is a summary of the forms and modifiers of indices. You can also get more details in the online reference documentation on the text widget.

Modifying an index

The modifiers in Table 4.2 do not exist on their own, but must follow the description of an index, such as "end -3 lines", or "1.2 wordstart." You can combine modifiers. For example, "3.12 wordend -1 chars" points to the second to last character of the end of the word that contains the index 3.12.

Table 4.1 Different forms of an index

Index	Function
@x,y	Points to the character covering the pixel located at x and y
end	Points to the end of the text (not the last character, but the position after the newline)
line.char	Points to the character at position char on line. Lines are numbered starting at 1; characters on lines are numbered starting at 0
tag.first	Points to the first character in the text that has been tagged with tag. See the following sections for more information on tags
tag.last	Points to the character after the previous one in the text that has been tagged with tag. See the follow ing sections for more information on tags
mark	Points to the character to the right of mark. See the following sections for more information on marks
widgetname	Points to the position of the embedded window whose name is widgetname

Introduction to tags

A *tag* is a string that you assign to an object in a text widget. You can tag a single letter, word, or phrase, and give the same tag to many words or phrases. Tags let you manipulate selected elements of your text box. For example, you can bind a tag to the mouse but-ton and a Tcl procedure, so that when you click on a tagged word, a Tcl command is executed. In this way you can link individual words and phrases to events and Tcl procedures.

A tag can be any string that you specify. For example, you might tag a piece of text that changes from red to black with the word "red." As in writing Tcl procedures, you should create your own naming scheme that makes sense to you. You should not use special characters like "$" and "%."

You can tag a string when you create the string, or at any time after you create a string. A word or phrase can have a number of tags associated with it.

Table 4.2 Modifiers of an index

Modifer	Function
`+ count chars`	Adjusts the index forward by `count` characters
`- count chars`	Adjusts the index backward by `count` characters
`+ count lines`	Adjusts the index forward by `count` lines. The character position on the line remains the same
`- count lines`	Adjusts the index backward by `count` lines. The character position on the line remains the same
`linestart`	Adjusts the index to the first character on the line
`lineend`	Adjusts the index to the last character on the line (the newline)
`wordstart`	Adjusts the index to refer to the first character of the word containing the current index
`wordend`	Adjusts the index to refer to the character just after the last one of the word containing the current index

Tag commands

This is an overview of commands that you can use to add, delete, manage, and find tags, and to manipulate tagged characters. The following applications will use some of these commands. You can get more details in the online reference documentation on the text widget.

In the following descriptions, "item" refers to something that can be tagged. It can be a single character or string of characters.

All the commands that manipulate tags have the syntax:

```
widgetname tag option
```

Adding a tag to an item

```
widgetname tag add name index1 ?index2
```

assigns the tag named by `name` with all characters starting with `index1` and ending just before `index2`. You can list any number of `index1  index2` pairs, assigning the tag to each pair. If you omit `index2`, then just be sure that the single character at `index1` is tagged.

Removing a tag from an item

```
widgetname tag remove tag_name index1 ?index2
```

removes the tag named by `tag_name` from all of the characters starting at `index1` and ending just before `index2`. You can list any number of `index1  index2` pairs. If you omit `index2`, then the tag at the single character at `index1` is deleted.

```
widgetname tag delete tag_name
```

deletes the tag named by `tag_name`, including removing it from all characters and deleting any bindings associated with it.

Locating a tag or tagged item

```
widgetname tag names ?index?
```

returns a list of all the tags at `index`. If you omit an index description, then this command will return all the tags that exist for the text box that you have created but not explicitly deleted, even if no characters are currently assigned to a tag.

```
widgetname tag ranges tag_name
```

returns a list describing all of the ranges of text that have been tagged with `tag_name`, in the form `{ index1 index2 index1 index2.... }`. Each "`index1 index2`" pair indicates a range of characters tagged with `tag_name`.

```
widgetname tag nextrange tag_name index1 ?index2?
```

searches the text between `index1` and `index2` (including `index1` but not including `index2`) for a range of characters tagged with `tag_name`. It returns the first pair that it finds in the form "`index1  index2`," indicating the range of characters tagged with `tag_name`.

```
widgetname tag prevrange tag_name index1 ?index2?
```

searches the text before `index1` but not before `index2` for a range of characters tagged with `tag_name`. It returns the pair closest to `index1` in the form "`index1  index2`," indicating the range of characters tagged with `tag_name`.

Managing tags

A text widget remembers tags in a specific order. This affects the order in which tag names are returned by commands such as `widgetname tag names`, described above. You can change the order of the list with the following two commands.

```
widgetname tag lower tag_name ?below_tag?
```

changes the priority of `tag_name` so that it is just lower in priority than the tag whose name is `below_tag`. If you omit the `below_tag`, then the tag will be placed at the lowest priority of all tags.

```
widgetname tag raise tag_name ?above_tag?
```

changes the priority of `tag_name` so that it is immediately higher in priority than the tag whose name is `above_tag`. If you omit the `above_tag`, then the tag will be placed at the highest priority of all tags.

Configuring a tagged item

```
widgetname tag cget tag_name option
```

returns the current value of `option` associated with `tag_name`. For example, "`text_box tag cget red -foreground`" will return the value of the foreground color of the characters tagged with the tag "`red.`"

```
widgetname tag configure tag_name ?option? ?value?
```

configures an `option` for all characters tagged with `tag_name`. For example, "`text_box tag configure red -foreground red`" will assign all characters tagged with "`red`" with the option "`-foreground red,`" coloring their text red.

Binding a tagged item

```
widgetname tag bind tag_name ?sequence? ?script?
```

This command associates a Tcl script with the tag named by `tag_name`. It is similar to the binding process that we discussed in Chapter 3. But here, only certain characters are bound to an event, not the entire widget. Events can be anything associated with the mouse or keyboard. For example, a word can be bound to a mouse click. A string of characters can have many tags, and each tag can have bindings.

Introduction to marks

A *mark*, like an index, isn't associated with a particular character. A mark is a position between two indices. The characters at those indices may change, but the mark will remain unless you delete it.

A mark has something called *gravity*, which indicates if a character should appear to the right or left of the mark when you insert a character. The default gravity is right.

You will learn more about marks in the next chapter. When you create an interactive text widget, you need to know about two special marks, `insert` and `current`. `Insert` is the location of the insertion cursor. `Current` is the location of the character closest to the mouse. It automatically adjusts itself and follows the mouse. These two marks are handy when working with interactive text widgets.

You can set, unset, and manipulate marks with Tcl commands similar to the commands that were used for tags. See the online reference documentation for details.

Building text applications

When you build dynamic or interactive text applications, you can consider your text in several different ways. You may need to think about the letters of your words as individual elements. Or you may think of the text as separate words or phrases. You might think of the spaces between the words as elements as well, or you may want to disregard them.

In the following applications, we use an array to manage the text elements. Sometimes the elements of the array are strings of text, and sometimes they are individual characters. Chapter 2 on Basic Tcl introduced you to arrays and array commands. We see the application of that data structure here.

App I: The Tcl/Tk ticker tape

The first application that we examine is the Tcl/Tk ticker tape. The Tcl/Tk ticker tape was created by developers at Sun Microsystems. It is one of the many demos included with the Tcl/Tk package.

This is a great introduction to how you can manage strings in the text widget. The ticker tape creates an array of different text messages, using a single procedure to cycle through the elements of the array. It places an element of the array in the text box, then deletes the first character of the text box (index 1.0) at a specified pace, as it continually adds the remaining elements to the text box. This has the effect of text scrolling across the screen.

This program uses the Tcl command `after` to execute commands after a specific time period. This command is essential to most of the text widget applications that we'll build in this chapter.

Steps to create a ticker tape

Step 1: Creating a text box

You first create a text box as the backdrop of the ticker tape. It is disabled because the user is not able to type anything into the text box. The ticker procedure will activate it, insert the text, and disable it.

You can create a text box of any size and color for this application.

```
text .t -relief ridge -bd 2 -wrap none -bg white      \
                    -state  disabled
pack .t
```

Step 2: Creating an array of text messages

Each individual text message is an element of the array. You will
use the command `array  set` with pairs of numeric array variables and strings of text.

Remember that this is an associative array. The numeric values
that you are using as variables provide an artificial ordering to the
array, but the Tcl interpreter does not actually store the elements
in any particular order. You will be able to access the array elements through the variables that you set.

```
array set text_messages {
        0       "What a nice day! Get away from the \
                    computer!"
        1       "Use the Spynergy Web Developer to cut \
                    your development time by 90%"
        2       "Simply the fastest, easiest and most \
                    powerful way to develop \
                    interactive Web content"
        3       "Cross platform, secure and rapid \
                    application development"
}
```

Step 3: Writing the ticker procedure

The Tcl procedure used in the Tcl/Tk ticker tape is called `ticker`.
It performs several functions.

- Checks to see if there are any more elements in the text
  message array since its last iteration. If not, it sets the array
  variable 0, the first message in the array. This lets the procedure cycle through all the text messages continuously.
- Scans the length of the text in the text box. If the length is
  under a specified amount, it enables the text box, inserts
  the next text message of the array, and disables the text
  box.

- Increases the array variable, so the next element of the array will be used in the next cycle.
- Deletes the first character of the text box. This shifts all characters in the text box by one. This also decreases the length of the text in the text box, so when the procedure scans the box again, as mentioned above, the next array element will be inserted.
- Specifies a time after which the procedure is run again.

```
proc ticker {t d f e} {
    global index text_messages

#  ---------------------------------------------------
# Scans the contents of the widget
#---------------------------------------------------

      scan [$t index 1.end] %d.%d line len
#  ---------------------------------------------------
# If the length is below e, continue
#  ---------------------------------------------------

    if { $len < $e} {

#  ---------------------------------------------------
# If there is not a value of the array element

# (such as text_messages(5)), set the index 0
#  ---------------------------------------------------
        if {![info exists text_messages($index)]} {
            set index 0
                }
#  ---------------------------------------------------
# Sets the message to the current array element,
# insert the message and tag it, insert the
# divider string
#  ---------------------------------------------------
        set message $text_messages($index)
```

```
        $t configure -state normal
        $t insert end $message tag$index
        $t insert end "$f" fill
        $t configure -state disabled
#  ─────────────────────────────────────────────────────
#  Increase the index and close the if loop
#  ─────────────────────────────────────────────────────

        incr index
    }
#  ─────────────────────────────────────────────────────
#  Delete the first character
#  ─────────────────────────────────────────────────────
    $t configure -state normal
    $t delete 1.0
    $t configure -state disabled
#  ─────────────────────────────────────────────────────
#  After a specified time, call the ticker procedure
#  ─────────────────────────────────────────────────────
after $d [list ticker $t $d $f $e]
}
```

Notice the last command in the procedure. Use the command [list ticker $t $d $f $e] instead of using the command [ticker $t $d $f $e] to avoid an infinite loop that the Tcl interpreter will not accept. List adds an extra step for the interpreter to evaluate. It returns the list {ticker $t $d $f $e} which will then start the procedure.

Step 4: Starting it up

The last lines of the program initialize the index and start the ticker procedure for the first time. The initial arguments specify the name of the widget, the time period (in milliseconds) that it waits to run itself again, the string that divides the array elements, and the length of text that should be maintained in the text box.

```
set index 0
ticker .t 200 " ****** " 95
```

Step 5: Configuring the text

You can configure your text messages in different ways. The ticker tape shows you how easily this is done. When you insert each string into the text box, it has a tag associated with it, depending on its array variable: `tag0`, `tag1`, `tag2`, or `tag3`. The string of characters that separates each phrase (in this case, "******"), was assigned the tag `fill` in the ticker procedure. You can configure each tag with different characteristics.

These are the examples provided by the ticker tape:

```
.t tag configure fill -foreground red
.t tag configure tag0 -font *-times-bold-r-*-18-*          \
          -foreground blue1
.t tag configure tag1 -font *-times-medium-i-*-18-*        \
          -foreground blue4
.t tag configure tag2 -font *-times-medium-r-*-18-*        \
          -foreground RoyalBlue4
.t tag configure tag3 -underline true                      \
        -foreground SlateBlue3 \
        -font *-times-medium-i-*-18-*
```

 Note: Not all font descriptions work on all platforms. These font descriptions work under Tcl 7.6 and Tk 4.2. Tcl/Tk 8.0 supports these descriptions, as well as an easier-to-read font naming system.

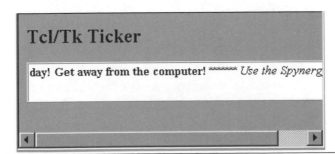

Figure 4.1 The Tcl/Tk ticker tape

The complete code to the ticker application:

```
proc ticker {t d f e} {
    global index text_messages
# ─────────────────────────────────────────────
# Scans the contents of the widget
# ─────────────────────────────────────────────
    scan [$t index 1.end] %d.%d line len
# ─────────────────────────────────────────────
# If the length is below e, continue
# ─────────────────────────────────────────────
    if { $len < $e} {
# ─────────────────────────────────────────────
# If there is not a value of the array element

# (such as text_messages(5)), set the index 0
# ─────────────────────────────────────────────
    if {![info exists text_messages($index)]} {
            set index 0
                }
# ─────────────────────────────────────────────
# Sets the message to the current array element,
# insert the message and tag it, insert the
# divider string
# ─────────────────────────────────────────────
        set message $text_messages($index)
        $t configure -state normal
        $t insert end $message tag$index
        $t insert end "$f" fill
        $t configure -state disabled
# ─────────────────────────────────────────────
# Increase the index and close the if loop
# ─────────────────────────────────────────────
    incr index
```

```
      }
# ─────────────────────────────────────────────
# Delete the first character
# ─────────────────────────────────────────────
    $t configure -state normal
    $t delete 1.0
    $t configure -state disabled
# ─────────────────────────────────────────────
# After a specified time, call the ticker procedure
# ─────────────────────────────────────────────
    after $d [list ticker $t $d $f $e]
}
# ─────────────────────────────────────────────
# Creates a text box
# ─────────────────────────────────────────────
text .t -relief ridge -bd 2 -wrap none -bg white    \
                          -state   disabled
pack .t
#─────────────────────────────────────────────
# Creates a message array
# ─────────────────────────────────────────────
array set text_messages {
        0       "What a nice day! Get away from the \
                computer!"
        1       "Use the Spynergy Web Developer to cut \
                your development  time by 90%"
        2       "Simply the fastest, easiest and most \
                powerful way to develop \
                interactive Web content"
        3       "Cross platform, secure and rapid \
                application development"
}
# ─────────────────────────────────────────────
# Configures text
# ─────────────────────────────────────────────
```

```
.t tag configure fill -foreground red
.t tag configure tag0 -font *-times-bold-r-normal-18-* \
            -foreground blue1
.t tag configure tag1 -font *-times-medium-i-normal-18-* \
            -foreground blue4
.t tag configure tag2 -font *-times-medium-r-normal-18-* \
        -foreground RoyalBlue4
.t tag configure tag3 -underline true \
        -foreground SlateBlue3 \
-font *-times-medium-i-normal-18-*
# ————————————————————————————————————
# Set initial index value and call procedure
# ————————————————————————————————————
set index 0
ticker .t 400 " ******* " 95
```

App II: The Tcl/Tk typewriter

This program creates a typewriter simulator that prints each character of a phrase separately, so that it looks like the text is being typed out.

The typewriter takes each character as a separate member of an array. Its code is even simpler than the ticker tape.

Steps to create a typewriter

Step 1: Creating the text box

The text widget will be the base for the typed text. The option -wrap specifies how the text will be wrapped. If you don't specify this option, the text box will break up words indiscriminately. This text box is also disabled, so the user can't edit the text in it.

```
text .t -relief ridge -bd 2 -wrap word -bg white   \
                -state disabled -height 5 -width 30
pack .t
```

Step 2: Creating the letters array

Each element of the `letters` array is a separate character of a string that will appear in the text box. Some elements are specified by { }, which represents a space. Each element is paired with an array variable, 0, 1, 2, etc, that indicates its position in the message. Note that this relationship is one that we have constructed, and we don't rely on the Tcl interpreter to order the array in the same way that we do.

To create the `letters` array, we could use the command `array set`, and type in each index with each accompanying letter. However, there is an easier way of creating an array with only a few lines of code. This method allows you to assign a string of text to a variable which then provides elements to an array. You can change this variable when you want to change the message, or this variable can receive its value from an outside source, as we will see in the next section.

This code will construct the letters array for you:

```
set original "Hello. I am the Tcl/Tk typewriter."
set letter_list [split $original {}]
set index 0
foreach ltr $letter_list {
      set letters($index) $ltr
      incr index
      }
```

1. Sets the original message to a string:

```
set original "Hello. I am the Tcl/Tk typewriter."
```

2. Splits the string into a list:

```
set letter_list [split $original {}]
```

The resulting list has the form { H e l l o . { } I { } a m { } t h e { } T c l / T k { } t y p e w r i t e r .}

3. Sets the initial value of the index:

```
set index 0
```

4. Creates a member of the `letters` array for each element of the letter list. Elements include spaces as well as letters:

```
foreach ltr $letter_list {
       set letters($index) $ltr
       incr index
       }
```

The array now has 33 elements, each of which is paired with a numeric variable that corresponds to its place in the message.

Step 3: Writing the typewriter procedure

The typewriter procedure accomplishes these tasks:

- Scans the text in the box. If the number of letters is less than a specified length (in this case, the length of the `letter_list`),then it enables the text box, inserts the next character of the array specified by index, and disables the text box.
- Increases the index (array variable) for the next iteration of the loop.
- After a specified time period, it calls the `typewriter` procedure again. However, unlike the ticker tape, this comand is included in the `if` statement described above. If there are no more letters to print, the procedure will not call itself again.

```
proc typewriter {w time length} {
# ——————————————————————————————————
# Declare the index and letters array as global
# ——————————————————————————————————
    global index letters
# ——————————————————————————————————
# Scan the text in the text box
# ——————————————————————————————————
```

```
        scan [$w index 1.end] %d.%d line len
#  ————————————————————————————————————————————
# If the length of the text is shorter than the
# specified length, then continue
#  ————————————————————————————————————————————
     if { $len < $length} {
#  ————————————————————————————————————————————
# Set let to the element of the array
#  ————————————————————————————————————————————
        set let $letters($index)
#  ————————————————————————————————————————————
# Insert the letter
#  ————————————————————————————————————————————
        $w configure -state normal
        $w insert end $let
        $w configure -state disabled
#  ————————————————————————————————————————————
# Increase the index (array variable)
#  ————————————————————————————————————————————
        incr index
#  ————————————————————————————————————————————
# After a time period, call the typewriter procedure
# again, using the same arguments
#  ————————————————————————————————————————————
        after $time [list typewriter $w $time $length]
#  ————————————————————————————————————————————
# Close the if loop and procedure
#  ————————————————————————————————————————————
        }
}
```

Step 4: Starting it up

To start the typewriter, we call the procedure and provide values
for the arguments. We also need to assign an initial value to the

array variable. (We can't do this as part of the procedure, or the index would always return a value of 0, and the first character would always be selected.)

```
set index 0
typewriter .t 20 [llength $letters_list]
```

Step 5: Configuring text

How would you modify the text in the typewriter? Unlike the ticker tape, each character of the typewriter is inserted separately. If you wanted to modify all text in the same way, you could tag each text with the same tag when you insert the text in the typewriter procedure:

```
$t insert end $let tag
```

Then you could configure the tag:

```
.t tag configure tag -foreground red
```

However, if all the text will have the same characteristics, then you could just configure the entire widget for those characteristics using the widgetname configure command. But if you want only one word to have a certain characteristic, then you will need to tag each letter of the word, and then configure each tag for that characteristic.

To do this, you could tag each element with its specific index when you insert is as part of the typewriter procedure:

```
$t insert end $message tag$index
```

Then, you can write a for loop that configures each tagged item. This particular loop colors the fifth word of the text, index 16-21.

```
for { set i 16} { $i <=21} {incr i} {
    .t2 tag configure tag$i -foreground red
    }
```

Figure 4.2 The Tcl/Tk typewriter

Here's the complete code for the Tcl/Tk typewriter program:

```
proc typewriter {w time length} {
# ————————————————————————————————————————
# Declare the index and letters array as global
# ————————————————————————————————————————
    global index letters
# ————————————————————————————————————————
# Scan the text in the text box
# ————————————————————————————————————————
    scan [$w index 1.end] %d.%d line len
# ————————————————————————————————————————
# If the length of the text is shorter than the
# specified length, then continue
# ————————————————————————————————————————
    if { $len < $length} {
# ————————————————————————————————————————
# Set let to the element of the array
# ————————————————————————————————————————
        set let $letters($index)
# ————————————————————————————————————————
# Insert the letter
# ————————————————————————————————————————
```

```
        $w configure -state normal
        $w insert end $let
        $w configure -state disabled
# ─────────────────────────────────────────
# Increase the index (array variable)
# ─────────────────────────────────────────
        incr index
# ─────────────────────────────────────────
# After a time period, call the typewriter
# procedure again, using the same values
# ─────────────────────────────────────────
        after $time [list typewriter $w $time
        $length]
# ─────────────────────────────────────────
# Close the if loop and procedure
# ─────────────────────────────────────────
        }
}
# ─────────────────────────────────────────
# Create the list of letters
# ─────────────────────────────────────────
set original "Hello. I am the Tcl/Tk \
typewriter."
set letter_list [split $original {}]
set index 0
foreach ltr $letter_list {
        set letters($index) $ltr
        incr index
        }
# ─────────────────────────────────────────
# Create the text box
# ─────────────────────────────────────────
```

```
text .t -relief ridge -bd 2 -wrap word -bg
white -state disabled \
                    -height 5 -width 30
pack .t -side left
# ────────────────────────────────────────────
#
# Create initial value and call the procedure
#
# ────────────────────────────────────────────
set index 0
typewriter .t 50 [llength $letter_list]
# ────────────────────────────────────────────
#
# Configuring text
#
# ────────────────────────────────────────────
for { set i 16} { $i <=21} {incr i} {
     .t tag configure tag$i -foreground red
     }
```

App III: An entry Tcl/Tk typewriter

As mentioned previously, you could change the original typed phrase of the Tcl/Tk typewriter directly in your code without having to change anything else about your script. The variable letter_list and the letters array are all generated from the original phrase.

But if the message is dynamic, meaning that it is continually changing, you would need change things in your code as well. We can give our typewriter an entry field that would provide the value of the original message. The original message would come from a user input, and change each time a user entered a new phrase.

This application will show you a few things that you need to consider when applications become interactive.

Steps to create an entry typewriter

Step 1: Building a GUI

First, we need to construct a user interface. This includes a label telling the user what to do, and two text widgets. One is the text field where the user will enter the script, and the other is the typewriter. The first text box is active and waiting for user input; the second text box has user input disabled.

```
label .l1 -text "Enter your message and press return" \
                 -background white -anchor nw
pack .l1  -side top
text .text1 -height 1 -width 50 -bg white -wrap word
pack .text1 -side top
focus .text1
text .text2 -relief ridge -bg white -wrap word \
        -state disabled -width 50 -height 4
pack .text2 -side top
```

Note: The focus command places the insertion cursor in the text box each time that the script runs.

Step 2: Writing the typewriter procedure

We can use a typewriter procedure similar to the one from the previous application.

```
proc typewriter {t d e} {
        global index words

        if {$index < $e} {
        set message $words($index)
        $t configure -state normal
        $t insert end $message tag$index
        $t configure -state disabled
        incr index
```

```
            after $d [list typewriter $t $d $e]
        }
}
```

Step 3: Preparing the message

We now need to consider a few issues that arise because the original message is dynamic. Each time the user types something different in the user field, the variables letter_list and
list_length need to be reset. Our original typewriter application only did this once.

Also, we want to strip out any newlines that are entered by the
user. And do we want to erase the text that is already in the text
box, or add to it? Should users delete the text or should we do it
for them?

These are only a few of the issues you should consider when
building a GUI. The procedure go assigns the variables, clears the
text, and starts the typewriter.

```
proc go { message } {
# ─────────────────────────────────────────────────────
# Declares the index and letters array as global
# ─────────────────────────────────────────────────────
global index letters
# ─────────────────────────────────────────────────────
# Strips the original message of its newline
# character that was added when the user pressed
# return. Checks to see if the beginning character
# (string index $original 0) is a not an
# alphabetic or numeric character with the regexp
# Tcl command.
# ─────────────────────────────────────────────────────
set original $message
set original [string trimright $original]
if {![regexp -nocase {[a-z]} [string index $original
0]]} {
        set original [string trimleft $original]
    }
```

```
#  ─────────────────────────────────────────────────
# Creates the list of letters and sets the elements
# of the array letters
#  ─────────────────────────────────────────────────
set letter_list [split $original {}]
set index 0
foreach ltr $letter_list {
        set letters($index) $ltr
        incr index
        }
#───────────────────────────────────────────────────
# Sets the variable list_length
#  ─────────────────────────────────────────────────

set list_length [llength $letter_list]

#  ─────────────────────────────────────────────────
# Sets the initial value of index to 0
#  ─────────────────────────────────────────────────

set index 0

#  ─────────────────────────────────────────────────
# Deletes any text in the typewriter text box and
# entry text box
#  ─────────────────────────────────────────────────
.text2 config -state normal
.text2 delete 1.0 end
.text2 config -state disabled
.text1 delete 1.0 end
#  ─────────────────────────────────────────────────
# Starts it up
#  ─────────────────────────────────────────────────
typewriter .text2 50 $list_length
}
```

Step 4: Binding the entry field procedure to the entry field

Now you can bind the entry field to the Return key of the keyboard. When you enter `text` and press Return, the procedure `go`
is called. It takes as its argument the contents of the first text box.

```
bind .text1 <Return>  {go [.f.text1 get 1.0 end]}
```

Note: When you set variables to the `letters` array, any variables
that are not replaced remain in the array. Therefore, if you enter a
long message and then enter a shorter one, characters from the
long message remain in the array. Because the typewriter stops
printing text after the text is as long as `list_length`, a variable
that is determined by the original message, those characters do not
appear. But it is good to understand that they are still there, especially if you modify or build on this application.

Figure 4.3 The entry Tcl/Tk typewriter

Here's the complete entry typewriter code:

```
proc go { message } {
global index letters var

# ───────────────────────────────────────────
# Trim original string of newline characters
# ───────────────────────────────────────────

set original $message
set original [string trimright $original]

if {![regexp -nocase {[a-z]} [string index $original
0]]} {
```

```
        set original [string trimleft $original]
    }

# ───────────────────────────────────────────────
# Create list of letters
# ───────────────────────────────────────────────

set letter_list [split $original {}]
set index 0
foreach ltr $letter_list {
    set letters($index) $ltr
    incr index
}

set list_length [llength $letter_list]

# ───────────────────────────────────────────────
# Set index to 0
# ───────────────────────────────────────────────
set index 0

# ───────────────────────────────────────────────
# Delete any text in text widget
# ───────────────────────────────────────────────

.text2 config -state normal
.text2 delete 1.0 end
.text2 config -state disabled

# ───────────────────────────────────────────────
# Call typewriter procedure
# ───────────────────────────────────────────────

typewriter .text2 50 $list_length

# ───────────────────────────────────────────────
# Delete text in entry field
# ───────────────────────────────────────────────
```

```
        .text1 delete 1.0 end

    }

proc typewriter {t d e} {
        global index letters

    # ────────────────────────────────────────────────
    # Place each letter in text field until end of
    # message is reached
    # ────────────────────────────────────────────────

        if {$index < $e} {
                set message $letters($index)
                $t configure -state normal
                $t insert end $message
                $t configure -state disabled
                incr index
                after $d [list typewriter $t $d $e]
        }

    }

    # ────────────────────────────────────────────────
    # Create label and text widgets. Focus on entry field
    # ────────────────────────────────────────────────

label .l1 -text "Enter your message and press \
            return" -background white -anchor nw
pack .l1  -side top

text .text1 -height 1 -width 50 -bg white -wrap word
pack .text1 -side top
focus .text1

text .text2 -relief ridge -bg white -wrap word - \
            state disabled -width 50 -height 4
pack .text2 -side top
```

```
# ─────────────────────────────────────────
# Bind return key to text field.
# ─────────────────────────────────────────

bind .text1 <Return>  {go [.text1 get 1.0 end]}
```

App IV: The Tcl/Tk text slider

The text slider is a slightly more complicated application than the Tcl/Tk typewriter or ticker tape, though still simple compared with what you could do with the text widget. The slider takes each letter of a message and slides it from the end position of the text widget to its correct position in the text. The tricky part of the Tcl slider is remembering that the end of the text changes whenever you add or delete letters.

The text slider is versatile. You can change its parameters - how quickly the letters appear, or how fast they disappear - and create different types of effects. The text slider has an echoing effect as the letters are created and destroyed. It can look like the text is skittering across the page. If you don't like this effect, you might prefer the canvas slider that we look at later in this chapter. With the canvas slider, the text objects are actually moving, and there is no echoing effect.

Steps to create a text slider

Step 1: Creating the text widget

Create a text widget for the text. You can create a variable for the width of the text box that you will use in other procedures and can change easily.

```
set textwidth 40
text .t -relief ridge -bd 2 -wrap word -bg white \
     -height 5  -width $textwidth
pack .t -side left
```

Step 2: Creating the message

Now you can create the message that will appear in the text widget. Each character is a separate element of the list. You can also set the length of the list to a variable that is used in other procedures.

```
set original "Hello. I am the Tcl/Tk slider."
set letter_list [split $original {} ]
set list_length [llength $letter_list]
```

Step 3: Creating space in the text widget

When you create a text widget, the index end is located at 2.0. That is because there is nothing occupying the space of the previous line except a newline character. So 2.0 is the next index after the last character of the widget, a newline character. For the slider to work, you need to create space in the text widget to increase the initial index of the end.

This `for` loop places empty space in the text widget equal to the amount specified by the variable `list_length`.

```
for {set i 0} {$i < [expr $textwidth-2]} \
{incr i} {.t insert end " "}
```

Step 4: Writing procedures

The slider is easier to visualize using more than one procedure. These procedures consider the case of one character going through a continual loop until it reaches its destination, its place in the text widget. In the next step, we will extend the procedures for all the characters.

The `show_and_delete` procedure inserts a character at a specified index, then schedules it for deletion after 5 milliseconds. The procedure requires the character and its current position to be passed to it.

```
proc show_and_delete {char currentPosition} {
    .t insert 1.$currentPosition $char tag1
    after 5 {.t delete tag1.first}
}
```

The slide procedure requires the character and its position in the text string to be passed. In this case, the position is the final position in the complete letter_list, not the dynamic position as in the previous procedure. How far the character travels is determined by the width of the text box. The show_and_delete procedure is called at a periodic rate with the dynamic position of the character. Then the character is inserted at its acual position after a specific time that depends on how far the character travelled.

```
proc slide {char position} {
  set width [lindex [.t configure -width] 4]
  incr width -2
  set time 1
  for {set i $width} {$i > $position} {incr i -1} {
    after $time [list show_and_delete $char $i]
    incr time 10;
    }
  after $time [list .t insert 1.$position $char]
  incr position;
  after $time [list .t delete 1.$position]
  }
```

Step 5: Starting it up

The procedures of the text slider are for one element of the letter_list. We now need to call the slide procedure for each element.

The final code to complete the application accomplishes these tasks:

- Sets the initial values of the position and start time.
- Starts a foreach loop that examines each element of the letter_list.
- Sets the delay for the element as a product of the total length of text and its position in that text.
- Checks if the element is an empty space. If it is not, it calls the slide procedure for that element after a particular time period.

- Increases the position variable for the next element. This
  will cause the next element to delay longer than the previous element.

```
set position 0;
set starttime 1;
foreach letter $letter_list {
  set delay [expr (($textwidth - $position) *5) \
      + 200]
  if {$letter != " "} {
    after $starttime [list slide $letter $position]
    incr starttime $delay
    }
  incr position;
  }
```

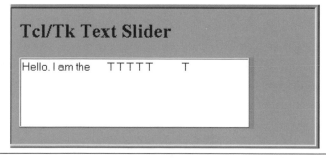

Figure 4.4 The Tcl/Tk text slider

Here's the complete text slider code:

```
# -----------------------------------------------------
# Shows a character at a position on line 1, and
# schedules it for deletion in 5 milliseconds.
# -----------------------------------------------------

proc show_and_delete {char currentPosition} {
    .t insert 1.$currentPosition $char tag1
    after 5 {.t delete tag1.first}
  }
```

```
# ─────────────────────────────────────────────
# Schedules characters to be displayed at given
# positions at times in the future. Schedules the
# character to be displayed in it's final location
# after the sliding is complete. Deletes the space
# replaced by this character.
# ─────────────────────────────────────────────
proc slide {char position} {
    set width [lindex [.t configure -width] 4]
    incr width -2
    set time 1
    for {set i $width} {$i > $position} {incr i -1} {
      after $time [list show_and_delete $char $i]
      incr time 10;
       }
    after $time [list .t insert 1.$position $char]
    incr position;
    after $time [list .t delete 1.$position]
    }
# ─────────────────────────────────────────────
# Creates the list of letters
# ─────────────────────────────────────────────

set original "Hello. I am the Tcl/Tk slider."
set letter_list [split $original {} ]
set list_length [llength $letter_list]
set textwidth 40
# ─────────────────────────────────────────────
# Creates the text widget
# ─────────────────────────────────────────────

text .t -relief ridge -bd 2 -wrap word -bg white \
        -height 5 -width $textwidth
pack .t -side left
```

```
#  ------------------------------------------------------------
# Fill line with spaces.
#  ------------------------------------------------------------

for {set i 0} {$i < [expr $textwidth-2]} {incr i}
{.t insert end " "}
set position 0;
set starttime 1;

#  ------------------------------------------------------------
# Slides each letter
#  ------------------------------------------------------------

foreach letter $letter_list {
   set delay [expr (($textwidth - $position) *5) +
200]
   if {$letter != " "} {
     after $starttime [list slide $letter $position]
     incr starttime $delay
     }
   incr position;
   }
```

Conclusion

The text widget applications that we've described in the first section of this chapter show you a few ways that you can use the text widget to create simple applications. These applications are really only the beginning of what you can do with the text widget. In the next chapter we will look at the text widget in an interactive role. The rest of this chapter is devoted to an introduction of the canvas widget.

The Canvas Widget

The canvas widget is similar to the text widget because you can use tags to specify objects. However, a canvas widget does not have prearranged indices. When you place text on a text widget, the text lines up in rows and columns. On a canvas widget, you place text and objects by x and z coordinates. You can place objects anywhere, and even overlap them. This makes the canvas widget more difficult to work with, but much more flexible than the text widget.

In the previous chapter on Tk commands, we created a small picture of a smiling face with a circle, two ovals, and an arc on a canvas. You have a whole palette available to you of lines, ovals, arcs, images, polygons, and text objects. The tricky part is placing them exactly where you want.

This section will introduce you to the various objects that you can create on a canvas widget, and the commands you can use to manipulate them. When you create an object on a text widget, the object is assigned a specific ID. You can use this ID or a tag that you assign to the object to refer to it in these commands.

You will also see how to create simple moving and "nervous" text. The next chapter will introduce more canvas commands and will use them to build an interactive canvas application.

Creating objects

The following sections describe the type of objects that you can create on a canvas widget. All objects in a canvas widget are ordered in a list. If objects overlap, then an object that is before another object in the display list obscures the object that follows it.

You create a new object with the command:

```
widgetname create type x y ?x y ...? ?option value
...?
```

Most objects require two sets of x y coordinates, specifying the opposite vertices of the object's bounding box (the box that contains it.) The options that you use with this command depend on the type of object you are creating.

The following sections will give you a brief introduction to the types of geometrical objects you can create, including arcs, ovals, rectangles, polygons, lines, and text objects.

Types of objects

Arc

An arc is a section of an oval delimited by two angles (specified by the -start and -extent options) and displayed in one of several ways (specified by the -style option). Arcs are created with the widget command:

```
widgetname create arc x1 y1 x2 y2 ?option value
option value ...?
```

The two pairs of x and y values are the upper left-hand and lower right-hand corners of the box that contains the arc. This box is not visible, but provides a method to place the arc.

Table 4.3 Options of arc

Option	Function
-extent degrees	Size of the angular range occupied by the arc
-fill color	Fill the region of the arc with color
-outline color	Color of arc's outline
-outlinestipple bitmapbitmap	Indicates that the outline for the arc should be drawn with a stipple pattern
-start degrees	Specifies the beginning of the angular range occupied by the arc
-stipple bitmap	Arc filled in stipple pattern specified by bitmap
-style type	Specifies how to draw the arc: pie-slice (the default), chord, or arc
-tags tagList	Specifies a set of tags to apply to the arc
-width outlineWidth	Specifies the width of the arc's outline

Examples of arcs

Here are a few example of arcs. The following commands created
the arcs in the following figure, from left to right.

Arc style:

```
.c create arc 50 50 100 100 -style arc -extent 180 \
-start 0
```

Pieslice style:

```
.c create arc 125 50 175 100 -style pieslice \
-extent 45    -start 180
```

Chord style:

```
.c create arc 180 50 230 100 -style chord \
-extent 190    -start 270 -outline red
```

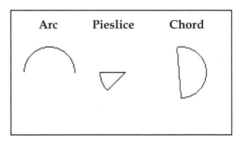

Line

You can specify one or more connected line segments. Lines can be
straight or curved. Each endpoint is specified by an x y pair.

```
widgetname create line x1 y1... xn yn ?option
value option value ...?
```

Table 4.4 Options for lines

Option	Function
`-arrow where`	Indicates if arrowheads are drawn at one or both ends of the line: none (no arrowheads), first (at the first point), last (at last point), or both (both ends)
`-arrowshape shape`	Shape of arrowheads. The shape argument is a list with three elements: the distance from the neck of the arrowhead to its tip, the distance from the trailing points of the arrowhead to the tip, and the distance from the outside edge of the line to the trailing points
`-capstyle style`	Specifies the ways in which caps are to be drawn at the endpoints of the line: butt, projecting, or round
`-fill color`	Color of line. Defaults to black
`-joinstyle style`	Specifies how the joints are drawn at the vertices of the line: bevel, miter, or round
`-smooth beboolean`	Indicates whether or not the line should drawn as a curve. If so, the line is rendered as a set of Bezier splines
`-splinesteps number`	Specifies the degree of smoothness desired for curves: each spline will be approximated with number line segments
`-stipple bitmap`	Indicates that the line is filled in a stipple pattern
`-tags tagList`	Specifies a set of tags to apply to the item
`-width lineWidth`	Specifies the width of the line

Examples of lines

Here are some examples of lines. Each of the commands that follows created a line in the following figure, from left to right.

Jointed line with arrow:

```
.c create line 50 50 80 70  90 100 -fill black \
-arrow last -joinstyle round
```

Curved line:

```
.c create line 100 50 70 70 180 80 -fill black \
-smooth 1
```

Thick line:

```
.c create line 200 50 200 100 -fill black -width 10
```

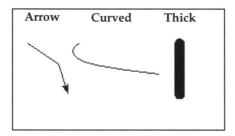

Ovals

Ovals may have an outline, filled color, both, or only an outline. To create an oval on your canvas, you use this command:

```
widgetname create oval x1 y1 x2 y2 ?option value
option value ...?
```

The two x y pairs specify the opposite vertices of the bounding box that contains the oval.

Examples of ovals

Here are a few examples of ovals. These commands created the ovals in the following figure, from left to right,

```
.c create oval 50 50 100 100 -fill red -outline \
white
```

```
.c create oval 120 50 150 70   -outline black
.c create oval 180 50 190 100
```

Table 4.5 Options for the oval

Option	Function
`-fill color`	Fill the area of the oval with color
`-outline color`	Specifies a color to use for drawing the oval's outline
`-stipple bitmap`	Indicates that the oval should be filled in a stipple pattern
`-tags tagList`	Specifies a set of tags to apply to the item
`-width outlineWidth`	Width of the outline to be drawn around the oval

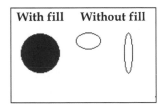

Polygons

Polygons can be curved or straight, filled or clear. You can create a polygon with this command:

```
widgetname create polygon x1 y1 ... xn yn ?option
value option value ...?
```

You can have any number of x y pairs. Each specify a vertex of the polygon.

The polygon will automatically close itself by connecting its first x y pair with the last. By default, it is filled.

Examples of polygons

Here are some examples of polygons. The following commands created the polygons in the following figure, from left to right.

Three vertices:

```
.c create polygon 50 50 100 100 30 150
```

Four vertices:

```
.c create polygon 100 20 100 90 150 110 170 30  \
            -fill white -outline red
```

Smooth polygon:

```
.c create polygon 200 50 230 80 240 110 190 70  \
            -fill white -outline black -smooth 1
```

Table 4.6 Options of polygons

Option	Function
`-fill color`	Color filling area of the polygon
`-outline color`	Color of outline
`-smooth boolean`	Indicates if polygon should be drawn with a curved perimeter
`-splinesteps number`	Specifies the degree of smoothness for curves
`-stipple bitmap`	Indicates that the polygon should be filled in a stipple pattern
`-tags tagList`	Specifies a set of tags to apply to the item
`-width outlineWidth`	Width of the polygon's outline

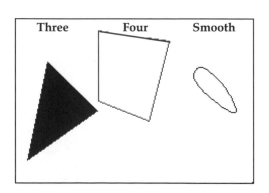

Rectangle

Rectangles may have an outline, a fill, or both. You can create rectangles with this command:

```
widgetname create rectangle x1 y1 x2 y2 ?option
value option value ...?
```

To create a rectangle, you only need to specify two pairs of x y coordinates.

Table 4.7 Options of rectangles

Option	Function
-fill color	Fill the area of the rectangle with color
-outline color	Color of rectangle's outline
-stipple bitmap	Indicates that the rectangle should be filled in a stipple pattern specified by bitmap
-tags tagList	Specifies a set of tags to apply to the item
-width outlineWidth	Width of the outline

Examples of rectangles

Here are a few examples of rectangles. The following commands created the rectangles in the following figure, from left to right.

```
.c create rectangle 50 50 100 100
.c create rectangle 140 50 160 200 -fill red
.c create rectangle 220 50 280 60
```

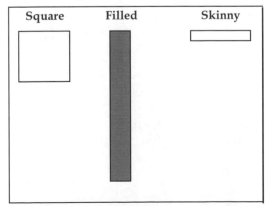

Text

A text object displays a string of characters on the screen in one or more lines. Text objects support indexing and selection. You can create a text object with this command:

```
widgetname create text x y ?option value option
value ...?
```

The text object is placed at the point specified by the x y pair. The text item is centered on this point, unless specified differently with the anchor option.

Table 4.8 Options for text

Option	Function
-anchor anchorPos	Positions the text relative to the positioning point for the text
-fill color	Color of text
-font fontName	Specifies the font to use for the text object
-justify how	Specifies how to justify the text within its bounding region
-stipple bitmap	Indicates that the text should be drawn in a stippled pattern rather than solid
-tags tagList	Specifies a set of tags to apply to the item
-text string	String specifies the characters to be displayed in the text item. Newline characters cause line breaks
-width lineLength	Specifies a maximum line length for the text

Examples of text

Here are a few examples of text objects. The following commands created the text objects in the following figure, from left to right.

```
.c create text 40 50 -text A

.c create text 100 50  -text "Hello there!" \
-fill red

.c create text 200 100  -text "This is a line broken\
 up into different lines by the canvas widget" \
-fill blue -width 60 -justify right
```

```
┌──────────────────────────────────┐
│                          This is  │
│                          a line   │
│      A  Hello there!     broken   │
│                          up into  │
│                          differen │
│                          t lines  │
│                          by the   │
│                          canvas   │
│                          widget   │
│                                   │
└──────────────────────────────────┘
```

Indices of the text objects

You have as many of the index options available to you as you did when working with text widgets. Text objects of a canvas widget recognize indices and a *selection*. We will look at the selection in the next chapter.

Two commands that you can use to work indices are as follows:

```
widgetname insert tagOrId beforeThis string
```

The `string` is inserted into the text just before the character whose index is `beforeThis`.

```
widgetname index tagOrId index
```

returns a decimal string giving the numerical index within `tagOrId` corresponding to `index`.

The different forms you can use to refer to an index are similar to the forms employed by the text widget.

Table 4.9 Forms of the index

Option	Function
number	A decimal number giving the position of the desired character within the text item. 0 refers to the first character, 1 to the next character, and so on
end	Refers to the character just after the last one in the item (same as the number of characters in the item)
insert	Refers to the character just before which the insertion cursor is drawn in this item
sel.first	Refers to the first selected character in the item
sel.last	Refers to the last selected character in the item
@x,y	Refers to the character at the point given by x and y

Other objects: bitmap, image, window

All the objects explained in this chapter cover the geometrical objects of a canvas widget: ovals, polygons, rectangles, lines, arcs, and text objects.

There are three other types of objects that you can create in a canvas widget: the bitmap, the image, and the window. Bitmaps and images let you place two-color or full-color images on your canvas. A window can hold an embedded Tk widget.

We will discuss these objects in the next chapter. The rest of this chapter explains how you can animate the simple geographical objects that we have looked at so far.

Object commands

These commands enable you to manipulate objects by referring to their tags, IDs, or coordinates.

Each object that you create is assigned a specific ID by the canvas widget. You can assign any number of tags to an object, and assign the same tag to numerous objects.

Adding tags to existing objects

```
widgetname addtag tag_name option
```

adds a tag named by tag_name to each item that meets the constraints specified by option. (All options are described in the following section.)

Finding an object with a tag, ID, or within specific coordinates

```
widgetname find option
```

returns a list consisting of all the objects that meet the constraints specified by option. All options are described below.

Table 4.10 Options for the commands addtag and find

Option	Function
above tagOrId	The object just after (above) the one given by tagOrId in the display list
all	All the objects in the canvas
below tagOrId	The object just before (below) the one given by tagOrId in the display list
closest x y ?halo??start?	The object closest to the point given by x and y, within halo, if it is specified. Halo is given in pixels. The start argument is used to step circularly through all the closest objects. It names an object using a tag or ID
enclosed x1 y1 x2 y2	All the objects completely enclosed within the rectangular region given by x1, y1, x2, and y2
overlapping x1 y1 x2 y2	All the objects that overlap or are enclosed within the rectangular region given by x1, y1, x2, and y2
withtag tagOrId	All the objects given by tagOrId

Retrieving all the tags from an object

```
widgetname gettags tagOrId
```

returns a list whose elements are the tags associated with the object specified by `tagOrId`.

Binding objects with particular tags or IDs

```
widgetname bind tagOrId ?sequence? ?command?
```

This command associates a Tcl script with the object specified by `tagOrId`. It is similar to the binding process that we discussed in Chapter 2 on basic Tcl. But here, only the object is bound to an event, not the entire widget. Events can be anything associated with the mouse or keyboard.

Deleting objects

```
widgetname delete ?tagOrId tagOrId ...?
```

deletes each of the objects specified by each `tagOrId`.

Deleting tags from objects

```
widgetname dtag tagOrId ?tag_name?
```

deletes the `tag_name` from each object that has `tagOrId`.

Managing objects

The canvas widget maintains a display list. When you overlap objects, the ordering of the display list determines which objects obscure, or are "in front of," other objects. Also, the ordering of the display list determines which objects are specified first when you find objects using the `find` command described previously. These two commands can change the ordering of the display list.

```
widgetname lower tagOrId ?belowThis?
```

moves all of the objects given by `tagOrId` to a new position in the display list just before the object given by `belowThis`.

```
widgetname raise tagOrId ?aboveThis?
```

moves all of the objects given by `tagOrId` to a new position in the display list just after the object given by `aboveThis`.

Configuring objects

```
widgetname itemcget tagOrId option
```

returns the current value of the option for the object specified by `tagOrId`. For example, `.c itemcget tag1 foreground` returns the foreground color of objects in the canvas `.c` tagged with `tag1`.

```
widgetname itemconfigure tagOrId ?option?
?value? ?option value ...?
```

configures an object specified with `tagOrId`. For example, `.c itemconfigure tag1 -foreground red` changes the foreground color of the item tagged with `tag1` to red.

```
widgetname type tagOrId
```

returns the type of the object that is specified by `tagOrId` (text, oval, rectangle, etc.)

Moving objects

```
widgetname move tagOrId x y
```

moves each of the objects specified by `tagOrId` by adding x to the object's x coordinate and y to the object's y coordinate.

App V, Part 1: Creating animated text and objects

This application will show you how easy it is to create and manipulate text objects and other figures.

When working with text objects, you can use similar principles as you did while working with text in text widgets. For example, you can easily create multiple text objects using an array. Each text object, however, must be tagged with a different tag if you want to move or change it separately from the others.

This application creates "nervous" text. You can expand on this application to create other types of moving text. You can also create graphical displays simply by substituting the text objects with graphic objects.

Steps to create animated text and objects

Step 1: Creating a canvas

```
canvas .c -bg white -width 200 -height 75
pack .c
```

Step 2: Creating text

The following code creates two sets of text objects that represent different words. Each text object, or letter, is an element of an array. You can use a for loop to create each text object. Each object is at the same y coordinate. The x coordinate increases with each iteration of the loop. The loop command also tags each element with a different tag.

```
# ────────────────────────────────────────
# Creates a list of letters "H E L L O"
# ────────────────────────────────────────

set word1 "Hello"
set wordlist_1 [split $word1 {}]
# ────────────────────────────────────────
# Creates a text object using each letter in the
# list of letters. Each is at the same y position,
# spaced evenly by x. Each is tagged with a distinct
# tag "m$i"
# ────────────────────────────────────────
for {set i 0} {$i < [llength $wordlist_1]} {incr i}
```

```
            set letter  [lindex $wordlist_1 $i]
            set x_position [expr 10 * $i + 50]
            .c create text $x_position 20 -text $letter    \
                -tags m$i -fill purple
}
# ─────────────────────────────────────────────────────
# Creates a list of letters "W O R L D"
# ─────────────────────────────────────────────────────
set word2 "World"
set wordlist_2 [split $word2 {}]
# ─────────────────────────────────────────────────────
# Creates a text object for each element of the
# letter list. Each is placed at the same y position,
# spaced with an even x distance. Each is tagged
# with a distinct tag
# ─────────────────────────────────────────────────────
for {set i 0} {$i < [llength $wordlist_1]} {incr i}
            set letter  [lindex $wordlist_2 $i]
            set x_position [expr 10 * $i + 100]
            set tag m[expr $i +5]
            .c create text $x_position 50 -text $letter \
                -tags $tag -fill red
}
```

Step 3: Writing the procedures

The following two procedures use the `after` command to move
specified text.

The `nervous` procedure moves an object a specified distance,
waits 1 second, and then moves it back again. The `nervous_text`
procedure repeats the `nervous` procedure in specified time incre-
ments.

```
proc nervous { w x y } {
        .c move $w $x $y
        after 100 ".c move $w [expr -$x] [expr -$y]"
```

```
}
proc nervous_text { w x y d } {
      for {set i 0} {$i < 1000} {incr i $d} {
      after $i "nervous $w $x $y"
      }
#  ─────────────────────────────────────────────────
# Calls the procedure again to create a loop
#  ─────────────────────────────────────────────────
   after $i [list nervous_text $w $x $y $d]
}
```

Step 4: Applying the procedure

Now we need to apply the nervous_text procedure to each text
object. However, in this case we want each object to move a different amount with a different time period, for erratically moving
text. So we repeat the procedure for each text element, providing
different arguments for each letter.

```
nervous_text m0 5 5 500
nervous_text m1 3 2 300
nervous_text m2 4 -6 700
nervous_text m3 -4 -3 600
nervous_text m4 -7 5 200
nervous_text m5 4 6 600
nervous_text m6 -9 3 200
nervous_text m7 -7 -5 400
nervous_text m8 8 4 200
nervous_text m9 6 -2 700
```

If you wanted to move an entire word together, you could use a
for loop to apply the nervous_text procedure to each letter,
using the same parameters.

For example:

```
for { set i 0} { $i < 4} { incr i } {
    nervous_text m$i 5 5 500
    }
```

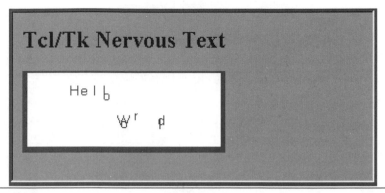

Figure 4.5 Nervous text on a canvas widget

The nervous text application:

```
# ─────────────────────────────────────────────
# Moves an object from one place to another
# ─────────────────────────────────────────────
proc nervous { w x y } {
      .c move $w $x $y
      after 100 ".c move $w [expr -$x] [expr -$y]"
      }
# ─────────────────────────────────────────────
# Continually calls the nervous procedure
# ─────────────────────────────────────────────
proc nervous_text { w x y d } {
      for {set i 0} {$i < 1000} {incr i $d} {
      after $i "nervous $w $x $y"
            }
      after $i [list nervous_text $w $x $y $d]
}
# ─────────────────────────────────────────────
# Creates the canvas
# ─────────────────────────────────────────────
canvas .c -bg white -width 200 -height 75
pack .c
```

```
# ─────────────────────────────────────────
# Creates the text objects
# ─────────────────────────────────────────
set word1 "Hello"
set wordlist_1 [split $word1 {}]
for {set i 0} {$i < [llength $wordlist_1]} {incr i}
{
      set letter  [lindex $wordlist_1 $i]
      set x_position [expr 10 * $i + 50]
      .c create text $x_position 20 -text $letter \
            -tags m$i -fill purple
}
# ─────────────────────────────────────────
# Creates the text objects for the second word
# ─────────────────────────────────────────
set word2 "World"
set wordlist_2 [split $word2 {}]
for {set i 0} {$i < [llength $wordlist_1]} {incr i}
{
      set letter  [lindex $wordlist_2 $i]
      set x_position [expr 10 * $i + 100]
      set tag m[expr $i +5]
      .c create text $x_position 50 -text $letter  \
            -tags $tag -fill red
      }
# ─────────────────────────────────────────
# Calls the procedure for each text object
# ─────────────────────────────────────────
nervous_text m0 5 5 500
nervous_text m1 3 2 300
nervous_text m2 4 -6 700
nervous_text m3 -4 -3 600
nervous_text m4 -7 5 200
```

```
nervous_text m5  4  6  600
nervous_text m6  -9  3  200
nervous_text m7  -7  -5  400
nervous_text m8  8  4  200
nervous_text m9  6  -2  700
```

App V, Part 2: Creating bubbles

You can easily animate any objects simply by substituting the text objects of this application with other objects.

In the following code, we've modified the for loops that created the text objects in the animated text application. We create ovals by substituting "oval" for "text" and removing any text-specific options, such as the font and text option. Also, we create an additional x y coordinate pair to specify the bounding box of the oval.

Other than these changes, we can use the same procedures to create animated objects as easily as text.

```
for {set i 0} {$i < 5} {incr i} {
    set x_position [expr 10 * $i + 50]
    .c create oval $x_position 20   \
        [expr $x_position + 10] 30 \
        -tags m$i -outline purple
}
for {set i 0} {$i < 5} {incr i} {
    set x_position [expr 20 * $i + 50]
    set tag m[expr $i +5]
    .c create oval $x_position 30 \
        [expr $x_position + 20] 50 \
        -tags $tag -outline red
}
```

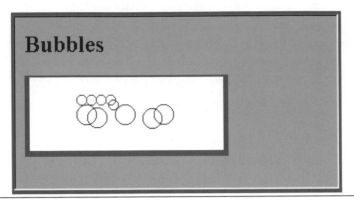

Figure 4.6 Moving objects on a canvas widget

App VI: The Tcl/Tk canvas slider

Unlike the text slider, this application has one procedure. It is actually doing what it looks like it is doing - sliding the text across the page. You can create the list of letters with only a few commands.

Steps to create a canvas slider

Step 1: Creating the canvas

The canvas can be as large or small as you would like.

```
canvas .c -bg white -width 200 -height 75
pack .c
```

Step 2: Creating the words

Each element of the list of letters will provide a different value for the -text option when we create the text objects in the procedure.

```
set words "Hello World"
set letter_list [split $words {}]
set list_length [llength $letter_list]
```

Step 3: Writing the procedure

The slide procedure accomplishes these tasks:

- After a certain time period, it creates a text object for an element of the letter_list if it is not an empty space " ".

- It moves that letter from its initial position to its final position, after a specific time period.
- It increases the time period between each movememnt of a letter object.
- It increases the time period that it waits before creating a new letter object.

In this procedure, the time periods are determined by the place of the letter in the `letter_list` (the variable k), and how many times a letter object has moved (the variable i).

```
proc slide { } {
global letter_list list_length


# ────────────────────────────────────────────────
# Starts the for loop that examines each member of
# letter_list
# ────────────────────────────────────────────────

for {set k 0} {$k < $list_length} {incr k} {
# ────────────────────────────────────────────────
# Sets the letter to an element of the letter_list
# ────────────────────────────────────────────────

        set letter [lindex $letter_list $k]
# ────────────────────────────────────────────────
# If the element is a space, it goes to the next
# iteration of the for loop, else creates a text
# for loop, else creates a text object at the right
# of the canvas
# ────────────────────────────────────────────────

      if {$letter == " "} { continue } else {
         after [expr 25 * $k * $k]                \
         ".c create text 150 40-text $letter -tags m$k"
# ────────────────────────────────────────────────
# Starts a for loop that  moves the text object
# (specified by its tag) a distance to the left.
# Increases the time period each iteration.
# ────────────────────────────────────────────────
```

```
          for {set i 0} {$i < 14 } {incr i} {
              after [expr 25 * $k *$i] ".c move\
              m$k -10 0"
                  }
              }
}
}
```

Step 4: Starting it up

The slide procedure requires no arguments.

```
slide
```

Here's the complete Tcl/Tk canvas slider:

```
# ──────────────────────────────────────────────
# Examine each of the letters, create a text object
# and move that object the length of the canvas.
# ──────────────────────────────────────────────
proc slide { } {
global letter_list list_length
for {set k 0} {$k < $list_length} {incr k} {
        set letter [lindex $letter_list $k]
    if {$letter == " "} { continue } else {
        after [expr 25 * $k * $k] ".c create text
150 40 -text \
                $letter -tags m$k"
            for {set i 0} {$i < 14} {incr i} {
            after [expr 25 * $k *$i] ".c move m$k -
10 0"
                }
    }}
}
# ──────────────────────────────────────────────
# Create the canvas
# ──────────────────────────────────────────────
```

```
canvas .c -bg white -width 200 -height 75
pack .c
# ─────────────────────────────────────
# Create the word list
# ─────────────────────────────────────
set words "Hello World"
set letter_list [split $words {}]
set list_length [llength $letter_list]
# ─────────────────────────────────────
# Start it up
# ─────────────────────────────────────
slide
```

Conclusion

This section of the chapter has given you an overview of the canvas widget and some examples of how you can animate and manipulate text objects and other graphics. In the next chapter, we will focus on the canvas widget in an interactive role, responding to the input of a user.

5

Interactive Applications

This chapter focuses on interactive applications that respond to the keyboard and the mouse. Examples of interactive applications include forms, text editors, and interactive animations.

We look at how to use the canvas widget to create animations, including how to embed windows and images and how to create objects that can be moved, created, or changed through actions of the mouse and keyboard. We also describe interactive applications using multiple widgets such as the entry widget, text widget, and button widget.

As we study the applications of this chapter, we assume that you've read the previous chapter that outlines some basic characteristics of the canvas widget, or that you can reference the online documentation about the canvas and other widgets.

Canvas Animations

The canvas widget and its geometrical objects are introduced in the previous chapter. You can use the following on the canvas widget: arcs, lines, ovals, polygons, rectangles, and text objects. This section will introduce images, bitmaps, and window objects.

You can manipulate these objects so that they can be moved and created by the mouse button or your keyboard. These applications depend heavily on the use of *tags* and *bindings*. The previous chapter covers more details about tags and bindings.

About focus

In an interactive application, a widget must have *focus* to receive keyboard events. Sometimes the widget will receive focus when the mouse button initially clicks on it to perform some function. You can also explicitly give a widget focus with the `focus widgetname` command. We used this command in the previous chapter while constructing the entry typewriter.

Only one widget at a time has focus in an application. When you create an application that has multiple widgets, then focus can be obtained either by entering that widget with the mouse or clicking on the widget with the mouse button. The widget has default bindings which determine how it behaves when it receives focus.

Several types of widgets, such as the button widget, will change their colors to active colors when they receive focus. These colors are determined by their `activeforeground` and `activebackground` attributes.

Percent substitutions in bindings

To create interactive animations and applications, your application needs to know what widget is involved in a keyboard or mouse event, and the location of the mouse when a button is clicked. Tcl/Tk recognizes the percent sign (%) as a special character that identifies *event keywords* that provide this type of information. When the interpreter encounters a percent sign, it substitutes the value of the keyword when the event occurs.

For example, the keyword %x is the x coordinate. If you use this keyword in a binding for the first mouse button, then when the user clicks the mouse button, the keyword %x is substituted for the actual x coordinate of the mouse. We use this keyword in the first examples of this chapter.

There is a large group of event keywords that you can use when binding scripts to Tk widgets. You can find a list of these keywords in the online documentation under the description of the `bind` command. Event keywords let you determine such issues as which mouse button is pressed and what the current state of a widget is, as well as x and y coordinates.

For the applications of this chapter, we use only three event keywords: the keywords that identify the x and y coordinates of the mouse, and a keyword that identifies the widget in which the event occurs.

%W   The widget in which the event occurs. (Must be capitalized.)

%x   The x coordinate.

%y   The y coordinate.

App I: Creating movable objects

After you create an object on a canvas widget, you can create a binding for it that enables a user to "pick up" the object and move it with a mouse button.

The following application is a demo bundled with the standard release of Tcl/Tk. It shows how you can enable a user of your application to move two text objects with the mouse. You can apply these principles to any type of object of the canvas widget.

Steps to create movable objects

Step 1: Creating bindings

The application creates two bindings for objects with the tag "movable." One binds the mouse button to a procedure; another binds the motion of the mouse (with the button pressed) to a procedure.

```
.c bind movable <Button-1> {dragstart %W %x %y}
.c bind movable <B1-Motion> {dragit %W %x %y}
```

Step 2: Writing the moving procedures

Each procedure takes three arguments. The values of the w , x, and y arguments are supplied by the location of the cursor. W represents the widget that has focus, and x and y are the x and y coordinates of the mouse location on the canvas.

The procedure `dragstart` determines the object that will be dragged by finding the closest object to the x and y coordinates given by the position of the mouse. It also sets the original location of the coordinates to the x and y coordinates of the mouse.

```
proc dragstart {w x y} {
    global draglocation

    catch {unset draglocation}
    set draglocation(obj) [$w find closest $x $y]

    set draglocation(x) $x
    set draglocation(y) $y
}
```

The procedure `dragit`, bound to the motion of the mouse, checks to see if there really is an object near the x and y coordinates in the widget identified by the variable w, and then moves the object the distance that the mouse moves from its original location.

The object moves the *difference* of the initial position of the mouse (determined in the `dragit` procedure) and the final position of the mouse. This final position is continually changing as long as the mouse is in motion.

```
proc dragit {w x y} {
    global draglocation

    #-------------------------------------------------
    # If the variable draglocation(obj) has no value,
    # then no object was near the specified
    # coordinates.
    #-------------------------------------------------
        if {"$draglocation(obj)" != ""} {
```

```
#--------------------------------------------------
# Set the distance equal to the final position
# minus the initial position and move the
# object that distance.
#--------------------------------------------------

        set dx [expr $x - $draglocation(x)]
        set dy [expr $y - $draglocation(y)]
        $w move $draglocation(obj) $dx $dy


#--------------------------------------------------
# Set the final position of the object to the
# position of the mouse.
#--------------------------------------------------

        set draglocation(x)  $x
        set draglocation(y)  $y
    }
}
```

Step 3: Creating the moving objects

You can create any type of object and use it with these procedures.
The "Hello World" application creates two text objects.

```
canvas .c -bg bisque -width 400 -height 400
.c create text 50 50 -text Hello \
            -font *-times-bold-r-*-18-* \
            -tags {movable color=red} -fill red
.c create text 100 100 -text World \
            -font *-times-medium-i-*-18-* \
            -tags {movable color=blue} -fill blue
pack .c
```

Here are two screen shots of this demo.

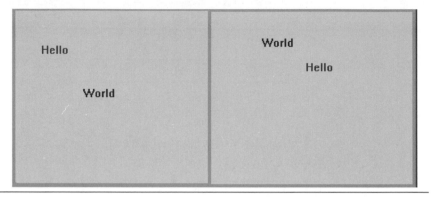

Figure 5.1 Movable objects

The complete code for this demo:

```
proc dragstart {w x y} {
    global draglocation

    catch {unset draglocation}
    set draglocation(obj) [$w find closest $x $y]
    set draglocation(x) $x
    set draglocation(y) $y
}

proc dragit {w x y} {
    global draglocation

    if {"$draglocation(obj)" != ""} {
      set dx [expr $x - $draglocation(x)]
      set dy [expr $y - $draglocation(y)]
      $w move $draglocation(obj) $dx $dy
      set draglocation(x) $x
      set draglocation(y) $y
    }
}
```

```
canvas .c -bg bisque -width 400 -height 400
.c create text 50 50 -text Hello \
        -font *-times-bold-r-*-18-* \
        -tags {movable color=red} -fill red
.c create text 100 100 -text World \
        -font *-times-medium-i-*-18-* \
        -tags {movable color=blue} -fill blue
.c bind movable <Button-1> {dragstart %W %x %y}
.c bind movable <B1-Motion> {dragit %W %x %y}
pack .c
```

App Ii: Animated puppy

We use similar procedures in this application to move a polygon object with a mouse button. This application also responds to the mouse button by configuring other objects on the canvas.

Here are two screen shots of the application. When the bone moves, the puppy's eyes follow the bone and the puppy sticks out its tongue. When the bone stops moving, the puppy's tongue appears and disappears to mimic panting.

Bone still   **Bone in motion**

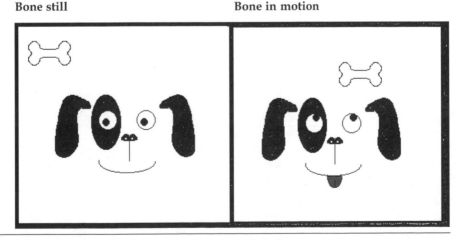

Figure 5.2 Animated puppy on a canvas widget

Steps to create animated puppy

Step 1: Creating the picture

The following code creates the picture in this application. Each object is tagged with an obvious name, such as "bone" or "eye."

```
#─────────────────────────────────────────────
# Creates the parent canvas widget
#─────────────────────────────────────────────
canvas .c -height 500 -width 500 -background white
pack .c


#─────────────────────────────────────────────
#  Creates the eyes. Notice the patch is listed last
# in the display list with the command ".c lower
# patch", so it won't cover up the other elements
# of the eye.
#─────────────────────────────────────────────
.c create oval 150 150 175 175 -outline black \
      -fill white
.c create oval 200 150 225 175 -outline black \
      -fill white

.c create oval 155 155 165 165 -fill black -tag eyel
.c create oval 205 155 215 165 -fill black -tag eyer

.c create oval 140 130 180 200 -outline black    \
      -fill black -tag patch
.c lower patch


#─────────────────────────────────────────────
# Creates the tongue. The parts of the tongue are
# initially the same color as the background. The
# procedures of the application will change their
# color, causing them to appear.
#─────────────────────────────────────────────

.c create arc 180 215 200 245 -style pieslice \
```

```
        -extent 180 -start 180 -tag tongue \
        -outline white -fill white

.c create line 190 235 190 245 -tag tongueline \
      -fill white


#————————————————————————————————————————————
# Creates the smile
#————————————————————————————————————————————

.c create arc 150 200 225 230 -style arc \
      -extent 180  -start 180 -tag smile \
      -outline black


#————————————————————————————————————————————
# Creates the nose. The nostrils are 4 pixels wide.
# Notice the -smooth attribute determines the poly-
# gon will be curved.
#————————————————————————————————————————————
.c create polygon 180 188 180 184 184 180 188 180 \
      190 184 192 180 196 180 200 184 200 188 \
      -outline black -fill black -smooth 1
.c create oval 184 184 188 188 -fill white
.c create oval 192 184 196 188 -fill white
.c create line 190 188 190 215


#————————————————————————————————————————————
# Creates the ears
#————————————————————————————————————————————

.c create polygon 100 140 110 130 120 130 \
      130 135 140 140 140 150 120 145 125 \
      190 120 200 110 210 100 210 90 200 \
       -fill black -smooth 1
.c create polygon 230 140 250 130 260 130 \
      270 140 280 200 270 210 260 210 250 \
      200 245 190 250 145 230 150  \
```

```
        -fill black -smooth 1

#————————————————————————————————————————————————

# Creates the bone

#————————————————————————————————————————————————

.c create polygon                      \
      5 10 10 5 15 5 20 10 20 15 45 15 45 10\
      50 5 55 5 60 10 60 15 55 20 60 25 60 30\
      55 35 50 35 45 30 45 25 20 25 20 30\
      15 35 10 35 5 30 5 25 10 20 5 15     \
      -fill white -outline black -tag bone -smooth 1
```

Steps to shape polygons

When working with the canvas widget, it may be difficult to place
and shape your geometrical objects exactly where you want them.
You'll find that the job is easier if you use graph paper and an
appropriate scale to sketch your shapes out before drawing them
on your canvas.

For example, the puppy's bone is a polygon with 26 sides. That
is a lot of vertices to specify. But with sketching, it is easy to determine the coordinates that will create the shape.

Here is the polygon on a graph. Each block represents five pixels.

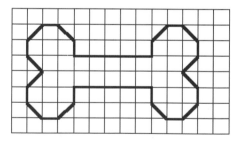

Step 2: Creating the bindings

The polygon that represents the bone has three bindings: the
mouse button, the motion of the mouse with the mouse button
pressed down, and the release of the mouse button.

```
.c bind bone <Button-1> {grab_bone %x %y}
.c bind bone <B1-Motion> {move_bone %x %y}
.c bind bone <ButtonRelease-1> {pant}
```

Step 3: Writing the moving procedures

The procedures grab_bone and move_bone are similar to the procedures of the previous application, except that they don't require the name of the canvas widget as an argument. Also, both procedures call a third procedure, move_eyes, described below.

```
proc grab_bone { x y } {
    global draglocation
    move_eyes $x $y
    set draglocation(x) $x
    set draglocation(y) $y
    }
proc move_bone { x y } {
  global draglocation
   move_eyes $x $y
   set dx [expr $x - $draglocation(x)]
   set dy [expr $y - $draglocation(y)]
   .c move bone $dx $dy
   set draglocation(x) $x
   set draglocation(y) $y
    }
```

The procedure move_eyes accomplishes these tasks:

• It causes the tongue to appear.
• It positions the two eyes at their original coordinates. This is done so the eyes will not be continually displaced, but will return to their original position each time the procedure is called before they are displaced.
• It determines in what general area of the canvas the bone is located. Notice that this is done loosely, and you could

make this procedure more precise if you wanted to. It sets the displacement distances according to the relative direction of the bone. For example, if the bone is located directly to the right, then the displacement distance for x is set at +5, and the y distance is set at 0, because the eyes will not move up or down.

- It moves the eyes their displacement distances in the general direction of the bone.

```
proc move_eyes { x y } {

    #—————————————————————————————————————————
    # Colors the tongue, causing it to appear
    # —————————————————————————————————————————

    tongue

    #—————————————————————————————————————————
    # Puts the eyes in their place
    #—————————————————————————————————————————

    .c coords eyel 155 155 165 165
    .c coords eyer 205 155 215 165

    #—————————————————————————————————————————
    # Determines the general direction and sets
    # the displacement values.
    #—————————————————————————————————————————

    if {$x > 225} {
        set dx 5
        } elseif {$x > 150} {
        set dx 0
          } else {
        set dx -5
          }
    if {$y > 175} {
        set dy 5
```

```
        } elseif { $y > 150} {
        set dy 0
        } else {
        set dy -5
    }


#─────────────────────────────────────
# Moves the eyes the displacement distances
#─────────────────────────────────────

.c move eyel $dx $dy
.c move eyer $dx $dy
}
```

The polygon that represents the bone also has a binding of the release of the mouse button. When the mouse button is released, the pant procedure is called.

This procedure calls the no_tongue procedure, then waits a specified time, and alternatively calls the tongue or no_tongue procedure after waiting a specified time that increases with each iteration of a for loop.

```
proc pant { } {
    no_tongue
    for {set i 100} {$i < 1000} {incr i 100} {
        after $i {tongue}
        incr i 100
        after $i { no_tongue}
    }
}
```

The tongue and no_tongue procedure simply configure the parts of the tongue to be colored the color of the background, or to be rendered in a color that distingushes them from the background.

You need to specify the parts of the tongue separately. They are two different types of objects: an arc and a line. If you tagged them both with the same name to refer to them without any differentiation, the line would not recognize the outline attribute, and it would generate an error.

```
proc no_tongue { } {
        .c itemconfigure tongue -outline white \
            -fill white
        .c itemconfigure tongueline -fill white
        }
proc tongue { } {
        .c itemconfigure tongue -outline black \
            -fill red
        .c itemconfigure tongueline -fill black
        }
```

Here is the complete code for the animated puppy:

```
#————————————————————————————————————————
# Colors the tongue, moves eyes
#————————————————————————————————————————

proc move_eyes { x y } {

   tongue

.c coords eyel 155 155 165 165
.c coords eyer 205 155 215 165
if {$x > 225} {
        set x 5
} elseif {$x > 150} {
        set x 0
            } else {
        set x -5
        }
```

```
if {$y > 175} {
     set y 5
     } elseif { $y > 150} {
       set y 0
      } else {
        set y -5
          }
.c move eyel $x $y
.c move eyer $x $y


}

#————————————————————————————————————
# Moves bone with the x y coordinates of the mouse
#————————————————————————————————————

proc move_bone { x y } {
   global draglocation
    move_eyes $x $y
    set dx [expr $x - $draglocation(x)]
    set dy [expr $y - $draglocation(y)]
    .c move bone $dx $dy
    set draglocation(x) $x
    set draglocation(y) $y

}

#————————————————————————————————————
# Picks up the bone and moves the eyes
#————————————————————————————————————

proc grab_bone { x y } {
     global draglocation
     move_eyes $x $y
     set draglocation(x) $x
```

```
        set draglocation(y) $y
        }


#————————————————————————————————————
# Colors the tongue and hides it again
#————————————————————————————————————

proc pant { } {
        no_tongue
        for {set i 100} {$i < 1000} {incr i 100} {
                after $i {tongue}
                incr i 100
                after $i { no_tongue}
        }
}


#————————————————————————————————————
# Procedures to color or hide the tongue
#————————————————————————————————————

proc no_tongue { } {
.c itemconfigure tongue -outline white \
        -fill white
.c itemconfigure tongueline -fill white
}

proc tongue { } {
.c itemconfigure tongue -outline black \
        -fill red
.c itemconfigure tongueline -fill black
}


#————————————————————————————————————
# Creates the parent canvas widget
#————————————————————————————————————
```

```
canvas .c -height 500 -width 500 -background white
pack .c

#————————————————————————————————————————————————————
#   Creates the eyes. Notice the patch is listed last
#   in the display list with the command ".c lower
#   patch", so it won't cover up the other elements
#   of the eye.
#————————————————————————————————————————————————————

.c create oval 150 150 175 175 -outline black \
      -fill white
.c create oval 200 150 225 175 -outline black \
      -fill white

.c create oval 155 155 165 165 -fill black -tag eyel
.c create oval 205 155 215 165 -fill black -tag eyer

.c create oval 140 130 180 200 -outline black     \
      -fill black -tag patch
.c lower patch

#————————————————————————————————————————————————————
#   Creates the tongue. The parts of the tongue are
#   initially the same color as the background. The
#   procedures of the application will change their
#   color, causing them to appear.
#————————————————————————————————————————————————————

.c create arc 180 215 200 245 -style pieslice \
      -extent 180 -start 180 -tag tongue \
      -outline white -fill white

.c create line 190 235 190 245 -tag tongueline \
      -fill white

#————————————————————————————————————————————————————
# Creates the smile
#————————————————————————————————————————————————————
```

```
.c create arc 150 200 225 230 -style arc \
        -extent 180 -start 180 -tag smile \
        -outline black

#————————————————————————————————————————————

# Creates the nose. The nostrils are 4 pixels wide.
# Notice the -smooth attribute determines the
# polygon will be curved.
#————————————————————————————————————————————

.c create polygon 180 188 180 184 184 180 188 180 190\
        184 192 180 196 180 200 184 200 188 \
        -outline black -fill black -smooth 1
.c create oval 184 184 188 188 -fill white
.c create oval 192 184 196 188 -fill white
.c create line 190 188 190 215
#————————————————————————————————————————————

# Creates the ears
#————————————————————————————————————————————

.c create polygon 100 140 110 130 120 130 \
        130 135 140 140 140 150 120 145 125 \
        190 120 200 110 210 100 210 90 200 \
           -fill black -smooth 1

.c create polygon 230 140 250 130 260 130 \
        270 140 280 200 270 210 260 210 250 \
        200 245 190 250 145 230 150  \
        -fill black -smooth 1

#————————————————————————————————————————————

# Creates the bone
#————————————————————————————————————————————

.c create polygon                 \
        5 10 10 5 15 5 20 10 20 15 45 15 45 10 \
```

```
           50 5 55 5 60 10 60 15 55 20 60 25 60 30 \
           55 35 50 35 45 30 45 25 20 25 20 30\
           15 35 10 35 5 30 5 25 10 20 5 15    \
           -fill white -outline black -tag bone -smooth 1

#————————————————————————————————————
# Bindings for the bone polygon
#————————————————————————————————————
.c bind bone <Button-1> {grab_bone %x %y}
.c bind bone <B1-Motion> {move_bone %x %y}
.c bind bone <ButtonRelease-1> {pant}
```

App III: Drawing objects with the mouse button

The next few applications will show how you can enable a user to draw shapes with the mouse button. We will look at two demos that use similar procedures and different shapes, and then we will combine these applications and create an application with embedded buttons.

Steps to draw ovals

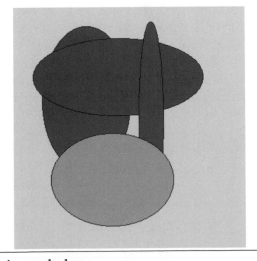

Figure 5.3 Drawing ovals demo

This application lets the user draw ovals on a canvas by clicking and dragging with the mouse.

Step 1: Creating the bindings

In this application, the canvas is assigned three bindings: pressing the mouse button, moving the mouse while the mouse button is pressed, and releasing the mouse button. Unlike the previous application, the bindings are associated with the entire canvas widget, and not with a particular object.

```
canvas .c -width 400 -height 400 -background bisque \
     -relief groove -highlightt 0
pack .c
focus .c


bind .c <Button-1> {startoval %W %x %y}
bind .c <B1-Motion> {dragoval %W %x %y}
bind .c <ButtonRelease-1> {endoval %W %x %y}
```

Step 2: Writing the drawing procedures

The three procedures bound to these events behave as you might expect: startoval begins drawing an oval, dragoval continues it, and endoval finishes the oval.

Ovals are created by specifying their bounding box. Two vertices are needed to specify this box. The procedures take the location of the mouse when the button is pressed as the first vertex and the current location of the mouse.

The startoval procedure determines the original location of the mouse when the button is pressed. These coordinates will be the first pair of vertices that determine the bounding box of the oval. It creates a tiny oval.

```
proc startoval {w x y} {
     global ovallocation

     #─────────────────────────────────────
     # If the ovallocation variable is already set,
     # it unsets it and catches any errors.
     #─────────────────────────────────────
```

```
catch {unset ovallocation}
set ovallocation(xorig) $x
set ovallocation(yorig) $y
set tx [expr $x + 1]
set ty [expr $y + 1]
set ovallocation(obj) \
   [$w create oval $x $y $tx $ty -fill red \
   -stipple gray25]
}
```

The `dragoval` procedure creates an oval with a bounding box of the original vertex (determined by the mouse click and the `start-oval` procedure) and the x y coordinates whose values it gets from its arguments. These values are continually changing as the mouse is dragged.

```
proc dragoval {w x y} {

   global ovallocation
   $w coords $ovallocation(obj)\
          $ovallocation(xorig) \
          $ovallocation(yorig) $x $y
}
```

The `endoval` procedure deletes the oval that was created by the previous procedure, and then creates an oval with a bounding box of the original coordinates and of the x y coordinates whose value is the location of the mouse when the mouse button is released.

The procedure also creates a binding for each specific oval involving the Enter and Leave events of the mouse. When the mouse enters or leaves the object, the object will change color. In the next application, you will see how you can create the bindings differently.

```
proc endoval {w x y} {
   global ovallocation
```

```
#  ————————————————————————————————————————
# Delete original oval
#  ————————————————————————————————————————

$w delete $ovallocation(obj)

  #  ————————————————————————————————————————
  # Creates the new oval
  #  ————————————————————————————————————————

set ovallocation(obj) \
  [$w create oval $ovallocation(xorig) \
        $ovallocation(yorig) \
        $x $y -fill blue]
  #  ————————————————————————————————————————
  # Add tags to the current oval
  #  ————————————————————————————————————————

$w addtag tag$ovallocation(obj) \
        withtag $ovallocation(obj)

$w bind tag$ovallocation(obj) <Enter> \
  [list %W itemconfigure $ovallocation(obj)\
        -fill yellow]
$w bind tag$ovallocation(obj) <Leave> \
  [list %W itemconfigure $ovallocation(obj) \
        -fill blue]
}
```

The canvas also includes a binding of the delete key, calling the command "%W delete current." The tag current is a special format understood by the canvas widget to be the object that is currently selected. The canvas widget has a default binding that enables you to select an object by clicking on it with the mouse button. When the object is selected, it is automatically assigned the tag current.

```
bind .c <Delete> {%W delete current}
```

Here's the complete code for the ovals demo:

```tcl
# ————————————————————————————————————————

proc startoval {w x y} {
    global ovallocation
    catch {unset ovallocation}
    set ovallocation(xorig) $x
    set ovallocation(yorig) $y
    set tx [expr $x + 1]
    set ty [expr $y + 1]
    set ovallocation(obj) \
      [$w create oval $x $y $tx $ty -fill red \
            -stipple gray25]
}
proc dragoval {w x y} {
    global ovallocation
    $w coords $ovallocation(obj) \
      $ovallocation(xorig) \
      $ovallocation(yorig) $x $y
}

proc endoval {w x y} {
    global ovallocation
    $w delete $ovallocation(obj)
    set ovallocation(obj) \
      [$w create oval $ovallocation(xorig) \
            $ovallocation(yorig) \
            $x $y -fill blue]
    $w addtag tag$ovallocation(obj) withtag \
            $ovallocation(obj)

    $w bind tag$ovallocation(obj) <Enter> \
      [list %W itemconfigure \
            $ovallocation(obj) -fill yellow]
```

```
    $w bind tag$ovallocation(obj) <Leave> \
      [list %W itemconfigure \
          $ovallocation(obj) -fill blue]
}

canvas .c -width 400 -height 400 -background bisque \
      -relief groove -highlightt 0
bind .c <Button-1> {startoval %W %x %y}
bind .c <B1-Motion> {dragoval %W %x %y}
bind .c <ButtonRelease-1> {endoval %W %x %y}
bind .c <Delete> {%W delete current}
pack .c
focus .c
# ─────────────────────────────────────────────
```

Steps to draw lines

This demo application accomplishes the same thing as the drawing ovals application, but the object that it draws is a line. There are also several other differences.

Figure 5.4 Drawing lines demo

Each line is drawn by creating and deleting many individual lines. It has similar bindings; however, the Enter and Leave events are not bound to each specific line, but to all objects with the tag line.

Step 1: Creating the bindings

The bindings that this demo uses are similar to the ovals demo:

```
canvas .c -width 400 -height 400 -highlightt 0 \
            -background bisque

bind .c <Button-1> {StrokeBegin %W %x %y}
bind .c <B1-Motion> {Stroke %W %x %y}
bind .c <ButtonRelease-1> {StrokeEnd %W %x %y}
bind .c <Delete> {%W delete [%W find closest %x %y]}

.c bind line <Enter> {%W itemconfigure \
            [%W find closest %x %y]  \
            -fill blue}
.c bind line <Leave> {%W itemconfigure \
            [%W find closest %x %y]  \
            -fill red}

pack .c
focus .c
```

Step 2: Writing the drawing procedures

The procedure that begins the line sets the initial coordinates of the first segment of the line. The values of the coordinates are expressed in an array. The initial coordinates are represented by stroke(0).

```
proc StrokeBegin {w x y} {
    global stroke
    catch {unset stroke}
    set stroke(N) 0
    set stroke(0) [list $x $y]
}
```

The `stroke` procedure creates a line segment using the coordinates specified by an array variable and the coordinates of the current position of the mouse. It saves the values of the end coordinates of this segment to use as the beginning coordinates for the next segment.

```
proc Stroke {w x y} {
    global stroke
    set last $stroke($stroke(N))
    incr stroke(N)
    set stroke($stroke(N)) [list $x $y]
    eval {$w create line} $last \
            {$x $y -tag segments -fill blue}
}
```

The result of the `stroke` procedure gives you an array of coordinates with variables numbering 0 through the value of N.

The final procedure deletes the segments produced by the `stroke` procedure and creates a line using the point list containing all the coordinates.

```
proc StrokeEnd {w x y} {
    global stroke
    set points {}
    for {set i 0} {$i <= $stroke(N)} {incr i} {
      append points $stroke($i) " "
    }
    $w delete segments
    eval {$w create line} $points \
      {-smooth true -tag line -fill red -width 5}
}
```

Using an array of coordinates lets the user draw curvy or wavy as well as straight lines, because the lines are made up of individual segments.

Here's the complete code for the stroker demo:

```
# ──────────────────────────────────────────────────

proc StrokeBegin {w x y} {
    global stroke
    catch {unset stroke}
    set stroke(N) 0
    set stroke(0) [list $x $y]
}
proc Stroke {w x y} {
    global stroke
    set last $stroke($stroke(N))
    incr stroke(N)
    set stroke($stroke(N)) [list $x $y]
    eval {$w create line} $last\
            {$x $y -tag segments -fill blue}
}
proc StrokeEnd {w x y} {
    global stroke
    set points {}
    for {set i 0} {$i <= $stroke(N)} {incr i} {
      append points $stroke($i) " "
    }
    $w delete segments
    eval {$w create line} $points \
      {-smooth true -tag line -fill red -width 5}
}

canvas .c -width 400 -height 400 -highlight 0 \
            -background bisque
bind .c <Button-1> {StrokeBegin %W %x %y}
bind .c <B1-Motion> {Stroke %W %x %y}
bind .c <ButtonRelease-1> {StrokeEnd %W %x %y}
bind .c <Delete> {%W delete [%W find closest %x %y]}
```

```
.c bind line <Enter> {%W itemconfigure \
          [%W find closest %x %y] \
          -fill blue}
.c bind line <Leave> {%W itemconfigure \
          [%W find closest %x %y] \
          -fill red}
pack .c
focus .c
#  ─────────────────────────────────────────────
```

App IV: Working with window objects

This application combines the two drawing applications into one application. We embed three buttons that let the user control what types of shapes to draw.

You can embed buttons by creating window objects on your canvas. Window objects are embedded widgets. To create the widget, you only need to create a widget with the `widget name` command. But then you do not pack the widget to embed it into the canvas; you use the widget's name with the window attribute of the `widgetname create window` command.

This command has the syntax:

```
widgetname create window x y ?option value
option value ...?
```

The x and y coordinates place the widget on the canvas. You can use the optional `-anchor` attribute to position the widget. For example, if you use the argument `-anchor sw`, then the southwest corner of the widget would be placed at the x and y coordinates.

You can manipulate a window object like any other canvas object, and you can also configure its options directly using the `widgetname` commands that we discussed in Chapter 3.

Table 5.1 Options of the window object

Option	Function
`-window widgetname`	Specifies the window to associate with this object. May not be a toplevel window
`-anchor anchorPos`	Positions the window relative to the positioning point, such as n, se , nw, etc.
`-height pixels`	Specifies the height of the window
`-tags tagList`	Provides a set of tags to apply to the object
`-width pixels`	Specifies the width of the window

Steps for window objects

Step 1: Creating the canvas and buttons

We can begin this application by creating a canvas and embedding the buttons. Our application will have three buttons: one to draw ovals, one to draw lines, and one that will clear the canvas of all objects.

```
canvas .c -height 500 -width 500 -background white \
     pack .c

button .b1 -text Ovals -background yellow        \
     -command   {press_button oval}
button .b2 -text Strokes -background white        \
     -command {press_button stroke}
button .b3 -text Clear -background white          \
          -command clear
```

These buttons are not packed or placed, but are used to create window objects:

```
.c create window 0 0 -window .b1 -anchor nw
.c create window 60 0 -window .b2 -anchor nw
.c create window 130 0 -window .b3  -anchor nw
```

Step 2: Writing the procedures

The ovals and strokes button invokes the press_button procedure. It configures the button as raised or sunken, as "off" or "on," and sets the global variable type. The value of this variable determines which object will be drawn.

```
proc press_button { tag } {
global type
if {$tag == "oval"} {
        .b1 configure -relief sunken
        .b2 configure -relief raised
        set type oval
} else {
        .b2 configure  -relief sunken
        .b1 configure -relief raised
        set type stroke
  }
}
```

The clear procedure simply deletes all objects tagged with oval and line. If you used the tag all, which is a special tag that the canvas understands to include all objects, the buttons would be deleted as well.

```
proc clear { } {
.c delete line
.c delete oval
 }
```

These last three procedures are similar to those used for the ovals and strokes demos. Each procedure works with the line object or the oval object, depending on the value of the variable type.

Because the methods to create the objects are different, it is easier to combine them in this way rather than to attempt to create generic procedures that could be used for either type of object.

```
# ————————————————————————————————————————————
# Create the initial oval or stroke
# ————————————————————————————————————————————

proc begin {w x y} {
   global type stroke ovallocation
   if {$type == "stroke"} {
        set stroke(N) 0
        set stroke(0) [list $x $y]
      } else {
        set ovallocation(xorig) $x
          set ovallocation(yorig) $y
          set tx [expr $x + 1]
          set ty [expr $y + 1]
          set ovallocation(obj) \
      [$w create oval $x $y $tx $ty -fill purple]
      }
}


# ————————————————————————————————————————————
# Create a list of indices for a line if the type if
# stroke, or create an oval with the current x and y
# coordinates.
# ————————————————————————————————————————————

proc go {w x y} {
global type stroke ovallocation
   if {$type =="stroke"} {
        set last $stroke($stroke(N))
          incr stroke(N)
          set stroke($stroke(N)) [list $x $y]
          eval {$w create line} $last \
            {$x $y -tag segments -fill green}
        } else {
           $w coords $ovallocation(obj) \
           $ovallocation(xorig) \
```

```
                    $ovallocation(yorig) $x $y
}
}
```

In this procedure, we tag the resulting ovals with the tag oval,
and we remove the object-specific tags that the original application
uses.

```
proc end {w x y} {
  global thing stroke ovallocation
    if {$type =="stroke"} {
        set points {}
      for {set i 0} {$i <= $stroke(N)} {incr i} {
        append points $stroke($i) " "
            }
      $w delete segments
      if {[llength $points] < 4} {  } else {
        eval {$w create line} $points \
          {-smooth 1 -tag line -fill green -width 5}
          }
} else {
      $w delete $ovallocation(obj)
      set ovallocation(obj) \
        [$w create oval $ovallocation(xorig)\
               $ovallocation(yorig) \
            $x $y -fill yellow -tag oval]


  }}
```

Step 4: Creating the bindings

Now we can bind these procedures to the mouse actions, as in the
previous demos. We can also bind the Enter and Leave events to
change the colors of drawn objects when the mouse enters or
leaves them. (This makes for a very flashy picture.)

```
bind .c <Button-1> {begin %W %x %y}
```

```
bind .c <B1-Motion> {go %W %x %y}
bind .c <ButtonRelease-1> {end %W %x %y}
bind .c <Delete> {%W delete [%W find closest %x %y]}

.c bind line <Enter>  \
           {%W itemconfigure \
           [%W find closest %x %y]  -fill green}
.c bind line <Leave> \
           {%W itemconfigure \
           [%W find closest %x %y] -fill orange}
.c bind oval <Enter>   \
           {%W itemconfigure \
           [%W find closest %x %y] -fill purple}
.c bind oval <Leave>      \
           {%W itemconfigure \
           [%W find closest %x %y] -fill yellow}
```

To complete this application, we need to specify the initial value of the variable type and "pre-press" a button by changing its relief.

```
set type oval
.b1 configure -relief sunken
```

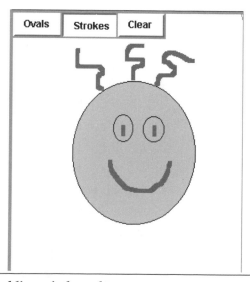

Figure 5.5 Embedding windows demo

Here's the complete code for the embed demo:

```
# ─────────────────────────────────────────────

proc begin {w x y} {
   global thing
   global stroke
   global ovallocation
   # catch {unset stroke}
   if {$thing == "stroke"} {
        set stroke(N) 0
        set stroke(0) [list $x $y]
      } else {
        set ovallocation(xorig) $x
          set ovallocation(yorig) $y
          set tx [expr $x + 1]
          set ty [expr $y + 1]
          set ovallocation(obj) \
       [$w create oval $x $y $tx $ty -fill purple]
      }
}

proc go {w x y} {
global thing
global stroke
  global ovallocation
    if {$thing =="stroke"} {
         set last $stroke($stroke(N))
           incr stroke(N)
           set stroke($stroke(N)) [list $x $y]
           eval {$w create line} $last \
              {$x $y -tag segments -fill green}
         } else {
           $w delete $ovallocation(obj)
           set ovallocation(obj) \
```

```
                     [$w create oval $ovallocation(xorig) \
                            $ovallocation(yorig) \
                            $x $y -fill purple]
     }
     }

     proc end {w x y} {
         global thing
       global stroke
         global ovallocation
     if {$thing =="stroke"} {
         set points {}
         for {set i 0} {$i <= $stroke(N)} {incr i} {
           append points $stroke($i) " "
                 }
         $w delete segments
       if {[llength $points] < 4} {  } else {
           eval {$w create line} $points \
             {-smooth 1 -tag line -fill green -width 5}
             }
     } else {
         $w delete $ovallocation(obj)
         set ovallocation(obj) \
           [$w create oval $ovallocation(xorig) \
                  $ovallocation(yorig) \
                  $x $y -fill yellow -tag oval]

     }}

     proc press_button { tag } {
     global thing
     if {$tag == "oval"} {
     .b1 configure -relief sunken
     .b2 configure -relief raised
     set thing oval
```

```
} else {
.b2 configure  -relief sunken
.b1 configure -relief raised
set thing stroke
 }
}

proc clear { } {
.c delete line
.c delete oval
}

canvas .c -height 500 -width 500 -background white
pack .c

button .b1 -text Ovals -background white \
            -command {press_button oval}
button .b2 -text Strokes -background white \
            -command {press_button stroke}
button .b3 -text Clear -background white -command
clear

set thing oval

.c create window 0 0 -window .b1 \
            -anchor nw -tag obutton
.c create window 60 0 -window .b2 \
            -anchor nw -tag sbutton
.c create window 130 0 -window .b3 \
            -anchor nw -tag clearbutton

bind .c <Button-1> {begin %W %x %y}
bind .c <B1-Motion> {go %W %x %y}
bind .c <ButtonRelease-1> {end %W %x %y}
bind .c <Delete> {%W delete [%W find closest %x %y]}
.b1 configure -relief sunken
```

App V: Tcl/Tk wordsearch game

The Tcl/Tk wordsearch game is built on one canvas widget. It uses principles similar to those used in the previous examples for drawing objects with the mouse. When a player finds a word to circle, the player clicks on the beginning letter and then clicks on the last letter of the word. The application circles the word by first creating the arc that is the beginning of the circle, then by creating the sides of the circle as the mouse is moved by the player. The "circle" consists of two line objects capped by two arc objects.

Each letter is a separate text object created from an array of objects. Each word in the word list is also in an array, and has a set of coordinates associated with it.

If the coordinates of the circle that the player has drawn do not correspond to a word, then the circle is deleted. When the coordinates match the coordinates of a word, then the circle appears around the word and the corresponding word "dims" on the word list by fading to gray.

You can find the complete source code of the Tcl/Tk wordsearch game on the CD included with this book.

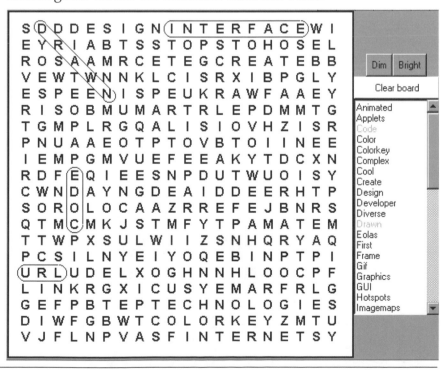

Figure 5.6 Tcl/Tk wordsearch game

One of the features of the wordsearch applet is the player can draw all over the canvas, but, when a word is found, that the circle "snaps" to a predefined circle. All the words are actually already circled with line and arc objects, but all the objects are the color of the background are and placed at the bottom of the display list, so they do not interfere with the letters. When a word is found, the line and arc objects that form its circle turn from white to black.

This code creates all the circles around the words. It examines each set of coordinates from the coords array and draws a circle horizontally, vertically, or diagonally, depending on the values of the coordinates. The w variable in this code is the name of the canvas.

```
for {set i 0} {$i <= 48} { incr i} {


#  ─────────────────────────────────────────────────

# Each set of coordinates are in the form
# {x1, y1, x2, y2} where the two x,y pairs are the
# the first and last letter of the word.

#  ─────────────────────────────────── ──────────────
set bx [lindex $coords($i) 0]

set by [lindex $coords($i) 1]

set x [lindex $coords($i) 2]

set y [lindex $coords($i) 3]


if {$by < $y} {


    if { $bx == $x} {


        #  ─────────────────────────────────────────

        # Creates a vertical circle

        #  ─────────────────────────────────────────


        $w create arc [expr $bx-10] [expr $by-10] \
              [expr $bx+10] [expr $by+10] \
              -start 0 -extent 180 -style arc \
                    -outline white -tags "origarc($i)"
        $w create line [expr $bx-10] $by \
                    [expr $x-10] $y \
```

```
                        -fill white -tags "origline($i)"
$w create line [expr $bx+10] $by \
                    [expr $x+10] $y \
             -fill white -tags "origline($i)"
$w create arc [expr $x-10] [expr $y-10]
            [expr $x+10] [expr $y+10] \
      -start 180 -extent 180 -style arc \
            -outline white -tags "origarc($i)"

} else {

# ————————————————————————————————————
# Creates a diagonal circle
# ————————————————————————————————————

$w create arc [expr $bx - 10] [expr $by -10] \
            [expr $bx+5] [expr $by +5] \
           -start 35 -extent 210 -style arc \
           -outline white -tags "origarc($i)"
$w create line [expr $bx-5] [expr $by+5] \
            [expr $x-5] [expr $y +5] \
           -fill white -tags "origline($i)"
$w create line [expr $bx+5] [expr $by-5]\
              [expr $x +5] [expr $y-5] \
           -fill white -tags "origline($i)"
$w create arc [expr $x -5] [expr $y-5] \
             [expr $x +10] [expr $y +10] \
           -start 210 -extent 215 -style arc \
           -outline white -tags "origarc($i)"

     }

} elseif  {$bx <$x} {

if {$by ==$y} {
```

```
# ─────────────────────────────────────────────
# Creates a horizontal circle
# ─────────────────────────────────────────────

$w create arc [expr $bx-10] [expr $by-10] \
            [expr $bx+10] [expr $by+10] \
            -start 90 -extent 180 -style arc \
            -outline white -tag "origarc($i)"
$w create line $bx [expr $by-10] \
                $x [expr $y-10] \
            -fill white -tag "origline($i)"
$w create line $bx [expr $by+10] \
                $x [expr $y+10] \
            -fill white -tag "origline($i)"
$w create arc [expr $x-10] [expr $y-10] \
            [expr $x+10] [expr $y+10] \
        -start 270 -extent 180 -style arc /
            -outline white -tag "origarc($i)"
} else {

# ─────────────────────────────────────────────
# Creates a diagonal circle
# ─────────────────────────────────────────────

$w create arc [expr $bx -10] [expr $by -10] \
            [expr $bx+10] [expr $by +10] \
            -start 315 -extent 180 -style arc \
            -outline white -tags "origarc($i)"
$w create line [expr $bx-5] [expr $by+5] \
            [expr $x-5] [expr $y +5] \
            -fill white -tags "origline($i)"
$w create line [expr $bx+5] [expr $by-5] \
            [expr $x +5] [expr $y-5] \
            -fill white -tags "origline($i)"
$w create arc [expr $x -10] [expr $y-10] \
```

```
                        [expr $x +10]  [expr $y +10]  \
                        -start 135 -extent 180 -style arc \
                        -outline white -tags "origarc($i)"
        }


        }

}
```

Each of the arcs and lines have been tagged to identify the word
that they circle and the coordinates they have used. When a particular word is found, the circle for that word is blackened using
those tags.

In the following example code, the flag accept indicates that
the word circled is an actual word. The application determines if
there is an actual word by examining the set of coordinates of the
drawn circle with the array of coordinates. If the flag is true, then
the temporary circle that the player had drawn is deleted and the
arcs and lines for that particular word are blackened and raised.
The word on the word list in the text box is grayed. Also, two more
tags are added to the finished circle. These tags are used in the buttons that dim or brighten the existing circles.

```
if {"$accept"} {
        $w delete temp
        $w itemconfigure "origline($i)" \
                -fill black
        $w addtag final withtag origline($i)
        $w itemconfigure "origarc($i)" \
                -outline black
        $w addtag arc withtag origarc($i)
        $w raise origarc($i)
        $w raise origline($i)
        .top1.f1.text1 tag configure word$i \
                -foreground LightGrey
        }
```

You can find the complete source code for the wordsearch game
on the CD included with this book in the programs directory.

Advanced Animations

Using images

Tcl/Tk supports bitmaps and full-color images in PPM (Portable Pixel Map) and GIF (Graphics Interchange Format) formats. You can use images on the face of buttons and on label widgets. You can place bitmaps and images on your canvas as bitmap and image objects. These objects act like other canvas objects in that you can tag and move them.

But to create image and bitmap objects, you first must create an image using the Tk command `image create`. Images created with this command can be placed on a canvas as objects.

Creating images

You create images with the command:

```
image create type ?options
```

The type can be *bitmap* or *photo.* Photos are full-color images. Bitmaps are two-color images; each pixel has the value of 1 or 0.

The image command has several other options such as `image delete`, `image width`, and `image names` that enable you to manipulate images. See the online documentation for details. For purposes of using them on the canvas widget, you only need to use `image create`.

Working with images: image create photo

When you create a photo image, you need to specify the image data, or you can specify in what file the image data is located. You use the `-data` or `-file` attributes to specify image data.

For example, the following creates a photo image from the file `picture.gif`:

```
image create photo -file picture.gif -gamma 1 \
    -palette 5/5/4
```

However, the Tcl Plug-in will not allow you to access files. If you create images for the Web under this plug-in, you should specify all your image data *inline*, which means directly in the code.

Using the data attribute

When you specify inline image data in an application, it must be in the form of BASE64 encoded ASCII. This format is understood by many e-mail programs. For example, when you send an image file over e-mail, then your mail program may encode the file to BASE64 to send over the Internet. Then the mail program of your recipient decodes the file for reception.

You can convert your images with the conversion tool that is included on the CD. See the online documentation for details. There are also many other software programs available that will convert images to BASE64 and other formats. One program is Wincode from Snappy Software, Inc., available from `http://snappy-software.com`.

When you convert a GIF or other image file into BASE64, the data comes out looking something like this:

```
set leaf {
```

```
R0lGODlhegDIAPcAAAAAAAAMwAAZgAAmQAAzAAA/zMAADMAMzMAZjMAmTMAzDMA/2Y
AAGYAM2YAZmYAmWYAzGYA/5kAAJkAM5kAZpkAmZkAzJkA/8wAAMwAM8wAZswAmcwAzM
wA//8AAP8AM/8AZv8Amf8AzP8A/wAzAAAzMwAzZgAzmQAzzAAz/zMzADMzMzMzZjMzm
TMzzDMz/2YzAGYzM2YzZmYzmWYzzGYz/5kzAJkzM5kzZpkzmZkzzJkz/8wzAMwzM8wz
ZswzmcwzzMwz//8zAP8zM/8zZv8zmf8zzP8z/wBmAABmMwBmZgBmmQBmzABm/zNmADN
mMzNmZjNmmTNmzDNm/2ZmAGZmM2ZmZmZmmWZmzGZm/5lmAJlmM5lmZplmmZlmzJlm/8
xmAMxmM8xmZsxmmcxmzMxm//9mAP9mM/9mZv9mmf9mzP9m/wCZAACZMwCZZgCZmQCZz
ACZ/zOZADOZMzOZZjOZmTOZzDOZ/2aZAGaZM2aZZmaZmWaZzGaZ/5mZAJmZM5mZZpmZ
mZmZzJmZ/8yZAMyZM8yZZsyZmcyZzMyZ//+ZAP+ZM/+ZZv+Zmf+ZzP+Z/wDMAADMMwD
MZgDMmQDMzADMzPMADPMMzPMZjPMmTPMzDPM/2bMAGbMM2bMZmbMmWbMzGbM/5nMAJ
nMM5nMZpnMmZnMzJnM/8zMAMzMM8zMZszMmczMzMzM///MAP/MM//MZv/Mmf/MzP/M/
wD/AAD/MwD/ZgD/mQD/zAD//zP/ADP/MzP/ZjP/mTP/zDP//2b/AGb/M2b/Zmb/mWb/
zGb//5n/AJn/M5n/Zpn/mZn/zJn//8z/AMz/M8z/Zsz/mcz/zMz/////AP//M///Zv/
/mf//zP///wAAAAAAAAAAAAAAAAAAAAAAAAAAAAAAAAAAAAAAAAAAAAAAAAAAAAAAAA
AAAAAAAAAAAAAAAAAAAAAAAAAAAAAAAAAAAAAAAAAAAAAAAAAAAAAAAAAAAAAAAAAAA
AAAAAAAAAAAAAAAAAAAAAAAAAAAAAAAACH5BAEAAAAALAAAAAB6AMgAAAj+AAEI
HEiwoMGDCBMqXMiwocOHECNKnEixosWLGDNq3IjRj8ePHjmKHNkx5MGPJEGqXGmS5EW
WfhTG3AizJkqXFW3KnPnSpk6cFH3yPGlRqE+gQYXKTGq0J1KJMY0uhdj06FOqAqVObV
```

```
j151WHQ7UmHDq2q9OvXAuKHcvQLEy0adUqbbvTrUq4cQmuZYuwKoCzeLfqnUvXoN+/b
wPzPWk1b1atXhXLJTs5sWPESiNLHni3r+aFPAl/3oy5peHRfL0SJj34pmfLYFdWRk26
82uWEe2CZF3XNGPcXHX75v17+OzdbYVTJn7a9W3bxe0yj+38efXWsKcXRd6b+/GoIZf
+a8/tvSz0x7hRih//8Lz56k6Rr2ef/Pp7sm87z6ffnarv/PrxN5FsOaVH4F8CkucedX
dZtl+CzZUXnIEHIgghg/Z1t1t2D17I2YIahsehh+1JGKKIwOlVknFwgWgdihVy1pOJL
bL4IngpqjVjhgLG152M29HYI4G0dfgiieg1CBhRTAlJH4A5Mg1VlAlCGWNfU1I55GGF
najlk2aBdd9eWzbVXnRcQthVbt+dZSRzaYr5oVg2shennKUd5aSdZkKVpFU8gkkmhpn
tOR5kykl1ZZWJNjpnoII22mebSGInqaSVjnnpmpm2uemdlYKq6aBI+vXplyT++Oepb0
a6Iav+qGYKq5WtejjrgbWmeqttuV64K3S9qvkrZcEyeiuWnYI2q2DJ3igdns3CGe2h0
05XbLUiXYstTdvypm23HYFbm7ibfUtuUOcqZmSswpKKrLOLuupWl3lyWqaj7yZ6L6ZE
8cvnspbqe+ivj25q7bAEe4twwqwtfCxx8frnMJyseipdxIENW7CLEdaJ18Nh+QsxyAZ
rR/Kl8p48b8oqi0pxy5PKSnK6G38KJM0d45sVzi3yjJa5Pl8WtEtAD82s0SMVjbSUMg
uskdI/o/x0sgCj26nGbFLNMLRXY01v1wh/3bRqTjOtdcz1oq3itMLVXGS1joZpNtjKu
a011BlLfSf+3nlLnXaMfPft92qBC26waN3Cuiqv4C6rmsXufvVwfAGXXaPjPiqu7rEt
S8Z555srDnPhyp7698ShHz466V6ubnnUKi8usuELV64z5LSNuvWOy5U8oet153w7ocA
3hrtuQI3e+uw0xb4880/PXN/D2aL+O/Xchl1i7VOfDn3pFNr80vFyD7gkvLkL7b3L2z
/7rNVopt8k8uuze/TLApef9b/+2sv1wOJjn2GMZTrZcUxHBKxY/f4HwMmd7137wpyqE
JjAXZ1ObPzT2APX1q7aTXBnvppZrFgXPRFGjIQZ6dz5UFhCkHmPg2Mj2JJYmLSJOSha
JmQcDl1IJLjl0CRYNMTJD2cSxOR5cEPnOpmFkuhCnDWRZ9pDGvaWpsClxU9/VlxREWm
2xSRmMSVfzFYYOdJFL46xe2cMVxrVuMaitHF8b8xJHOdIR4jV8Y54zKMe98jHoAUEAA
A7
```

```
}
```

You could use this image data to create an image with the `-data` attribute.

```
image create photo -data $leaf -format GIF \
        -height 200 -width 122 -gamma 1 -palette 5/5/4
```

Using the file attribute

If you specify both a `-data` attribute and a `-file` attribute, the file attribute will take precedence. If you specify a `-file` attribute and the file is not available, then the command will generate an error, even if there is a `-data` attribute specified.

You can avoid this error by using the Tcl command `catch`, which will not let the error interupt the application. See Appendix A for more information about using the `-data` and `-file` attributes for creating images in an application.

Naming an image

You can name the image with the `image create photo` command, or the Tk interpreter will name the image for you. You can also set a variable to the value of the command.

The following command creates an image with the name "picture." You can use this name in other commands such as creating image objects on a canvas. This name is a fixed value, and you do not need to use the $ sign to perform variable substitution.

```
image create photo picture -data $data
```

The following command sets the value of the variable `picture` to the name of the image. If you used this variable in other commands, you would need to perform variable substitution using the $ sign.

```
set picture [image create photo -data $data]
```

You use the name or variable that represents the name to create image objects on canvases.

Options of image create photo

The `image create photo` command creates full-color images. Besides specifying the image data by `-file` or `-data`, you can provide values for several other attributes. These attributes are optional and have default values.

```
-format
```

is the name of the file format for the data specified with the `-data` or `-file` option. The only supported format is GIF. This is the original format of the data, not the BASE64-encoded data.

```
-gamma value
```

This value is the gamma exponent that specifies how the colors displaying this image should be corrected for a nonlinear display. The default value is 1, which specifies no correction. The value must be greater than 0. In general, values greater than 1 will make the image lighter, and values less than 1 will make it darker.

```
-height number
```

is the height of the image, in pixels. This is optional; if you don't specify a height, the image will expand or shrink to fit the image data.

```
-palette palette-spec
```

is the resolution of the color cube to be allocated for displaying this image. The palette-spec can be a single decimal number, specifying the number of shades of gray to use to result in a grayscale image. For a full-color image, the palette-spec should be three decimal numbers separated by slashes (/), specifying the number of shades of red, green, and blue to use, respectively. In the above example, the palette-spec is 5/5/4, so the image is displayed using 5 shades of red, 5 shades of green, and 4 shades of blue. This is a good choice for most images.

```
-width number
```

is the width of the image, in pixels. This is optional; if you don't specify a width, the image will expand or shrink to fit the image data.

Creating image objects

After you've created a photo image, you can create an image object on the canvas. This command takes this form:

```
widgetname create image x y ?option value option
value ...?
```

The x and y coordinates specify the location of the image. You can position this point in the center of the image, or in a particular corner, depending on the -anchor attribute.

The height and width of an image object are determined by the image that you created with the image create photo command.

Options of the image object

You need to provide the name of the image to the -image attribute. The name of the image can be a variable or the name that you set when you created the image. The other attributes are optional.

Table 5.2 Options of the image object

Option	Function
-anchor anchorPos	Positions the image relative to the positioning point for the item, such as n, se, sw,etc. Default is center
-image name	Specifies the name of the image to display in the item
-tags tagList	Provides set of tags to apply to the object

You can see more examples of the image object in the next application.

Working with bitmaps: image create bitmap

A bitmap consists of two colors. It can also have transparent pixels. It is made up of two files: a *source* and a *mask*. These two bitmaps must be the same size. The mask specifies whether each pixel is transparent or opaque. The source bitmap specifies each pixel as either the foreground color or the background color.

Built-in bitmaps

Tk has a number of built-in bitmaps. The bitmaps and their names are shown in the following figure.

You can use these built-in bitmaps on canvas widgets simply by specifying a name with the widgetname create bitmap command. You do not need to use image create to create the bitmap. See the next section for more details of this command.

Figure 5.7 Built-in Tcl/Tk bitmaps

Creating your own bitmaps

If you create your own bitmaps from data or a file, then it must be in X11 bitmap format. Files in this format have the extension .xbm. The data for this format look like this:

```
#define home_width 26
#define home_height 18
static char home_bits[] = {
0x00,0x00,0x00,0x00,0x00,0x0c,0x00,0x00,0xc0,0xf3,0x0
f,0x00,0xe0,0xf3,0x1f,0x00,0x50,0xff,0x3f,0x00,0x28,0
xfe,0x7f,0x00,0x14,0xfc,0xff,0x00,0x0a,0xf8,0xff,0x01
,0x06,0x10,0x80,0x00,0x34,0xd3,0xb6,0x00,0x34,0xd3,0x
b6,0x00,0x04,0x10,0x80,0x00,0x04,0x10,0x80,0x00,0x34,
0xd3,0xb6,0x00,0x34,0xd3,0xb6,0x00,0x04,0x10,0x86,0x0
0,0xfc,0xff,0xff,0x00,0x00,0x00,0x00,0x00};
```

You can simply set a variable to the value of these data and use the `image create` command to create a bitmap:

```
set data {
#define home_width 26
#define home_height 18
static char home_bits[] = {
0x00,0x00,0x00,0x00,0x00,0x0c,0x00,0x00,0xc0,0xf3,0x0
f,0x00,0xe0,0xf3,0x1f,0x00,0x50,0xff,0x3f,0x00,0x28,0
xfe,0x7f,0x00,0x14,0xfc,0xff,0x00,0x0a,0xf8,0xff,0x01
,0x06,0x10,0x80,0x00,0x34,0xd3,0xb6,0x00,0x34,0xd3,0x
b6,0x00,0x04,0x10,0x80,0x00,0x04,0x10,0x80,0x00,0x34,
0xd3,0xb6,0x00,0x34,0xd3,0xb6,0x00,0x04,0x10,0x86,0x0
0,0xfc,0xff,0xff,0x00,0x00,0x00,0x00,0x00};
```

```
}
image create bitmap home -data $data
```

Options of image create bitmap

Options of image create bitmap include the following. Only the -data or -file attribute is required. If you specify both, then the -file attribute will be considered first.

Table 5.3 Options of image create bitmap

Option	Function
-background color	Specifies color of the background. If it is an empty string, then all background pixels are transparent
-data string	Data must be in X11 bitmap format
-foreground color	Specifies color of the foreground
-file name	Name of .xbm file
-maskdata string	Data to use as mask
-maskfile name	Name of .xbm file to use as mask

Where to find bitmap files

You can find a lot of bitmaps on the Web in .xbm format that you can download and use. Many sites on the Web have directories full of bitmaps for use on Web pages.

You can also create your own two-color images with the X Window program called "bitmap" if your platform is UNIX. You can convert images to .xbm format on UNIX using one of the many converters available. One such converter is called Netpbm, available at ftp://sunsite.unc.edu/pub/Linux/apps/graphics/convert/.

If your platform is Windows and Macintosh, then you may not be able to create bitmaps in .xbm or convert bitmaps, but you can still obtain them on the Web and use them in your Tcl/Tk applications.

Creating bitmap objects

You can use Tcl/Tk's ready made bitmaps and bitmaps that you've created on canvas, button, and label widgets. But there is a big difference between the way that Tcl/Tk treats built-in bitmaps and bitmaps that are created by you.

Built-in bitmaps use the `widgetname create bitmap` command to create bitmap objects on canvas widgets, and the `-bitmap` attribute to place bitmaps on button and label widgets. However, bitmaps that you've created with X11 bitmap data are treated as other images, and use the `widgetname create image` command and the `-image` attribute for button and labels, rather than `widgetname create bitmap` and the `-bitmap` attribute.

You use the `widgetname create bitmap` command only for Tcl/Tk's built-in bitmaps. This command has the form:

```
widgetname create bitmap x y ?option value
option value ...?
```

The x and y coordinates specify the location of the bitmap. You can position this point in the center of the bitmap, or in a particular corner, depending on the `anchor` attribute.

Table 5.4 Options for creating bitmap objects

Option	Function
`-anchor anchorPos`	Positions the bitmap relative to a positioning point, such as center, nw or sw
`-background color`	Specifies a background color
`-bitmap bitmap`	Specifies the bitmap to display
`-foreground color`	Specifies the foreground color
`-tags tagList`	Specifies a set of tags

To create canvas objects using bitmaps you have created using xbm data and the `image create bitmap` command, you create image objects rather than bitmap objects.

Here's a short example of the difference between images and built-in bitmaps.

```
canvas .c  -height 100 -width 100 -background white
pack .c

#--------------------------------------------------------
# Set the inline data to a variable
#--------------------------------------------------------

set data {
#define home_width 26
#define home_height 18
static char home_bits[] = {
0x00,0x00,0x00,0x00,0x00,0x0c,0x00,0x00,0xc0,0xf3,0x0
f,0x00,0xe0,0xf3,0x1f,0x00,0x50,0xff,0x3f,0x00,0x28,0
xfe,0x7f,0x00,0x14,0xfc,0xff,0x00,0x0a,0xf8,0xff,0x01
,0x06,0x10,0x80,0x00,0x34,0xd3,0xb6,0x00,0x34,0xd3,0x
b6,0x00,0x04,0x10,0x80,0x00,0x04,0x10,0x80,0x00,0x34,
0xd3,0xb6,0x00,0x34,0xd3,0xb6,0x00,0x04,0x10,0x86,0x0
0,0xfc,0xff,0xff,0x00,0x00,0x00,0x00,0x00};
}

#--------------------------------------------------------
# Create a bitmap using inline data
#--------------------------------------------------------

image create bitmap home -data $data

#--------------------------------------------------------
# Create two canvas objects. One is a bitmap object
# using the built-in bitmap named error. The other
# is an image object using the bitmap just created.
#--------------------------------------------------------

.c create bitmap 20 20 -bitmap error
.c create image 50 50 -image home
```

App VI: Fish

You can find the fish applet on the CD included with this book. This is a reduced image of it.

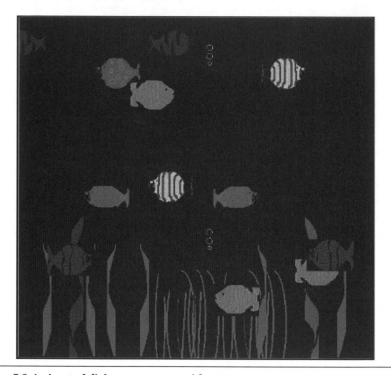

Figure 5.8 Animated fish on a canvas widget

The fish animation applet is an example of a complicated animated image that uses photo images on a single canvas widget.

When the applet runs, each fish swims across the screen at a different rate. Some blow bubbles.

The use of color on Tcl/Tk Web applications

When you develop Tcl/Tk applications that use full-color images such as this fish applet, you should consider your use of color. Images that you create may be viewed by others using different operating systems and screens with different resolution and color palettes. If you use a color in your image that does not exist for a viewer's platform, then dithering will occur. The color will be imitated with a combination of other colors. This usually does not look as good as simply using a color that is available on all operating systems.

You should also be aware that many colors that Tk uses are not cross-platform. You can get more information about browser-safe and cross-platform colors in one of the several books available on Web graphics and color. One book is *Coloring Web Graphics* by Weinman and Heavin. This book includes a CD-Rom with a Paintshop Pro browser-safe palette ready for you to use.

Steps to create fish

Step 1: Creating the fish

Each fish and each leaf is specified with image data converted into BASE64. Specifying this data makes up the bulk of the application. There are not many procedures.

For example, these are the data for the green fish:

```
set gfish {
```

```
R01GODlhTwA4ALMAAP///zGlGCl7GCFaGAgQCBApEBhCGAAAAAAAA
AAAAAAAAAAAAAAAAAAAAAAAAAACH5BAEAAcALAAAAABPADgAAA
T+0JRDq70416m7/5hBgCRFGIPAYWcxlnBlGHGWCkKgC2yq64NV7UN
41V6En5JmIeSUP+bQY4wRBqbnj9eEegfV6eU0dJq+xazXKwiLTdNC
YJSEGnQT+XrtFrtKBSJ6eVADdwFYWntQQm9kJIFKWHpRV211i14ib
xswIgM/k1BVh1ACPoWBnBSqJAISWweUiAczIqU7HFejcqu1fRh6mD
yzIlG4bU1aWKBSJWF/RE+KskoElIaSIT8u3DGtrM4ZTnvXsaWvW25
6xEoqgEEws16RQAegUbHbtLgBmyAnsJhoZKEfPUoT7ITK8CSRkjyQ
CoBhRbCWIhyaShUp1BBDihb+mAJweeRBwj8LBU4FUgTGYDaR1SThE
8jKkBFcgg6QzFDAxQpVcjB245byyyEs/dLRKngBH8w7E04Ay7MiDc
sDWhRJOnrPC7lkFa6FdYcVD0UWeYz0LBtr3pZDSmloDVCvilgKuMA
8HCiEiZA/uKLuGaq0yFy9/i4AthPSWSCqAXkawMGhKCOdOw6NWMPj
0BiJ/WB5GyMhIM1aNMRJ1CpwmMiNbHTmEJfGqT9KXFjoBD1mwOlav
i/LHhXSWi0dfYrhpjLjtMTfKYPrG64E8xoOOXIrC4WNygnHKJz5lq
5DCjl1xRda117BKeLEHp4rvqtzvG0j6WF/kQEkDDqn4gT+MwNpTYT
nlHZ1BHfJHqfhAxYrg30QyG+yjHENKqcliI9+pmyH3FhbjNbBhMG4
oZ9z5R0yVGxNOGVEQ6UEqNgMjewEIl0olTdIejuwMM0LDsYooS0h8
PRDFYOoyKMO46h3VCkUwqFTc8EQRAkpeOghF2d9aHScSN3NSONu8V
wQIFxmZmnPIn1gIspr0+Glyz/gbBDGjxZsqIdDfGjgYExtaBHWSVP
aSeAG1VnwBGzMlKNBKdbN4VRU0aD0QkWPnAcTiO3QYtteRuKByQyh
2BhWT/Qp1lM/+B1ZR2eONilqQ+ygOuIVMvI1gkQ4QgjTqzGZcqkzo
56nQmKVjjMmDL7d8fdrj259SME7Z5R3wBJUEeEbMB1I8ScmHCYqG0
2YuLCMLBX1lmt8UU0TqWFspFEWoh8qMgO3eeI7YrBYgMuWO1dQIO2
3F+lrgsEauHBgpDR8+ppJH4YZxSu+gNCTNuchxYYLmFBHCznrVqxY
```

```
IZF2KskER2k6B2YPikzFVcMEy90uInUoW8gu50lWSJHOvIhAKeX8z
MLFdIXtkvClKvQHGs2isTXmxrr0EaCQx+QsPBTh8FJTxzGXaNCa41
XXnPC6xTw6sZJVumRbMdnZJ6hQlURstz1FQPhNZLcFEQAAOw==
}
```

The data for each fish are defined in a similar fashion. The make_fish procedure creates a fish with the image data, specific x and y coordinates, and tags. The fish is created as an image, which is then placed on the canvas as an image object.

```
proc make_fish { fish x y tag } {

    #───────────────────────────────────────
    # Creating the image
    #───────────────────────────────────────

    set im [image create photo -data $fish \
            -format GIF -gamma 1  \
            -height 56 -width 79 -palette 5/5/4]

    #───────────────────────────────────────
    # Creating the image object
    #───────────────────────────────────────

    .c create image $x $y -image $im -tag $tag \
                -anchor center
}
```

For example, the green fish is placed at (700, 300) and tagged "g" to differentiate it from the other fish.

```
make_fish $gfish 700 300 g
```

The fish that will move from right to left have a tag that ends in 'r.' This lets us determine the direction the fish will travel in the move_fish procedure, described in the next step.

Step 2: Moving the fish

Each fish is moved with the move_fish procedure. This procedure determines which way the fish is going and moves the fish
according to its place on the canvas and its time period. The time
period is how long the fish will wait before moving to a new position. This procedure allows for different time periods, so the fish
can move at different speeds.

When the fish get to the other side of the canvas, the procedure
deletes the image object and creates a new object using the same
image data.

```
proc move_fish { fishtag period place fish x1 y1 } {

#  ─────────────────────────────────────────────────────────
# Checks to see if the fish is tagged with an r
# character. If so, then the x direction is nega-
# tive, because it is traveling from right to left.
#  ─────────────────────────────────────────────────────────

if {[string match *r $fishtag]} {
     set x 10
     } else {
     set x -10
     }

#  ─────────────────────────────────────────────────────────
# Moves the fish in the x direction after the time
# period. Each fish can have different time periods.
# The for loop continues until the end of the canvas
# is reached, which is calculated by multiplying the
# beginning position of the object and the time
# period, then dividing by the 10 (the absolute
# value of the x direction).
#  ─────────────────────────────────────────────────────────

for {set i 0} {$i < [expr $place *$period/10]} \
           {incr i $period} {
     after $i ".c move $fishtag $x 0"
     }
```

```
#  ──────────────────────────────────────
# After the time it takes to travel the length of
# the canvas, the object is deleted. A new object is
# created using the same data and initial coordinates.
# That object is moved using this same procedure.
#  ──────────────────────────────────────


after $i "

        .c delete $fishtag

        make_fish {$data} $x1 $y1 $fishtag

        move_fish $fishtag $period $place {$data}
$x1 $y1

            "

}
```

Step 3: Creating the background

The application also creates and places each patch of grass and leaf. Different image objects can use the same image.

```
set im [image create photo -data $leaf \
            -format GIF -gamma 1  \
            -height 200 -width 16 -palette 5/5/4]


#  ──────────────────────────────────────
# Each of the following image objects are created
# using the same data.
#  ──────────────────────────────────────


.c create image 50 500 -image $im -tag leaf \
            -anchor center
.c create image 215 500 -image $im -tag leaf \
            -anchor center
.c create image 415 500 -image $im -tag leaf \
            -anchor center
.c create image 550 500 -image $im -tag leaf \
            -anchor center
```

```
set im [image create photo -data $leaf2 \
            -format GIF -gamma 1  \
            -height 300 -width 24 -palette 5/5/4]
.c create image 100 500 -image $im -tag leaf \
            -anchor center

set im [image create photo -data $leaf6 \
            -format GIF -gamma 1 \
            -height 200 -width 16 -palette 5/5/4]
.c create image 125 500 -image $im -tag leaf \
            -anchor center
.c create image 160 500 -image $im -tag leaf \
            -anchor center

set im [image create photo -data $leaf5 \
            -format GIF -gamma 1 \
            -height 175 -width 120 -palette 5/5/4]
.c create image 285 525 -image $im -tag leaf \
            -anchor center
.c create image 400 525 -image $im -tag leaf \
            -anchor center

set im [image create photo -data $leaf4 \
            -format GIF -gamma 1 \
            -height 300 -width 24 -palette 5/5/4]
.c create image 500 500 -image $im -tag leaf \
             -anchor center
```

Step 4: Blowing bubbles

You can have some of your fish blow bubbles with the following
procedures. These procedures require that you know when a fish
will be in a particular place. It creates a few oval objects that
appear out of the fish's mouth and travel to the top of the screen.

```
proc bubble { x y} {
.c create oval $x $y \
```

```
                    [expr $x+10] [expr $y+10] \
                    -outline white \
                    -tag bubble$x
.c create oval $x [expr $y+15] \
                    [expr $x+10] [expr $y+25] \
                    -outline white \
                   -tag bubble$x
.c create oval [expr $x+3] [expr $y+30] \
                       [expr $x +8] [expr $y +35]\
                    -outline white \
                    -tag bubble$x
for {set k 0} {$k < [expr $y * 100/ 5]} \
            {incr k 100} {
        after $k ".c move bubble$x 0 -5"
        }
after $k ".c delete bubble$x"
}

proc bubbling { x y period } {
for {set i 0} {$i < [expr $period * $x] } \
        {incr i   [expr $period * 15] } {
        after $i "bubble $x $y"
        incr x -150
        }
}

bubbling 620 275 300
bubbling 620 450 400
```

Here's the complete code for the fish applet (excluding the image data).

```
# ─────────────────────────────────────────
#
#   Creates each fish by creating an image and
#   image canvas object.
#
# ─────────────────────────────────────────
```

```
proc make_fish { fish x y tag } {

set im [image create photo -data $fish \
            -format GIF -gamma 1 \
            -height 56 -width 79 -palette 5/5/4]
.c create image $x $y -image $im \
            -tag $tag -anchor center
}


# ————————————————————————————————————————
# Moves a fish from a particular starting point with
# a specific time period.
# ————————————————————————————————————————

proc move_fish { fishtag period place data x1 y1 } {
if {[string match *r $fishtag]} {
     set x 10
     } else {
     set x -10
     }
for {set i 0} {$i < [expr $place *$period/10]} \
            {incr i $period} {
            after $i ".c move $fishtag $x 0"
}

after $i "
     .c delete $fishtag
     make_fish {$data} $x1 $y1 $fishtag
     move_fish $fishtag $period $place {$data} $x1
$y1
         "

}


# ————————————————————————————————————————
# Creates bubbles for specific fish
# ————————————————————————————————————————
```

```
proc bubble { x y} {
.c create oval $x $y [expr $x+10] [expr $y+10] \
            -outline white \
            -tag bubble$x
.c create oval $x [expr $y+15] \
            [expr $x+10] [expr $y+25] \
            -outline white -tag bubble$x

.c create oval [expr $x+3] [expr $y+30] \
            [expr $x +8] [expr $y +35] \
            -outline white -tag bubble$x
for {set k 0} {$k < [expr $y * 100/ 5]} \
            {incr k 100} {
    after $k ".c move bubble$x 0 -5"
    incr x -150
    }
after $k ".c delete bubble$x"
}

proc bubbling { x y period } {

for {set i 0} {$i < [expr $period * $x] } \
    {incr i  [expr $period * 15] } {

    after $i "bubble $x $y"
    }
}

# ─────────────────────────────────────────
# Create the canvas and the leaves in the back-
# ground.
# ─────────────────────────────────────────

canvas .c -height 600 -width 600 \
            -background black
pack .c
```

```
set im [image create photo -data $leaf \
     -format GIF -gamma 1 \
     -height 200 -width 16 -palette 5/5/4]

.c create image 50 500 -image $im -tag leaf -anchor
center

set im [image create photo -data $leaf2 \
          -format GIF -gamma 1 \
          -height 300 -width 24 -palette 5/5/4]
.c create image 100 500 -image $im -tag leaf \
          -anchor center


set im [image create photo -data $leaf6 \
          -format GIF -gamma 1 \
          -height 200 -width 16 -palette 5/5/4]
.c create image 125 500 -image $im -tag leaf \
          -anchor center

set im [image create photo -data $leaf6 \
          -format GIF -gamma 1 \
          -height 200 -width 16 -palette 5/5/4]
.c create image 160 500 -image $im -tag leaf \
          -anchor center
set im [image create photo -data $leaf \
          -format GIF -gamma 1 \
     -height 200 -width 16 -palette 5/5/4]
.c create image 215 500 -image $im -tag leaf \
          -anchor center

set im [image create photo -data $leaf5 \
     -format GIF -gamma 1 \
     -height 175 -width 120 -palette 5/5/4]
.c create image 285 525 -image $im -tag leaf \
     -anchor center
```

```
set im [image create photo -data $leaf5 \
            -format GIF -gamma 1 \
            -height 175 -width 120 -palette 5/5/4]
.c create image 400 525 -image $im -tag leaf \
            -anchor center

set im [image create photo -data $leaf \
            -format GIF -gamma 1 \
            -height 200 -width 16 -palette 5/5/4]
.c create image 415 500 -image $im -tag leaf \
            -anchor center

set im [image create photo -data $leaf4 \
            -format GIF -gamma 1 \
            -height 300 -width 24 -palette 5/5/4]
.c create image 500 500 -image $im -tag leaf \
            -anchor center



set im [image create photo -data $leaf \
            -format GIF -gamma 1 \
            -height 200 -width 16 -palette 5/5/4]
.c create image 550 500 -image $im -tag leaf \
            -anchor center
# ───────────────────────────────────────────────
# Create and move the fish. The procedure is called
# for each fish because each fish is placed at
# different location and moves at a different speed.
# ───────────────────────────────────────────────


make_fish $gfish 700 300 g
make_fish $rainfish 750 50 rain
make_fish $bfish 600 100 b
make_fish $yfish 600 420 y
make_fish $rfish 700 500 re
```

```
make_fish $ofish 800 320 o
make_fish $gfish_r -200 100 gr
make_fish $ofish_r -150 320 or
make_fish $rainfish_r 0 50 rainr
make_fish $bfish_r -100 140 br
make_fish $yfish_r -200 430 yr
make_fish $rfish_r 0 450 rr


move_fish   g      300 700 "$gfish"      700 300
move_fish   gr     200 800 "$gfish_r" -200 100
move_fish   rain   175 750 "$rainfish" 750 50
move_fish   y      260 600 "$yfish"      600 420
move_fish   b      300 600 "$bfish"      600 100
move_fish   re     400 700 "$rfish"      700 500
move_fish   o      200 800 "$ofish"      800 320
move_fish   or     250 850 "$ofish_r" -150 320
move_fish   rainr  500 800 "$rainfish_r" 0 50
move_fish   br     400 800 "$bfish_r"  -100 140
move_fish   yr     450 900 "$yfish_r"  -200 430
move_fish   rr     250 800 "$rfish_r"  0 450
move_fish   y      200 600 "$yfish"      600 420


# ────────────────────────────────────────────
# Place some bubbles
# ────────────────────────────────────────────

bubbling 620 275 300
bubbling 620 450 400
```

Using bitmaps in an applet

The fish applet uses full-color image data. For an interesting use of bitmaps, you should try the Tcl/Tk solitaire game created by Michael J. McLennan. You can find the Tcl/Tk solitaire game on Lucent's Tcl/Tk Web site at http://www.tcltk.com.

Tcl/Tk Forms and Processors

Now we will turn from the canvas widget and look at interactive applications that you can create using buttons, entry widgets, and text widgets.

App VII: Tcl/Tk calculator

This is an application created to show how Tcl/Tk can work with numbers. A calculating application can be useful on a Web page because it can provide immediate feedback to a user. You can calculate, for example, how much something is worth or the amount of time it will take to complete a task.

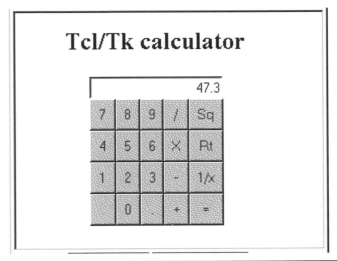

Figure 5.9 Tcl/Tk calculator embedded in a Web page

When you design a calculator or other application that has many buttons interacting with one another, you need to consider the multiple pathways that the application may take.

For example, this is a simple calculator that adds, subtracts, multiplies, and divides. It lets you input decimals and provides answers in decimal format. It also lets you input a single number and square it, take the square root of it, or invert it. It seems pretty straightforward, but there are a number of things to consider. When you enter a number, how will the application know if it is a single number or a digit of a larger number? How does the application recognize decimals? How should the application behave when you enter one function after another without pressing the "=" button?

One typical path that the calculator applet may take is expressed by the following diagram.

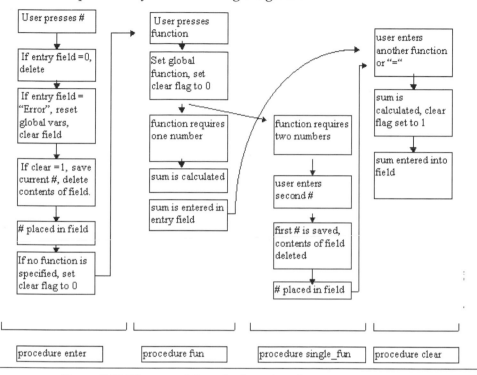

Figure 5.10 Diagram of the calculator functions

Scan command

The calculator works with decimals by *scanning* numbers using the Tcl command `scan`. The Tcl command `scan` parses a string and converts it using a conversion specifier.

The format of this command is:

```
scan string format variable
```

The `format` option is a conversion specifier, the `string` is the number or string that we want to scan. The `variable` is the name of the variable set to the result of the scan.

For this application, we want to convert integers into decimal numbers. We can use the command

```
scan $number %e decimal
```

The value of the number variable is an integer or other number. As a result of this command, the value of the decimal variable is a floating point number that has the same value as the original number, but now it can contain a decimal point, an exponent, and a sign.

For details and a list of conversion specifiers, see the online reference documentation.

Steps to using calculator

Step 1: Entering a number

Each button that enters a number executes the enter procedure when pressed. Besides placing the number in the entry field, it accomplishes these tasks:

- It checks the entry field. If it contains 0, it deletes the number. If it contains "Error," it calls the clear procedure, described below.
- It checks the clear flag. If there is already another number in the entry field, it saves it in the number list and clears the field if the clear flag is 1, or it appends the existing number if the clear flag is 0.
- It sets the clear flag to 0 if no function is specified (if the global variable function = "none").

```
proc enter { n } {
global clear number_list function

# ────────────────────────────────────────
# If the contents of the entry box is 0, delete it,
# or if the contents is Error, invoke the clear pro-
# cedure.
# ────────────────────────────────────────

if {[.e get] == 0} {
    .e delete 0
    } elseif {[.e get] == "Error"} {
    clear}
```

```
# _____
# If the clear flag is 1, saves the current number
# in the number list if there is one and clears
# the entry field.
# _____

if {$clear == 1} {
    if {[.e get] != ""} {
        set number [.e get]
        scan $number %e number
        set number_list \
            [lappend number_list $number]
        }
    .e configure -state normal
     .e delete 0 end
    }


# _____
# Inserts the number in the entry field
# _____

.e configure -state normal
.e insert end $n

.e configure -state disabled
# _____
# If the function is specified, then sets the clear
# flag to 0.
# _____

if {$function != "none"} {
    set clear 0}
}
```

Step 2: Entering the function

The procedure fun executes when you press one of "+", "*", "-", or "/". It calls the equals procedure, and then sets the global variable function to the specified function. It also sets the clear flag to 1, so when the user enters another number that calls the enter procedure, the previous number is saved in the number_list.

```
proc fun { fun } {
global function clear
equals
set function $fun
set clear 1
}
```

The procedure single_fun executes when you press a function that requires only one number: "square," "square root," or inversion. The procedure scans the contents of the entry box into a floating point number. It then calculates the final result and places it in the entry box. It resets the global variables number_list and function.

```
proc single_fun { fun } {
global sum clear function number_list
if {[.e get] == ""} {return} else {
    scan [.e get] %e sum
if {$fun == "square"} {
    set sum [expr $sum * $sum]
    } elseif {$fun == "sqrt"} {
    set sum [expr sqrt($sum)]
    } elseif {$fun == "invert"} {
    set sum [expr 1 / $sum]
    }
.e configure -state normal
.e delete 0 end
.e insert end $sum
set number_list {}
set function none
set sum 0
.e configure -state disabled
```

```
}
}
```

Step 3: Calculating the result

The procedure `equals` executes when you press the "=" button. It is also called by the `fun` procedure when you press a function button. If there is a value in the entry field and a number already saved in the number list, then a sum is determined between those two values using the specified function.

If the function specified is division, then the procedure checks to make sure the denominator is not 0.

```
proc equals { } {
global sum clear function number_list

# ─────────────────────────────────────────────
# If there is no function specified, or if there is
# nothing in the entry box, or if there is no number
# saved, the procedure returns and nothing more is
# done.
# ─────────────────────────────────────────────

if {$function == "none"} {
    return
    } elseif {[.e get] == ""} {
    return
    } elseif {[lindex $number_list 0] == ""} {
    return
    } else  {

# ─────────────────────────────────────────────
# The sum and next numbers are set, and the final
# sum iscalculated based on the value of the
# function variable.
# ─────────────────────────────────────────────

            set sum [lindex $number_list 0]
            scan $sum %e sum
            set next [.e get]
```

```
        scan $next %e next

            if {$function == "add"} {
            set sum [expr $sum + $next]
            }
            if {$function == "minus"} {
            set sum [expr $sum - $next]
            }
            if {$function == "mult"} {
            set sum [expr $sum * $next]
            }
            if {$function == "div"} {
                if {$next != 0} {
                set sum [expr $sum / $next]}
            }
            if {$function == "square"} {
            set sum [expr $sum * $next]
            }


#  ————————————————————————————————————————
# The contents of the field are deleted
#  ————————————————————————————————————————

    .e configure -state normal
    .e delete 0 end


#  ————————————————————————————————————————
# If the function is division, the procedure
# checks the denominator. If it is 0, it enters
# Error into the field.
#  ————————————————————————————————————————

    if {$function == "div"} {
        if {$next == 0} {
        .e insert end "Error"
        set function none
        } else {
```

```
            .e insert 0 $sum
            }
    } else {
            .e insert 0 $sum }

# ─────────────────────────────────────────────
# Resets global variables
# ─────────────────────────────────────────────

    set number_list {}
    set function none
    set sum 0
    set next 0
    .e configure -state disabled
    }


}
```

Step 4: Clearing the entry field

The clear procedure resets all the global variables and deletes the contents of the entry field. It is called when the clear button is pressed.

```
proc clear { } {
global number_list function clear

.e configure -state normal

.e delete 0 end
set number_list {}
set clear 0
set function none
.e configure -state disabled

}
```

Step 5: Entering decimals

The decimal procedure is called when you press the decimal button. If the clear flag is 1, it saves the current number in the number list and inserts a new number starting with a decimal point. If
the clear flag is 0, it scans the current number in the entry field
into a floating point number and inserts a decimal point.

```
proc decimal { } {
global clear function number_list
.e configure -state normal

if {[.e get] == ""} {
     set num 0
     set clear 0
     } elseif  {$clear == 1} {
     if {[.e get] != ""} {
          scan [.e get] %e number
          set number_list \
               [lappend number_list $number]
          }
     set num 0
     set clear 0
     } else {
     set num [.e get]
}

scan $num %e num
set num [string trimright $num 0]
.e delete 0 end
.e insert end $num
.e configure -state disabled
}
```

Step 6: Creating the user interface

The user interface is simple with an entry field and five buttons in four rows arranged using the grid command. Each button calls the appropriate procedure. The foreground color of the buttons is different for the numbers and functions.

```
entry .e -width 18 -background white \
        -justify right -state disabled

grid .e -row 0 -column 0 -columnspan 5

button .b1 -text 7 -command {enter 7} \
        -foreground red -background lightgrey
button .b2 -text 8 -command {enter 8} \
        -foreground red -background lightgrey
button .b3 -text 9 -command {enter 9} \
        -foreground red -background lightgrey
button .b4 -text / -command {fun div} \
        -foreground purple -background lightgrey
button .b5 -text Sq -command {single_fun square} \
        -foreground purple -background lightgrey

grid .b1 .b2 .b3 .b4 .b5 \
        -columnspan 1 -sticky we

button .b6 -text 4 -command {enter 4} \
        -foreground red -background lightgrey
button .b7 -text 5 -command {enter 5} \
        -foreground red -background lightgrey
button .b8 -text 6 -command {enter 6} \
        -foreground red -background lightgrey
button .b9 -text X -command {fun mult} \
        -foreground purple -background lightgrey
button .b10 -text Rt -command {single_fun sqrt} \
        -foreground purple -background lightgrey
```

```
grid .b6 .b7 .b8 .b9 .b10 \
    -columnspan 1 -sticky we

button .b11 -text 1 -command {enter 1} \
    -foreground red -background lightgrey
button .b12 -text 2 -command {enter 2} \
    -foreground red -background lightgrey
button .b13 -text 3 -command {enter 3} \
    -foreground red -background lightgrey
button .b14 -text - -command {fun minus} \
    -foreground purple -background lightgrey
button .b15 -text 1/x -command {single_fun invert} \
    -foreground purple -background lightgrey

grid .b11 .b12 .b13 .b14 .b15 \
    -columnspan 1 -sticky we

button .b16 -text C -command { clear } \
    -foreground yellow -background lightgrey
button .b17 -text 0 -command {enter 0} \
    -foreground red -background lightgrey
button .b18 -text . -command {decimal} \
    -foreground blue -background lightgrey
button .b19 -text + -command {fun add} \
    -foreground purple -background lightgrey
button .b20 -text = -command {equals} \
    -foreground purple -background lightgrey

grid .b16 .b17 .b18 .b19 .b20 \
    -columnspan 1 -sticky we
```

Step 7: Creating the bindings

The bindings let you use the calculator with the number pad. Using the command "focus." will allow the calculator to accept the bindings without requiring that the user give the explicit focus by entering the application with the mouse.

```
# The number buttons

bind . <KeyPress-1> {enter 1}
bind . <KeyPress-2> {enter 2}
bind . <KeyPress-3> {enter 3}
bind . <KeyPress-4> {enter 4}
bind . <KeyPress-5> {enter 5}
bind . <KeyPress-6> {enter 6}
bind . <KeyPress-7> {enter 7}
bind . <KeyPress-8> {enter 8}
bind . <KeyPress-9> {enter 9}
bind . <KeyPress-0> {enter 0}

# The function buttons
bind . <BackSpace> {clear}
bind . <equal> {equals}
bind . <Return> {equals}
bind . <slash> {fun div}
bind . <asterisk> {fun mult}
bind . <minus> {fun minus}
bind . <plus> {fun add}
bind . <space> {clear}
bind . <Delete> {clear}
bind . <period> {decimal}
focus .
```

Step 8: Setting initial values

As part of the application, you need to declare the initial values of
the global variables: the clear flag, the function, and the number
list.

```
set clear 0
set function none
set number_list {}
```

For another example of an application that works with numbers, you can look at a demo on the Sun Microsystem's SunScript Web site at `sunscript.sun.com` that computes the wheel diameter of a bike given a gear setup.

Here's the code for the Tcl/Tk calculator (excluding the user interface):

```
# ─────────────────────────────────────────────────
# Entering a number
# ─────────────────────────────────────────────────

proc enter { n } {
global clear number_list function

if {[.e get] == 0} {
    .e delete 0
    } elseif {[.e get] == "Error"} {clear}

if {$clear == 1} {
    if {[.e get] != ""} {
        set number [.e get]
        scan $number %e number
        set number_list \
            [lappend number_list $number]
        }
    .e configure -state normal
    .e delete 0 end
    .e insert end $n
    .e configure -state disabled
} else {
    .e configure -state normal
    .e insert end $n
    .e configure -state disabled
}
```

```tcl
if {$function != "none"} {
     set clear 0}


}



# ─────────────────────────────────────
# Entering a function
# ─────────────────────────────────────



proc fun { fun } {
     global function clear
     equals
     set function $fun
     set clear 1
     }



# ─────────────────────────────────────
# Entering a single function that requires
# an immediate answer.
# ─────────────────────────────────────



proc single_fun { fun } {
global sum clear function number_list
     if {[.e get] == ""} {return} else {

     scan [.e get] %e sum
     if {$fun == "square"} {
      set sum [expr $sum * $sum]
     } elseif {$fun == "sqrt"} {
      set sum [expr sqrt($sum)]
     } elseif {$fun == "invert"} {
      set sum [expr 1 / $sum]
     }
```

```
.e configure -state normal
.e delete 0 end
.e insert end $sum
set number_list {}
set function none
set sum 0
set next 0

.e configure -state disabled
}
}


# ─────────────────────────────────────────────
# The "=" button
# ─────────────────────────────────────────────

proc equals { } {
        global sum clear function number_list

        if {$function == "none"} {
        return
        } elseif {[.e get] == ""} {
        return
        } elseif {[lindex $number_list 0] == ""} {
        return
        } else  {

                set sum [lindex $number_list 0]
                scan $sum %e sum
                set next [.e get]
                scan $next %e next

                        if {$function == "add"} {
                        set sum [expr $sum + $next]
                        }
                        if {$function == "minus"} {
```

```
                                set sum [expr $sum - $next]
                                }
                                if {$function == "mult"} {
                                set sum [expr $sum * $next]
                                }
                                if {$function == "div"} {
                                        if {$next != 0} {
                                        set sum [expr $sum / $next]}
                                }
                                if {$function == "square"} {
                                set sum [expr $sum * $next]
                                }

                .e configure -state normal
                .e delete 0 end
                if {$function == "div"} {
                        if {$next == 0} {
                        .e insert end "Error"
                        set function none
                        } else {
                        .e insert 0 $sum
                        }
                } else { .e insert 0 $sum }
                set number_list {}
                set function none
                set sum 0
                set next 0

                .e configure -state disabled
                }
        }


#   ───────────────────────────────────────────────
#   The clear button
#   ───────────────────────────────────────────────
```

```
proc clear { } {
global number_list function clear

.e configure -state normal

.e delete 0 end
set number_list {}
set clear 0
set function none

.e configure -state disabled

}
# ————————————————————————————————————————————
# The decimal button
# ————————————————————————————————————————————


proc decimal { } {
global clear function number_list
.e configure -state normal

if {[.e get] == ""} {
    set num 0
    set clear 0
    } elseif  {$clear == 1} {
    if {[.e get] != ""} {
        set number [.e get]
        scan $number %e number
        set number_list \
            [lappend number_list $number]
        }
    set num 0
    set clear 0
    } else {
    set num [.e get]
```

```
}
scan $num %e num
set num [string trimright $num 0]
.e delete 0 end
.e insert end $num
.e configure -state disabled


}


# ────────────────────────────────────────────────
# The bindings for keyboard entry
# ────────────────────────────────────────────────

bind . <KeyPress-1> {enter 1}
bind . <KeyPress-2> {enter 2}
bind . <KeyPress-3> {enter 3}
bind . <KeyPress-4> {enter 4}
bind . <KeyPress-5> {enter 5}
bind . <KeyPress-6> {enter 6}
bind . <KeyPress-7> {enter 7}
bind . <KeyPress-8> {enter 8}
bind . <KeyPress-9> {enter 9}
bind . <KeyPress-0> {enter 0}
bind . <BackSpace> {clear}
bind . <equal> {equals}
bind . <Return> {equals}
bind . <slash> {fun div}
bind . <asterisk> {fun mult}
bind . <minus> {fun minus}
bind . <plus> {fun add}
bind . <space> {clear}
bind . <Delete> {clear}
bind . <period> {decimal}
focus .
```

```
#  ─────────────────────────────────────────────
# Global variables
#  ─────────────────────────────────────────────

set clear 0
set function none
set number_list {}
```

App VIII: Tcl/Tk crossword

You can find the full source code of the Tcl/Tk crossword on the CD included with this book.

Figure 5.11 Tcl/Tk crossword

The Tcl/Tk crossword is an interactive application built out of entry widgets. Each entry widget is either normal or disabled. The disabled entry widgets are black.

The entry widgets and their characteristics are managed with arrays. Each entry widget is identified with an array variable that corresponds to arrays of words, letters, and horizontal and vertical clues. Each entry widget has bindings that specify its ID, what words it is a part of, how long those words are, and what its position is in the horizontal and vertical words.

Each entry widget has a number of bindings that call procedures when the user clicks on the widget. We examine a few of the procedures here.

Entering a letter box

When a player clicks on an active entry widget, the procedure enter_or_focus is called with arguments that specify the word length for both the horizontal and vertical words, and the position of the letter in those words. It uses these values to highlight the specific word and go to the next entry box of the correct word when the player is done typing in a letter. It determines which word the player is entering through use of the global variable dir.

```
#───────────────────────────────────────────────
# Entering letters. The enter_or_focus procedure
# calls the enter_box and give_clue procedures.
# The values it provides to these procedures
# depend on the value of the global direction
# variable.
#───────────────────────────────────────────────

proc enter_or_focus { index lengthx positionx \
                 cluex lengthy positiony cluey }   {
global ID glob_dir
bindings $W $index
set W $ID ($index)

if {$glob_dir == "x"} {
     enter_box $W $index $lengthx $positionx
     give_clue $cluex
     } else {
     enter_box $W $index $lengthy $positiony
     give_clue $cluey
     }}
```

The enter_or_focus procedure is actually a wrapper procedure, calling other procedures to complete its work. It calls enter_box, which highlights the appropriate letters in the word.

It requires the length of the word, and the position of the current letter in the word.

```
proc enter_box { W index length position } {
        global glob_dir ID
        set s $length
        set t $index
        set p $position

        #————————————————————————————
        # This code determines what is the entry box
        # to the right and below the current entry
        # box. It accomodates the cases when
        # the current entry box is on the last row or
        # in the last column of the crossword. It
        # provides these values to the procedure
        # return_key, which specifies what entry box
        # is entered when the return key is pressed.
        #————————————————————————————

        if {[$W cget -state] != "disabled"} {
                $W config -background yellow
                } else {
                set right $ID([if {$t == 121} {
                expr $t-120
                } else {
                expr $t+1}])
                set down $ID([if {$t>110} {
                expr $t-110
                } else {
                expr $t+11}])
                return_key $right $down
                }

        #————————————————————————————
        # The following code colors the appropriate
        # entry boxes to highlight the word.
        #————————————————————————————
```

```
if {$glob_dir == "x"} {
    for {set i 1} {$i < $p} {incr i}  \
        {set box $ID([expr $t-$i])
        $box config -background pink
        }
    for {set i 1} {$i <= [expr $s-$p]} {incr i}  \
        {set box $ID([expr $t+$i])
        $box config -background pink
        }
        } else {
    for {set i 11} {[expr $i/11] < $p} {incr i 11}  \
        {set box $ID([expr $t-$i])
        $box config -background pink
        }
    for {set i 11} {[expr $i/11] <= [expr $s-$p]}\
        {incr i 11}  \
            {set box $ID([expr $t+$i])
        $box config -background pink
        }}
    }
```

Checking letters

If a player enters a wrong letter, the crossword puzzle will highlight the incorrect letter and will not let the player proceed to the next letter. The check_letters procedure is called when a letter is entered.

```
proc check_letter { t } {
global ID let
set entry [$ID($t) get]
set uplet [string toupper $let($t)]
if {$entry == $let($t)} {
    $ID($t) configure -background yellow
    } elseif {$entry ==$uplet} {
```

```
            $ID($t) configure -background yellow
            } else {
            $ID($t) configure -background orange
            }
    }

proc right_or_wrong { box letter } {
        set entry [ $box get ]
        if  {$entry == ""} {
        $box configure  -foreground black
        } elseif  [regexp -nocase $entry $letter] {
        $box configure -foreground black
         } else {
        $box configure -background orange
        }
    }
```

The Tcl/Tk crossword also has a number of procedures called
from these procedures that provide clues in the label widget (the
give_clue procedure), change the global direction variable
when the player presses and arrow key (the change_direction
procedure), and color specific boxes (the color_box and
empty_all procedures)

You can find the complete source code to this game, as well as
further explanation about how to build your own crosswords with
this applet, in the online documentation included on the CD.

App IX: Tcl/Tk notecards

In this example application, we build an Web applet that displays
the contents of text files on a Web page.

This application uses the Tcl 8.0 HTTP package. The program
cannot run under Tcl 7.6/Tk 4.2. If you want to build an application such as this that runs under the older versions of Tcl/Tk, you
can use the Spynergy Toolkit procedures that include the

fetchURL procedure. Chapter 7 will explain this procedure in more detail, when we discuss the Tcl/Tk Rolodex.

Because this application uses the HTTP package offered with Tcl 8.0, it needs the Tcl Plug-in 2.0 to run. It also requires the use of the security policy outside, which is bundled with the Plug-in. The outside security policy lets your application access remote servers. When using this or other security policies, be sure to read the latest documentation available at http://sunscript. sun.com.

In this application, we also show how to build a simple navigation system that responds to the mouse. When you click on a word in the table of contents, it creates a list of words in a separate text box as a secondary table of contents. When you click on one of these words, a text file is fetched using the ::http::geturl command.

The application presented here is an online cookbook that displays recipes to the user. But you can adapt this application to display any type of information. The simple text files can contain definitions, addresses, or any other information.

Namespaces

You may have noticed that the name of the procedure, ::http::geturl, does not look like any of the other Tcl/Tk built-in commands we've discussed so far. The HTTP package uses the *namespace* facility added in Tcl 8.0.

Throughout the applications presented in this book, we give procedures names that are identifiable and have some order within the application. For example, in Appendix A, we build procedures for the Tcl Code Editor with names such as ed_loadfile and ed_edit_copy and ed_edit_paste.

Namespaces simply provide another scope to your Tcl applications. As well as global scope for procedures, global variables, and the local scope that is within each procedure, namespaces let you group procedures and variables in larger scopes. This can be useful for managing large applications.

You create namespaces using the Tcl command namespace. Namespaces are specified using double colons. For example, the name ::http::geturl indicates that the namespace is http and the command is geturl. You can also nest namespaces.

The applications that we present in this book do not use namespaces, with the exception of using the HTTP package. For more information on creating and managing namespaces, view the online documentation on the `namespace` and `variable` commands.

Steps to using notecards

Step 1: Requiring http and outside

The `package require` command specifies that the application requires the use of the Tcl HTTP package. If you don't start off this application with this command, the interpreter will not recognize the command `::http::geturl`.

Also, because this tclet uses the HTTP package on the Web, it requires the use of the security policy outside. The `policy` command lets the application access a security policy.

```
policy outside
package require http
```

You may need to configure the Tcl Plug-in to use a specific security policy. See Sun's Tcl Web site at `http://sunscript.sun .com` for the most up-to-date information about the Tcl Plug-in.

Note: If you design a Tcl/Tk application that is not embedded in a Web page and running under the Tcl plug-in, then using the command `policy outside` would generate an error. For testing purposes, wrap the procedure in a `catch` command to avoid errors when you are running the program from the interpreter.

```
catch {policy outside}
```

Step 2: Building a GUI

These commands create three text widgets: two for the navigation system and one to display files. The table of contents is a simple string placed into the first text box. We also create a scrollbar to accompany the display text widgets.

```
#--------------------------------------------------------
# Creates the frames to hold the text widgets
#--------------------------------------------------------

set Name .top
frame $Name
pack $Name

set Name .top.side
frame $Name
pack $Name -side left

set Name .top.main
frame $Name
pack $Name -side left

#--------------------------------------------------------
# Creates the text widget and string for the toc.
# The regsub command replaces all empty spaces " "
# of the string with the newline character
# \n. This will cause all the words of the string
#  to be listed on top of each other.
#--------------------------------------------------------

set Name .top.side.nav
text $Name      -background pink\
    -borderwidth 2 -height 4 -width 15

pack $Name -side top

set toc "COOKIES PIES PUDDING CAKE"

regsub -all " " $toc " \n " title

$Name insert end $title
$Name configure -state disabled

#--------------------------------------------------------
# Creates the text box for the sub-toc.
# This text box will be destroyed
```

```
# and recreated each time a different item
# from the main toc is created.
#————————————————————————————————————————

set Name .top.side.subnav

text $Name -background white -width 15 -height 10

pack $Name -side left


#————————————————————————————————————————
# Creates the text widget and accompanying
# scrollbar that displays text files.
#————————————————————————————————————————

set Name .top.main.display

text $Name -background white -borderwidth 2 \
            -height 15 -width 30 \
            -padx 5 -pady 5 -state disabled -wrap
word

pack $Name -side left


set Name   .top.main.scroll

scrollbar $Name -background white \
            -command {.top.main.display yview}

pack $Name -anchor center -expand 0 -fill y \
                -ipadx 0 -ipady 0 \
              -padx 2 -pady 2 -side right


.top.main.display configure \
            -yscrollcommand {.top.main.scroll set}
```

Step 3: Creating the navigation system

These procedures tag the elements of the main table of contents
and the different secondary table of contents with the appropriate
commands.

The procedure `tag_toc` tags a specific position with the procedure `create_sub`, which creates a secondary table of contents.
Because each element of the table of contents is linked to a different list of words, the `tag_toc` procedure also requires the list of

words as an argument that it passes to the create_sub procedure.

```
proc tag_toc { w position tagname words num} {
#————————————————————————————————————————————
# Adds the tagname to the word sepecified
# by the position.
#————————————————————————————————————————————

$w tag add $tagname "$position wordstart" \
                 "$position wordend"


#————————————————————————————————————————————
# Creates bindings for the word that cause it to
# change color when the mouse passes over it.
#————————————————————————————————————————————

        $w tag bind $tagname <Enter> \
                    "$w tag configure $tagname \
                    -foreground green"
        $w tag bind $tagname <Leave> \
                    "$w tag configure $tagname \
                    -foreground black"


#————————————————————————————————————————————
# Creates a binding for the word to call
# create_sub when the mouse clicks on it.
# The num argument is the number of the word in
# main toc. This argument is used to identify
# the appropriate array of text files that the
# sub-toc will reference.
#————————————————————————————————————————————

        $w tag bind $tagname <Button-1> \
                    "create_sub {$words} $num"
        }
```

The create_sub procedure destroys the text widget that holds
the secondary table of contents, and then creates it with a new list
of words. It tags them using the tagging procedure.

```
proc create_sub { words num} {

    # ----------------------------------------
    # Destroys the .top.side.subnav if it exists.
    # Use catch to catch
    # any errors if the window does not exist
    # ----------------------------------------
    catch {destroy .top.side.subnav}


    # ----------------------------------------
    # Creates a text widget and places the word
    # string specified by  the procedure's argu-
    # ment. The regsub procedure places a
    # newline character in place of every space,
    # so the words will appear on separate rows.
    # ----------------------------------------

    set Name .top.side.subnav

    text $Name       -background Lightgrey \
         -borderwidth 2 -width 15 -height 10
    pack $Name -side top

    regsub   -all " "  $words   " \n "   title

    $Name insert end $title
    $Name configure -state disabled


    # ----------------------------------------
    # Tags each procedure using the tagging proce
    # dure. The procedure uses the num argument
    # the to name array of text files the words
    # are associated with.
    # ----------------------------------------

    set i 1
    foreach word  $words {
    tagging $Name [expr $i + 1].2 link($i) \
               $[join notes$num]($i)
    incr i
```

```
        }


    }
```

The tagging procedure provides each element of the secondary
table of contents with tags to access the text files.

```
proc tagging { w position tagname note } {

        # ─────────────────────────────────────
        # Adds a tag to the word specified by the
        # position.
        # ─────────────────────────────────────

        $w tag add $tagname "$position wordstart" \
                        "$position wordend"


        # ─────────────────────────────────────
        # Tags the word to turn from red to black when
        # the mouse passes over it.
        # ─────────────────────────────────────

        $w tag bind $tagname <Enter> \
                    "$w tag configure $tagname \
                     -foreground red"
        $w tag bind $tagname <Leave> \
                    "$w tag configure $tagname \
                     -foreground black"


        # ─────────────────────────────────────
        # Tags the word to call the ::http::geturl
        # command when the mouse clicks on it.
        # The url changes according to the note
        # argument - it is a separate text file
        # for each different word. The url must
        # be a complete and not relative url.
        # ─────────────────────────────────────

        $w tag bind $tagname <Button-1> \
            "::http::geturl \
```

```
http://www.company.com/$note \
-command get_notes"
```

```
}
```

Step 4: Retrieving data

The `tagging` procedure binds the `::http::geturl` procedure to the first mouse button. This procedure retrieves the file over the Web by calling its command option, `get_notes`, that takes as its argument the token returned by the HTTP transaction.

Specifying a command for `::http::geturl` is optional. You could call the `::http::geturl` command and set the token that it returns to a variable for use in other commands, using syntax such as `set id [::http::geturl` *url*`]`.

However, when you don't use the command option in the `::http::geturl` procedure, then the HTTP package calls the Tcl command `vwait`, and this command is not allowed by the Tcl Plug-in. When you design Tcl applications for a Web page that use the HTTP package, you must use the command option with the `::http::geturl` procedure. This causes the function to return immediately. It gives the command that you specify a *token* that represents the HTTP transaction that the `::http::geturl` procedure has completed. You do not need to specify the token argument when calling the procedure with the `::http::geturl` command, but when you define the procedure you need to include this argument.

The `get_notes` procedure that the `::http::geturl` command calls retrieves the data of the specified URL and places it into the text widget. To retrieve the data, it accesses the token that the HTTP transaction returns as the Tcl array `state`. This array includes useful information about the status, URL, size, and data of the transaction. The data that are contained in the retrieved file can be represented by the variable `state(body)`.

For more information about the HTTP package and the `state` array, see the manual page on HTTP. We also use the HTTP package in Chapter 10.

```
proc get_notes {token} {
```

```
#  ——————————————————————————————————————
#  Access  the  token  as  the  state  array
#  ——————————————————————————————————————

upvar  #0  $token  state

    #  ——————————————————————————————————————
    #  Retrieve  the  data  using  the  state  array
    #  ——————————————————————————————————————
    set  data  $state(body)

    #  ——————————————————————————————————————
    #  Inserts  the  data  into  the  text  widget
    #  ——————————————————————————————————————

    .top.main.display  configure  -state  normal
    .top.main.display  delete  1.0  end
    .top.main.display  insert  end  $data
    .top.main.display  -state  disabled
    }
```

Step 5: Creating arrays

The procedures of this application use array elements to create the secondary table of contents and to tag each word with the appropriate text file.

This array is used in the `tag_toc` and `create_toc` procedures, to create a separate list of words for each element of the main table of contents.

```
array set words {
1 " ChocolateChip Sugar PeanutButter \
          Oatmeal Brownies"
2 " Fruit Pumpkin LemonMeringue"
3 " Vanilla Chocolate Tapioca"
4 " Chocolate AngelFood Yellow"
}
```

These arrays specify the individual text files that are associated with each element of the secondary table of contents.

```
array set notes1 {
1 chip.txt
2 sugar.txt
3 peanut.txt
4 oat.txt
5 brown.txt
}

array set notes2 {
1 fruit.txt
2 pumpkin.txt
3 lemon.txt
}

array set notes3 {
1 vanilla.txt
2 choc.txt
3 tapi.txt
}

array set notes4 {
1 cake.txt
2 angel.txt
3 yellow.txt
}
```

Step 6: Tagging the toc

To finish the application, we call the `tag_toc` procedure for each element of the table of contents.

```
set i 1
foreach word  $toc {
      tag_toc .tp.sub.nav $i.2 link($i) $words($i) $i
```

```
        incr i
    }
```

The words and the text files can be modified for your own applications. You can create an online address book or a online manual using this application. It gives you mini nested frames on a Web page, and the ability to display text files without needing to modify them for the Web.

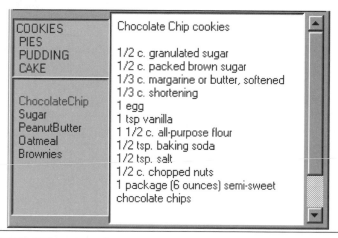

Figure 5.12 Tcl/Tk notecards

Here's the complete code for the Tcl notecards application:

```
# ─────────────────────────────────────────────
# Specify the necessary resources
# ─────────────────────────────────────────────

policy outside

package require http


# ─────────────────────────────────────────────
# Tag an element of  main table of contents
# to create a sub-toc
# ─────────────────────────────────────────────

proc tag_toc { w position tagname words num } {

    $w tag add $tagname "$position wordstart" \
```

```
                        "$position wordend"

        $w tag bind $tagname <Enter> \
                "$w tag configure $tagname \
                -foreground green"
        $w tag bind $tagname <Leave> \
                "$w tag configure $tagname \
                -foreground black"
        $w tag bind $tagname <Button-1> \
                "create_sub {$words} $num"

        }


# ─────────────────────────────────────────────────
# Create a sub-toc using a specific list of words
# ─────────────────────────────────────────────────

proc create_sub { words  num } {

        catch [destroy .top.side.subnav]
        set Name .top.side.subnav
        text $Name      -background Lightgrey \
            -borderwidth 2 -width 15 -height 10
        pack $Name -side top

        regsub  -all " "  $words  " \n "  title

        $Name insert end $title
        $Name configure -state disabled

        set i 1
        foreach word  $words {
        tagging $Name [expr $i + 1].2 link($i) \
                $[join notes$num]($i)
        incr i
        }

}
```

```
# ───────────────────────────────────────────
# Tag an element of a sub-toc to call the
# http_get function.
# ───────────────────────────────────────────

proc tagging { w position tagname note } {

        $w tag add $tagname "$position wordstart" \
                    "$position wordend"
        $w tag bind $tagname <Enter> \
                    "$w tag configure $tagname \
                     -foreground red"
        $w tag bind $tagname <Leave> \
                    "$w tag configure $tagname \
                     -foreground black"

        $w tag bind $tagname <Button-1> \
             "::http::geturl \
                    http://www.company.com/$note \
                    -command get_notes"
}


# ───────────────────────────────────────────
# Retrieve the data
# ───────────────────────────────────────────

proc get_notes {token} {

        upvar #0 $token state
        set data $state(body)
        .top.main.display configure -state normal
        .top.main.display delete 1.0 end
        .top.main.display insert end $data
        .top.main.display -state disabled
}
```

```
# ────────────────────────────────────────────
# Create the text widgets and insert the main toc
# ────────────────────────────────────────────

set Name .top
frame $Name
pack $Name

set Name .top.side
frame $Name
pack $Name -side left

set Name .top.main
frame $Name
pack $Name -side left

set Name .top.side.nav
text $Name      -background pink\
    -borderwidth 2 -height 4 -width 15

pack $Name -side top

set toc "COOKIES PIES PUDDING CAKE"

regsub -all " " $toc " \n " title

$Name insert end $title
$Name configure -state disabled

set Name .top.side.subnav
text $Name -background white -width 15 -height 10
pack $Name -side left

set Name .top.main.display
text $Name -background white -borderwidth 2 \
            -height 15 -width 30 \
            -padx 5 -pady 5 -state disabled \
            -wrap word
```

```
pack $Name -side left

set Name   .top.main.scroll
scrollbar $Name -background white \
          -command {.top.main.display yview}
pack $Name -anchor center -expand 0 -fill y \
          -ipadx 0 -ipady 0 \
            -padx 2 -pady 2 -side right


.top.main.display configure \
          -yscrollcommand {.top.main.scroll set}

# ————————————————————————————————————————
# Create arrays for each of the tocs
# ————————————————————————————————————————

array set words {
1 " ChocolateChip Sugar PeanutButter \
          Oatmeal Brownies"
2 " Fruit Pumpkin LemonMeringue"
3 " Vanilla Chocolate Tapioca"
4 " Chocolate AngelFood Yellow"
}

array set notes1 {
1 chip.txt
2 sugar.txt
3 peanut.txt
4 oat.txt
5 brown.txt
}

array set notes2 {
1 fruit.txt
2 pumpkin.txt
3 lemon.txt
}
```

```
array set notes3 {
1 vanilla.txt
2 choc.txt
3 tapi.txt
}

array set notes4 {
1 cake.txt
2 angel.txt
3 yellow.txt
}

# ─────────────────────────────────────
# Tag each element of the main table of contents
# ─────────────────────────────────────

set i 1
foreach word  $toc {
    tag_toc $Name $i.2 link($i) $nav($i) $i
    incr i


    }
```

The Tcl HTTP package allows you to access any public file on the Web. It does not render HTML, however, but simply retrieves data using HTTP. The Rouser application described in Chapter 11 will show you how to use an HTML rendering engine which is built entirely out of Tcl, and how you can use it to develop a simple Web browser using nothing but Tcl/Tk.

Conclusion

In this chapter we introduced a few different types of interactive Tcl/Tk applets. We also explained how to use images in Tcl/Tk applications. The next chapter gives you a brief introduction to HTML to help you publish your applications on Web pages.

6

Publishing Tcl/Tk Applications

The first section of the book, Basic Web applets, introduced Tcl/Tk and showed how to build several types of Web page applets. In Chapter 1, we presented an example of how to embed an application into a Web page. We end this section on Basic Web Applets with more detailed attention to creating Web pages and writing HTML. We also provide information about how servers and clients communicate with each other in anticipation of the next section of this book, Advanced Server-Based Applications. As we go through examples, we assume that you have access to a Web browser and know how to get around on the Web.

The topics that we touch on in this chapter are the main subjects of many other books. For more detailed information about any of these topics, you can access the Web references that we give you in this chapter or locate books at your local book store.

Creating HTML Documents

HTML documents are ASCII (plain-text) files with the extension .html. You can create HTML documents in any text editor, such as Notepad if your platform is Windows, or you could use the Ed Tcl Editor included on the CD to write plain-text files. If you use a word processor such as Microsoft Word to create HTML documents, then you should save your documents as "text only" with the extension .html.

Instead of writing HTML from "scratch," you might elect to use an HTML editor or HTML conversion tool. If you use one of these tools, it is still a good idea to have some HTML skills, or at least have a general understanding of the language. No conversion tool or editor is perfect, and you may find that you will have to tweak the HTML code to get your documents looking the way that you want them.

Fortunately, HTML is pretty straightforward and fun too. If you want to learn more, you can access one of many HTML resources that exist on the Web. One resource is the World Wide Web Consortium's HTML pages at `http://www.w3.org/pub/WWW/MarkUp/`. You probably can also find a number of books on HTML and Web page design in your local book store.

Working with tags

HTML is a simple markup language. It uses *tags* to format text, place images, and embed applications such as Tcl/Tk applets on Web pages. Examples of tags are `<B>` and `<IMG SRC="picture.gif">`. Tags begin and end with brackets. The brackets and the text that specify the tag do not appear on the Web page.

Many tags come in pairs, with a start and end tag. An end tag is the same as a start tag, except that it includes a slash (/) . For example, the tag `<B>` specifies that the text between the start and end characters of the tag should be bold. The phrase `<B> this is bold text</B>` will appear as **this is bold text** when interpreted by a Web browser. If you do not specify an end tag, then all the text that appears after the start tag will be bold until the end of the document is reached.

Other tags do not come in pairs, such as tags that specify the source and location of images, `<IMG SRC="picture.gif" HEIGHT=10 WIDTH=10>`.

HTML is not case-sensitive except when it is specifying special characters with escape sequences. Special characters include characters that are reserved for HTML tags that you want to display on a Web page, such as an ampersand or square bracket. Special characters also include accented characters. For example, the escape sequence `&amp` results in "&," and the escape sequence `&ntilde`

creates "(". These escape sequences are case sensitive. For a full list of escape sequences, see the W3 list at `http://www.w3.org/pub/WWW/MarkUp/html-spec/html-spec_13.html`.

Formatting text and documents

When a word or group of words is tagged, it behaves in a particular way. For example, it may change its format and become bold or italic. It may separate itself from other text, becoming a paragraph or header or list element. Or it may become a link to another document.

Here's a short example:

```
<H1> Hi, this is Header One </H1>
<P>This is a paragraph. </P>
<STRONG> I'm emphasized text</STRONG>
<H2> I'm Header Two </H2>
```

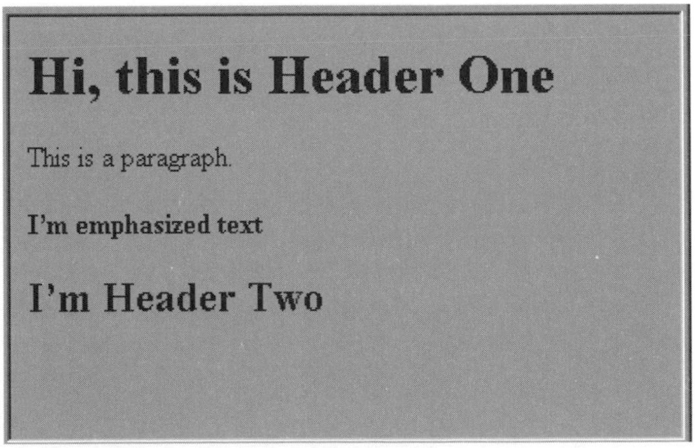

Hi, this is Header One

This is a paragraph.

I'm emphasized text

I'm Header Two

Figure 6.1 Example tags

In the above example, the text that is tagged with <H1> appears large and bold. The text tagged with <H2> is smaller relative to <H1>. Using these particular tags, you don't have control over the actual font and size of font; those preferences are determined by each viewer's Web browser. You can only determine how a selection of text will look relative to other text on the Web page.

The two other tags in the example are the paragraph and the text tag <STRONG>. The paragraph tag specifies the start and end of a paragraph. You need paragraph tags because HTML does not recognize carriage returns. A browser will ignore blank lines, multiple spaces, and tabs. The <STRONG> tag specifies emphasized text. Emphasized text usually appears as bold text, but it can appear as italic or a different color if the browser is configured to interpret strong tags in one of those ways.

In addition to formatting text, tags format documents. For example, the header tags also create line breaks before and after the text. The paragraph tags mark the beginning and end of a paragraph, placing a line break before and after the block of text between the beginning and ending tags.

The header and strong tags are *logical* tags. Logical tags specify styles of text, not the specific appearance of text. This is different from *physical* tags that describe how the text will appear. Physical tags override the preferences of a browser. Physical tags include the italics tag <I>, the bold tag <B>, and the <FONT> tag that specifies a particular font or color of text.

You could create a Web page consisting entirely of logical tags or entirely of physical tags. With logical tags, a Web page is flexible across many types of browsers, and the presentation of the Web page is separate from the content of the Web page. Traditionally, this is the best method to use when writing HTML. Yet because of the logical tags, the same Web page may look different from one browser to another. Web developers whose designs depend upon the appearance of text may elect to use the specific physical tags to keep their designs consistent.

Lists

HTML supports numbered lists, bulleted lists, and definition lists.

Bulleted lists start and end with the <UL> tag, for *unnumbered* list. Numbered lists begin and end with the <OL> tag, for *ordered* list. Each list element is specified with a <LI> tag, with no accompanying end tag. Each element can have multiple paragraphs and nested lists.

```
<P>Why should you use Tcl/Tk?</P>
```

```
<OL>
<LI> Easy to use
     <UL>
     <LI>Quick development cycle
     <LI>Ready made widgets
     </UL>
<LI>Powerful and flexible
<LI>Application integration
</OL>
```

The definition list is not as widely used as bulleted and numbered lists. A definition list begins and ends with <DL>. Each term to be defined begins with <DT>, and each definition of a term is tagged with <DD>.

```
<DL>
<DT> Tcl/Tk
<DD> The natural scripting language for the Web.
<DT> Spynergy Tcl/Tk
<DD> An enhanced version of Tcl/Tk that helps
you create powerful, interactive Web applica-
tions.
</DL>
```

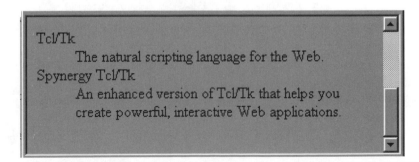

Figure 6.2 Example lists

Preformatted text

Although HTML does not recognize tabs or carriage returns, it does allow for preformatted text using the <PRE> tag.

With this tag you can shape a selection of text as you would using a word processor, without needing to use HTML tags. You can indent and add blank lines. This is useful for code examples and other situations in which you are restricted by the limits of HTML formatting.

```
<P>A short Tcl/Tk program</P>

<PRE>
button .b -text "Hello there!" -background white \
      -foreground red  -command {.b configure \
      -text "Goodbye!"}
pack .b -side left
</PRE>
```

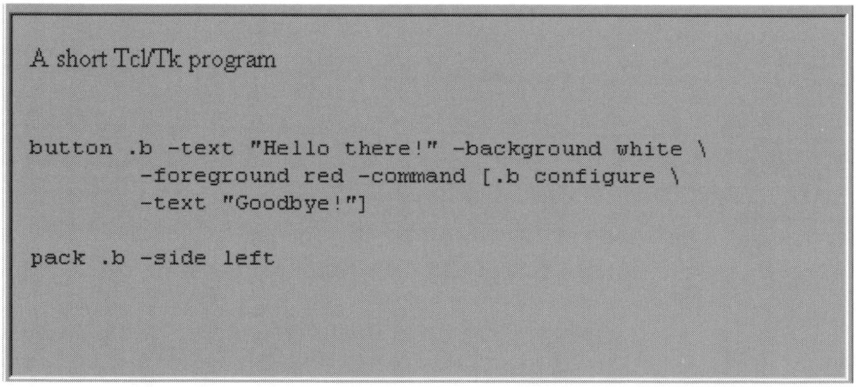

Figure 6.3 Preformatted text

Document tags

Document tags are tags that specify the heading and body of a Web page. Some browsers will supply the values of these tags and do not need them if they are provided, but other browsers need these tags to recognize an HTML document. Otherwise, they will display the HTML file as plain text without intepreting the HTML. It is good practice to always use the document tags, even if you are working with a browser that fills them in for you.

The examples that we have used so far in this chapter are not complete HTML files. An HTML file should begin and end with the <HTML> tag, indicating to the browser that the file contains HTML code. An HTML file should also contain two sections: a header described with the <HEAD> tag, and the body section described by the <BODY> tag.

In the header section, you can specify a title of the Web page with the <TITLE> tag. The title of the Web page typically appears in a text field of the Web browser window.

The <BODY> tag can have a number of arguments that specify the color of the background, foreground, and links of the Web page.

```
<HTML>
<HEAD>
<TITLE> A real Web page
</TITLE>
</HEAD>
<BODY BGCOLOR=#ffffff>
<H1> A Web page</H1>
      <P> This background is
<STRONG>white</STRONG>.</P>
<P> This is a paragraph. This is another line of
text.
      This line is not affected by the carriage
return in the source code.  </P>
<H3> HTML supports two types of styles:</H3>
<OL>
<LI>Logical tags include
      <UL>
      <LI> Header tags
      <LI> List tags
      <LI> Paragraph tags
      <LI> Strong and emphasized text
      </UL>
<LI>Physical tags include
      <UL>
      <LI> Italic tags
      <LI> Font tags
      <LI> Bold tags
```

```
        </UL>
    </OL>
    </BODY>
    </HTML>
```

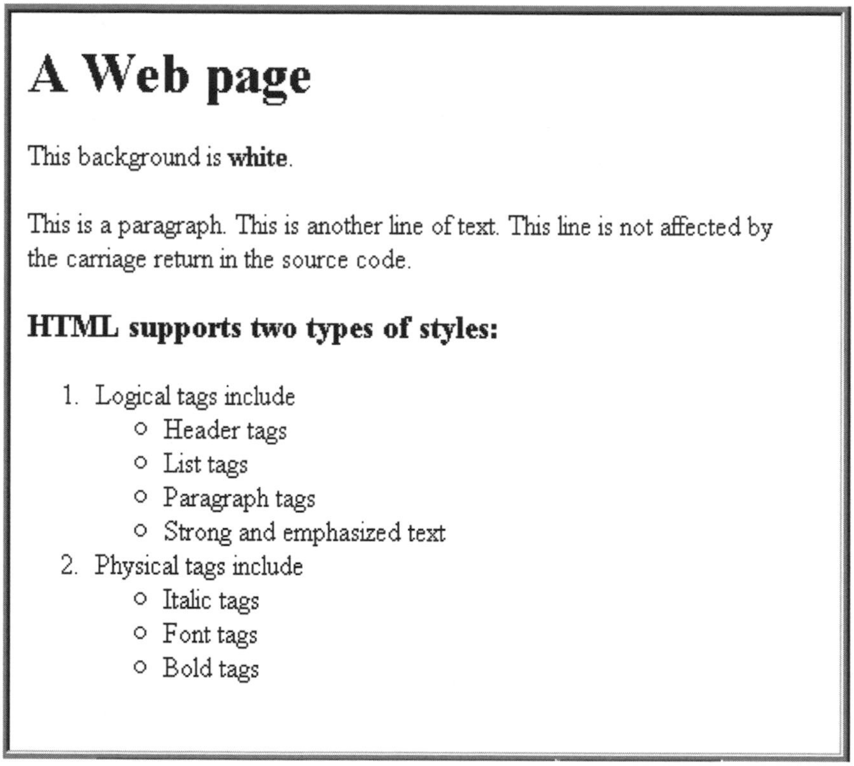

A Web page

This background is **white**.

This is a paragraph. This is another line of text. This line is not affected by the carriage return in the source code.

HTML supports two types of styles:

1. Logical tags include
   ○ Header tags
   ○ List tags
   ○ Paragraph tags
   ○ Strong and emphasized text
2. Physical tags include
   ○ Italic tags
   ○ Font tags
   ○ Bold tags

Figure 6.4 Example Web page

In this example, the background color is specified in the <BODY> tag. The default colors of a Web page are gray background with black text. You can change the default colors of the background, foreground, links, active links, and visited links by specifying hexadecimal RGB values for each component. A hexadecimal RGB value is a combination of six numbers and letters that represent the amount of red, green, and blue in the color.

You can find lists of hexadecimal values for particular colors on the Web. One resource that provides hexadecimal values is the ColorPro Web Server located at `http://www.biola.edu/cgi-bin/colorpro/`. This service lets you select a color and find its value.

Links

The nature of the Web depends on the ability to link documents to each other. You can link any line of text or image to another HTML file with the `<A HREF>` tag. The ending tag is `</A>`.

This link will take you to the home page of Eòlas Technologies.

```
<A HREF="http://www.eolas.com/"> Eolas Technologies</A>
```

The text of a link will appear in a different color. Each browser has a default color for links; and you can also set the color of the links on your Web page in the `<BODY>` tag, as discussed above.

```
<BODY BGCOLOR=#ffffff LINK=#00FF00>
```

The links of this Web page will be green, because the RBG values are specified as 00FF00, where the red value is 00, green is FF (the highest saturation), and the blue value is 00.

Links within the same document

You can also place links on a document that point to another place in a document. This is useful if you need a table of contents, for example. You use the number (#) sign to specify links within the same document.

For example, this link:

```
<A HREF="#DESC"> Description of service</A>
```

will jump to the place in the document tagged with this tag:

```
<A NAME="DESC">
```

The <A NAME> tag does not have an ending tag. If this tag does not appear within the document, then the link will have no effect.

Links to places in a different document

To jump to a specific place in a *different* document, you simply include the filename of the document before the # sign.

```
<A HREF="document.html#DESC>Description of service</A>
```

This tag will look for a section of document.html tagged with <A NAME="DESC">.

Mailto

You can invoke a browser e-mail window by using the "mailto" option in the <A HREF> tag. When you use this option and specify an e-mail address rather than a URL, the browser will open the e-mail window and allow the user to send an e-mail to the specified e-mail address.

```
<A HREF="mailto:support@eolas.com">Support</A>
```

Sounds and animations

You can also use the <A HREF> tag to link to movie and sound files such as .wav and .mpg files. Some sound and animation programs are not available for all platforms, and so your viewers may not always be able to view or hear them.

Images

Besides the ability to link documents, another appeal of the Web is the ability to place images on documents. To specify images, you only need to use the image tag, <IMG>. This tag has the form:

```
<IMG SRC="filename" HEIGHT=10 WIDTH=10 ALIGN=CENTER
ALT="Alternative text">
```

The SRC attribute is required. Image files can be .gif, .jpeg, or .xbm files. The image file can be located in a different directory than the

HTML file that references it, or even on a separate server. For example, the <IMG> tag <IMG SRC="http://www.company. com/images/logo.gif"> references the file "logo.gif" on the server specified by the URL http:\\www.company.com.

You should always specify a height and width attribute, even though some browsers do not require them. Some browsers will shrink or expand an image to fit the values given by the height and width attributes if they are not the actual dimensions of the image. But other browsers will not do this, so if you want to resize your image, you should change the size of the actual image instead of resizing it through the HTML code.

The ALT attribute is the text that is displayed when the image is not displayed. An image will not be displayed on browsers that cannot display images, or if a user configures his or her browser not to load images.

Images can be used with other HTML tags. For example, you can place images in the cells of tables. Tables are described in the next section. You can also link images to documents using the <A HREF> tag described in the previous section. To link an image, place the image tag in between the start and end tags of the link.

```
<A HREF="http://www.company.com/"><IMG SRC="logo.gif"
HEIGHT=15 WIDTH=30 ALT="Company"> </A>
```

Image maps

If an image is an image map, different sections of the image can be linked to different files.

There are two ways to create simple image maps. One way is the *server-side* image map, where the image references a separate file called a map file. The other way is the *client-side* image map, where you include all the coordinates and links to documents in the source of the HTML file.

Client-side image maps are preferred over server-side image maps in many cases because when the user selects a part of the image, the browser does not need to receive the separate map file from the server in order to get the correct URL. The URL is included in the source code of the HTML file. With server-side image maps, the server is "hit" many times. But some advanced image mapping software, such as the Eòlas MetaMAP server (see more on this later), is only available in server-side form. It gives you unique capabilities such as animated image maps that are not currently possible for client-side image maps.

However, not all browsers support client-side image maps. You can map an image map in both ways. If the browser supports client-side image maps, it will not access the separate map file from the remote server. If it does not support client-side image maps, then it will use the server-side mapping.

This example uses both server-side and client-side mapping. To create a server-side image map, you link the image to a file on your server, typically in your cgi-bin directory, and use the term ISMAP in the <IMG> tag. To create a client-side image map, you use the term USEMAP to point to a map tag within the HTML document.

```
<A HREF="/cgi-bin/imagemaps/navbar">
<IMG SRC="navbar.gif" HEIGHT=30 WIDTH=80
ISMAP USEMAP="navbar">
</A>
<MAP NAME="navbar">
<AREA SHAPE="RECT" COORDS="1,1, 20, 30"
HREF="home.html">
<AREA SHAPE="RECT" COORDS="21,1, 40, 30"
HREF="corporate.html">
<AREA SHAPE="RECT" COORDS="41,1, 60, 30"
HREF="products.html">
<AREA SHAPE="RECT" COORDS="61,1, 80, 30"
HREF="services.html">
</MAP>
```

When you map an image to use both server-side mapping and client-side mapping, then browsers that support client-side mapping will not access the server but use the information in the document for decoding the areas of the image. Browsers that do not support client-side mapping will ignore the <MAP> tags and use the specified map file.

For more information, see Netscape Navigator's online documentation on image maps.

MetaMAP® server

Both the server-side mapping and client-side mapping let you link sections of an image to different URLs. But if you are interested in creating very complicated image maps or animated image maps, or mapping images that will launch Tcl applets or create dynamically generated Web pages, then you will want to investigate the MetaMAP® server by Eòlas Technologies. See the MetaMAP® demo page at `http://www.eolas.com/metamap` for more information.

Background images

You can place an image in the background of your Web page. A background image is tiled, meaning that the browser takes the source of the image and repeats the image in a tile pattern. You specify a background image in the `<BODY>` tag.

```
<BODY BACKGROUND="picture.gif">
```

There are pros and cons to using a background image. It may add to the design of your Web page, but it may also add to the size of your file that users must download. Also, you should be careful that the image does not interfere with the text. If you look around on the Web, you will see many Web pages that are hard to read because of their background images.

Tables

Tables are a popular HTML extension. Some older browsers do not support tables, but most browsers do. You can create a table using the table tag `<TABLE>` that specifies the table, the table row tag `<TR>`, the table header tag `<TH>`, and the table cell tag `<TD>`. Each of these tags has an accompanying ending tag. You nest the table rows and table cells within the table tags, and you nest the table cells within the table rows.

Each table tag also has particular attributes. You can align text to the left, center, or right in a table, and you can specify specific height and width for each table cell. Each table row can have a different number of table cells. The table can have a thick, thin, or no border. You can place images and lists and other HTML elements in table cells.

```
<TABLE BORDER=1>
<CAPTION> A few TK widgets</CAPTION>
<TR>
     <TH>   Widget name </TH>
     <TH>   Picture        </TH>
     <TH>   Characteristics     </TH>
</TR>
<TR>
     <TD>   Button  </TD>
     <TD> <IMG SRC="button.gif" height=33 width =96 ></TD>
     <TD>     <UL>
             <LI> Executes  command when  pressed
             <LI>Displays  text  or  image
             <LI>Changes  relief  and  color  when  pressed
             </UL>
     </TD>
</TR>
<TR>
     <TD>Entry             </TD>
     <TD><IMG SRC="entry.gif" HEIGHT=29 WIDTH=84 ></TD>
     <TD> <UL>
           <LI> User  enters  text
         <LI>Width and  height  is  specified
     <LI> Can  be  disabled
            </UL>
     </TD>

</TR>
<TR>
     <TD>     Label          </TD>
     <TD><IMG SRC="label.gif" HEIGHT=22 WIDTH=64 ></TD>
     <TD> <UL>
           <LI> Displays  text  or  image
```

```
                          <LI>Shrinks to fit
                          </UL>

          </TR>
          </TABLE>
```

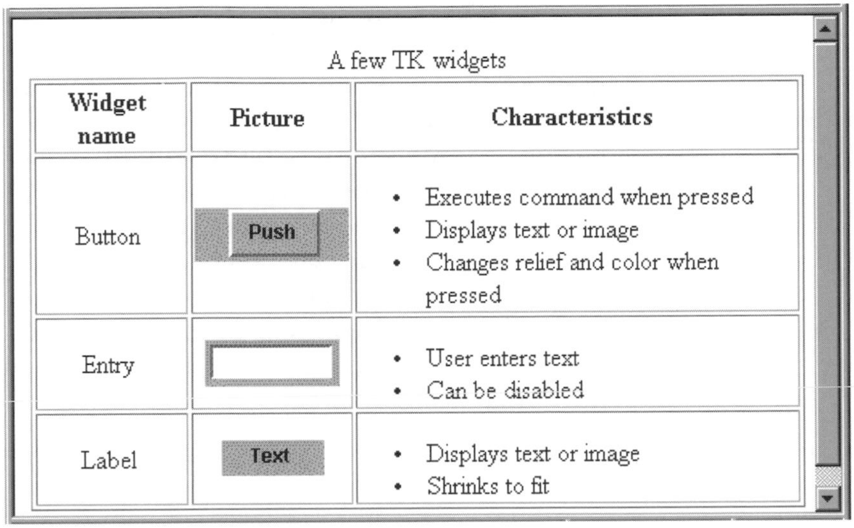

Figure 6.5 Example table

For more information on creating tables and the available attributes of the table tags, view the Netscape's table sampler at `http://home.netscape.com/assist/net_sites/table_sample.html`

Frames

Frames split the browser window into two or more sections. Each section of the window can load a different file. For example, you can have a navigation bar in one frame, with each link loading a separate page in another frame. Frames are very flexible and have a lot of creative uses.

Some older browsers do not support frames. Although that number is shrinking, you may want to consider how you handle your viewers that use these browsers. Some Web developers choose to provide alternate content that uses no frames. Using the <NOFRAMES> tag, this content will be displayed when the browser cannot interpret the other code that specifies frames. Other Web developers simply don't provide alternative content and tell viewers to come back when they can support frames. Your choice might depend on how much your design uses frames.

The first step in creating frames is to create an HTML document that splits the browser window and loads a file into each section. In this HTML document, you replace the <BODY> tag with the <FRAMESET> tag.

In the <FRAMESET> tag, you must specify values for the ROWS and COLUMNS attribute. You can specify a numeric value that is the fixed height (for rows) or width (for columns) in pixels, or you can specify a percentage of the window. Using the "*" character will give that frame all remaining space.

For example, this tag will create a frame with a fixed top row of height 100 pixels, and a bottom row that resizes to fill all available space. The frame has a thin column on the right. The columns will resize to the same proportions if the size of the browser window is changed.

```
<FRAMESET ROWS="100, *" COLUMNS="80%, 20%">
```

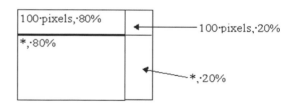

Placed within the <FRAMESET> start and end tag, a <FRAME> tag describes the attributes of a frame. You can also nest <FRAMESET> tags for frames within frames.

```
<FRAMESET COLUMNS="60, *">

<FRAME SRC="nav.html" NAME="left" MARGINWIDTH= 3
     MARGINHEIGHT=5 SCROLLING="auto" NORESIZE>

<FRAME SRC="main.html" NAME="right" MARGINWIDTH= 3
     MARGINHEIGHT=5 SCROLLING="auto" NORESIZE>

</FRAMESET>
```

The SRC attribute is required; it specifies the HTML document that will be loaded into the frame.

The NAME attribute enables you to target a specific frame from links within other documents. For example, you may include one frame that contains a navigation bar, as in the preceding example. The links from the navigation bar will load a file into a specific frame of the window.

```
<A HREF SRC="products.html" TARGET="right"> Products </A>
<A HREF SRC="services.html" TARGET="right"> Services </A>
```

This link will load the specified SRC into the framed named by TARGET. You specify the name of the frame, such as "right," when you create the frame.

Other attributes of the <FRAME> tag include the MARGIN-HEIGHT and MARGINWIDTH. They are optional and let you "pad" a frame to include margins specified in pixels.

The SCROLLING attribute lets you decide if the frame has a scrollbar. Auto, the default value, tells the browser to create a scrollbar only if needed. You can also specify yes, to create a scrollbar, and no, to prohibit creation of a scrollbar.

The NORESIZE flag instructs the browser not to let a user resize a frame. If the NORESIZE flag is not there, then the user will be able to resize a frame.

The NOFRAMES tag will let you provide content for those browsers that cannot support frames. All data between a NOFRAMES start and end tag will be ignored by browsers that support frames.

For more information on creating and working with frames, you can view the Netscape Navigators online documentation at http://home.netscape.com/assist/net_sites/frames.html.

Forms

Forms enable you to collect information from a person who visits your Web page. They can be composed of radio buttons, checkboxes, text fields, entry fields, and listboxes.

When a user submits a form, it typically executes a CGI (common gateway interface) program that is located on the server. A CGI script is a relatively simple program written in Perl, Tcl, or other scripting language. The script may gather the data to place in a database or to send to a specific e-mail address. It also may generate a HTML response page.

To construct a form on the Web page, you use the <FORM> tag that references a CGI script with the ACTION attribute. Each component of a form is created with a tag.

The <INPUT> tag allows you to specify a particular type of input field. Type can be a checkbox, a radiobox, a text field, or a submit button. The <SELECT> tag defines a pull-down selection list, each of which is defined with an <OPTION> tag. The <TEXTAREA> tag specifies a large text field that allows for multiple lines.

Each checkbox and radiobox is assigned a value with the VALUE attribute, much in the same way as you use variables for checkbox and radiobox Tk widgets.

The two <INPUT> tags at the end of this example create the buttons that submit or clear the form.

```
<FORM METHOD= POST ACTION="http://www.company.com/
    cgi-bin/script_name">

<INPUT NAME="select_1" TYPE=checkbox VALUE=one>
    Selection 1

<INPUT NAME="select_2" TYPE=checkbox VALUE=two>
Selection 2

<SELECT NAME="selection">

    <OPTION SELECTED> One

    <OPTION> Two

    <OPTION> Three

</SELECT>

<INPUT TYPE=submit> <INPUT TYPE=reset>

</FORM>
```

You can find many resources on the Web on creating forms and writing CGI scripts. One resource that includes links to other resources is on The University of Kansas Web site at http://kuhttp.cc.ukans.edu/info/forms/forms-intro.html.

The Second Edition of *Practical Programming in Tcl/Tk* by Brent Welch includes a complete section on writing CGI scripts. You can also write Tcl CGI scripts in Tcl using Don Libes's cgi.tcl library.

For more information on working with the cgi.tcl library, see `http://expect.nist.gov/cgi.tcl/`.

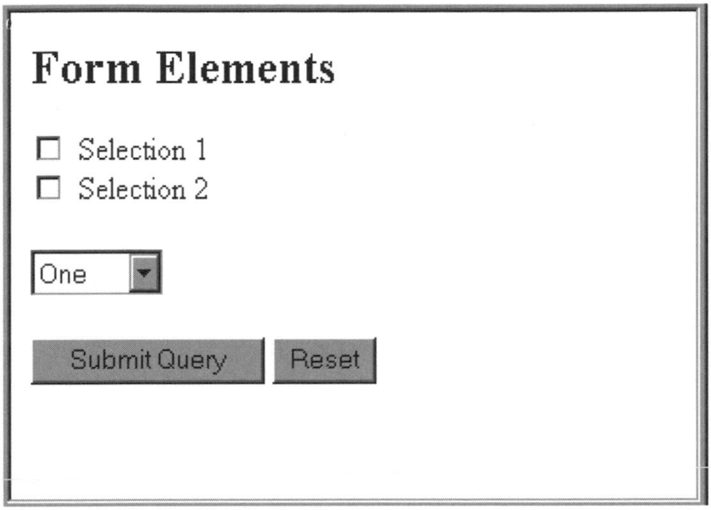

Form Elements

☐ Selection 1
☐ Selection 2

[One ▼]

[Submit Query] [Reset]

Figure 6.6 Form elements

There are also several software packages available that will help you create forms without needing to know how to create CGI script.

Embedding applications

In Chapter 1 we covered a short example of embedding an application into a Web page. This example is more detailed and uses frames.

To embed Tcl/Tk applications into your Web page, you simply use the <EMBED> tag. You must specify the height and width of an application.

The format of the <EMBED> tag is:

```
<EMBED SRC=filename HEIGHT=pixels WIDTH=pixels>
```

For example, to embed the animated puppy applet presented in Chapter 5, we could use the tag:

```
<EMBED SRC= "http://www.eolas.com/tcl/examples/
puppy.tcl HEIGHT=300 WIDTH=300>
```

In this example, we embed applications into different frames and tables. You can embed applications in any location that you can place an image, as long as you specify a height and width for that application.

Here's the source for the HTML file that specifies the initial frames. The top frame that we use as a navigation bar is named "top," the frame that loads different HTML files to display applets is named "main." The file head.html that this HTML code initially loads into the top frame acts as a navigation bar and remains in the top frame.

```
<HTML>
<HEAD>
<TITLE> Tcl/Tk applications </TITLE>
</HEAD>
<FRAMESET ROWS="50, *>
<FRAME SRC="head.html" NAME="top" SCROLLING="no">
<FRAME SRC="main.html" NAME="main" SCROLLING="auto">
</FRAMESET>
<NOFRAMES>
<P> This page best viewed using frames. Upgrade now!</P>
</NOFRAMES>
</HTML>
```

Here's the source for the page initially loaded into the top frame. Each link will load a different page into the main frame that includes an embedded applet. This navigation bar includes a type-writer applet that displays a message.

```
<HTML>
<HEAD>
<TITLE>Head</TITLE>
</HEAD>
<BODY BGCOLOR=#FFFFF>
<TABLE>
<TR>
<TD>
```

```
<EMBED SRC="typewriter.tcl" HEIGHT=30 WIDTH=130>
</TD>
<TD WIDTH=300>
<A HREF="puppy.html" TARGET="main">Puppy</A> *
<A HREF="crossword.html" TARGET="main">Crossword</A> *
<A HREF="calculator.html" TARGET="main">Calculator</A> *
<A HREF="wordsearch.html" TARGET="main">Wordsearch</A>
</TD>
</TR>
</TABLE>
</BODY>
</HTML>
```

Here's the source for the page initially loaded into the main window, `main.html`.

```
<HTML>
<HEAD>
<TITLE>Main</TITLE>
</HEAD>
<BODY BGCOLOR=#FFFFFF>
Tcl/Tk is an exciting innovative language for the
World Wide Web.
</BODY>
</HTML>
```

Each HTML file linked to the navigation bar contains an embedded Tcl application. This HTML code embeds the Tcl/Tk calculator into the Web page.

```
<HTML>
<HEAD>
<TITLE>Tcl/Tk Applets</TITLE>
</HEAD>
<BODY BGCOLOR=#FFFFFFF>
<P> You can use your keyboard or the mouse. </P>
```

```
<P><EMBED SRC="calculator.tcl" HEIGHT=163 WIDTH=214></P>
</BODY>
</HTML>
```

The other HTML files containing other applications are similarly coded, with appropriate height and width specified. These HTML files let a user view different Tcl/Tk applets in the main frame by clicking on the links in the navigation bar.

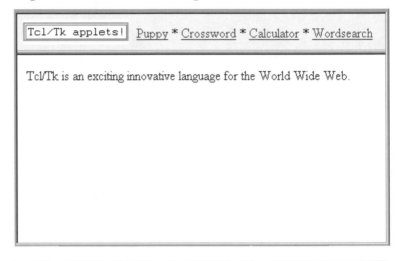

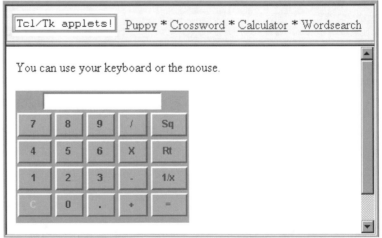

Figure 6.7 Frames and embedded Tcl/Tk applets

Browser-specific tags

One way to learn more about HTML is to look around on the Web, and when you see something you like, you can look at the source of the Web page to learn how that Web author accomplishes it.

But one thing to watch out for is HTML hacks and browser-specific tags. There may be things you can do with HTML that have a certain effect on one browser that will not translate to another. What seems like an interesting effect for one viewer will look like garbage to another.

If you use an HTML editor that is accompanied by a specific browser, then the Web pages you create with that HTML editor may be specific to that Web browser. It is good practice to make sure your Web page follows HTML standards, so all browsers will be able to interpret it.

URLs, IP Addresses, and Ports

How does the Web work? When you point your browser to the URL of a particular page, how does your browser know where to go among the millions of Web sites out there? And once located, how does your browser communicate with a Web server?

When you type a URL in your Web browser, your system signals your Internet connection to contact the remote server named by the URL. They communicate to each other through standard *protocols,* typically TCP/IP. TCP is Transmission Control Protocol and IP stands for Internet Protocol.

Each server, or *node,* on the Internet has a unique IP address that identifies it to all the other servers on the Internet. This address consists of four numbers, each between 0 and 255, separated by periods. In most cases, the first three numbers indicate the network that the particular node is connected to, and the final number defines the host. The Internet maintains a list of IP addresses and host names that can be used to access these hosts. For example, the server with the IP address 209.19.23.157 may also be accessed as http:\\www.eolas.com.

A URL is a Uniform Resource Locator. This is a mechanism for referencing files and other resources across the Internet. A URL consists of two parts, a *method* and a *resource,* separated by a colon. The method portion of the URL tells the browser what protocol to use to access the resource. The resource portion specifies the particular resource (usually a data file) to access. A method is usually HTTP (for Hypertext Transfer Protocol), but could also be FTP (for File Transfer Protocol), GOPHER (for gopher databases), or several other methods. Typing `http://www.eolas.com/` into your browser would cause the browser to open an HTTP session to `www.eolas.com`, and would load and display the Eòlas Technologies home page.

You can also connect to different *ports* of a server. A port offers a specific network service, such as e-mail or FTP; each network service of a server is provided on a different port. When you use a Web browser to request documents from a remote server, the Web browser accesses a particular port on the server. Typically, you connect to a server to download Web pages on port 80. When you use a Web browser to request documents via FTP, then your system will connect to a different port for that network service. Similarly, your e-mail is received and sent through yet another port on your server.

When your browser establishes a connection with a remote server using TCP/IP or other protocol, it then uses HTTP to request and download hypertext files, unless you specify FTP or another method to communicate with the server.

Conclusion

This chapter introduced HTML and writing Web pages, with references to resources you can go to for more information. We also introduced some concepts of how the Web works, in anticipation of the next section of this book, Advanced Server-Based Applications.

Part II

Advanced Server-Based Applications

The second section of this book focuses on server-side Web applications written in pure Tcl and using the Spynergy Toolkit. Chapter 7 discusses how to build a Tcl database and a Tcl/Tk Rolodex, and how to adapt the Tcl/Tk Rolodex into a client-server application. Chapter 8 shows how to build a basic Tcl Web server to use with server-side Web applications. In Chapter 9, you will learn to create a true server-push system that works with the Tcl Web server or another Web server, and connects with multiple clients.

Building a Client-Server Database

In this chapter, we will build a Tcl database that serves records over the Internet to a client application, the Tcl/Tk Rolodex. To build the Tcl/Tk Rolodex, we use two resources provided by the Spynergy Toolkit: remote procedure calls and Web Fusion database procedures.

In the first part of this chapter, we will build the Tcl database and Rolodex GUI that can be used on a single machine with Web Fusion database procedures. In the second part of this chapter, we will adapt the Rolodex into a client-server application using the Spynergy remote procedure calls. With this client-server application, the Tcl database is located on a server and keeps the records of the Rolodex, while the GUI is located on a client and displays records to a user. This adaptation of the Rolodex application into a client-server application was developed by Hengbing Duan.

Rolodex: The Tcl Database

The Tcl/Tk Rolodex is a fully functional online rolodex that we can easily construct using the Spynergy Toolkit database procedures. We build a front-end GUI in Tcl/Tk that lets a user add, delete, modify, sort, and view records of the Rolodex. These records are stored in the Tcl database that we can construct in just a few lines of code.

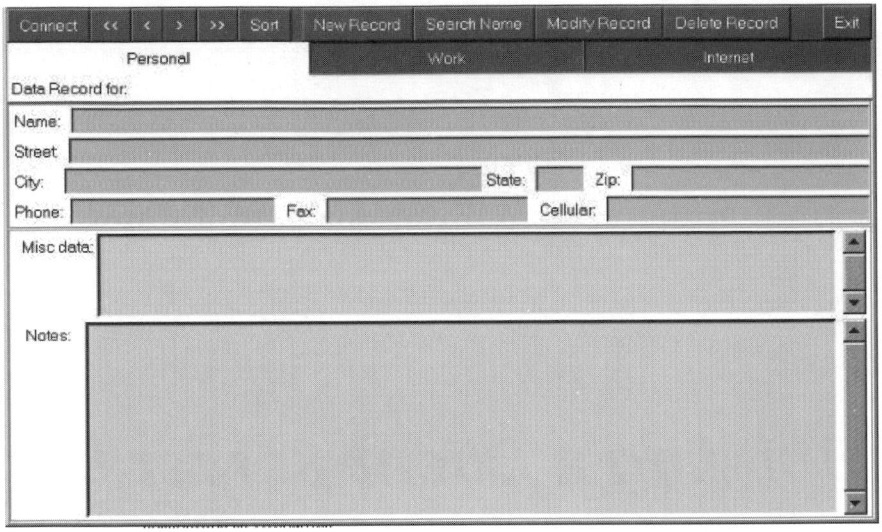

Figure 7.1 The Tcl/Tk Rolodex

The Tcl/Tk Rolodex uses the Spynergy Toolkit database procedures to create, open, and close a database and to create and modify database rows. The database that you create with these procedures is a robust and versatile tool that you can use as a back end to many types of applications.

If you have never worked with databases before, this is a good introduction. The Spynergy Toolkit Web Fusion procedures make it easy to understand how theTcl database is constructed and how you can manipulate it. This Tcl-based database is made up of one simple table. Each table row is a different database record, and each column is a different field for a record.

NAME	ADDRESS	COMPANY	PHONE
Susie	13 Washington	Silly Software, Inc	555-1345
Albert	27 First St	ISPs R US	555-8923

When you create a database, you specify the different columns for the table using dbCreate. Records can be added and retrieved using commands dbGetRow and dbPutRow.

When you create a new database, you also specify a database array variable, typically named db. You can easily access specific entries in the database table using this database variable. For example, an entry in the database table could be referenced by db(tablename, fieldname) where the tablename is the name of the database and the fieldname is the name of the field. We show you how to use this variable in the Rolodex procedures.

This is a summary of the Spynergy Toolkit database procedures. We explain these procedures when we use them to construct and manipulate the Rolodex. For a full specification of the database procedures, you can view the Spynergy online reference documentation that is on the CD. The Spynergy documentation is in HTML form that you can view with a Web browser, and also is contained in a Windows help file.

Table 7.1 Spynergy Toolkit database procedures

Procedure	Function
dbCreate	Creates a new database table
dbOpen	Opens a database and associates it with a variable
dbCleanup	Defragments and reorganizes the tables of a database
dbClose	Closes an open database, commits all pending changes
dbGetRow	Reads a row from a table using the row's sequence number as a key for the row to read
dbPutRow	Writes the current row for a table back to file
dbClearRow	Clears either current or specified row in a table
dbNewRow	Adds one or more new rows to a table
dbDelRow	Deletes the current or specified row from a table
dbFirstRow	Sets the current row to the first valid row in a table
dbLastRow	Sets the current row to the last valid row in a table
dbNextRow	Sets the current row to the next valid row in a table
dbPrevRow	Sets the current row to the previous valid row in a table
dbSetProc	Registers application procedures to call when problems arise
dbEOF	Determines if you have reached beyond the limits of a table

The Rolodex procedures

The Rolodex operates using the procedures in Table 7.2 which we will construct in the following sections:

Table 7.2 Procedures of the Tcl/Tk Rolodex

Procedure	Function
db_open	Opens an existing database, or creates a new database
db_display_record	Displays the selected record by placing the database variable values in the form field
db_capture_record	Pulls the form field data to place it into variables
db_clear_form	Clears the form fields of any data
db_sort	Sorts the records into a new database
db_add_record	Add the specifed record to the database
db_get_name	Selects the record from the database

db_open

The procedure db_open opens an existing database, or creates a new database if one does not exist, using dbCreate.

The Spynergy procedure dbCreate has the syntax:

```
dbCreate path var tablename fieldnames
```

The path indicates the path to the database. In this case, the path is the directory that the Rolodex application is located in. The var names the database array variable that we can use to access the database entries. The tablename names the database, and fieldnames specify the different columns of the database table.

This procedure also uses the Spynergy procedure dbOpen. This procedure has the syntax:

```
dbOpen path var
```

The path is the path to the database, and the var is the name of the database array variable. We will use this variable to access entries in the database table.

```
proc db_open {} {
   global db dir result
```

```
#  ---------------------------------------------------------------
# If the database is open, close it with dbClose
#  ---------------------------------------------------------------


    if {[info exists db]} {dbClose db}



#  ---------------------------------------------------------------
# If no database exists, create a new one using
# dbCreate and specify the form fields.
#  ---------------------------------------------------------------


  if {![file exist $dir/rolodex.idx]} {
        dbCreate $dir db rolodex "NAME STREET CITY STATE ZIP
PHONE  FAX CELL COMPANY C_STREET C_CITY C_STATE C_ZIP
C_PHONE C_FAX  C_CELL EMAIL PERSONALWEB WORKWEB PAGER
PGPFINGERPRINT PGPKEY NOTES"
            }

#  ---------------------------------------------------------------
# Open and refresh the database
#  ---------------------------------------------------------------

dbOpen $dir db

dbCleanup db

}
```

db_display_record and db_capture_record

The procedures db_display_record and db_capture
_record use the database array variable to pull specific values
from the selected record, or to write new values to the database
variables. These procedures are not interacting with the database,
but are simply retrieving or writing to variables.

The procedure db_display_record inserts each field of the
database record in the appropriate entry box on the Rolodex GUI.
It identifies each entry using the variable db(tablename,
fieldname), where tablename is the name of the database
table (in this case, rolodex) and fieldname is the name of the
entry.

We will build the entry fields of the form in the next section
when we build the Rolodex GUI.

```
proc db_display_record {} {
global db person_name

# ─────────────────────────────────────────────
# Each entry is pulled from the table row and placed in
# the appropriate entry field.
# ─────────────────────────────────────────────


.rolodex.form.personal.name.entry delete 0 end
.rolodex.form.personal.name.entry insert end \
      $db(rolodex,NAME)
.rolodex.form.personal.street.entry delete 0 end
.rolodex.form.personal.street.entry insert end \
      $db(rolodex,STREET)
.rolodex.form.personal.citystate.city delete 0 end
.rolodex.form.personal.citystate.city insert end \
      $db(rolodex,CITY)
.rolodex.form.personal.citystate.state delete 0 end
.rolodex.form.personal.citystate.state insert end \
      $db(rolodex,STATE)
.rolodex.form.personal.citystate.zip delete 0 end
.rolodex.form.personal.citystate.zip insert end \
      $db(rolodex,ZIP)
.rolodex.form.personal.phonefax.phone delete 0 end
.rolodex.form.personal.phonefax.phone insert end \
      $db(rolodex,PHONE)
.rolodex.form.personal.phonefax.fax  delete 0 end
.rolodex.form.personal.phonefax.fax insert end \
      $db(rolodex,FAX)
.rolodex.form.personal.phonefax.cellular delete 0 end
.rolodex.form.personal.phonefax.cellular insert end \
      $db(rolodex,CELL)
.rolodex.form.work.name.entry delete 0 end
.rolodex.form.work.name.entry insert end \
      $db(rolodex,COMPANY)
.rolodex.form.work.street.entry delete 0 end
.rolodex.form.work.street.entry insert end \
      $db(rolodex,C_STREET)
.rolodex.form.work.citystate.city delete 0 end
.rolodex.form.work.citystate.city insert end \
      $db(rolodex,C_CITY)
.rolodex.form.work.citystate.state delete 0 end
.rolodex.form.work.citystate.state insert end \
      $db(rolodex,C_STATE)
.rolodex.form.work.citystate.zip delete 0 end
.rolodex.form.work.citystate.zip insert end \
      $db(rolodex,C_ZIP)
```

```
.rolodex.form.work.phonefax.phone delete 0 end
.rolodex.form.work.phonefax.phone insert end \
       $db(rolodex,C_PHONE)
.rolodex.form.work.phonefax.fax delete 0 end
.rolodex.form.work.phonefax.fax insert end \
       $db(rolodex,C_FAX)
.rolodex.form.work.phonefax.cellular delete 0 end
.rolodex.form.work.phonefax.cellular insert end \
               $db(rolodex,C_CELL)
.rolodex.form.internet.email.entry delete 0 end
.rolodex.form.internet.email.entry insert end \
       $db(rolodex,EMAIL)
.rolodex.form.internet.personal_web.url delete 0 end
.rolodex.form.internet.personal_web.url insert end  \
       $db(rolodex,PERSONALWEB)
.rolodex.form.internet.work_web.url delete 0 end
.rolodex.form.internet.work_web.url insert end \
       $db(rolodex,WORKWEB)
.rolodex.form.internet.pagerpgp.pager delete 0 end
.rolodex.form.internet.pagerpgp.pager insert end \
       $db(rolodex,PAGER)
.rolodex.form.internet.pagerpgp.pgp delete 0 end
.rolodex.form.internet.pagerpgp.pgp insert end \
       $db(rolodex,PGPFINGERPRINT)
.rolodex.form.notes.misc.data delete 1.0 end
.rolodex.form.notes.misc.data insert end \
       $db(rolodex,PGPKEY)
.rolodex.form.notes.text delete 1.0 end
.rolodex.form.notes.text insert end \
       $db(rolodex,NOTES)
.rolodex.form.spacer0.data configure \
       -text [.rolodex.form.personal.name.entry get]
}
```

The procedure `db_capture_record` simply sets the value of each database array variable to the contents of the corresponding form field filled out by the user.

```
proc db_capture_record {} {
global db

set db(rolodex,NAME) \
       [.rolodex.form.personal.name.entry get]
set db(rolodex,STREET) \
       [.rolodex.form.personal.street.entry get]
set db(rolodex,CITY) \
       [.rolodex.form.personal.citystate.city get]
```

```
set db(rolodex,STATE) \
        [.rolodex.form.personal.citystate.state get]
set db(rolodex,ZIP) \
        [.rolodex.form.personal.citystate.zip get]
set db(rolodex,PHONE) \
        [.rolodex.form.personal.phonefax.phone get]
set db(rolodex,FAX) \
        [.rolodex.form.personal.phonefax.fax get]
set db(rolodex,CELL) \
        [.rolodex.form.personal.phonefax.cellular get]
set db(rolodex,COMPANY) [.rolodex.form.work.name.entry get]
set db(rolodex,C_STREET) \
        [.rolodex.form.work.street.entry get]
set db(rolodex,C_CITY) \
        [.rolodex.form.work.citystate.city get]
set db(rolodex,C_STATE) \
        [.rolodex.form.work.citystate.state get]
set db(rolodex,C_ZIP) [.rolodex.form.work.citystate.zip get]
set db(rolodex,C_PHONE) \
        [.rolodex.form.work.phonefax.phone get]
set db(rolodex,C_FAX) [.rolodex.form.work.phonefax.fax get]
set db(rolodex,C_CELL) \
        [.rolodex.form.work.phonefax.cellular get]
set db(rolodex,EMAIL) \
        [.rolodex.form.internet.email.entry get]
set db(rolodex,PERSONALWEB) \
        [.rolodex.form.internet.personal_web.url get]
set db(rolodex,WORKWEB) \
        [.rolodex.form.internet.work_web.url get]
set db(rolodex,PAGER) \
        [.rolodex.form.internet.pagerpgp.pager get]
set db(rolodex,PGPFINGERPRINT) \
        [.rolodex.form.internet.pagerpgp.pgp get]
set db(rolodex,PGPKEY) \
        [.rolodex.form.notes.misc.data get 1.0 end]
set db(rolodex,NOTES) \
        [.rolodex.form.notes.text get 1.0 end]
```

These two procedures are used by db_add_record and db_get_name to manage the form fields and database variables. The following procedures interact with the database to pull and place records into the table.

db_add_record

The procedure db_add_record uses dbNewRow to create a new row in the Rolodex database, and then uses db_capture _record to place all the values of the database variables into the appropriate database fields . It uses dbPutRow to place the record into the database.

```
proc db_add_record {} {
global db
        dbNewRow db rolodex
        db_capture_record
        set result [dbPutRow db rolodex]

}
```

db_get_name

The procedure db_get_name performs a string search of the database for the value entered in the name, company, or e-mail field. It determines the current tab of the Rolodex. (We will describe the different tabs of the Rolodex GUI in the next section.) It uses the Spynergy utility dbuSearchString to find the record according to a search criteria set according to the tab in the Rolodex table, then displays the record by using dbGetRow (to get the row in the database table) and db_display_record (to write the database variables to the entry fields of the GUI).

```
proc db_get_name {} {
global db current_type

# ──────────────────────────────────────────────
# Determine the current tab and set the field to that
# search type - so the search utility searches by
# NAME, COMPANY, or e-mail, depending if the tab is
# internet, work, or personal.
# ──────────────────────────────────────────────

switch $current_type \
        "internet" {
        set type EMAIL
         set field "internet.email.entry"
        } "work" {
        set type COMPANY
        set field "work.name.entry"
        } {
        set type NAME
        set field "personal.name.entry"
        }
```

```
# ────────────────────────────────────────────
# Set the sequence number list to the result of the
# search utility. Get the row and place it in the
# form fields using db_display_record.
# ────────────────────────────────────────────

set seqlist [dbuSearchString db rolodex $type \

[.rolodex.form.$field get]]
set seqno [lindex $seqlist 0]
dbGetRow db rolodex $seqno
db_display_record

}
```

db_sort

The procedure db_sort creates a new database table and sorts the records of the existing Rolodex database. It adds these records to its database table, then simply replaces the original Rolodex table with its sorted table of records, and loads the first record into the form.

To accomplish these tasks, the procedure uses dbGetRow and dbPutRow and the database utility dbuSort. The procedures dbGetRow and dbPutRow read a table row and write a table row, using the row's sequence number in the table to identify the row. The utility dbuSort returns a list of sequence numbers that is the order in which the existing table should be viewed using some criteria that we specify. The command has the form:

```
dbuSort var tablename fieldname [options]
```

In this application, we use the command dbuSort db rolodex NAME, so the command sorts the Rolodex table by the NAME field and returns a list of sequence numbers for ordering the records. We can use these sequence numbers to pull the ordered records from the database table and form the sorted table.

```
proc db_sort {} {

global db dir result
set first 1

# ────────────────────────────────────────────
# If the sorted database table does not exist, create a
# new one.
# ────────────────────────────────────────────
```

```
        if {![file exist $dir/sorted.idx]} {
            dbCreate $dir db sorted "NAME STREET CITY STATE
ZIP PHONE FAX CELL COMPANY C_STREET C_CITY C_STATE C_ZIP
C_PHONE C_FAX  C_CELL EMAIL PERSONALWEB WORKWEB PAGER
PGPFINGERPRINT PGPKEY NOTES"
            }


#  ------------------------------------------------------------
# For each sequence number returned by dbuSort, retrieve
# the record in the Rolodex table and set the sorted
# database variables to the appropriate form fields.
#  ------------------------------------------------------------


foreach seqno [dbuSort db rolodex NAME] {

dbGetRow db sorted $first
dbGetRow db rolodex $seqno
set db(sorted,NAME)  $db(rolodex,NAME)
set db(sorted,STREET) $db(rolodex,STREET)
set db(sorted,CITY) $db(rolodex,CITY)
set db(sorted,STATE) $db(rolodex,STATE)
set db(sorted,ZIP) $db(rolodex,ZIP)
set db(sorted,PHONE) $db(rolodex,PHONE)
set db(sorted,FAX) $db(rolodex,FAX)
set db(sorted,CELL) $db(rolodex,CELL)
set db(sorted,COMPANY) $db(rolodex,COMPANY)
set db(sorted,C_STREET) $db(rolodex,C_STREET)
set db(sorted,C_CITY) $db(rolodex,C_CITY)
set db(sorted,C_STATE) $db(rolodex,C_STATE)
set db(sorted,C_ZIP) $db(rolodex,C_ZIP)
set db(sorted,C_PHONE) $db(rolodex,C_PHONE)
set db(sorted,C_FAX) $db(rolodex,C_FAX)
set db(sorted,C_CELL) $db(rolodex,C_CELL)
set db(sorted,EMAIL) $db(rolodex,EMAIL)
set db(sorted,PERSONALWEB) $db(rolodex,PERSONALWEB)
set db(sorted,WORKWEB) $db(rolodex,WORKWEB)
set db(sorted,PAGER) $db(rolodex,PAGER)
set db(sorted,PGPFINGERPRINT) $db(rolodex,PGPFINGERPRINT)
set db(sorted,PGPKEY) $db(rolodex,PGPKEY)
set db(sorted,NOTES) $db(rolodex,NOTES)

#  ------------------------------------------------------------
# Place these records in the sorted database
#  ------------------------------------------------------------

dbPutRow db sorted
```

```
incr first
}
# ─────────────────────────────────────────────
# Copy the existing rolodex table and database file to
# a backup, and then copy the sorted table and database
# to the new rolodex table and database file.
# ─────────────────────────────────────────────

dbClose db
file copy rolodex.idx rolobak.idx
file copy rolodex.tbl rolobak.tbl
file copy sorted.idx rolodex.idx
file copy sorted.tbl rolodex.tbl
file del sorted.idx
file del sorted.tbl


# ─────────────────────────────────────────────
# Open the database and display the first record.
# ─────────────────────────────────────────────

db_open
set seqno 1
dbGetRow db rolodex $seqno
db_display_record
}
```

db_clear_form

The procedure db_clear_form deletes the strings in the entry
fields. It does not interact with the database.

```
proc db_clear_form {} {

.rolodex.form.personal.name.entry delete 0 end
.rolodex.form.personal.street.entry delete 0 end
.rolodex.form.personal.citystate.city delete 0 end
.rolodex.form.personal.citystate.state delete 0 end
.rolodex.form.personal.citystate.zip delete 0 end
.rolodex.form.personal.phonefax.phone delete 0 end
.rolodex.form.personal.phonefax.fax  delete 0 end
.rolodex.form.personal.phonefax.cellular delete 0 end
.rolodex.form.work.name.entry delete 0 end
.rolodex.form.work.street.entry delete 0 end
.rolodex.form.work.citystate.city delete 0 end
.rolodex.form.work.citystate.state delete 0 end
```

```
.rolodex.form.work.citystate.zip delete 0 end
.rolodex.form.work.phonefax.phone delete 0 end
.rolodex.form.work.phonefax.fax delete 0 end
.rolodex.form.work.phonefax.cellular delete 0 end
.rolodex.form.internet.email.entry delete 0 end
.rolodex.form.internet.personal_web.url delete 0 end
.rolodex.form.internet.work_web.url delete 0 end
.rolodex.form.internet.pagerpgp.pager delete 0 end
.rolodex.form.internet.pagerpgp.pgp delete 0 end
.rolodex.form.notes.misc.data delete 1.0 end
.rolodex.form.notes.text delete 1.0 end
.rolodex.form.spacer0.data configure -text ""

}
```

Rolodex GUI

In this section, we will construct the Rolodex GUI. The Rolodex has a button bar and three tabs. The buttons enable you to add, delete, modify, sort, and view records of the database using the Rolodex procedures. The tabs display personal, work, or Internet information for each record of the database.

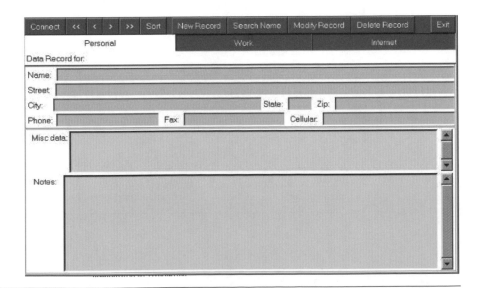

Figure 7.2 The Rolodex GUI

The buttons of the GUI call the procedures that we've described, and the procedures refer to the entry fields of the form that we build in this code.

Declaring global variables

The GUI is all inline code. To build the GUI, we first source in the Spynergy Toolkit and declare and initialize global variables.

```
source spynergy.tcl

global db dir result seqno current_type person_name


# ─────────────────────────────────────────────────────
# Result is the return value from dbPutRow
# ─────────────────────────────────────────────────────

set result 0

# ─────────────────────────────────────────────────────
# seqno is the sequence number of a record of the database
# table.
# ─────────────────────────────────────────────────────


set seqno 0

# ─────────────────────────────────────────────────────
# This global variable specifies what directory the
# rolodex table is located in. Here, we set it to the
# current directory.
# ─────────────────────────────────────────────────────

set dir [pwd]

# ─────────────────────────────────────────────────────
# This binding will bind the backspace key to all
# the entry fields, so you can delete letters.
# ─────────────────────────────────────────────────────


bind Entry <BackSpace> {tkEntryBackspace %W}
```

Creating the button bar

The following code creates the button bar. The button bar includes buttons to go to the first record of the database, the previous

record, the next record, or the last record of the database. You can
create a new record, search by name, modify a record, delete a
record, or exit the application.

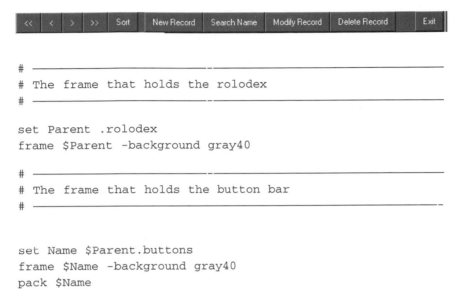

```
# --------------------------------------------------
# The frame that holds the rolodex
# --------------------------------------------------

set Parent .rolodex
frame $Parent -background gray40

# --------------------------------------------------
# The frame that holds the button bar
# --------------------------------------------------


set Name $Parent.buttons
frame $Name -background gray40
pack $Name
```

The First button opens the first record of the database. Its
command sets the sequence number to 1, gets the first row
of the table, and displays it using db_display_record.

```
set Name $Parent.buttons.first
button $Name       -activebackground  gray80 \
    -activeforeground black \
    -background gray40 \
    -command {
      set seqno 1
      dbGetRow db rolodex $seqno
      db_display_record
      } \
    -disabledforeground LightGray -foreground White \
    -highlightbackground LightGray \
    -highlightcolor LightGray \
    -padx 5 -pady 1 -text "<<"
pack $Name       -anchor nw -fill none -side left
```

The Back button displays the row just previous to the current row. It uses dbPrevRow to retrieve the sequence number of that row, then gets the row and displays it.

```
set Name $Parent.buttons.back
button $Name      -activebackground  gray80 \
    -activeforeground black \
    -background gray40 \
    -command {
      set row [dbPrevRow db rolodex]
      if {$row} {
            set seqno $row
            dbGetRow db rolodex $seqno
            db_display_record
            }
      } \
    -disabledforeground LightGray \
    -foreground White \
    -highlightbackground LightGray \
    -highlightcolor LightGray \
    -padx 5 -pady 1 -text "<"
pack $Name      -anchor nw -fill none \
    -side left
```

The Forward button uses dbNextRow to determine the sequence number of the next row, then gets the row and displays it.

```
set Name $Parent.buttons.forward
button $Name      -activebackground  gray80 \
    -activeforeground black \
    -background gray40 \
    -command {
      set row [dbNextRow db rolodex]
      if { $row} {
            set seqno $row
            dbGetRow db rolodex $seqno
            db_display_record
            }
      } \
    -disabledforeground LightGray \
    -foreground White \
    -highlightbackground LightGray \
    -highlightcolor LightGray \
    -padx 5 -pady 1 \
    -text ">"
pack $Name      -anchor nw \
    -fill none \
    -side left
```

The Last button displays the last record of the database. It determines the sequence number of the last row of the table using `dbLastRow` and displays it using `db_display_record`.

```
set Name $Parent.buttons.last
button $Name        -activebackground  gray80 \
    -activeforeground black \
    -background gray40 \
    -command {set seqno [dbLastRow db rolodex]
            db_display_record} \
    -disabledforeground LightGray \
    -foreground White \
    -highlightbackground LightGray \
    -highlightcolor LightGray \
    -padx 5 -pady 1 \
    -text ">>"
pack $Name        -anchor nw \
    -fill none -side left
```

The Sort button calls `db_sort` to sort and display the first record of the sorted database.

```
set Name $Parent.buttons.sort
button $Name        -activebackground  gray80 \
    -activeforeground black -background gray40 \
    -command "db_sort" \
    -disabledforeground LightGray \
    -foreground White \
    -highlightbackground LightGray \
    -highlightcolor LightGray \
    -padx 5 -pady 1 -text "Sort"
pack $Name        -anchor nw -fill none \
    -side left
```

```
# ─────────────────────────────────────────────
# This label spaces the buttons
# ─────────────────────────────────────────────

set Name $Parent.buttons.spacer
label $Name -text " " -background gray40
pack $Name -anchor nw -side left
```

The New Record button displays the personal tab and clears the form. It then unpacks itself and packs the Done button in its place.

```
set Name $Parent.buttons.new_record
button $Name        -activebackground  gray80 \
    -activeforeground black -background gray40 \
    -command {
      $Parent.datatype.personal invoke
      db_clear_form
      pack forget $Parent.buttons.new_record
      pack $Parent.buttons.new_record_done \
            -fill none -side left \
            -before $Parent.buttons.get_name
            } \
    -disabledforeground LightGray \
    -foreground White \
    -highlightbackground LightGray \
    -highlightcolor LightGray \
    -padx 5 -pady 1  -text "New Record"
pack $Name        -anchor nw -fill none \
    -side left
```

The Done button adds the record to the database using db_add_record. It clears the form and unpacks itself, packing the New Record button in its place.

```
set Name $Parent.buttons.new_record_done
button $Name        -activebackground  gray80 \
    -activeforeground black \
    -background gray60 -relief groove -border 1\
    -command {
      db_add_record;
      db_clear_form;
      pack forget $Parent.buttons.new_record_done
      pack $Parent.buttons.new_record -fill none \
            -side left -before $Parent.buttons.get_name
      after 1000 db_display_record
      } \
    -disabledforeground LightGray \
    -foreground Black -highlightbackground LightGray \
    -highlightcolor LightGray \
    -padx 5 -pady 1 \
    -text "        Done           "
```

The Search button retrieves the record matching the specified search criteria using db_get_name. The user can seach by name, company, or e-mail, depending on what tab is displayed.

```
set Name $Parent.buttons.get_name
button $Name       -activebackground  gray80 \
    -activeforeground black \
    -background gray40 -command "db_get_name" \
    -disabledforeground LightGray \
    -foreground White \
    -highlightbackground LightGray \
    -highlightcolor LightGray \
    -padx 5 -pady 1 \
    -text "Search Name"
pack $Name       -anchor nw -fill none \
    -side left
```

Modify Record

The Modify Record button captures the current record using db_capture_record and places it in the row of the table using dbPutRow. It clears the form and displays the current record after 1 second, allowing all procedures to complete.

```
set Name $Parent.buttons.modify_record
button $Name       -activebackground  gray80 \
    -activeforeground black -background gray40 \
    -command {
      db_capture_record
      dbPutRow db rolodex
      db_clear_form
      after 1000 db_display_record
      } \
    -disabledforeground LightGray \
    -foreground White -highlightbackground LightGray \
    -highlightcolor LightGray \
    -padx 5 -pady 1 -text "Modify Record"
pack $Name       -anchor nw -fill none \
    -side left
```

Delete Record

The Delete Record button deletes the current row of the Rolodex and clears the GUI form. It configures the text on the name label to an empty string.

```
set Name $Parent.buttons.delete_record
button $Name       -activebackground  gray80 \
    -activeforeground black \
    -background gray40 \
```

```
-command {
  if {$seqno} {
  dbDelRow db rolodex $seqno
  db_clear_form
  .rolodex.form.spacer0.data configure -text ""
  }
  } \
-disabledforeground LightGray \
-foreground White -highlightbackground LightGray \
-highlightcolor LightGray \
-padx 5 -pady 1 -text "Delete Record"
pack $Name       -anchor nw -fill none  -side left
```

```
# —————————————————————————————————————————
# This label spaces the buttons
# —————————————————————————————————————————

set Name $Parent.buttons.spacer2
label $Name -text "        " -background gray40
pack $Name -anchor nw -side left
```

Exit The Exit button closes the database using `dbClose` and exits the application using the Tk command `exit`.

```
set Name $Parent.buttons.exit
button $Name       -activebackground  gray80 \
    -activeforeground black -background gray40 \
    -command {dbClose db; exit} \
    -disabledforeground LightGray \
    -foreground White \
    -highlightbackground LightGray \
    -highlightcolor LightGray -padx 5 -pady 1 \
    -text "Exit"
pack $Name       -anchor nw -fill none -side right
```

Creating the tabs of the entry and display forms

Each of the separate tabs of a single record are identified with buttons. The buttons are configured to look like they are part of the frames that create the different pages of a record, but they are actually simple Tk buttons that pack and unpack the frames for personal, work, and Internet information.

This is an easy way to create a "tabbed notebook" visual effect through the use of nothing but frames and buttons.

Figure 7.3 Tabs of the Rolodex with the personal tab selected

The command of each button is the same: It packs and displays the appropriate frame and colors its background and changes its relief. It sets the global variable `current_type` to the appropriate value: personal, work, or Internet.

```tcl
# ————————————————————————————————————————————
# Frame that holds the three buttons
# ————————————————————————————————————————————

set Name $Parent.datatype
frame $Name
pack $Name -expand 1 -fill x


# ————————————————————————————————————————————
# The personal tab
# ————————————————————————————————————————————

set Name $Parent.datatype.personal
button $Name        -activebackground   white \
     -activeforeground black \
     -background white -relief flat \
     -command {
       $Parent.datatype.$current_type \
       configure -background gray40 \
             -relief sunken -foreground white
       $Parent.datatype.personal configure \
             -background white -relief flat \
             -foreground black
     pack forget $Parent.form.$current_type
     pack $Parent.form.personal   \
             -anchor nw -expand 1 \
             -fill x -before $Parent.form.notes
     set current_type personal
     } \
     -disabledforeground LightGray \
     -foreground black \
     -highlightbackground LightGray \
     -highlightcolor LightGray \
     -pady 1 -text "Personal"
pack $Name    -expand 1   -anchor nw   \
        -fill x   -side left
```

```
# -------------------------------------------------------- -----------
# The Work tab
# -------------------------------------------------------- ---------------

set Name $Parent.datatype.work
button $Name       -activebackground  white \
     -activeforeground black -background gray40 \
      -relief sunken \
     -command {
       $Parent.datatype.$current_type configure \
       -background gray40 -relief sunken \
       -foreground white
       $Parent.datatype.work configure\
             -background white -relief flat \
             -foreground black
       pack forget $Parent.form.$current_type
       pack $Parent.form.work  -anchor nw \
             -expand 1 -fill x \
             -before $Parent.form.notes
       set current_type work
        } \
     -disabledforeground LightGray \
     -foreground White \
     -highlightbackground LightGray \
     -highlightcolor LightGray \
     -pady 1 -text "Work"
pack $Name    -expand 1  -anchor nw  -fill x  -side left

# ------------------------------------------------------- --------------
# The Internet tab
# ------------------------------------------------------- --------------

set Name $Parent.datatype.internet
button $Name       -activebackground  white \
     -activeforeground black \
     -background gray40 -relief sunken \
     -command {
       $Parent.datatype.$current_type configure \
             -background gray40 -relief sunken
             -foreground white
       $Parent.datatype.internet configure \
             -background white -relief flat \
             -foreground black
       pack forget $Parent.form.$current_type
       pack $Parent.form.internet  -anchor nw \
             -expand 1 -fill x -before $Parent.form.notes
       set current_type internet
```

```
        } \
    -disabledforeground LightGray \
    -foreground White -highlightbackground LightGray \
    -highlightcolor LightGray \
    -pady 1 -text "Internet"
pack $Name    -expand 1   -anchor nw \
                -fill x   -side left
```

Creating the name label

Directly below the three buttons is a label that displays the name of the person in the current record. This lets the user know whom the record is for even when the personal tab is not displayed.

Data Record for:
_____

```
#————————————————————————————————————————————————————————————
# Frame of the form
#————————————————————————————————————————————————————————————

set Name $Parent.form
frame $Name -height 600 -background white
pack $Name -anchor nw -expand 1 -fill both
frame $Parent.form.spacer0  -background white \
            -relief flat -border 0
pack $Parent.form.spacer0 -expand 1 -fill x

label $Parent.form.spacer0.name -text "Data Record for:" \
        -background white -foreground black
pack $Parent.form.spacer0.name -side left -anchor w

#————————————————————————————————————————————————————————————
# Label for the name. This is configured each
# time a new record is displayed or removed.
#————————————————————————————————————————————————————————————

label $Parent.form.spacer0.data -text   " " \
            -background white -foreground black
pack $Parent.form.spacer0.data -side left -anchor w
```

The personal information tab

The personal information tab has entry fields for the name, street, city, state, zip, phone, and fax number. Each of these entry fields has a corresponding label, and is packed with a label in a frame.

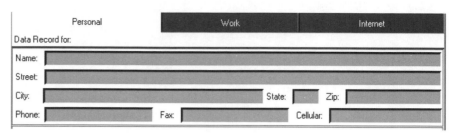

Figure 7.4 The personal information tab

```
# ─────────────────────────────────────────────
# The personal information frame
# ─────────────────────────────────────────────

set Form $Parent.form.personal
set Name $Form
frame $Name -background white -borderwidth 2 \
      -relief groove -height 300
pack $Name -anchor nw -expand 1 -fill x

# ─────────────────────────────────────────────
# The name frame, label, and entry field
# ─────────────────────────────────────────────

set Name $Form.name
frame $Name -background white
pack $Name -anchor nw -expand 1 -fill x -side top

set Name $Form.name.label
label $Name -text "Name:   " -background white
pack $Name -anchor nw -side left -pady 2

set Name $Form.name.entry
entry $Name -width 91 -background lightgray -borderwidth 3
pack $Name -anchor nw -side left -pady 2

# ─────────────────────────────────────────────
# The street frame, label, and entry field
# ─────────────────────────────────────────────

set Name $Form.street
frame $Name -background white
pack $Name -anchor nw -expand 1 -fill x -side top

set Name $Form.street.label
label $Name -text "Street:   " -background white
pack $Name -anchor nw -side left -pady 2
```

```
set Name $Form.street.entry
entry $Name -width 91 -background lightgray -borderwidth 3
pack $Name -anchor nw -side left -pady 2

# ————————————————————————————————————————————————
# The city, state, and zip frame, labels,
# and entry fields.
# ————————————————————————————————————————————————

set Name $Form.citystate
frame $Name -background white
pack $Name -anchor nw -expand 1 -fill x -side top

set Name $Form.citystate.city_l
label $Name -text "City:      " -background white
pack $Name -anchor nw -side left -pady 2

set Name $Form.citystate.city
entry $Name -width 50 -background lightgray -borderwidth 3
pack $Name -anchor nw -side left -pady 2
set Name $Form.citystate.state_l
label $Name -text "State:  " -background white
pack $Name -anchor nw -side left -pady 2

set Name $Form.citystate.state
entry $Name -width 5 -background lightgray -borderwidth 3
pack $Name -anchor nw -side left -pady 2

set Name $Form.citystate.zip_l
label $Name -text "  Zip:  " -background white
pack $Name -anchor nw -side left -pady 2

set Name $Form.citystate.zip
entry $Name -width 21 -background lightgray -borderwidth 3
pack $Name -anchor nw -side left -pady 2

# ————————————————————————————————————————————————
# The phone, fax, and cellular number frame,
# labels, and entry fields.
# ————————————————————————————————————————————————

set Name $Form.phonefax
frame $Name   -background white
pack $Name -anchor nw -expand 1 -fill x -side top

set Name $Form.phonefax.phone_l
label $Name -text "Phone: " -background white
pack $Name -anchor nw -side left -pady 2
```

```
set Name $Form.phonefax.phone
entry $Name -width 24 -background lightgray -borderwidth 3
pack $Name -anchor nw -side left -pady 2

set Name $Form.phonefax.fax_l
label $Name -text "  Fax:  " -background white
pack $Name -anchor nw -side left -pady 2

set Name $Form.phonefax.fax
entry $Name -width 24 -background lightgray -borderwidth 3
pack $Name -anchor nw -side left -pady 2

set Name $Form.phonefax.cellular_l
label $Name -text "  Cellular:  " -background white
pack $Name -anchor nw -side left -pady 2

set Name $Form.phonefax.cellular
entry $Name -width 25 -background lightgray -borderwidth 3

pack $Name -anchor nw -side left -pady 2
```

The work information tab

The work information tab includes the company name field, and
fields for the street, city, state, zip, phone, fax, and cellular numbers.

The frame is initally unpacked. It will be packed when the user
selects the work tab.

Figure 7.5 The work information tab

```
# ----------------------------------------------------------------
#   The frame of the work information tab
# ----------------------------------------------------------------

set Form $Parent.form.work
set Name $Form
```

```
frame $Name -background white -borderwidth 2 \
            -relief groove

# ─────────────────────────────────────────────────────
# The frame, label, and entry field of the company name
# ─────────────────────────────────────────────────────

set Name $Form.name
frame $Name -background white
pack $Name -anchor nw -expand 1 -fill x -side top

set Name $Form.name.label
label $Name -text "Company: " -background white
pack $Name -anchor nw -side left -pady 2

set Name $Form.name.entry
entry $Name -width 89 -background lightgray -borderwidth 3
pack $Name -anchor nw -side left -pady 2

# ─────────────────────────────────────────────────────
# The frame, label, and entry field of the street address
# ─────────────────────────────────────────────────────

set Name $Form.street
frame $Name -background white
pack $Name -anchor nw -expand 1 -fill x -side top

set Name $Form.street.label
label $Name -text "Street:        " -background white
pack $Name -anchor nw -side left -pady 2

set Name $Form.street.entry
entry $Name -width 89 -background lightgray -borderwidth 3
pack $Name -anchor nw -side left -pady 2

# ─────────────────────────────────────────────────────
# The frame, labels and entry fields of the city,
# state, and zip.
# ─────────────────────────────────────────────────────

set Name $Form.citystate
frame $Name -background white
pack $Name -anchor nw -expand 1 -fill x -side top

set Name $Form.citystate.city_l
label $Name -text "City:              " -background white
pack $Name -anchor nw -side left -pady 2

set Name $Form.citystate.city
```

```
entry $Name -width 50 -background lightgray -borderwidth 3
pack $Name -anchor nw -side left -pady 2

set Name $Form.citystate.state_l
label $Name -text "State:   " -background white
pack $Name -anchor nw -side left -pady 2

set Name $Form.citystate.state
entry $Name -width 5 -background lightgray -borderwidth 3
pack $Name -anchor nw -side left -pady 2

set Name $Form.citystate.zip_l
label $Name -text " Zip:   " -background white
pack $Name -anchor nw -side left -pady 2

set Name $Form.citystate.zip
entry $Name -width 19 -background lightgray -borderwidth 3
pack $Name -anchor nw -side left -pady 2

# ─────────────────────────────────────────────────────
# The frame, labels and entry fields of the phone,
# fax, and cellular numbers.
# ─────────────────────────────────────────────────────

set Name $Form.phonefax
frame $Name   -background white
pack $Name -anchor nw -expand 1 -fill x -side top

set Name $Form.phonefax.phone_l
label $Name -text "Phone:      " -background white
pack $Name -anchor nw -side left -pady 2

set Name $Form.phonefax.phone
entry $Name -width 24 -background lightgray -borderwidth 3
pack $Name -anchor nw -side left -pady 2

set Name $Form.phonefax.fax_l
label $Name -text "  Fax:   " -background white
pack $Name -anchor nw -side left -pady 2

set Name $Form.phonefax.fax
entry $Name -width 24 -background lightgray -borderwidth 3

pack $Name -anchor nw -side left -pady 2
set Name $Form.phonefax.cellular_l
label $Name -text "  Cellular:   " -background white
pack $Name -anchor nw -side left -pady 2

set Name $Form.phonefax.cellular
```

```
entry $Name -width 23 -background lightgray \
      -borderwidth 3
pack $Name -anchor nw -side left -pady 2
```

The Internet information tab

The Internet information tab includes entry fields for e-mail, Web site URLs, pager number, and PGP fingerprint.

The frame of the Internet page is initially not packed. It is only packed when the user selects the Internet tab.

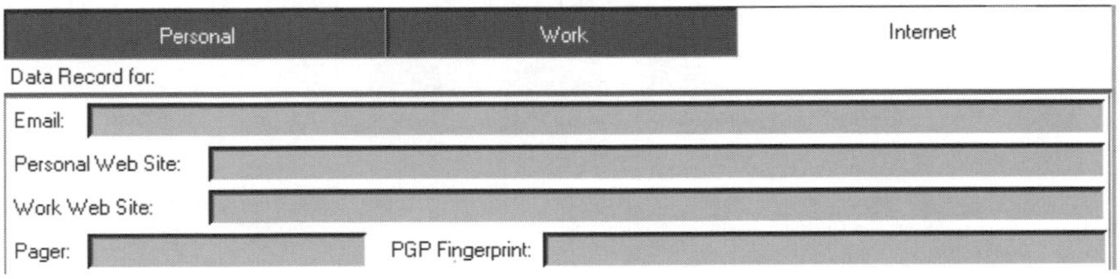

Figure 7.6 The Internet information tab

```
# ─────────────────────────────────────────────
# The frame of the Internet information page
# ─────────────────────────────────────────────

set Form $Parent.form.internet
set Name $Form
frame $Name -background white -borderwidth 2 \
      -relief groove


# ─────────────────────────────────────────────
# The frame, label, and entry field of the e-mail
# ─────────────────────────────────────────────

set Name $Form.email
frame $Name -background white
pack $Name -anchor nw -expand 1 -fill x -side top

set Name $Form.email.label
label $Name -text "Email:    " -background white
pack $Name -anchor nw -side left -pady 2

set Name $Form.email.entry
entry $Name -width 91 -background lightgray \
      -borderwidth 3
pack $Name -anchor nw -side left -pady 2
```

```
# ------------------------------------------------
# The frame, label, and entry field of the personal
# Web page.
# ------------------------------------------------

set Name $Form.personal_web
frame $Name -background white
pack $Name -anchor nw -expand 1 -fill x -side top

set Name $Form.personal_web.label
label $Name -text "Personal Web Site:     " \
        -background white
pack $Name -anchor nw -side left -pady 2

set Name $Form.personal_web.url
entry $Name -width 80 -background lightgray \
        -borderwidth 3
pack $Name -anchor nw -side left -pady 2

# ------------------------------------------------
# The frame, label, and entry field of the work Web site
# ------------------------------------------------

set Name $Form.work_web
frame $Name -background white
pack $Name -anchor nw -expand 1 -fill x -side top

set Name $Form.work_web.label
label $Name -text "Work Web Site:          " \
        -background white
pack $Name -anchor nw -side left -pady 2

set Name $Form.work_web.url
entry $Name -width 80 -background lightgray \
        -borderwidth 3
pack $Name -anchor nw -side left -pady 2

# ------------------------------------------------
# The frame, labels, and entry fields of the
# pager number and PGP fingerprint.
# ------------------------------------------------

set Name $Form.pagerpgp
frame $Name  -background white
pack $Name -anchor nw -expand 1 -fill x -side top

set Name $Form.pagerpgp.pager_l
label $Name -text "Pager:  " -background white
```

```
pack $Name -anchor nw -side left -pady 2

set Name $Form.pagerpgp.pager
entry $Name -width 24 -background lightgray \
        -borderwidth 3
pack $Name -anchor nw -side left -pady 2

set Name $Form.pagerpgp.pgp_l
label $Name -text "   PGP Fingerprint: " \
        -background white
pack $Name -anchor nw -side left -pady 2

set Name $Form.pagerpgp.pgp
entry $Name -width 50 -background lightgray \
        -borderwidth 3
pack $Name -anchor nw -side left -pady 2
```

The miscellaneous notes area

The Rolodex form also includes a miscellaneous data and notes area. The fields could contain a PGP signature or any other important data.

Figure 7.7 Miscellaneous notes

```
# ─────────────────────────────────────────────
# Frame for the notes area
# ─────────────────────────────────────────────

set Form $Parent.form.notes
set Name $Form
frame $Name -background white -borderwidth 2 \
        -relief groove
pack $Name -anchor nw -expand 1 -fill x
```

```
# ----------------------------------------------------------
# Frame, scrollbar, and label for the data area
# ----------------------------------------------------------

set Name $Form.misc
frame $Name  -background white
pack $Name -anchor nw -expand 1 -fill x -side top

set Name $Form.misc.scroll
scrollbar $Name -command {$Form.misc.data yview} \
       -orient vertical
pack $Name -side right -padx 4 -pady 2 -expand 1 \
       -fill y

set Name $Form.misc.data_l
label $Name -text "  Misc data:" -background white
pack $Name -anchor nw -side left -pady 2

set Name $Form.misc.data
text $Name -width 80 -background gray90 -borderwidth 3 \
       -height 4 -width 84 \
       -yscrollcommand \
       {.rolodex.form.notes.misc.scroll set}
pack $Name -anchor nw -side left -pady 2

# ----------------------------------------------------------
# Scrollbar, text widget, and label for notes area
# ----------------------------------------------------------

set Name $Form.scroll
scrollbar $Name -command {$Form.text yview} \
       -orient vertical
pack $Name -side right -padx 4 -pady 2 \
       -expand 1 -fill y

set Name $Form.text_l
label $Name -text "   Notes:   " -background white
pack $Name -anchor nw -side left -pady 2

set Name $Form.text
text $Name -width 45 -background gray90 \
       -borderwidth 3 \
       -height 10 -width 85 \
       -yscrollcommand {$Form.scroll set}
pack $Name -anchor nw -side left -pady 2
```

Starting it up

The last inline code of the Rolodex application sets the global variable, packs the Rolodex frame, and calls db_open to open or create the database.

```
set current_type personal
pack $Parent

db_open
```

The Internet Rolodex: A Client-Server Application

In this section, we modify the Tcl/Tk Rolodex to construct a client-server application. The Rolodex becomes a client that you can use on any computer with an Internet connection to connect with another computer on the Internet that hosts your Rolodex database. Using the Spynergy Toolkit remote procedure calls, we can easily build a server application to serve the Rolodex records to the client. This client-server application lets you access your Rolodex from any place on the Internet.

The procedure call that enables the client to execute commands on the server is dp_RPC. Using this command, the client can call a procedure which the server executes and then returns a result to the client.

Table 7.3 is a summary of Spynergy's remote procedure calls. For a full specification, see the online reference documentation.

Creating the Rolodex client

We can create a Rolodex client by building on the Rolodex application. We modify procedures with remote procedure calls and include global variables that specify the server and port.

Table 7.3 Remote procedure calls

Procedure	Function
dp_RPC	Arranges for a command and arguments to evaluate in remote Tcl/Tk interpreter
dp_RDO	Arranges for the command and arguments to evaluate in remote Tcl/Tk interpreter, without needed return token
dp_MakeRPCClient	Establishes RPC connection
dp_MakeRPCServer	Allows the current server to accept RPC connections
dp_CloseRPC	Closes the RPC connection
dp_CancelRPC	Cancels RPC transactions that are waiting for a return token
dp_Host	Determines the clients that are authorized to connect to this server
dp_SetCheckCmd	Checks the command

Global variables

The new variables that we introduce to the application specify the port and the server. They have default values that can be changed by the user.

```
set port 8088
set server localhost
```

Modified client procedures

The commands that open and sort the records, db_open and db_sort, in the database are defined in the server code. The following procedures have been modified to use remote call procedures to interact with the database that is on a remote server rather than on the local host. Instead of accessing a record directly using the database array variable, we use dp_RPC to contact the host and execute a procedure to retrieve the record.

db_display_record

The procedure db_display_record pulls the value of each field from the remote server using dp_RPC. It provides the utility with the host name and the field name, using the server procedure db_getfield. Instead of the field being specified by the database variable db(tablename, fieldname), the field is specified by [dp_RPC $host db_getfield fieldname]. For example, the contents of the name field are obtained by [dp_RPC $host db_getfield NAME].

```
proc db_display_record {} {
global db person_name host
.rolodex.form.personal.name.entry delete 0 end
.rolodex.form.personal.name.entry insert end \
      [dp_RPC $host db_getfield NAME]
.rolodex.form.personal.street.entry delete 0 end
.rolodex.form.personal.street.entry insert end \
      [dp_RPC $host db_getfield STREET]
.rolodex.form.personal.citystate.city delete 0 end
.rolodex.form.personal.citystate.city insert end \
      [dp_RPC $host db_getfield CITY]
.rolodex.form.personal.citystate.state delete 0 end
.rolodex.form.personal.citystate.state insert end \
      [dp_RPC $host db_getfield STATE]
.rolodex.form.personal.citystate.zip delete 0 end
.rolodex.form.personal.citystate.zip insert end \
      [dp_RPC $host db_getfield ZIP]
.rolodex.form.personal.phonefax.phone delete 0 end
.rolodex.form.personal.phonefax.phone insert end \
      [dp_RPC $host db_getfield PHONE]
.rolodex.form.personal.phonefax.fax  delete 0 end
.rolodex.form.personal.phonefax.fax insert end \
      [dp_RPC $host db_getfield FAX]
.rolodex.form.personal.phonefax.cellular delete 0 end
.rolodex.form.personal.phonefax.cellular insert end \
      [dp_RPC $host db_getfield CELL]
.rolodex.form.work.name.entry delete 0 end
.rolodex.form.work.name.entry insert end \
      [dp_RPC $host db_getfield COMPANY]
.rolodex.form.work.street.entry delete 0 end
.rolodex.form.work.street.entry insert end \
      [dp_RPC $host db_getfield C_STREET]
```

```
.rolodex.form.work.citystate.city delete 0 end
.rolodex.form.work.citystate.city insert end \
        [dp_RPC $host db_getfield C_CITY]
.rolodex.form.work.citystate.state delete 0 end
.rolodex.form.work.citystate.state insert end \
        [dp_RPC $host db_getfield C_STATE]
.rolodex.form.work.citystate.zip delete 0 end
.rolodex.form.work.citystate.zip insert end \
        [dp_RPC $host db_getfield C_ZIP]
.rolodex.form.work.phonefax.phone delete 0 end
.rolodex.form.work.phonefax.phone insert end \
        [dp_RPC $host db_getfield C_PHONE]
.rolodex.form.work.phonefax.fax delete 0 end
.rolodex.form.work.phonefax.fax insert end \
        [dp_RPC $host db_getfield C_FAX]
.rolodex.form.work.phonefax.cellular delete 0 end
.rolodex.form.work.phonefax.cellular insert end \
        [dp_RPC $host db_getfield C_CELL]
.rolodex.form.internet.email.entry delete 0 end
.rolodex.form.internet.email.entry insert end \
         [dp_RPC $host db_getfield EMAIL]
.rolodex.form.internet.personal_web.url delete 0 end
.rolodex.form.internet.personal_web.url insert end \
        [dp_RPC $host db_getfield PERSONALWEB]
.rolodex.form.internet.work_web.url delete 0 end
.rolodex.form.internet.work_web.url insert end \
        [dp_RPC $host db_getfield WORKWEB]
.rolodex.form.internet.pagerpgp.pager delete 0 end
.rolodex.form.internet.pagerpgp.pager insert end \
        [dp_RPC $host db_getfield PAGER]
.rolodex.form.internet.pagerpgp.pgp delete 0 end
.rolodex.form.internet.pagerpgp.pgp insert end \
        [dp_RPC $host db_getfield PGPFINGERPRINT]
.rolodex.form.notes.misc.data delete 1.0 end
.rolodex.form.notes.misc.data insert end \
        [dp_RPC $host db_getfield PGPKEY]
.rolodex.form.notes.text delete 1.0 end
.rolodex.form.notes.text insert end \
        [dp_RPC $host db_getfield NOTES]
.rolodex.form.spacer0.data configure \
        -text [.rolodex.form.personal.name.entry get]
}
```

db_capture_record

The procedure db_capture_record uses dp_RPC to evaluate the command db_setfield and set database variables on the remote server. The list command is used in order to insure that the contents of each field are passed as a single argument to the RPC server.

```
proc db_capture_record {} {
  global host
dp_RPC $host db_setfield NAME [list \
      [.rolodex.form.personal.name.entry get]]
dp_RPC $host db_setfield STREET [list \
      [.rolodex.form.personal.street.entry get]]
dp_RPC $host db_setfield CITY [list \
      [.rolodex.form.personal.citystate.city get]]
dp_RPC $host db_setfield STATE [list \
      [.rolodex.form.personal.citystate.state get]]
dp_RPC $host db_setfield ZIP [list \
      [.rolodex.form.personal.citystate.zip get]]
dp_RPC $host db_setfield PHONE [list \
      [.rolodex.form.personal.phonefax.phone get]]
dp_RPC $host db_setfield FAX [list \
      [.rolodex.form.personal.phonefax.fax get]]
dp_RPC $host db_setfield CELL [list \
      [.rolodex.form.personal.phonefax.cellular get]]
dp_RPC $host db_setfield COMPANY [list \
      [.rolodex.form.work.name.entry get]]
dp_RPC $host db_setfield C_STREET [list \
      [.rolodex.form.work.street.entry get]]
dp_RPC $host db_setfield C_CITY [list \
      [.rolodex.form.work.citystate.city get]]
dp_RPC $host db_setfield C_STATE [list \
      [.rolodex.form.work.citystate.state get]]
dp_RPC $host db_setfield C_ZIP [list \
      [.rolodex.form.work.citystate.zip get]]
dp_RPC $host db_setfield C_PHONE [list \
      [.rolodex.form.work.phonefax.phone get]]
dp_RPC $host db_setfield C_FAX [list \
      [.rolodex.form.work.phonefax.fax get]]
dp_RPC $host db_setfield C_CELL [list \
      [.rolodex.form.work.phonefax.cellular get]]
dp_RPC $host db_setfield EMAIL [list \
```

```
            [.rolodex.form.internet.email.entry get]]
dp_RPC $host db_setfield PERSONALWEB [list \
            [.rolodex.form.internet.personal_web.url get]]
dp_RPC $host db_setfield WORKWEB [list \
            [.rolodex.form.internet.work_web.url get]]
dp_RPC $host db_setfield PAGER [list \
            [.rolodex.form.internet.pagerpgp.pager get]]
dp_RPC $host db_setfield PGPFINGERPRINT [list \
            [.rolodex.form.internet.pagerpgp.pgp get]]
dp_RPC $host db_setfield PGPKEY [list \
            [.rolodex.form.notes.misc.data get 1.0 end]]
dp_RPC $host db_setfield NOTES [list \
            [.rolodex.form.notes.text get 1.0 end]]
}
```

db_add_record

The `db_add_record` procedure is redefined for the Rolodex client so that `dp_RPC` is called to execute `db_new_row` on the remote server. The record is captured and the result is placed in the database on the remote server using `dp_RPC $host db_put_row`.

```
proc db_add_record {} {
    global host result
    dp_RPC $host db_new_row
    db_capture_record
    set result [dp_RPC $host db_put_row]
}
```

db_get_name

The procedure `db_get_name` is changed for the client application so that the search function is evaluated on the remote server. The sequence list is retrieved using the command `[dp_RPC $host db_search_string $type [.rolodex.form. $field get]]`, rather than `[dbuSearchString db rolodex $type [.rolodex.form.$field get]]`.

```
proc db_get_name {} {
    global host current_type

    if {$current_type == "internet"} {
```

```
      set type EMAIL
      set field "internet.email.entry"
  } elseif {$current_type == "work"} {
      set type COMPANY
      set field "work.name.entry"
  }   else {
      set type NAME; set field "personal.name.entry"
  }

      set seqlist [dp_RPC $host db_search_string $type \
                    rolodex.form.$field get]]
  set seqno [lindex $seqlist 0]
  dp_RPC $host db_get_row $seqno
  db_display_record
}
```

connect

This procedure is called when the Connect button is selected. It opens a dialog box that accepts a host name or IP address. It then calls dp_MakeRPCClient with the server name that the user has entered into the entry field. This procedure opens the RPC connection to the host.

```
proc connect {} {
global host server port
if { [winfo exist .connect] == 0 } then {

        # ─────────────────────────────────────────────
        # Create the toplevel for the dialog box
        # ─────────────────────────────────────────────

        toplevel .connect
        wm title .connect "Remote Host:"

        # ─────────────────────────────────────────────
        # The frames, label, and entry box for the server
        # ─────────────────────────────────────────────

        frame .connect.f1
        pack .connect.f1 -fill x
        pack [entry .connect.f1.e1 \
              -width 20 -textvariable server] \
              -side right
        pack [label .connect.f1.l1 \
              -text "Hostname: "] -side right
```

```
    pack [frame .connect.f3] -fill x

    # ————————————————————————————————————————
    # The clear button that clears the entry field
    # ————————————————————————————————————————

pack [button .connect.f3.b1 -text Clear -command \
    { .connect.f1.e1 delete 0 end} ] -side left

    # ————————————————————————————————————————
    # The Connect button calls the dbMakeRPCClient
    # procedure using the server and port variables.
    # ————————————————————————————————————————

  pack [button .connect.f3.b2 -text "Connect" -command {
    wm withdraw .connect
    set host [dp_MakeRPCClient $server $port]
    if {![catch "dp_RPC $host db_open"]} {
        .rolodex.buttons.connect configure \
        -foreground green
        .rolodex.buttons.connect configure \
        -state disabled
      .rolodex.buttons.first invoke
    }
    }] -side left

  return

}
  wm deiconify .connect
}
```

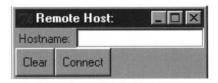

Figure 7.8 The dialog box displayed by the Connect button. The user enters the IP address or complete domain name of the server

disable_buttons and enable_buttons

These two commands enable and disable the buttons of the Rolodex GUI. Using these procedures with other commands lets the remote call procedures finish before the user can click on another button to execute another command. For example, the First button will disable buttons before proceeding to call dp_RPC to retrieve the first record from the database. It enables the buttons after the transaction is complete.

```
proc disable_buttons {} {

.rolodex.buttons.first configure -state disabled
.rolodex.buttons.back configure -state disabled
.rolodex.buttons.forward configure -state disabled
.rolodex.buttons.last configure -state disabled
.rolodex.buttons.sort configure -state disabled
.rolodex.buttons.new_record configure -state disabled
.rolodex.buttons.new_record_done configure -state disabled
.rolodex.buttons.get_name configure -state disabled
.rolodex.buttons.modify_record configure -state disabled
.rolodex.buttons.delete_record configure -state disabled
.rolodex.buttons.exit configure -state disabled
}

proc enable_buttons {} {

.rolodex.buttons.first configure -state normal
.rolodex.buttons.back configure -state normal
.rolodex.buttons.forward configure -state normal
.rolodex.buttons.last configure -state normal
.rolodex.buttons.sort configure -state normal
.rolodex.buttons.new_record configure -state normal
.rolodex.buttons.new_record_done configure -state normal
.rolodex.buttons.get_name configure -state normal
.rolodex.buttons.modify_record configure -state normal
.rolodex.buttons.delete_record configure -state normal
.rolodex.buttons.exit configure -state normal
}
```

The client Rolodex GUI

The only addition to the GUI is a Connect button that lets a user enter a server host. All the other buttons on the client GUI have modified commands to call dp_RPC and ask the server to execute the procedures to open, view, sort, and modify database records, rather than directly accessing the records with the database variable.

Figure 7.9 The Rolodex client button bar

Connect   The Connect button calls the connect procedure
described in the previous section.

```
set Name $Parent.buttons.connect
button $Name        -activebackground   gray80 \
    -activeforeground black \
    -background gray40 -command connect \
    -disabledforeground green \
    -foreground white -highlightthickness 0 \
    -highlightbackground LightGray \
    -highlightcolor LightGray \
    -padx 5 -pady 1  -text "Connect"
pack $Name        -anchor nw -fill none \
    -side left
```

«   The First button calls dp_RPC to execute db_get_row
with the first sequence number.

```
-command {
        disable_buttons
        set seqno 1
        dp_RPC $host db_get_row $seqno
        db_display_record
        enable_buttons
        }
```

<   The Back button calls dp_RPC to evaluate db_prev_row
and db_get_row to retrieve the records from the remote
server. It calls display_record to display the record.

```
-command {
    disable_buttons
    set row [dp_RPC $host db_prev_row]
    if {$row} {
        set seqno $row
        dp_RPC $host db_get_row $seqno
        db_display_record
        }
    enable_buttons
    }
```

>   The Forward button calls dp_RPC to evaluate
db_next_row and find the sequence number of the next
record. The db_get_row procedure is called through
dp_RPC and the record is displayed.

```
-command {
      disable_buttons
      set row [dp_RPC $host db_next_row]
      if {$row} {set seqno $row}
      if { $row} {
            dp_RPC $host db_get_row $seqno
            db_display_record
            }
      enable_buttons
      }
```

The Last button command calls `dp_RPC` to evaluate `db_last_row` to return the sequence number of the last row of the table. It displays that record.

```
-command {
    disable_buttons
    set seqno [dp_RPC $host db_last_row]
    db_display_record
    enable_buttons
    }
```

The Sort button calls `dp_RPC` to evaluate `db_sort` on the server and display the record that is returned by the procedure.

```
-command {
    disable_buttons
    dp_RPC $host db_sort
    db_display_record
    enable_buttons
    }
```

The New Record button remains the same, except that it disables the buttons until it has finished executing the commands.

```
-command {
    disable_buttons
    $Parent.datatype.personal invoke
    db_clear_form
    pack forget $Parent.buttons.new_record
    pack $Parent.buttons.new_record_done \
          -fill none -side left \
          -before $Parent.buttons.get_name
```

```
        enable_buttons
}
```

Done The Done button adds the record using the new `db_add_record` and clears the form.

```
-command {
  disable_buttons
  db_add_record;
  db_clear_form;
  pack forget $Parent.buttons.new_record_done
  pack $Parent.buttons.new_record -fill none \
        -side left \
        -before $Parent.buttons.get_name
  after 1000 db_display_record
  enable_buttons
  }
```

Search Name The Search button uses the new `db_get_name` to search the records and display the form.

```
-command {
  disable_buttons
  db_get_name
  enable_buttons
  }
```

Delete Record The Modify Record button calls `dp_RPC` to evaluate `db_put_row` on the remote server. It clears the form and displays the current record.

```
-command {
  disable_buttons
  db_capture_record
  dp_RPC $host db_put_row
  db_clear_form
  after 1000 db_display_record
  enable_buttons
  }
```

Delete Record The Delete button calls `dp_RPC` to evaluate `db_del_row` on the remote server.

```
-command {
  disable_buttons
```

```
if {$seqno} {
        dp_RPC $host db_del_row $seqno
        db_clear_form
        .rolodex.form.spacer0.data configure -text ""
        }
enable_buttons
}
```

 The Exit button closes the database and closes the RPC connection using db_CloseRPC. It calls the Tk command exit to exit the application.

```
-command {
  disable_buttons
    dp_RPC $host db_close
  dp_CloseRPC $host
    exit
  }
```

Creating the Rolodex Server

The code that follows is the program for the Rolodex Server. It can be run on any computer with an IP address. You need to specify the hosts that are allowed to connect to the server in this code, insuring that no other clients can connect. The Rolodex Server has no user interface and passes all of its status messages and error messages directly to the Tcl console.

Sourcing Spynergy Toolkit

It requires the Spynergy Toolkit to use the Web Fusion and remote call procedures.

```
source spynergy.tcl
```

Setting global variables

The variables include the directory of the Rolodex (the current directory), the database variable db, the port number, and the result variable. The default port is 8088.

```
set port 8088
global db dir result port

set dir [pwd]
```

Rolodex server procedures

start_server

The `start_server` procedure calls the `dp_MakeRPCServer` procedure and returns the response to the Tcl console. In this procedure, you explicitly state the IP addresses that are allowed to connect to this server using `dp_Host`.

The `dp_Host` procedure requires IP addresses. In this code, we specify the IP address 127.0.0.1, the IP address for the local host. The command `[dp_Host -]` that we use before specifying clients insures that no other clients will be allowed to connect to this server.

```
proc start_server {} {
global port

puts "Rolodex Server started on port: [dp_MakeRPCServer $port]"

# ─────────────────────────────────────────────
# Add approved client hostname — one line for each host
# ─────────────────────────────────────────────

puts [dp_Host -]
puts [dp_Host +localhost]
}
```

stop_server

The `stop_server` procedure closes the RPC connection.

```
proc stop_server {} {
global port

dp_CloseRPC $port
puts "Server stopped on port $port"

}
```

quit

The `quit` procedure lets the user stop the server from the console's command line.

```
proc quit {} {

stop_server
exit
}
```

db_open and db_sort

These procedures are called from the client using `dp_RPC`.

The procedure `db_open` creates or opens a new database.

```
proc db_open {} {
global db dir result
if {[info exists db]} {dbClose db}
if {![file exist $dir/rolodex.idx]} {
      dbCreate $dir db rolodex "NAME STREET CITY STATE
ZIP PHONE FAX CELL COMPANY C_STREET C_CITY C_STATE C_ZIP
C_PHONE C_FAX  C_CELL EMAIL PERSONALWEB WORKWEB PAGER
PGPFINGERPRINT PGPKEY NOTES"
    }
    dbOpen $dir db
}
```

The procedure `db_sort` sorts the records into a new database.

```
proc db_sort {} {
   global db dir result
   set first 1
   if {![file exist $dir/sorted.idx]} {
       dbCreate $dir db sorted "NAME STREET CITY STATE
ZIP PHONE FAX CELL COMPANY C_STREET C_CITY C_STATE C_ZIP
C_PHONE C_FAX  C_CELL EMAIL PERSONALWEB WORKWEB PAGER
PGPFINGERPRINT PGPKEY NOTES"
   }

   foreach seqno [dbuSort db rolodex NAME] {
      dbGetRow db sorted $first
      dbGetRow db rolodex $seqno
      set db(sorted,NAME)   $db(rolodex,NAME)
```

```
        set db(sorted,STREET) $db(rolodex,STREET)
        set db(sorted,CITY) $db(rolodex,CITY)
        set db(sorted,STATE) $db(rolodex,STATE)
        set db(sorted,ZIP) $db(rolodex,ZIP)
        set db(sorted,PHONE) $db(rolodex,PHONE)
        set db(sorted,FAX) $db(rolodex,FAX)
        set db(sorted,CELL) $db(rolodex,CELL)
        set db(sorted,COMPANY) $db(rolodex,COMPANY)
        set db(sorted,C_STREET) $db(rolodex,C_STREET)
        set db(sorted,C_CITY) $db(rolodex,C_CITY)
        set db(sorted,C_STATE) $db(rolodex,C_STATE)
        set db(sorted,C_ZIP) $db(rolodex,C_ZIP)
        set db(sorted,C_PHONE) $db(rolodex,C_PHONE)
        set db(sorted,C_FAX) $db(rolodex,C_FAX)
        set db(sorted,C_CELL) $db(rolodex,C_CELL)
        set db(sorted,EMAIL) $db(rolodex,EMAIL)
        set db(sorted,PERSONALWEB) $db(rolodex,PERSONALWEB)
        set db(sorted,WORKWEB) $db(rolodex,WORKWEB)
        set db(sorted,PAGER) $db(rolodex,PAGER)
        set db(sorted,PGPFINGERPRINT) $db(rolodex,PGPFINGERPRINT)
        set db(sorted,PGPKEY) $db(rolodex,PGPKEY)
        set db(sorted,NOTES) $db(rolodex,NOTES)
        dbPutRow db sorted
        incr first
    }

dbClose db
file copy rolodex.idx rolobak.idx
file copy rolodex.tbl rolobak.tbl
file copy sorted.idx rolodex.idx
file copy sorted.tbl rolodex.tbl
file del sorted.idx
file del sorted.tbl

db_open
set seqno 1
dbGetRow db rolodex $seqno

}
```

wrapper procedures

The following procedures are wrapper functions for the manipulation of database variable. They are used when the Rolodex client makes dp_RPC requests.

```
# -----------------------------------------------------
# Returns the entry of a record
# -----------------------------------------------------

proc db_getfield { fieldname } {
    global db
    return $db(rolodex,$fieldname)
}

# -----------------------------------------------------
# Sets the value for a single field of current row
# -----------------------------------------------------

proc db_setfield { fieldname value } {
    global db
    set db(rolodex,$fieldname) $value
}

# -----------------------------------------------------
# Creates a new row in the database
# -----------------------------------------------------


proc db_new_row {} {
  global db
  dbNewRow db rolodex
}


# -----------------------------------------------------
# Puts a row into the database
# -----------------------------------------------------

proc db_put_row {} {
  global db
  dbPutRow db rolodex
}

# -----------------------------------------------------
# Searches for a particular row
# -----------------------------------------------------

proc db_search_string { type value } {
  global db
  dbuSearchString db rolodex $type $value
}
```

```
# ---------------------------------------------------------
# Retrieves a row from the database
# ---------------------------------------------------------

proc db_get_row { seqno } {
  global db
  dbGetRow db rolodex $seqno
}

# ---------------------------------------------------------
# Retrieves the previous row from the database
# ---------------------------------------------------------

proc db_prev_row {} {
  global db
  dbPrevRow db rolodex
}

# ---------------------------------------------------------
# Retrieves the next row from the database
# ---------------------------------------------------------

proc db_next_row {} {
  global db
  dbNextRow db rolodex
}

# ---------------------------------------------------------
# Retrieves the last row from the database
# ---------------------------------------------------------

proc db_last_row {} {
  global db
  dbLastRow db rolodex
}

# ---------------------------------------------------------
# Deletes the specified row
# ---------------------------------------------------------

proc db_del_row { seqno } {
  global db
  dbDelRow db rolodex $seqno
}

# ---------------------------------------------------------
# Closes the database
# ---------------------------------------------------------
```

```
proc db_close {} {
  global db
  dbClose db
}
```

The last line of the Rolodex Server code starts the server.

```
start_server
```

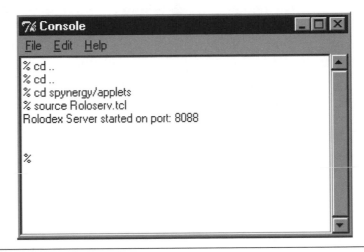

Figure 7.9 The Rolodex Server has no GUI. Status messages are displayed in the console

Adding security

While building the Rolodex Server, we use the command dp_Host to determine the clients that are allowed to access the server and to prevent all other clients from accessing the server.

You can build added security into your client-server applications using the Spynergy procedure dp_SetCheckCmd. This command calls a procedure to check commands called when a client makes a RPC or RDO request. You can create checking procedures that return Tcl codes or error messages when a client makes a specified request. For example, you can prevent a client from setting variables or from evaluating a Tcl script. The command dp_SetCheckCmd could also be useful in allowing access with Pretty Good Privacy signatures, or with password authentication. See the online Spynergy reference documentation for more details and an example of this command.

Conclusion

This chapter presented the Internet Tcl/Tk Rolodex to introduce you to the Tcl database and client-server applications. Using the Spynergy Toolkit's Web Fusion database procedures, you can easily create database tables for many different Tcl/Tk applications. The remote call procedures enable your applications to communicate between different hosts. In the next chapter, we will build a basic Tcl Web server that you can use to host your server-side Web applications.

8

The Tcl Web Server

The Tcl Web Server is a fully functional Web server. It creates log files that use the industry-standard National Computer Security Association (NCSA) format and serves data specified in standard Multipurpose Internet Mail Extensions (MIME) type definitions. You can use this Web server to construct server-side Web applications such as the applications we discuss in the next chapter.

The Tcl Web Server depends on the use of the socket and vwait Tcl commands. The socket command opens up a Transmission Control Protocol (TCP) network connection and returns an ID. With this ID you can execute other commands such as read, puts, and flush that manipulate the connection. You can specify a server name with the socket command, or open a socket on your own client. See the online documentation for more details of the socket command.

The vwait command is a powerful command that simply waits until a variable is written, no matter how long it takes. While it is waiting, Tcl enters into an "event loop." This means that Tcl continues to process events, such as responding to data coming in or out of a socket, until the variable is written.

Using the Spynergy Toolkit

This program also uses a group of Spynergy Toolkit procedures. It simply sets up a server socket and a vwait event loop to call the `httpd_accept` Spynergy Toolkit procedure whenever a request comes in on the socket. As long as you source *spynergy.tcl* in your program code, the only `httpd` procedure that you need to call explicitly in your program is `httpd_accept`. The others are called by procedures in the Spynergy Toolkit..

Table 8.1 The Spynergy Toolkit procedures used by the Tcl Web Server

Procedure	Function
`httpd_accept` *port*	Accepts a client connection to an HTTP server socket on the designated port. Calls `http_process_request` to respond to client request
`httpd_process_request` *sock*	Manages the server-side processing of HTTP requests on a server socket. Parses the request and reponds with appropriate error messages if necessary, or calls `http_send_it` to initiate transfer of requested data to the Web browser client
`httpd_send_it` *sock key item* `httpd_send_buf` *sock*	Httpd_send_it reads the data in the file designated by "key" and calls `httpd_send_buf` to send data to the client on the designated socket
`httpd_not_found` *sock item* `httpd_bad_request` *sock item*	These two procedures will send the specified error message out on the designated socket if the file requested is not found (or is restricted, such as log file) or if the HTTP request is malformed
`httpd_log_error` *sock message* `httpd_log_access` *sock getmessage ip codelength* `httpd_log_agent` *sock agent*	These three procedures handle writing to the error, access, and agent logs, in order to track activity on the Web server. These log files are in NCSA-standard format and can be analyzed using any of the popular utilities available for Web server log analysis
`httpd_cleanup_connection` *sock*	Cleanly closes out the HTTP session and closes the log files

Using a MIME data table

As the following code indicates, a MIME-type data file must be specified prior to calling `httpd_accept` in the server. A list of MIME-type definitions comprises the different types of data that the Web server recognizes.

You can use the `mime.typ` file that is located on the CD in the examples directory to build your applications. Just make sure that it is in the same directory as the Web server when you start the server. You can modify or add to the MIME types, if your application requires it. The definitions in this file will determine what MIME type is specified in the content headers of files sent using HTTP.

You can get more information about MIME and MIME type definitions on the NCSA's Web site at

```
http: //www.ncsa.uiuc/SDC/Software/Mosiac/Docs/
rfc1521.txt.
```

Building the Web Server

Step 1: Make sure to run the appropriate release level

Because of the powerful Tcl commands we use, the program requires Tcl 7.5 or higher.

```
global tcl_version
if {[info exists tcl_version] == 0 || \
        $tcl_version < 7.5} {
    error "webservr:  This program requires Tcl 7.5 \
or higher"
}
```

Step 2: Search for and locate the MIME table

Our Web server requires a MIME table so that it can recognize and specify different types of data.

```
global auto_path env
```

```
set mimepath "mime.typ"
if {(![file exists $mimepath]) || \
    (![file readable $mimepath])} {
    error "webservr:  could not find $mimepath file"
}
```

Step 3: Accommodate different versions of Tcl

This program can be run under Tcl 8.0, Tcl 7.6, or Tcl 7.5. One difference between Tcl 8.0 and other versions is the use of the fcopy and unsupported0 command. The fcopy command replaced the unsupport0 command in Tcl 8.0. Tcl 8.0 no longer recognizes the unsupported0 command. The following code accommodates all Tcl versions by using the unsupported0 command if the fcopy command is not recognized.

```
if {[info commands fcopy] == ""} {
  if {[info commands unsupported0] != ""} {
    rename unsupported0 fcopy
  } else {
    error "webservr: could not find the fcopy command"
  }
}
```

Step 4: Source the Spynergy Toolkit

```
source spynergy.tcl
```

Step 5: Set defaults

The following code specifies the defaults to the server socket and the locations of the log files if used. The log files that the Tcl Server creates are standard server log files that can be analyzed using statistical software tools like any other Web server log files.

These defaults are changed if options are specified in the command line of the Web server. For example, if you run the server specifying a port number:

```
webservr.tcl -port 80
```

then the variable HTTPD(serversocket) is changed to 80.

```
# ————————————————————————————————————————
# Port number of server socket
# ————————————————————————————————————————

set HTTPD(serversocket) 8080

# ————————————————————————————————————————
# Use of log files
# ————————————————————————————————————————

set HTTPD(use_log_files) 1
set HTTPD(logdir) "."
set HTTPD(webdir) "."
set HTTPD(access_log) "access.log"
set HTTPD(agent_log) "agent.log"
set HTTPD(error_log) "error.log"
set HTTPD(pid_file) "webservr.pid"
```

Step 6: Create an interface to shut down the server

You can use this interface to stop the server. This interface is not required. You can delete this code from your application if you don't want to give the user control over the operation of the server, or if you don't want your server to need Tk to run (if you want to run it under tclsh, rather than wish, for example.)

```
set Name .top0
catch "destroy .top0"
```

```
        toplevel $Name
        wm title $Name "Tcl Web Server"
        wm geometry $Name 170x36

set Parent .top0

set Name $Parent.b
button $Name      -background bisque \
    -relief raised \
    -text "Shut down server" -command "exit" \
    -activebackground red

pack $Name -side top
```

Step 7: Read contents of MIME file

This code reads in the contents of the MIME file. The file requires NCSA-standard MIME definitions. You can use or modify the mime.typ file that we provide on the CD, or you can create your own.

```
set fd [open $mimepath r]
while {![eof $fd]} {
    set line [gets $fd]
    if {[string index $line 0] != "#" && \
            [string index $line 0] != " " && \
            [string index $line 0] != "\n" && \
            [string index $line 0] != "\t"} {
        set content [lindex $line 0]
        set exts [lrange $line 1 end]
        foreach ext $exts {
            if {[string index $ext 0] != "#"} {
                set HTTPD(mime~~$ext) $content
            }
```

```
                }
            }
        }
    close $fd
    unset fd
    unset mimepath
```

Step 8: Examine and process command options

This code examines any options that are given when the server is
run. The options that can be specified at startup are the Web directory, log file directory, and the port number.

```
webservr.tcl ?-webdir path? ?-logdir path? \
        ?-port port?


# ────────────────────────────────────────────────
# Look for arguments
# ────────────────────────────────────────────────


if {$argc > 0} {
    set i 0
    while {$i < $argc} {
        switch -glob — [string tolower [lindex $argv $i]] {

# ────────────────────────────────────────────────
# If the log directory is specified, merge the
# path to the current path and set the resulting
# path  to the HTTPD(logdir) variable
# ────────────────────────────────────────────────


    -logdir {
        incr i
        set HTTPD(logdir) [lindex $argv $i]
        set path [file split [eval file join \
```

```
                    [file split [pwd]] \
                    [file split $HTTPD(logdir)]]]
        set outpath ""
        foreach item $path {
           switch -exact — $item {
              . {}
              .. {
                    set outpath [lrange $outpath 0 \
                             [expr [llength $outpath] - 2]]
                             }
                             default {lappend outpath $item}
                          }
                   }
        set HTTPD(logdir) [eval file join \
                 [split $outpath " "]]
        if {(![file isdirectory $HTTPD(logdir)])|| [file\
             writable $HTTPD(logdir)])} {
               error "webservr: logging directory \
                         may not be written to"
           }
           incr i
       }


#   ────────────────────────────────────────────
# If the Web directory is specified, merge the path
# with the path of the current directory and set
# the resulting path to the HTTPD(webdir) variable.
#   ────────────────────────────────────────────

   -webdir {
       incr i
       set HTTPD(webdir) [lindex $argv $i]
       set path [file split [eval file join \
          [file split [pwd]] \
          [file split $HTTPD(webdir)]]]
```

```
            set outpath ""
            foreach item $path {
                switch -exact — $item {
                    . {}
                    .. {
                        set outpath [lrange $outpath 0 \
                            [expr [llength $outpath] - 2]]
                            }
                            default {lappend outpath $item}
                    }
                }
                set HTTPD(webdir) [eval file join \
                        [split $outpath " "]]
                if {(![file isdirectory $HTTPD(webdir)])||\
                    (![file writable $HTTPD(webdir)])} {
                    error "webservr: WEB directory may \
                            not be written to"
                }
                incr i
        }
#  ———————————————————————————————————————————————————————————
# If the port number is specified, set it to the
# HTTP(serversocket) variable.
#  ———————————————————————————————————————————————————————————

    -port {
        incr i
        set HTTPD(serversocket) [lindex $argv $i]
        incr i
    }
    default {

#  ———————————————————————————————————————————————————————————
# If the option is not specified, then issue an
# error.
#  ———————————————————————————————————————————————————————————
```

```
            puts stderr "webservr: unrecognized option \
                    [[lindex $argv $i]\]"
                    incr i
            }
        }
    }
}


# ─────────────────────────────────────────────────
# Set related variables to the results of these
# processes.
# ─────────────────────────────────────────────────


set HTTPD(access_log)  "$HTTPD(logdir)/$HTTPD(access_log)"
set HTTPD(agent_log)   "$HTTPD(logdir)/$HTTPD(agent_log)"
set HTTPD(error_log)   "$HTTPD(logdir)/$HTTPD(error_log)"
set HTTPD(pid_file)    "$HTTPD(logdir)/webservr.pid"
set HTTPD(serverfd)   ""
set HTTPD(activesessions) 0
```

Step 9: Start up the server

To start the server after the variables have been set, we create a
process ID file that will record process Ids (useful for debugging),
and we open a "listening socket" that will wait for requests. The
forever variable will never be written to, so the command vwait
forever insures that the server will continue running until manually shut down by the user or by the application that is using it.

```
global forever HTTPD


# ─────────────────────────────────────────────────
#  Create or overwrite the process ID (pid) file
# ─────────────────────────────────────────────────


    set pidfd [open $HTTPD(pid_file) w]
```

```
      puts $pidfd "[pid]"
      flush $pidfd
      close $pidfd
      set outfd "dummy"



#  ─────────────────────────────────────────
# Create a listening socket and issue errors if
# there's a problem.
#  ─────────────────────────────────────────

if {[catch "socket -server [list "httpd_accept \
     $HTTPD(serversocket)"] $HTTPD(serversocket)" \
     outfd]} {
   puts stderr "webservr: Unable to open a \
     server socket"
   catch "close $outfd"
   exit 1
   }
if {[string range $outfd 0 3] != "sock"} {
   puts stderr "webservr: Unable to open a \
     server socket"
   catch "close $outfd"
   exit 1
   }
vwait forever
```

Conclusion

We have built a fully functional Web server out of a few pages of
Tcl code.   This is an excellent example of the power and flexibility of the Tcl/Tk platform. To the outside world, this server will be
indistinguishable from commercial Web servers costing thousands

of dollars. Since the log files use the industry-standard NCSA format, you can use any of the popular log analysis tools on the market to see who has accessed your site and to look for useful patterns in the data.

The next chapter presents a server-push application that can be supported by this Tcl Web Server.

9

Building a Server-Push Application

In Chapter 7, the Rolodex client-server application included a client with a GUI that requests files from a server. The Rolodex server simply waits for requests and gives records to the client when it is asked to. The server has no control over what records are requested or when it provides records.

With a server-push application, the relationship is reversed. All the action is on the server with a server-push application. The server provides a GUI that an administrator can use to select files and clients to push files to. Each one of the clients runs a small Tcl application that lets the client machine accept files from the server. The clients do not decide which files are sent to them, or when any files are sent. This is handled by the push server.

This is a true server-push application. You may have heard of other server-push systems that are actually client-pull applications. In a client or browser pull (such as the stockticker application or the weather map retrieval system discussed in the next section), the client periodically requests information from the server. In this application, the server is pushing the files to particular directories of specified clients. The push client machine only needs to be running a small application to allow it to accept the files.

There is one tricky concept that needs to be grasped to fully understand how the push system works. Although we are creating a push server program, called `pushserv.tcl`, this program actually uses the `dp_MakeRPCClient` command to act as an RPC "client" when it connects to the push client programs running on the remote machines listed in its client list. These remote push client applications actually act as RPC "servers," allowing the push server program to connect and disconnect, at will, in order to "push" files to those client machines by remotely invoking the Spynergy `fetchURL` procedure using the `dp_RPC` command (the `fetchURL` procedure is introduced in this chapter.) Because `fetchURL` is used to do the actual file transfers, the `pushserv.tcl` program must be launched from the HTML root directory of a Web server in order to work correctly. Any files within the tree of subdirectories under the Web server can then be set up to be pushed by `pushserv.tcl`. Of course, the Tcl Web Server that we built in Chapter 8 could act as the necessary Web server, so you could use the push system with any directory on your system, merely by launching both `webserv.tcl` and `pushserv.tcl` from the same directory.

One good application of such a system might be to perform automatic updates of various applications within a corporate Intranet. Whenever a new copy of a given program's files is put into a specific directory on the server machine, the required files would be automatically copied to the client machines. Your users would then automatically always have the lastest version of the application.

As written, the application will not allow the file push system to go beyond certain specified directories. Each of the clients needs to have the same file directory structure as the server for the files to be replaced for the clients.

Using `fetchURL`

The file push system uses the Spynergy Toolkit procedure `fetchURL` to transfer files from the push server to the client. The push server invokes the `fetchURL` procedure on the client machine using `dp_RPC`, causing the client machine to pull files from the server. This procedure implements a remote HTML document retrieval function from atop the Tcl socket command.

In Chapter 5, we looked at a demo that used the Tcl 8.0 HTTP package to retrieve files over the Internet. The Spynergy fetchURL procedure is similar to the HTTP package. One important difference is that Tcl/Tk applications do not need to be running under Tcl 8.0 to use this procedure, while the HTTP package is exclusive to Tcl 8.0. Another difference is that, while the primary command of the HTTP package, ::http::geturl, returns a token from the HTTP transaction, the fetchURL procedure returns the data contained in the URL.

The syntax of fetchURL is:

```
fetchURL -url  url -outfile filename -timeout secs
-initialtimeout secs
```

The only required option is the URL.

Table 9.1 Options of fetchURL

Option	Function
-url url	url to retrieve
-outfile filename	Place output in named file rather than returning it from this procedure
-timeout secs	Timeout between I/O buffers before assuming a connection closure (default 5 seconds)
-initialtimeout secs	Timeout to wait for initial connection establishment and 1st buffer retrieval (default 30 seconds)

The Push Server

This is true server-push system for unattended file distribution. The server includes a GUI that lets a user select files and clients.

This system requires that PushClnt.tcl (the client application) is running on all desired clients. The clients and the server must have Internet access. If files are pushed from subdirectories, then those subdirectory names must preexist on the client machine.

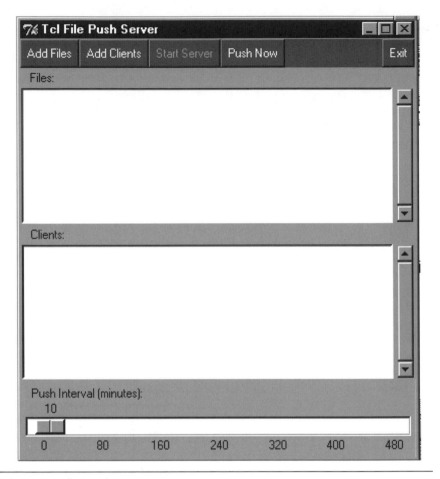

Figure 9.1 The push server

The File Push GUI

This is the inline code of the application. We will explain the GUI and then cover the procedures that let the user specify files to be pushed and the clients to push them to.

Sourcing the Spynergy Toolkit

Both the server-push application and the client application require the Spynergy Toolkit to use the remote call procedures and the `fetchURL` procedure

```
source spynergy.tcl
```

Setting the global variables

```
global _F loadsave interval i password _PUSH started \
        new_files push_status current_connection
set password "theSunalsosets"
set push_status idle
set time 10
set interval 600000
set started 0
set _PUSH(file~~name) ""
set _PUSH(file~~time) ""

bind Entry <BackSpace> {tkEntryBackspace %W}

# ─────────────────────────────────────────────────────────
# These variables are needed for the directory browser
# ─────────────────────────────────────────────────────────

    set _F(start_dir) [pwd]
    set _F(pwd) [pwd]
    set _F(directory) [pwd]
    set _F(file) ""
    set _F(filefilter) "*.*"
    set _F(keyname) ""
    set _F(status) ""
    set _F(permstatus) ""
    set _F(blockflag) 0

      if {$tcl_platform(platform) == "windows"} {
          set _F(courierfont) {{Courier New} 11 {normal}}
      } else {
          set _F(courierfont) \
          "-*-Helvetica-Medium-R-Normal—12-*-*-*-*-*-*-*"
      }
```

Creating the button bar

The buttons let you add files and clients, start the server, start the push loop, and exit the application.

```
# ─────────────────────────────────────────────────────────
# The toplevel parent
# ─────────────────────────────────────────────────────────
```

```
set Parent .filepush
set Name $Parent

# ─────────────────────────────────────────────────────────────
# Create the toplevel
# ─────────────────────────────────────────────────────────────


    toplevel $Name      -background LightGray
    wm title $Name "Tcl File Push Server "

# ─────────────────────────────────────────────────────────────
# Create the buttons for the button bar
# ─────────────────────────────────────────────────────────────

set Name $Parent.buttons
frame $Name      -relief flat -border 0 \
      -background gray40
pack $Name -anchor nw -side top -expand yes \
      -fill both
```

Add Files   The Add Files button calls the `file_load` procedure. This opens the directory browser to select the files to push, and then places the files into the file list.

```
set Name $Parent.buttons.files
button $Name      -activebackground lavender \
    -background gray40  \
    -command {file_load} \
    -foreground white \
    -highlightbackground LightGray \
    -text "Add Files"
pack $Name -anchor nw -side left \
            -expand 1 -fill x
```

Add Clients   The Add Clients button calls the `add_client` procedure. It opens a dialog box for the user to add clients. The clients are placed into the client list.

```
set Name $Parent.buttons.clients
button $Name      -activebackground lavender \
    -background gray40  \
    -command {add_client} \
    -foreground white \
    -highlightbackground LightGray \
    -text "Add Clients"
```

```
pack $Name -anchor nw -side left -expand 1 -fill x
```

 The Start Server button starts the server when pressed. It starts the `push_loop`, which begins to push files to the clients.

```
set Name $Parent.buttons.start
button $Name      -activebackground green \
    -background gray40  \
    -command {
      start_server
      } \
    -foreground green \
    -highlightbackground LightGray \
    -text "Start Server"
pack $Name -anchor nw -side left \
        -expand 1 -fill x
```

 The Stop button is packed in place of the Start Server button when the server is started by the `start_server` procedure.

```
set Name $Parent.buttons.stop
button $Name      -activebackground red \
    -background gray40  \
    -command {
      stop_server
      pack forget $Parent.buttons.stop
      pack $Parent.buttons.start \
      -anchor nw -side left /
      -expand 1 -fill x -after $Parent.buttons.clients
      } \
    -foreground red \
    -highlightbackground LightGray \
    -text "Stop Server"
```

 The Push Now button calls `push_files` that will immediately push to the clients without waiting for the push loop.

```
set Name $Parent.buttons.push
button $Name      -activebackground lavender \
    -background gray40  \
    -command {push_files} \
    -foreground white \
```

```
        -highlightbackground LightGray \
        -text "Push Now"
pack $Name -anchor nw -side left \
        -expand 1 -fill x

# ────────────────────────────────────────────────
# This is a spacer for the buttons
# ────────────────────────────────────────────────

set Name $Parent.buttons.spacer
label $Name -text "                          " \
        -background gray40 -foreground white
pack $Name -anchor w -side left
```

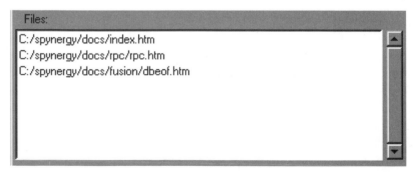 The Exit button calls the Tk command `exit` to exit the application.

```
set Name $Parent.buttons.exit
button $Name      -activebackground lavender \
    -background gray40 \
    -command exit \
    -foreground white \
    -highlightbackground LightGray \
    -text Exit
pack $Name -anchor nw -side left -expand 1 -fill x
```

Creating the file list

The following code sets up the listbox area of the GUI. This listbox displays the files to be pushed after they have been selected through the directory browser. The listbox does not allow user input, so the user cannot enter any file from the server to push to the client, but must use the restricted directory browser.

Figure 9.2 List of files

```
set Name $Parent.lists
frame $Name -border 0
pack $Name

set Name $Parent.lists.files
frame $Name -border 0
pack $Name


label $Name.label -text "  Files:"
pack $Name.label -anchor nw -side top

listbox $Name.filelist -width 60 -height 8 \
        -yscrollcommand \
        "$Parent.lists.files.scrollbar set" \
        -background white
pack $Name.filelist -anchor nw -side left

bind $Name.filelist <Double-ButtonRelease-1> \
        {foreach i \
        [$Parent.lists.files.filelist curselection] \
{$Parent.lists.files.filelist delete $i}
        }

set Name $Parent.lists.files.scrollbar
        scrollbar $Name  -activebackground plum \
                -activerelief sunken \
                -background LightGray \
                -command \
                "$Parent.lists.files.filelist yview" \
                -highlightbackground LightGray \
                -troughcolor gray40
pack $Name -anchor nw -expand 0 -fill y \
        -ipadx 0 -ipady 0 \
        -padx 2 -pady 2 -side left2
```

Creating the client list

The following code constructs the listbox that lists the domain names or IP addresses of the clients to push the files to.

Figure 9.3 List of clients

```
set Name $Parent.lists.clients
frame $Name -border 0
pack $Name

label $Name.label -text "  Clients:"
pack $Name.label -anchor nw -side top

listbox $Name.clientlist -width 60 -height 8 \
        -yscrollcommand \
        "$Parent.lists.clients.scrollbar set" \
        -background white
pack $Name.clientlist -anchor nw -side left

bind $Name.clientlist <Double-ButtonRelease-1> \
        {foreach i \
        [$Parent.lists.clients.clientlist curselection]
{$Parent.lists.clients.clientlist delete $i}
        }


set Name $Parent.lists.clients.scrollbar
scrollbar $Name  -activebackground plum \
        -activerelief sunken \
        -background LightGray \
        -command \
        "$Parent.lists.clients.clientlist yview" \
        -highlightbackground LightGray \
        -troughcolor gray40
pack $Name -anchor nw -expand 0 -fill y \
        -ipadx 0 -ipady 0 \
        -padx 2 -pady 2 -side left
```

Creating the push interval scale

The following constructs the scale that sets the push interval. When you change the push interval, the new interval is reflected after the next push.

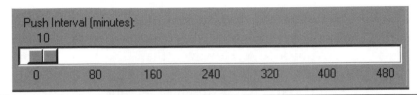

Figure 9.4 The files are pushed every 10 minutes at this setting

```
set Name $Parent.timing
frame $Name -border 0
pack $Name

scale $Name.scale -from 0 -to 480 -length 380 \
        -variable time -orient horizontal\
        -label "Push Interval (minutes):"\
         -tickinterval 80 -showvalue true \
        -troughcolor white
pack $Name.scale -expand 1 -fill x
```

Selecting files

The file_add procedure adds a file to the push list. It determines if the file is readable, calls the filepush_error procedure to issue an error if it is not readable, then inserts the filename into the listbox.

```
proc file_load {} {
global _F _PUSH

set _F(file) [loadsave 1]

if {$_F(file) == ""} {return}

if {![file readable $_F(file)]} {
  filepush_error "File \[$_F(file)\] is not readable."
  return
}

.filepush.lists.files.filelist insert end $_F(file)
```

```
.filepush.lists.files.filelist yview end
set _PUSH($_F(file)~~time) ""
}
```

Building the directory browser

We build the file push directory browser using the same proce-dures that we use for the Ed Tcl Editor directory interface in Appendix A. However, there are a few important modifications that restrict the browsing capabilities. The entry field that specifies the directory is disabled so that no other directories can be accessed but the directory and subdirectories specified by the file server application. You cannot access files from directories further up the tree.

We will not go into the details of the directory browser proce-dures here, except to point out the modifications that we have made for the file push application. For a full discussion of these procedures, see Appendix A on the Ed Tcl Code Editor.

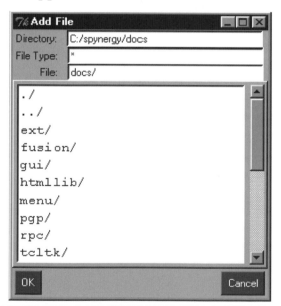

Figure 9.5 The directory browser interface

loadsave

The loadsave procedure creates the directory browser GUI.

```
proc loadsave {loadflag} {

#————————————————————————————————————————————————
# Declare and set variables that will be used in this
# procedure. The loadsave(pwd) vaiable is set to the
# current working directory using the Tcl command pwd.
#————————————————————————————————————————————————


global loadsave _F
if {![info exists loadsave(pwd)]} {
        set loadsave(pwd) [pwd]
        set loadsave(filter) "*"
        set loadsave(file) ""
}

set loadsave(path) ""
set loadsave(done) 0


#————————————————————————————————————————————————
# Create a toplevel for the dialog file selection box.
# Withdraw it until the rest of the GUI is built.
#————————————————————————————————————————————————


toplevel .loadsave  -background LightGray
wm withdraw .loadsave
wm title .loadsave "Add File"
wm geometry .loadsave +[expr ([winfo screenwidth .]/2)\
        - 173]+[expr ([winfo screenheight .]/2) - 148]

set Name .loadsave
set Parent $Name

set Name $Parent.f1
frame $Name -background lightgray
pack $Name -anchor nw -side top
```

This entry field is disabled so the user cannot manually enter a file-name to push.

```
set Name $Parent.f1.e3
entry $Name  -background white -foreground black \
        -highlightbackground LightGray -width 35 \
        -textvariable loadsave(pwd) -state disabled
pack $Name -side right -anchor nw -padx 5
bind $Name <Return> {loadsavegetentries}
bind $Name <Delete> {
```

```
            if [%W selection present] {
            %W delete sel.first sel.last
            } else {
            %W delete insert
            }
}


set Name $Parent.f1.l1
label $Name  -background LightGray  -text "Directory: "
pack $Name -side right -anchor nw

set Name $Parent.f2
frame $Name -background lightgray
pack $Name -anchor nw -side top -fill x

#─────────────────────────────────────────────────────
# This code creates an entry field that will display
# the type of file. The value of the text variable is the
# loadsave(filter).
#─────────────────────────────────────────────────────

set Name $Parent.f2.e7
entry $Name  -background white -foreground black \
        -highlightbackground LightGray -width 35 \
        -textvariable loadsave(filter)
pack $Name -side right -anchor nw -padx 5


#─────────────────────────────────────────────────────
# Create bindings that  will let you delete text and call
# the ed_loadsavegetentries procedure by pressing the
# Return key.
#─────────────────────────────────────────────────────

bind $Name <Return> {loadsavegetentries}
bind $Name <Delete> {
        if [%W selection present] {
        %W delete sel.first sel.last
        } else {
        %W delete insert
        }
}


set Name $Parent.f2.l5
label $Name  -background LightGray -text "File Type: "
pack $Name -side right -anchor nw
```

```
#————————————————————————————————————————
set Name $Parent.f3
frame $Name -background lightgray
pack $Name -anchor nw -side top -fill x

#————————————————————————————————————————
# This code creates an entry field that displays the
# filename file. The value of the text variable is the
# loadsave(file).
#————————————————————————————————————————

set Name $Parent.f3.e11
entry $Name  -background white -foreground black \
        -highlightbackground LightGray -width 35 \
        -textvariable loadsave(file)
pack $Name -side right -anchor nw -padx 5

#————————————————————————————————————————
# Place the value of the _F(keyname) in the entry field
#————————————————————————————————————————

.loadsave.f3.e11 delete 0 end
.loadsave.f3.e11 insert 0 $_F(keyname)


#————————————————————————————————————————
# Create bindings that  will let you delete text and call
# the loadsavevalentry procedure by pressing the Return
# key.
#————————————————————————————————————————

bind $Name <Delete> {
 if [%W selection present] {
        %W delete sel.first sel.last
} else {
        %W delete insert
}
}

bind $Name <Return> {if {[loadsavevalentry]} \
        {set loadsave(done) 1}
        }

#————————————————————————————————————————
set Name $Parent.f3.19
label $Name  -background LightGray -text "File: "
pack $Name -side right -anchor nw
```

```
#—————————————————————————————————————————
set Name $Parent.f13
frame $Name  -background LightGray -borderwidth 2 \
        -height 50 \
        -highlightbackground LightGray \
        -relief raised -width 50
pack $Name -side top -anchor nw -expand yes -fill both

#—————————————————————————————————————————
# Create a listbox to display the directory listing
#—————————————————————————————————————————


set Name $Parent.f13.lb1
listbox $Name   -background white \
        -font $_F(courierfont) \
        -foreground black \
        -highlightbackground LightGray \
        -selectbackground LightBlue \
        -selectforeground black \
        -yscrollcommand "$Parent.f13.sb2 set" \
        -selectmode browse
pack $Name -anchor center -expand 1 -fill both \
        -ipadx 0 -ipady 0 \
        -padx 2 -pady 2 -side left

#  ————————————————————————————————————————
# Listbox bindings
#  ————————————————————————————————————————


bind $Name <Any-ButtonPress> {loadsaveselbegin %W %y}
bind $Name <Any-ButtonRelease> {loadsaveselbegin2 %W}
bind $Name <Any-Motion> {loadsaveselbegin %W %y}
bind $Name <Any-Double-ButtonPress> {loadsaveselbegin %W %y}
bind $Name <Any-Double-ButtonRelease> {set _F(keyname) \
                  $seld_file; loadsaveselend %W %y}
bind $Name <Any-Triple-ButtonPress> {break}
bind $Name <Any-Triple-ButtonRelease> {break}
bind $Name <Return> {loadsaveselend %W %y}
bind $Name <Up> {
        tkCancelRepeat
        tkListboxBeginSelect %W [%W index active]
        %W activate [%W index active]
}
bind $Name <Down> {
        tkCancelRepeat
```

```
                tkListboxBeginSelect %W [%W index active]
                %W activate [%W index active]
}


#————————————————————————————————————————————————
# Scrollbar for the listbox
#  ————————————————————————————————————————————

set Name $Parent.f13.sb2
scrollbar $Name  -activebackground plum \
        -activerelief sunken \
        -background LightGray -command \
            "$Parent.f13.lb1 yview" \
        -highlightbackground LightGray \
        -troughcolor gray40
pack $Name -anchor center -expand 0 -fill y \
        -ipadx 0 -ipady 0 \
        -padx 2 -pady 2 -side left


#————————————————————————————————————————————————
set Name $Parent.f14
frame $Name -background lightgray
pack $Name -side top -anchor nw -fill x


#————————————————————————————————————————————————
# This code creates the OK button. The command
# sets the name of the file to the contents of
# the entry field. If the procedure loadsavevalentry
# returns True, then it sets the done flag to 1.
#————————————————————————————————————————————————


set Name $Parent.f14.b15
button $Name  -activebackground lavender \
        -background gray40 \
        -foreground white \
        -highlightbackground LightGray \
         -text OK \
        -command {set _F(keyname) \
              [.loadsave.f3.e11 get]  \
              if {[loadsavevalentry]} {
                     set loadsave(done) 1}
              }
pack $Name -side left -anchor nw -padx 3 -pady 3


#————————————————————————————————————————————————
# The Cancel button destroys the dialog box
#————————————————————————————————————————————————
```

```
set Name $Parent.f14.b17
button $Name  -activebackground lavender \
      -background gray40 \
      -foreground white \
      -highlightbackground LightGray \
      -text Cancel \
      -command {destroy .loadsave}
pack $Name -side right -anchor nw -padx 3 -pady 3

#-----------------------------------------------------------
# Call loadsavegetentries to display the file list
#-----------------------------------------------------------

loadsavegetentries

#-----------------------------------------------------------
# Display the dialog box, wait until the variable is
# written, then destroy the dialog box.
#-----------------------------------------------------------

wm deiconify .loadsave
vwait loadsave(done)
destroy .loadsave


if {[file isdirectory $loadsave(path)]} {
      set loadsave(path) ""
      }
return $loadsave(path)
}
```

These procedures aid in the mouse button bindings in the load-save procedure.

```
proc loadsaveselbegin {win ypos} {
      $win select anchor [$win nearest $ypos]
}

proc loadsaveselbegin2 {win} {
global seld_file

set seld_file [$win get [$win curselection]]
.loadsave.f3.e11 delete 0 end
.loadsave.f3.e11 insert 0 $seld_file
set _F(keyname) $seld_file

}
```

loadsaveselend

This procedure allows you to maneuver among the displayed
directories. The If statement insures that you can't move up the
tree beyond the launch directory (the directory that the file push
application is located in).

```
proc loadsaveselend {win ypos} {
       global loadsave _F


  if { [$win get [$win curselection]] == "../" } {
       if { [.loadsave.f1.e3 get] == $_F(start_dir) } {
            return
       }
       }

$win select set anchor [$win nearest $ypos]
set fil [.loadsave.f13.lb1 get [lindex [$win curselection] 0]]
if {-1 == [string last "/" $fil]} {
       set loadsave(file) $fil
       set loadsave(path) \
       [eval file join $loadsave(pwd) $loadsave(file)]
        set loadsave(done) 1
       return ""
}
set loadsave(pwd) [loadsavemergepaths \
       $loadsave(pwd) [string trimright $fil "/"]]
loadsavegetentries
return ""
}
```

loadsavegetentries, loadsavevalentry, loadsavemergepaths

These procedures refresh the directory browser list, retrieve the
filename, and merge file and directory filenames. For a complete
description of these procedures, see Appendix A.

```
proc loadsavegetentries {} {
       global loadsave tcl_version
       set e 0

#───────────────────────────────────────────────
# If the path is not a directory, issue error and
# set e variable to 1.
#───────────────────────────────────────────────
```

```tcl
if {![file isdirectory $loadsave(pwd)]} {
  gui_error "\"$loadsave(pwd)\" is not a valid directory"
  .loadsave configure -cursor {}
  set e 1
}


#————————————————————————————————————————————————
# Configure the cursor in the dialog box to the
# watch icon, indicating that the application is
# processing, and update the application.
#————————————————————————————————————————————————

.loadsave configure -cursor watch
update


#————————————————————————————————————————————————
# Set the sort mode to -dictionary. This mode ignores case
# and treats integers as integers and not numbers. This
# option is only supported under Tcl 8.0 and higher, so
# the program checks the tcl version and sets the mode to
# -ascii if the version is less than 8.0.
#————————————————————————————————————————————————


set sort_mode "-dictionary"
if {[info exists tcl_version] == 0 || $tcl_version < 8.0} {
        sort_mode "-ascii"
        }

#————————————————————————————————————————————————
# If there is no specific file type, set the
# file type to a wildcard character, *.
#————————————————————————————————————————————————

if {$loadsave(filter) == ""} {set loadsave(filter) "*"}

#————————————————————————————————————————————————
# Sort files in directory using the specified sort mode
#————————————————————————————————————————————————

set files [lsort $sort_mode "[glob -nocomplain \
      loadsave(pwd)/.*]\
        [glob -nocomplain $loadsave(pwd)/*]"]

#————————————————————————————————————————————————
# Delete the contents of the listbox
#————————————————————————————————————————————————
```

```
                .loadsave.f13.lb1 delete 0 end

#———————————————————————————————————————
# If the e variable is 1, then return and do no more. The
# e variable is set to 1 only when the directory is|
# not valid.
#———————————————————————————————————————


if {$e} {
        .loadsave configure -cursor {}
        update
        return
}


#———————————————————————————————————————
# Set initial values of the list of directories "d"
# and the list of files, "fils". These lists will be
# augmented in the following code.
#———————————————————————————————————————


set d "./ ../"
set fils ""


# ——————————————————————————————————————
# Examine each object in the directory. If it is a
# directory, append its name with "/" and add it to the
# "d" list. If it is a file, then add it to the "fils"
# list only if it matches the filtering variable, i.e.
# the file type.
#———————————————————————————————————————

foreach f $files {
        set ff [file tail $f]
        if {$ff != "." && $ff != ".."} {
                if {[file isdirectory $f]} {
                        lappend d "$ff/"
                } else {
                        if {[string match $loadsave(filter) $ff]} {
                                lappend fils "$ff"
                        }
                }
        }
}
```

```
#————————————————————————————————
# Set the list of files to the d variable, which
# is the list of directories created in the above
# foreach loop, and the fils variable, which is the
# list of files created in the above foreach loop.
#————————————————————————————————

set files "$d $fils"


#————————————————————————————————
# List each object of the "files" list in the listbox
#————————————————————————————————


foreach f $files {
        .loadsave.f13.lb1 insert end $f
}

#————————————————————————————————
# Configure the cursor to its normal state and update the
# application.
#————————————————————————————————

.loadsave configure -cursor {}
update
}


proc loadsavevalentry {} {
global loadsave _F

if {"." != [file dirname $loadsave(file)]} {


#————————————————————————————————
# If the file selected is not the directory, then set its
# path to the merge of the directory and the file name.
#————————————————————————————————


set path [loadsavemergepaths \
        $loadsave(pwd) $loadsave(file)]

#————————————————————————————————
# Set the working directory variable to the path
#————————————————————————————————


        set loadsave(pwd) [file dirname $path]
```

```
#
# If the file has an extension, set the file type
# variable to the file's extension. Else set the file type
# variable to the wildcard character.
#

if {[file extension $path] != ""} {
        set loadsave(filter) "*[file extension $path]"
} else {
        set loadsave(filter) "*"
}



#
# Set the current file variable to the selected file name
#

        set loadsave(file) [file tail $path]

#
# Call the loadsavegetentries procedure, refreshing
# the directory display.
#

        loadsavegetentries
        return 0
}

#
# Set the filename to the merge of the directory and
# the filename.
#

set fil [loadsavemergepaths $loadsave(pwd) $loadsave(file)]


if {(![file exists $fil]) || (![file readable $fil])} {
        gui_error "\"$fil\" cannot be loaded."
        set loadsave(path) ""
        return 0
} else {

#
# If file is readable, set the _f(file) global variable
# (the file being manipulated) to the actual file,
# and return 1.
#

        set loadsave(path) $fil
```

```
            set _F(file) $fil
            set loadsave(done) 1
            return 1
    }


    }

proc loadsavemergepaths {patha pathb} {


#─────────────────────────────────────────────────
# Split the pathnames up into a list of components
#─────────────────────────────────────────────────

set pa [file split $patha]
set pb [file split $pathb]

#─────────────────────────────────────────────────
# If the  first element of the second path is not ":",
# then return the joined filename. Else, continue with
# modifications.
#─────────────────────────────────────────────────

if {[string first ":" [lindex $pb 0]] != -1} \
        {return [eval file join $pb]}

#─────────────────────────────────────────────────
# If the first element of the second path is "/", then
# return the joined filename.
#─────────────────────────────────────────────────

if {[lindex $pb 0] == "/"} {return [eval file join $pb]}

#─────────────────────────────────────────────────
# Examine each item in the second pathname. If it
# indicates to go up a directory "..", then delete the
# last element of the first pathname. Else append the
# item to the first pathname.
#─────────────────────────────────────────────────

set i [expr [llength $pa] - 1]
foreach item $pb {
if {$item == ".."} {
                incr i -1
                set pa [lrange $pa 0 $i]
} elseif {$item == "."} {
        # — do nothing
        } else {
```

```
        lappend pa $item
        }
}


#————————————————————————————————————————
# Return the completed file name
#————————————————————————————————————————

return [eval file join $pa]
}
```

Error message procedures

These procedures are called by the directory browser procedures
when an error has occurred.

```
proc gui_error {message} {
      catch "destroy .xxx"
      bell
      tk_dialog .xxx "Error" "$message" warning 0 Close
}

if {[info procs bgerror] == ""} {
      proc bgerror {{message ""}} {
      global errorInfo
      puts stderr $errorInfo
      }
}
```

Adding clients to the client list

This procedure is called by the Add Client button. It uses a simple
entry box to add clients to the client list . You can specify clients by
full domain names or by IP addresses.

```
proc add_client {} {
toplevel .add_client
wm title .add_client "Add Client to List"
entry .add_client.entry -background white -width 60
pack .add_client.entry -anchor nw -side top -expand 1 \
        -fill x -padx 4 -pady 4

# ─────────────────────────────────────────────────────
# The Add button places the entry into the client list
# ─────────────────────────────────────────────────────

button .add_client.add -text Add -command {
                .filepush.lists.clients.clientlist \
                insert end [.add_client.entry get]
                .add_client.entry delete 0 end
                .filepush.lists.clients.clientlist yview end
                destroy .add_client
        } -background gray40 -foreground white
pack .add_client.add -side left -padx 4 -pady 4

button .add_client.close -text Close \
        -command {destroy .add_client} \
          -background gray40 -foreground white
pack .add_client.close -side right -padx 4 -pady 4

}
```

Starting the server

This procedure is called by the Start Server button. The Server will start only if there are clients specified. It calls the push_loop procedure that starts pushing files to the server.

```
proc start_server {} {
global _PUSH started push_status

if { ! $started } {
        if {[.filepush.lists.clients.clientlist \
        get 0 end] != ""} {
        set started 1
        wm title .filepush "Tcl File Push Server: waiting"
        push_loop
        pack forget .filepush.buttons.start
        pack .filepush.buttons.stop \
        -anchor nw -side left \
```

```
        -expand 1 -fill x \
        -after .filepush.buttons.clients
                }
        }
}
```

Stopping the server

This procedure is called by the Stop Server button. It sets the `started` variable to 0 which will stop the file push loop.

```
proc stop_server {} {
global started

set started 0
wm title .filepush "Tcl File Push Server: idle"

}
```

Pushing files

This procedure starts the main push loop. It is called by `start_server`. It calls `push_files`.

```
proc push_loop {} {
global interval push_status
wm title .filepush "Tcl File Push Server: pushing files"
push_files
wm title .filepush "Tcl File Push Server: waiting"
after $interval push_loop

}
```

push_files

This procedure determines which files to push, and then pushes them to each client machine, if they have been changed. It pushes all of the files in the file list at the first server startup. Then it looks for changes in either the file size or the time stamp for each file. The `string range` command strips the launch path from each filename prior to pushing, thereby converting the absolute path to a Web-centric relative path.

The actual pushing is accomplished through calling dp_RPC of the fetch_file procedure in the PushClnt.tcl script.

```
proc push_files {} {
global _PUSH started _F new_files interval time \
        current_connection



# ─────────────────────────────────────────────
# If the server has started, set the appropriate
# variables and post the time the push has started.
# ─────────────────────────────────────────────


if { $started } {
        set new_files ""
        set interval [expr $time * 60000]
        puts "\npush started: [clock format [clock seconds]]"

# ─────────────────────────────────────────────
# Start a foreach loop that will execute the following
# commands for each file on the file list.
# ─────────────────────────────────────────────

foreach listed_file \
                [.filepush.lists.files.filelist get 0 end] {
                set fileinfo [file dir -long $listed_file]

# ─────────────────────────────────────────────
# If the timestamp has changed for the file, then
# add the file name to the file list.
# ─────────────────────────────────────────────

if {$_PUSH($listed_file~~time) \
        != [lindex $fileinfo 5] &&
$_PUSH($listed_file~~time)\
        != [lindex $fileinfo 2]} {

        set _PUSH($listed_file~~time) [lindex $fileinfo 5]
        set rel_file [string range $listed_file \
                [string length $_F(start_dir)] end]
        lappend new_files $rel_file
        }
        }
```

```
# --------------------------------------------------------
# If the file list is not an empty string, post the list
# --------------------------------------------------------

 if {$new_files != ""} {puts "Files to push: $new_files"}

# --------------------------------------------------------
# Start a foreach loop to execute the following commands
# for each element of the client list.
# --------------------------------------------------------


foreach listed_client \
        [.filepush.lists.clients.clientlist get 0 end] {

# --------------------------------------------------------
# If connection is refused, issue an error
# --------------------------------------------------------


if {[catch "set current_connection [dp_MakeRPCClient   \
       $listed_client 7658]"]} {
 puts "Error: Could not connect to $listed_client"
       continue
       }

# --------------------------------------------------------
# If the new file list is not empty, then foreach
# of the new files, call dp_RPC to executre fetch_file
# on the client machine.
# --------------------------------------------------------


if {$new_files != ""} {foreach file_to_push $new_files {
       dp_RPC $current_connection fetch_file $file_to_push
       }
}

# --------------------------------------------------------
# Close the RPC connection for the client
# --------------------------------------------------------

       dp_CloseRPC $current_connection
       }
}
}
```

Push Client

The push client is a simple daemon that allows the push server to serve files to it. It has a simple GUI - just one button - that lets you stop the application. It requires the Spynergy Toolkit.

The "push client" is actually a small server, while the "push server" is actually a client application. Instead of one server connecting to multiple clients, the client is connecting to multiple servers.

Setting the server URL or IP address

First, we specify the server URL. The push client will not allow files from any other push server than the one specified here. In this code, the URL is set to the local host.

```
global url

set url "http://127.0.0.1"
```

Fetch_file procedure

The `fetch_file` procedure is invoked through RPC by the push server. It calls the Spynergy procedure `fetchURL`, introduced earlier in this chapter, and places the returned data in the file, replacing any existing data in that file on the client machine.

```
proc fetch_file {file_sent} {
global url
set cur_path [pwd]
if {[catch "fetchURL $url$file_sent \
     -outfile $cur_path$file_sent"]} {
     puts "$cur_path$file_sent: FetchURL ERROR" } else {
     puts "$cur_path$file_sent: File fetched"
}

}
```

Source the Spynergy Toolkit

Because the client machine uses the `fetchURL` procedure, the Spynergy Toolkit must be available to the push client script. An alternative to sourcing the `spynergy.tcl` file would be to include all the Spynergy procedures that construct and support the `fetchURL` procedure and the remote call procedures in the source code of the push client. This would allow the `push-clnt.tcl` script to operate independent of any extra files. The different sections of the Spynergy Toolkit are clearly labeled in the `spynergy.tcl` file. You can copy any section of the Spynergy Toolkit and place them in your Tcl code.

```
source spynergy.tcl
```

Creating the button to close the connection

This button appears on the client's machine and allows the client to close the connection. It exits the application.

```
set Parent .pushclnt
frame $Parent
pack $Parent

set Name $Parent.gui
frame $Name
pack $Name

button $Name.button  -text "stop Push Client daemon" \
       -command {dp_CloseRPC $server_port; after 1000 exit}

pack $Name.button
```

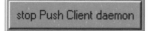

Allowing the server to connect

The code allows the push server to connect through the command `dp_MakeRPCServer`. It calls "`dp_Host -`" to forbid any hosts from connecting to the client, and then calls "`dp_Host + ipad-dress`" to specify the hosts that are allowed to connect to the client.

Note: You must call "`dp_Host  -`" before specifying other hosts, otherwise, other hosts will be allowed to connect to the push client.

```
set server_port [dp_MakeRPCServer 7658]
dp_Host -
dp_Host +127.0.0.1


# ─────────────────────────────────────────────
# Issues status message to the console
# ─────────────────────────────────────────────

puts "Push client port: $server_port"
```

Conclusion

You can use this file-push system for any number of purposes. It is ideal for administering background updates of various files across a corporate Intranet, for example. You could use it to automatically push files to an archive server, to create an automatic backup system for your critical data. You could combine it with the Tcaster program and the Webservr application to create a pure-Tcl news distribution service. Or you could use it to automatically distribute new versions of your Tcl/Tk applications to your users, to simplify your life as a developer. The possibilities really are endless.

Part III

Integrating with the Web

The last section of this book examines Tcl/Tk Internet applications that can exist as stand-alone applications or as application add-ons. In Chapter 10, we will show you how to work with an HTML data stream, how to build a stockticker applet that updates itself, and how to create an e-mail agent that will notify you of changes in stock prices. In Chapter 11, we will build a complete Tcl/Tk Web browser with the aid of the Spynergy Toolkit. We discuss how you can modify this Web browser to become a Tcl/Tk applet, or part of a Tcl/Tk graphical application. With this Web browser, we also create several browser-pull applications, including an animated image map client.

10

Automated Data Retrieval and Agent Technology

In this chapter we present an application, the stockticker, that periodically fetches and formats data from a Web page. It automatically parses HTML code and refreshes a display. This application can be a Web applet using the Tcl 8.0 HTTP package, an application add-on using the Spynergy Toolkit or HTTP package, or a stand-alone application running under Tcl/Tk 7.6/4.2 or Tcl/Tk 8.0. The stockticker application was largely developed by Clif Flynt.

In the second part of this chapter, we add e-mail notification to the stockticker. The stockticker sends e-mail when a particular stock price drops or rises out of a specified range.

Stockticker

We can build the stockticker applet using the Tcl 8.0 HTTP package or the Spynergy Toolkit. The applet fetches data from a freely accessible Web page that displays stock quotes and updates every 20 minutes. The program strips the data of HTML formatting tags, and displays the data using a ticker tape such as the one we introduced in Chapter 4. Retrieving and displaying the data are simple;

the bulk of the application is the code that strips the data of HTML tags and formats it for display.

The following section explains the procedures to build a stock-ticker application that you can embed on a Web page as an applet to run under the Tcl 2.0 Plug-in, or that you can run as a stand-alone application under versions of Tcl/Tk from 7.5/4.1 to 8.0.

Requiring the HTTP package, the outside security policy, or the Spynergy Toolkit

The first lines of our program specify the outside resources that the application will need. We specify the HTTP package so this applet can be used on a Web page. We use the catch statement so the application will continue running if the resource is not available. For example, the HTTP package would not be recognized if the application was running under Tcl/Tk 7.6/4.2..

```
catch {package require http}
```

We also source in the Spynergy Toolkit. This enables the application to run under versions of Tcl that are earlier than 8.0. The catch command insures that the program will continue if the command returns an error, as it will if the Spynergy Toolkit is not available.

```
catch {source spynergy.tcl}
```

To build an applet to run on the Web, we need to specify the out-side security policy. This will allow the functioning of the HTTP package under the Tcl Plug-in.

```
catch {policy outside}
```

Be sure to read the latest information about security policies on Sun's Tcl Web site at http://www.sunscript.sun.com.

Retrieving data

To retrieve the data, you can use either the command ::http::geturl or the fetchURL procedure of the Spynergy Toolkit that we introduced in Chapter 9.

As we explained in Chapter 5, the `::http::geturl` procedure needs a command option to give the token of the HTTP transaction, so the procedure will return immediately. If there is no
command option, then the HTTP package will use `vwait`. That
command is not allowed under the Tcl Plug-in, so the application
will not be allowed to function as an applet on a Web page. You
must use the command option to use `::http::geturl` for
applications that use the Tcl Plug-in.

The `display_stocks` procedure simply uses either the
Spynergy procedure or the HTTP package to retrieve data, and
then calls the appropriate procedure to format and place the data.
After 15 minutes, the `display_stocks` procedure calls itself
again. This continually refreshes the data as the stockticker runs.

```
proc display_stocks {stock_list} {

foreach symbol $stock_list {

# _____
# If the command returns an error, then use the
# fetchURL Spynergy procedure to retrieve the data.
# The command will return an error if
# the Http package is not available.
# _____

    if {[catch "::http::geturl \
      http://www.newsalert.com/free/stocknews?Symbol=$symbol \
        -command get_data"]} {

# _____
# Retrieve the data with fetchURL if the HTTP
# package is not available.
# _____
    set data [fetchURL \
      http://www.newsalert.com/free/stocknews?Symbol=$symbol]

# _____
# Call the format_data procedure to format and place
# the data (only called if the procedure is using
# the Spynergy Toolkit).
# _____
  format_data $symbol $data $stock_list
    }
  }
```

```
# ------------------------------------------------
# Call the procedure to refresh the data
# ------------------------------------------------

after 900000 "display_stocks [list $stock_list]"
}
```

The get_data procedure is called by ::http::geturl if the program is using the HTTP package. It specifies the data of the transaction and the symbol of the list of stocks. It then calls the format_data procedure to format and place the retrieved data.

```
proc get_data { id } {

   global messages formatstr stock_list state

# ------------------------------------------------
# Access the token as the state array
# ------------------------------------------------

 upvar #0 $id state

# ------------------------------------------------
# Set the symbol to the last few characters of the
# URL of the transaction.
# ------------------------------------------------

 set symbol [string range $state(url) 47 end]

# ------------------------------------------------
# Set the data to the state(body)
# ------------------------------------------------

set data $state(body)

# ------------------------------------------------
# Call the format_data procedure
# ------------------------------------------------

format_data $symbol $data $stock_list
}
```

Whether the program uses fetchURL or HTTP to retrieve the data, it calls format_data to format and place the data in the stockticker.

Formatting data

This `format_data` procedure examines the data returned by the `get_data` procedure, or by the `fetchURL` procedure. It strips out HTML formatting and then calls the `doticker` procedure. It is specifically tailored to the HTML page that it retrieves, looking for a single HTML table and isolating the data by determining the start and end tags of the table rows. If you access data from a different source than this particular Web page, then you would need to modify this procedure to isolate the data from that source.

For a discussion on building heuristics for extracting information from Web pages, see *A Scalable Comparison-Shopping Agent for the World-Wide Web,* by Doorenbos, Etzioni, and Weld. (Proceedings of the First International Conference on Autonomous Agents, ACM, 1997).

The data that the application fetches comprise a large HTML page. We are interested in an HTML table of data. The table that this procedure isolates looks something like this.

```
<TABLE BORDER=1 CELLSPACING=0 CELLPADDING=1 BGCOLOR="#FFFFFF">
<TR bgcolor="#ccccff">
<TD ALIGN=CENTER><font size=-1>
  <B>Co.<BR>Digest</B></FONT></TD>
<TD ALIGN=CENTER><font size=-1><B>Symbol</B></FONT></TD>
<TD ALIGN=CENTER><font size=-1><B>Company</B></FONT></TD>
<TD ALIGN=CENTER><font size=-1><B>Last<BR>Sale</B></FONT></TD>
<TD ALIGN=CENTER><font size=-1>
  <B>Net<BR>Change</B></FONT></TD>
<TD ALIGN=CENTER><font size=-1><B>%<BR>Chg</B></FONT></TD>
<TD ALIGN=CENTER><font size=-1>
  <B>Last<BR>Sale<BR>Time</B></FONT></TD>
<TD ALIGN=CENTER><font size=-1><B>Open</B></FONT></TD>
<TD ALIGN=CENTER><font size=-1><B>High</B></FONT></TD>
<TD ALIGN=CENTER><font size=-1><B>Low</B></FONT></TD>
<TD ALIGN=CENTER><font size=-1><B>Volume<BR>(in<BR>000)</B>
  </FONT></TD>
</TR>
<TR VALIGN=TOP>
<TD align=center valign=middle>
<A HREF=/free/digest?Symbol=AAPL>
<IMG SRC="/gifs/pencil.gif" alt="Co Digest"
width=20 height=18  border=0></a></TD>
<TD NOWRAP ALIGN=LEFT><font size=-1>
<A HREF=/free/headlines?Query=AAPL&SearchOption=ticker>
AAPL</a></FONT></TD>
```

```
<TD ALIGN=CENTER><font size=-1>
<A HREF=/free/charts?Symbol=AAPL>APPLE COMPUTER INC</a>
</FONT> </TD>
<TD NOWRAP ALIGN=RIGHT><font size=-1> 22 3/8</FONT></TD>
<TD NOWRAP ALIGN=RIGHT><img src="/gifs/uparrow.gif"
height=14 width=14><font color="#006600" size=-1>7/16
</FONT></TD>
<TD NOWRAP ALIGN=RIGHT> <font size=-1> 2.0%</FONT></TD>
<TD NOWRAP ALIGN=RIGHT> <font size=-1> 14:30</FONT></TD>
<TD NOWRAP ALIGN=RIGHT> <font size=-1> 22 1/8</FONT></TD>
<TD NOWRAP ALIGN=RIGHT> <font size=-1> 22 1/2</FONT></TD>
<TD NOWRAP ALIGN=RIGHT> <font size=-1> 22</FONT></TD>
<TD NOWRAP ALIGN=RIGHT> <font size=-1> 939</FONT></TD>
</TR>
</TABLE>
```

The table's format is not predictable. This procedure isolates this table of data, reorganizes it with the help of other procedures, and then strips out the table tags and isolates the information contained in the individual cells.

```
proc format_data { symbol data stock_list } {

global messages formatstr

# _____
# Extract the table with the stock values from the output.
# This is the portion of the data between Symbol=XXX and
# the end of the table. Set the upsym variable to the
# symbol in uppercase letters.
# _____

set upsym [string toupper $symbol]
set st1 [string first "Symbol=$symbol" $data]
set st2 [string first "</TABLE>" $data]
incr st1

set data [string range $data $st1 $st2]

# _____
# Skip the first two rows in the table
# _____

set st1 [string first "</TR" $data]
incr st1
set data [string range $data $st1 end]

set st2 [string first "</TR" $data]
```

```
set data [string range $data 0 $st2]

#  ─────────────────────────────────────────────────
# Convert this to a list for ease in further processing.
# This list is composed of single elements separated by
# line breaks.
#  ─────────────────────────────────────────────────

    set lst [split $data "\n"]

#  ─────────────────────────────────────────────────
# Reformat the original list into a list with each list
# entry being a separate column in the table. (See the
# following section for more information about the
# reform_table procedure).
#  ─────────────────────────────────────────────────

set tdlst [reform_table $lst]

#  ─────────────────────────────────────────────────
# The table columns are:
# symbol Name last change percentChange open high low
# Examine these columns one at a time, and extract the
# value.
#  ─────────────────────────────────────────────────

set line [lindex $tdlst 2]
set st1 [string first "$upsym>" $line]
set line [string range $line $st1 end]
set st1 [string first ">" $line]
set st2 [string first "<" $line]
incr st1
incr st2 -1

set company [string range $line $st1 $st2]"

#  ─────────────────────────────────────────────────
# The numeric values are extracted using a regular
# expression that looks for a string of numbers between
# a ">", and a "<". See the following section for more
# information on the extract_number procedure.
#  ─────────────────────────────────────────────────
set last [extract_number [lindex $tdlst 3]]
set chg  [extract_number [lindex $tdlst 4]]
set pct  [extract_number [lindex $tdlst 5]]
set open [extract_number [lindex $tdlst 7]]
set high [extract_number [lindex $tdlst 8]]
set low  [extract_number [lindex $tdlst 9]]
```

```
#   ————————————————————————————————————
# Set the stockinfo string to a formatted string
# of all the set variables.
#   ————————————————————————————————————

set stockinfo [format $formatstr \
  $upsym [string range $company 0 11] $last $chg $pct \
      $open $high $low

#   ————————————————————————————————————
# If the stockinfo is not an empty string, then set the
# index number of the message array to the position of the
# symbol in the stock list, and set the stockinfo string
# to the mesage array variable.
#   ————————————————————————————————————

if {$stockinfo != ""} {

    set in   [expr [lsearch -exact $stock_list $symbol]]
    set messages($in) "$stockinfo"

#   ————————————————————————————————————
# If all the array items have been specified, then call
# the doticker procedure that will place the data in
# the text window. Notice that this assumes that each
# symbol will return viable data.
#   ————————————————————————————————————

if {[info exists \
        messages([expr [llength $stock_list]-1])]} {
        doticker .f.t 1000 "  *****  " 250
          }
        }
}
```

The `reform_table` procedure is called by the `format_data` procedure. It takes a list that is composed of single elements separated by line breaks and returns a list of elements where each element is one row of an HTML table, including the start and end tags that specify the table row.

For example, given this input:

```
<TD>
  one two
</TD>
```

The procedure would return a single line of data:

```
<TD> one two </TD>
```

With the data returned in a predictable format, the `format_data` procedure can continue to process and set variables.

```
proc reform_table {lst} {

    if {[string length $lst] < 5} {return ""}
    set tdState 0
    set tdline ""

# ─────────────────────────────────────────────────────
# Loop through the list items checking for Table
# markers (<TD> </TD>) Append the text between
# <TD> and </TD> (inclusive) into a singlelist item
# in a new list.
#
# The automata is in one of these states:
#  0) No <TD seen. (outside of a table definition.)
#  1) <TD seen, and no </TD seen (inside a table
# definition.)
#
# Transitions are:
#  See a <TD : Go to state 1
#  See a </TD       : If in state 1, go to state 0
#
# Simple rules:
#  if state 0, discard current text
#  if state 0 & <TD go to state 1, append
#  <TD to holding string
#  if state 1, append current text to holding
#  string if state 1, & </TD, add accumulated
#  list, text to go to state 0.
# ─────────────────────────────────────────────────────

    for {set i 0} {$i < [llength $lst]} {incr i} {
      set line [lindex $lst $i]

# ─────────────────────────────────────────────────────
# If this line contains no <TD or </TD, we don't change
# states. If we are in state 1, save the text, else
# discard it.
# ─────────────────────────────────────────────────────
```

```
while {[string length $line] > 2} {
        if {([string first "<TD" $line] < 0) &&
          ([string first "</TD" $line] < 0)} {
    if {$tdState == 1} {
        append tdline $line
        set line ""
    } else {
        set line ""
    }
        }


#   ──────────────────────────────────────────────
# If there is a <TD in this line, convert from state 0 to
# state 1.  Strip the <TD from the line being scanned, and
# add that text to the holding space.
#   ──────────────────────────────────────────────

if {[set st1 [string first "<TD" $line]] >= 0} {

set st2 [expr $st1+4]
    set tdline [string range $line $st1 $st2]
    set line [string range $line $st2 end]
    set tdState 1
}


#   ──────────────────────────────────────────────
# If there is a </TD in this line, convert from state 1
# to state 0.  Any text up to the end of the </TD> should
# be transfered to the holding space, before the holding
# string is lappended to the list of table definitions.
#   ──────────────────────────────────────────────

if {[set st1 [string first "</TD" $line]] >= 0} {
        }
  set st2 [expr $st1+5]
  if {$tdState} {
      append tdline [string range $line 0 $st2]
      lappend tdlst $tdline
      set tdline ""
      set tdState 0
      }
      set line [string range $line $st2 end]
      }
      }
    }
```

```
#  ─────────────────────────────────────────────────
# Return the formatted list to the format_data procedure
#  ─────────────────────────────────────────────────

    return $tdlst
}
```

This procedure extract_number is called by format_data as a helper procedure. It simply extracts the specific numerical data needed to set the values of the variables that make up the stock information.

```
proc extract_number {line} {

#  ─────────────────────────────────────────────────
# The numeric values are extracted using a regular
# expression that looks for a string of numbers between
# a ">", and a "<".
#  ─────────────────────────────────────────────────

set xx [regexp {>([ ]*)([0-9%\./-]+ *[0-9%\./-]*)([ ]*)<} \
            $line mat p1 p2 p3]
    if {$xx == 0} {
       return "XX"
       } else {
       return $p2
       }
   }
```

After all the data has been received and formatted, the format_data procedure calls the doticker procedure to display the stocks.

Including the ticker procedure

This procedure is almost the same as the one used for the ticker demo in Chapter 4. It scans the text window to find the length of text and inserts each message. It deletes the first character of the text window as it continues to add messages. After a specified amount of time, it calls itself to continue the ticker tape.

The only modification to this procedure is that the text box carries two lines of text rather than one: the header that labels the data, as well as the strings of stock information.

```
proc doticker {textWindow delay text width} {
    global index messages header once

    # ─────────────────────────────────────────
    # Find the location of the last character on the
    # second line and if that is less than the possible
    # last character, add a new set of strings to the
    # scrolling text in the window.
    # ─────────────────────────────────────────

        scan [$textWindow index 2.end] %d.%d line len

        if {$len < $width} {
           if {![info exists messages($index)]} {
                set index 0
           }
           set message $messages($index)
           $textWindow configure -state normal
           $textWindow insert 1.end "$text" fill
           $textWindow insert 1.end $header

           # Insert a newline at the end of the line 1.

           if {$len == 0} {
                $textWindow insert 1.end "\n"
             }

           $textWindow insert 2.end "$text" fill
           $textWindow insert 2.end $message tag$index
           $textWindow configure -state disabled

           incr index
        }


    # ─────────────────────────────────────────
    # Delete the first characters in the first and
    # second line,to scroll the text one position to
    # the left.
    # ─────────────────────────────────────────


        $textWindow configure -state normal
        $textWindow delete 2.0
        $textWindow delete 1.0
        $textWindow configure -state disabled


    # ─────────────────────────────────────────
    # Call again to continue the ticker display
    # ─────────────────────────────────────────
```

```
    after $delay [list doticker $textWindow $delay $text $width]
}
```

Starting it up

The init_ticker procedure is the last procedure to complete the application. It starts the program by accomplishing these tasks:

- Sets and formats the header for the stockticker
- Creates the text box
- Calls the display_stocks procedure

```
proc init_ticker {win} {

#  ─────────────────────────────────────────────────
# Define the globals that the stock subsystem uses,
# and initialize them.
#  ─────────────────────────────────────────────────


    global index messages header formatstr

    set index 0; set messages(0) ""; set header "";

#  ─────────────────────────────────────────────────
# Sets the variable that helps format the header
# and data to correct string lengths.
#  ─────────────────────────────────────────────────

set formatstr "%-10s %-12s %10s %10s %12s %12s %12s %12s"

#  ─────────────────────────────────────────────────
# Set and format the header that labels the data in
# the stockticker.
#  ─────────────────────────────────────────────────


set header [format $formatstr \
        Symbol "Company Name" Lst Chg Pct Open High Low ]

    text $win.t -relief ridge -bd 2 -wrap none \
                -bg black -fg green -state disabled -height 2
    pack $win.t

#  ─────────────────────────────────────────────────
# Set the list of stocks
#  ─────────────────────────────────────────────────
```

```
set stock_list [list aapl gwrx ibm mot msft nscp pkt spyg sunw]

#  ─────────────────────────────────────────────────────────────
# Call the display_stocks procedure to get things going
#  ─────────────────────────────────────────────────────────────

  display_stocks $stock_list
}
```

Finally, we create a frame to hold the text widget and call the init_ticker procedure.

```
frame .f -height 10
pack .f -anchor nw -side top -expand 1 -fill x

#  ─────────────────────────────────────────────────────────────
# Call the init_ticker procedure to begin the application.
#  ─────────────────────────────────────────────────────────────

init_ticker .f
```

Figure 10.1 The stockticker under Tcl 7.6

Enhancements to the stockticker

There are several things that we could do to enhance the stockticker application. We could provide entry fields for a user to add or delete stocks to the list of stocks. We could create buttons to speed up or stop the stockticker.

In the next section, we will enhance the stockticker by giving it the ability to send a user an e-mail when the price of a stock gets above or below a specified range. To do this, we take advantage of an anonymous remailer demo which can be found on the Neosoft Web site.

The Neosoft Web Site at http://www.neosoft.com is a rich resource for Tcl/Tk developers. You can find the source code for Neotcl, a compilation of Tcl/Tk and extensions, as well as other programs and pointers to Tcl/Tk resources. The demo that we use here is a form built with NeoWebScript™, a programming language that enables you to do server-based interactive programming directly in your Web pages. For more information about

NeoWebScript, see `http://www.neosoft.com/neoweb-script/`.

Stockticker That Sends E-mail

When you fill out a form on a Web page, you may notice that a form will sometimes append the values that you provide the form fields to the URL. For example, if you go through several screens of a form, the URL of the final screen before you press the Submit button may be in the form `www.company.com/cgi-bin/script?Name+address+order+date`, where the words appended to the end are the values of the form fields. This is the result of a `GET` request to a server. The values that you provide are posted to the server using the URL of the Web page.

We can take advantage of this format by using the `::http::geturl` command or `fetchURL` procedure with a URL that includes variables providing the form fields with values. This submits the form to the server which processes the data that we provide. In this case, the server sends an e-mail to the person specified in the URL.

This procedure can be called from the `format_data` procedure for each stock. It requires the symbol of the stock, the company name, and the current price of the stock specified by the last variable set by `format_data`.

The first part of the procedure sets the values of variables that we use in the URL request.

```
proc check_stocks { symbol price company } {

    global stock_list

# ─────────────────────────────────────────────
# Sets the range of prices that we are interested
# in for each stock.
# ─────────────────────────────────────────────

    array set range {
      aapl {15 20}
      gwrx {5 30}
      ibm {5 120}
      mot {25 100}
```

```
        msft {25 200}
        nscp {20 150}
        pkt {20 80}
        spyg {6 20}
        sunw {25 75}
        }

#  ─────────────────────────────────────────────
# Scans the price into a whole number that we can
# use for comparison.
#  ─────────────────────────────────────────────


scan "$price" %d last

#  ─────────────────────────────────────────────
# Set the start and end variables to the matching
# array values.
#  ─────────────────────────────────────────────

set start [lindex $range($symbol) 0]
set end [lindex $range($symbol) 1]


#  ─────────────────────────────────────────────
# Set the separate parts of the price - the whole number
# and the fraction - to different variables to use in the
# URL request. Use the catch command that will catch an
# error if the current price does not include a fraction.
#  ─────────────────────────────────────────────


set pricelist [split "$price"]
set wholeprice [lindex $pricelist 0]
set fraction " "
catch "set fraction [lindex $pricelist 1]"

#  ─────────────────────────────────────────────
# Set the separate words of the company name to variables
# to use in the URL form request. Use the catch command
# that will catch an error if the company does not have
# a second word in the name.
#  ─────────────────────────────────────────────

set companylist [split "$company"]
set compfirst [lindex $companylist 0]
set compsec " "
catch "set compsec [lindex $companylist 1]"
```

```
# ─────────────────────────────────────────────
# Set the name and e-mail variables to use in the
# URL request.
# ─────────────────────────────────────────────

set name First+last
set email you@isp.com
```

The second part of the procedure compares the whole number to the start and end variables determined by the specified range. It sends an HTTP request to the remailer if the price falls outside the range.

The URL is structured so that the message includes the company name and the current price of the stock, including the whole number and any fraction.

If the HTTP request returns an error, the application uses the `fetchURL` procedure.

```
if { $last < $start } {


    if {[catch "::http::geturl \
http://www.neosoft.com/neowebscript/demos/emailscript.html?
name=$name&recipient=$email&email=$email&comments=The+$comp
first+$compsec+stock+is+down%0D%0Alast+price+is+$wholeprice
+$fraction%0D%0A"]} {


        fetchURL    \
http://www.neosoft.com/neowebscript/demos/emailscript.html?
name=$name&recipient=$email&email=$email&comments=The+$comp
first+$compsec+stock+is+down%0D%0Alast+price+is+$wholeprice
+$fraction%0D%0A
        }
    } elseif  { $last > $end } {

        if {[catch "::http::geturl \
http://www.neosoft.com/neowebscript/demos/emailscript.html?
name=$name&recipient=$email&email=$email&comments=The+$comp
first+$compsec+stock+is+up%0D%0Alast+price+is+$wholeprice+$
fraction%0D%0A"]} {


        fetchURL \
http://www.neosoft.com/neowebscript/demos/emailscript.html?
name=$name&recipient=$email&email=$email&comments=The+$comp
first+$compsec+stock+is+down%0D%0Alast+price+is+$wholeprice
+$fraction%0D%0A
        }
```

```
  } else {
}
}
```

We can add a line to the `format_data` procedure to call this procedure for each stock.

```
check_stocks $symbol "$last" "$company"
```

Each time that data are retrieved with `format_data`, the `check_stocks` procedure will send an e-mail to the specified e-mail address if the stock price falls outside the specified range. Because the `format_data` procedure is called every 15 minutes, when `display_stocks` is called, the stockticker will notify a user every 15 minutes if the stock price is above or below the specified range.

You will notice that, in the `check_stocks` procedure, we have explicitly specified the range of prices and the recipient e-mail and address. However, you could build an application and create entry fields to supply the application with values for those variables. For example, you could provide an entry field for you or another user to enter a recipient name or e-mail address, or a range of prices for the stockticker to check. You could also introduce a flag into this procedure that will determine if you have already been notified of the price of a particular stock, so it will not send you e-mail every 15 minutes. You could create a button to turn e-mail notification on or off.

Because the sending e-mail feature uses `::http::geturl` without a command option, this application would not work on a Web page with this enhancement, but it operates as a stand-alone application on your computer using your Internet connection.

Conclusion

This is an example of "agent" technology. Typically, the term "agent" refers to some sort of application that automatically fetches information at regular intervals, performs analysis on that information, and then uses a set of rules to determine an action to take in response to the information involved. The enhanced stockticker application we have just built shows how easy it is to use Tcl/Tk to create useful and sophisticated agent applications.

11

Building a Browser-Pull Application

In this chapter, we build a complete Tcl/Tk Web browser using the Spynergy Toolkit, and then focus on how you can customize this application to behave as a Spynergy applet running under the Spynergy Tcl/Tk Plug-in, a complete application, or as an integral part of an existing application.

We can also use this application, called the Rouser, to build several browser-pull applications, including a weather map retrieval system and an animated image map client.

Using the Spynergy Toolkit

The Spynergy Toolkit procedures used to create the Rouser are outlined in the following section. You can view the source code for these procedures in the file spynergy.tcl that is included on the CD in the examples directory. We do not go into detail about the code that constructs these procedures, but we provide the full source code so that you can examine them yourself and see how they work.

To call these procedures in any of your Tcl applications, you need only source in the spynergy.tcl file using the command source spynergy.tcl.

Table 11.1 The Spynergy Toolkit procedures used by the Rouser

Procedure	Function
HB_init *win*	Sets up a group of variables that allow GUI widgets to be attached to the various URL navigational functions in the Spynergy library. The win argument is the name of the text window that displays the Web page
HB_resolve_url *win url*	Transforms relative URL pathnames into absolute pathnames that the HTML library functions can handle. The URL argument is the relative URL. The procedure returns the absolute URL as a string
HB_load_url *win url*	Loads the given URL into the text widget defined by *win*
HB_home *button*	Loads the default home URL into the text widget that displays the Web page. The argument specifies the name of the button that calls this procedure
HB_back *button*	Causes reloading of the URL that immediately preceded the URL being currently viewed, if applicable. The argument specifies the name of the button that calls this procedure
HB_forward *button*	If the Back button has been pushed, causes reloading of the URL that immediately follows the URL being currently viewed. The argument specifies the name of the button that calls this procedure
HB_go_form *button*	Causes the display of a scrolling listbox and a "history list" of all of the URLs that the user has visited. Clicking on any URL in the list will cause that URL to be immediately fetched and rendered into the text widget. The argument specifies the name of the button that calls this procedure
HB_Stop *button*	Interrupts the fetching and rendering of HTML into the Web browser text widget

Creating a Basic Rouser

The following code constructs a basic Rouser. It has six buttons that load and interrupt HTML files, a status label that tells the user what file the application is processing, and an entry field that accepts URLs or filenames.

Step 1: Sourcing the Spynergy Toolkit

Before writing the rest of the application, we need to make the Spynergy functions available to the Rouser program and the various widgets that call the Spynergy procedures.

```
source spynergy.tcl
```

Step 2: Creating the Rouser GUI

This code creates a simple user interface with six buttons, an entry field, and a status bar. The buttons are Back, Forward, Home, Go, Stop, and Exit.

```
set Name .rouser
# ─────────────────────────────────────────
# Destroy any previous instances of the rouser
# ─────────────────────────────────────────
catch "destroy .rouser"
# ─────────────────────────────────────────
# Create a toplevel
# ─────────────────────────────────────────

    toplevel $Name      -background LightGray
    wm title $Name "Rouser, the Tcl Web browser"
    wm geometry $Name 624x447
    wm geometry $Name +20+20

# ─────────────────────────────────────────
# Set the path of the toplevel window to the
# Parent variable.
# ─────────────────────────────────────────
```

```
set Parent .rouser

# ----------------------------------------------------
# Create frames for the widgets
# ----------------------------------------------------

set Name $Parent.main
frame $Name      -relief ridge
pack $Name -anchor nw -side top \
           -expand yes -fill both

set Name $Parent.main.top
frame $Name      -background LightGray \
     -borderwidth 2 -height 50 \
     -relief raised -width 50
pack $Name       -side top

set Name $Parent.main.top.buttons
frame $Name      -background LightGray
pack $Name       -anchor nw -expand 1 \
           -fill x -side top

# ----------------------------------------------------
# Creates the back button. It calls the HB_back
# procedure which reloads the most recent URL.
# ----------------------------------------------------

set Name $Parent.main.top.buttons.back
button $Name     -activebackground  gray40 \
    -activeforeground green \
    -background gray40 \
    -command "HB_back $Parent.main.top.buttons.back" \
    -disabledforeground LightGray -foreground White \
    -highlightbackground LightGray \
    -highlightcolor LightGray -padx 5 \
    -pady 1 -text Back
pack $Name       -anchor nw -fill none -side left
```

```
# ─────────────────────────────────────
# Creates the Forward button that calls the
# HB_forward procedure.
# ─────────────────────────────────────

set Name $Parent.main.top.buttons.forward
button $Name      -activebackground gray40 \
  -activeforeground green \
  -background gray40 \
  -command "HB_forward $Parent.main.top.buttons.forward" \
  -disabledforeground LightGray \
  -foreground White \
  -highlightbackground LightGray \
  -highlightcolor LightGray\
  -padx 5 -pady 1 -text Forward
pack $Name      -anchor nw \
  -fill none -side left


# ─────────────────────────────────────
# Creates the Home button that loads the
# default URL specified by the ROUSERURL(1) variable.
# ─────────────────────────────────────

set Name $Parent.main.top.buttons.home
button $Name      -activebackground gray40 \
    -activeforeground green -background gray40
    -command "HB_home $Parent.main.top.buttons.home" \
    -disabledforeground LightGray -foreground White \
    -highlightbackground LightGray \
    -highlightcolor LightGray \
    -padx 5 -pady 1 -text Home
pack $Name      -anchor nw -fill none -side left


# ─────────────────────────────────────
# Creates the Go button that calls the HB_go_form
# procedure that creates a listbox with a list
```

```
# of previously viewed URLs for the user to select.
# ———————————————————————————————————

set Name $Parent.main.top.buttons.go
button $Name        -activebackground gray40 \
    -activeforeground green \
    -background gray40 \
    -command "HB_go_form $Parent.main.top.buttons.go" \
    -disabledforeground LightGray \
    -foreground White \
    -highlightbackground LightGray \
    -highlightcolor LightGray \
    -padx 5 -pady 1 -text Go
pack $Name        -anchor nw -fill none -side left

# ———————————————————————————————————
# Creates the Stop button that calls HB_Stop,
# interrupting the fetchng and rendering of an
# HTML file.
# ———————————————————————————————————
set Name $Parent.main.top.buttons.stop
button $Name        -activebackground gray40 \
    -activeforeground red -background gray40 \
    -command "HB_Stop $Parent.main.top.buttons.stop" \
    -disabledforeground LightGray \
    -foreground White \
    -highlightbackground LightGray \
    -highlightcolor LightGray \
    -padx 5 -pady 1 -text Stop
pack $Name        -anchor nw -fill none -side left

# ———————————————————————————————————
# Creates a status label widget
# ———————————————————————————————————

set Name $Parent.main.top.buttons.122
```

```
label $Name      -anchor w -background LightGray \
    -foreground white -justify left
pack $Name       -anchor nw -fill none -side left

set Name $Parent.main.top.buttons.status
label $Name      -anchor w -background LightGray \
    -foreground white \
    -justify left
pack $Name       -anchor nw -fill none -side left


# ————————————————————————————————————————————————
# Creates the Exit that destroys the application
# when pressed.
# ————————————————————————————————————————————————

set Name $Parent.main.top.buttons.exit
button $Name      -activebackground lavender \
    -background gray40 \
    -command exit -foreground white \
    -highlightbackground LightGray \
    -text Exit
pack $Name -anchor nw -side right


# ————————————————————————————————————————————————
# Creates the label and field for the URL
# ————————————————————————————————————————————————

set Name $Parent.main.top.ubar
frame $Name      -background LightGray
pack $Name       -anchor nw -expand 1 \
    -fill x -side top

set Name $Parent.main.top.ubar.113
label $Name      -background LightGray \
    -foreground black -text URL:
```

```
pack $Name      -anchor w -side left



# ----------------------------------------------------------
# Creates the URL entry widget
# ----------------------------------------------------------

set Name $Parent.main.top.ubar.url
entry $Name      -background white \
     -highlightbackground LightGray \
     -highlightcolor cyan \
     -selectbackground skyblue -width 0
pack $Name      -anchor nw -expand yes \
     -fill x -side left

set Name $Parent.main.txt
frame $Name      -background LightGray \
     -borderwidth 2 \
     -highlightbackground lightgray \
     -relief raised
pack $Name      -anchor nw -expand 1 \
     -fill both -side top



# ----------------------------------------------------------
# Creates the text widget that displays the
# Web document, including scrollbars.
# ----------------------------------------------------------

set Name $Parent.main.txt.win
text $Name      -background white \
     -cursor arrow -foreground black \
     -height 100 \
     -highlightbackground lightgray \
     -insertbackground black \
     -selectbackground LightGray \
     -selectforeground black \
```

```
        -takefocus 0 -width 20 \
        -yscrollcommand "$Parent.main.txt.scroll set"
$Name insert end {


}
pack $Name      -anchor nw -expand 1 \
        -fill both -padx 2 -pady 2 \
        -side left

set Name $Parent.main.txt.scroll
scrollbar $Name      -activebackground plum \
        -activerelief sunken \
        -background LightGray \
        -command "$Parent.main.txt.win yview" \
        -highlightbackground LightGray \
        -troughcolor gray40 -width 16
pack $Name          -anchor center -fill y \
        -padx 2 -pady 2 -side right
```

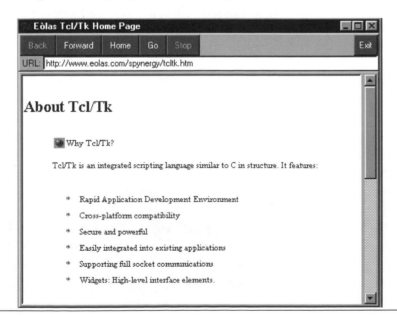

Figure 11.1 The basic Rouser

This is a basic user interface for this application. You can also add icons for the buttons and menubars to configure options. This application allows you to set different options, such as the default URL and the color of the background and frame, by changing the default variables in the program code. In the next few sections of this chapter, we will see how we can modify these options for different uses of the Rouser.

Step 3: Configuring the GUI array variables

We need to set the variables below so the Spynergy Toolkit procedures will be able to work with the GUI elements of the Rouser. The procedures use the _url array variables to load the HTML page into the appropriate text widget, or to retrieve the URL from the appropriate entry widget, among other uses. You can build your GUI any way you want, as long as you set these specific variables in your program.

```
set win $Parent.main.txt.win
global _url
set base .rouser.main
set _url($win~~statuslabel)  "$base.top.buttons.status"
set _url($win~~entrywidget)  "$base.top.ubar.url"
set _url($win~~backbut)      "$base.top.buttons.back"
set _url($win~~forwardbut)   "$base.top.buttons.forward"
set _url($win~~homebut)      "$base.top.buttons.home"
set _url($win~~gobut)        "$base.top.buttons.go"
set _url($win~~stopbut)      "$base.top.buttons.stop"
```

Step 4: Writing the Rouser procedure

This procedure calls several Spynergy Toolkit functions to load HTML into the text widget and display the Web page. It uses the _url global array set by HB_init. This function determines the paths to the widgets involved in the loading and display of the HTML file.

```
proc LoadHTML {w url} {
```

```
        global _url

#  ────────────────────────────────────────────

# Set the _url variables using the path
# to the text widget.

#  ────────────────────────────────────────────


    HB_init $w

#  ────────────────────────────────────────────

# If the URL is not an empty string, place it in
# the entry field and determine its non-relative
# path using HB_resolve_url. Call HB_load_url
# to fetch the file.

#  ────────────────────────────────────────────
    if {$url != ""} {
        $_url($w~~entrywidget) configure \
                -text $url
        update
        set urllist [HB_resolve_url $w $url]
        HB_load_url $w [lindex $urllist 0] \
            [lindex $urllist 1] 1
        if {[lindex $urllist 1] != ""} {
            HMgoto [lindex $urllist 1]
            }
        }
    }
}
```

Step 5: Configuring the options

This section allows you to set several configuration options. These options include:

•   The URL that the browser loads at startup and when the Home button is pressed

•   Whether or not to display the navigation buttons, URL window, and scrollbar

- The color of the HTML document background
- The color and width of the frame surrounding the Web page
- If the Rouser fills a specified area when used as an applet

You should place this code at the beginning of the Tcl file for your Rouser applications if these options are set by you. These options can also be dynamically set by external sources, such as a choice on a menubar or an argument for an embed tag on a Web page.

```
# ————————————————————————————————————————
# Declare global variables
# ————————————————————————————————————————

global ROUSERURL BASE BUTFLAG BORDWID BG
global FRMBG SCROLFLAG FILLAREA

# ————————————————————————————————————————
# The Home URL of the Rouser
# ————————————————————————————————————————

set ROUSERURL(1) "http://www.eolas.com/spynergy/tcltk.htm"
set BASE(1) .rouser.main

# ————————————————————————————————————————
# The button flag determining if button bar will
# be displayed. The scroll flag determining if
# the scrollbar will be displayed.
# ————————————————————————————————————————

set BUTFLAG(1) "1"
set SCROLFLAG(1) "1"

# ————————————————————————————————————————
# The frame background color, the width of the
# frame border, the background color.
# ————————————————————————————————————————

set FRMBG(1) "LightGray"
```

```
set BORDWID(1) "0"
set BG(1) "white"


#  ─────────────────────────────────────────
# The fillarea variable fills the specified area
# on a web page when the Rouser is used as an
# applet.
#  ─────────────────────────────────────────
set FILLAREA(1)   "0"
```

Step 6: Starting it up

The final code of this application examines the values of the options that you set, and packs and configures the widgets accordingly. It then loads the default URL into the text widget unless there is no default URL specified.

```
#  ─────────────────────────────────────────
# Packs the button bar if the button flag is true
#  ─────────────────────────────────────────

if {!$BUTFLAG(1)} {
    pack forget .rouser.main.top
} else {
    pack .rouser.main.top \
            -before .rouser.main.txt -anchor nw   \
            -expand 1  -fill x -side top
}


#  ─────────────────────────────────────────
# Packs the scrollbar if the scrollbar flag is true
#  ─────────────────────────────────────────

if {!$SCROLFLAG(1)} {
    pack forget .rouser.main.txt.scroll
```

```
} else {
    pack .rouser.main.txt.scroll \
            -after .rouser.main.txt.win \
            -anchor center -expand 0 -fill y \
            -padx 2 -pady 2 -side right
}

# ─────────────────────────────────────
# Configures the borderwidth and colors to the
# options. Fills the application with the text
# widget is the fillarea is true.
# ─────────────────────────────────────
.rouser.main configure -borderwidth $BORDWID(1)
.rouser.main.txt configure -background $FRMBG(1)
.rouser.main.txt.win configure -background $BG(1)

if {$FILLAREA(1)} {
    place .rouser.main -x 0 -y 0 -width 0 \
            -height 0 -relx 0 -rely 0 \
            -relwidth 1.0 -relheight 1.0 -anchor nw
}

# ─────────────────────────────────────
# Updates the application and loads the default
# URL if it exists.
# ─────────────────────────────────────

update

if {$ROUSERURL(1) != ""} {
    LoadHTML .rouser.main.txt.win "$ROUSERURL(1)"
}
```

The Rouser was designed so that you can adapt it for your own
purposes using the configuration options. We look at three ways
that you can adapt it in this chapter: enhancing it as a complete

application, integrating it into an existing application, and embedding it as a applet on a Web page.

Complete code for the basic Rouser:

```
#———————————————————————————————————————————————————--

global ROUSERURL BASE BUTFLAG BORDWID BG
global FRMBG SCROLFLAG FILLAREA

set ROUSERURL(1) "http://www.eolas.com/spynergy/tcltk.htm"
set BASE(1) .rouser.main
set BUTFLAG(1) "1"
set BORDWID(1) "0"
set FILLAREA(1)  "0"
set BG(1) "white"
set FRMBG(1) "LightGray"
set SCROLFLAG(1) "1"
### End of Rouser Configuration Section

#———-This section sets up the GUI———-
set Name .rouser
catch "destroy .rouser"
toplevel $Name      -background LightGray
    wm title $Name "Rouser, the Tcl Web browser"
    wm geometry $Name 624x447
    wm geometry $Name +20+20
set Parent $Name


set Name $Parent.main
frame $Name       -relief ridge
pack $Name -anchor nw -side top -expand yes -fill both

set Name $Parent.main.top
frame $Name       -background LightGray \
```

```
              -borderwidth 2 -height 50 \
              -relief raised -width 50
pack $Name      -side top

set Name $Parent.main.top.buttons
frame $Name     -background LightGray
pack $Name      -anchor nw -expand 1 -fill x -side top


# ————————————————————————————————————————————————————
# The Back button
# ————————————————————————————————————————————————————

set Name $Parent.main.top.buttons.back
button $Name       -activebackground  gray40 \
      -activeforeground green \
      -background gray40 \
      -command "HB_back $Parent.main.top.buttons.back" \
      -disabledforeground LightGray -foreground White
      -highlightbackground LightGray \
      -highlightcolor LightGray \
      -padx 5 -pady 1 -text Back
pack $Name      -anchor nw -fill none -side left

# ————————————————————————————————————————————————————
# The Forward button
# ————————————————————————————————————————————————————
set Name $Parent.main.top.buttons.forward
button $Name      -activebackground gray40 \
  -activeforeground green \
  -background gray40 \
  -command "HB_forward $Parent.main.top.buttons.forward" \
  -disabledforeground LightGray \
  -foreground White \
  -highlightbackground LightGray \
  -highlightcolor LightGray\
```

```
      -padx 5 -pady 1 -text Forward
pack $Name      -anchor nw -fill none -side left


# ─────────────────────────────────────────────
# The Home button
# ─────────────────────────────────────────────


set Name $Parent.main.top.buttons.home
button $Name      -activebackground gray40 \
   -activeforeground green \
   -background gray40 \
   -command "HB_home $Parent.main.top.buttons.home" \
   -disabledforeground LightGray \
   -foreground White \
   -highlightbackground LightGray \
   -highlightcolor LightGray \
   -padx 5  -pady 1  -text Home
pack $Name      -anchor nw -fill none \
       -side left


# ─────────────────────────────────────────────
# The Go button (pops up the history listbox)
# ─────────────────────────────────────────────
set Name $Parent.main.top.buttons.go
button $Name      -activebackground gray40 \
   -activeforeground green \
   -background gray40 \
   -command "HB_go_form $Parent.main.top.buttons.go" \
   -disabledforeground LightGray \
   -foreground White \
   -highlightbackground LightGray \
   -highlightcolor LightGray \
   -padx 5 -pady 1 -text Go
pack $Name      -anchor nw  -fill none -side left
```

```
# ──────────────────────────────────────────────
# The Stop button
# ──────────────────────────────────────────────

set Name $Parent.main.top.buttons.stop
button $Name       -activebackground gray40 \
    -activeforeground red \
    -background gray40 \
    -command "HB_Stop $Parent.main.top.buttons.stop" \
    -disabledforeground LightGray \
    -foreground White \
    -highlightbackground LightGray \
    -highlightcolor LightGray \
    -padx 5 -pady 1   -text Stop
pack $Name       -anchor nw -fill none   \
        -side left


set Name $Parent.main.top.buttons.122
label $Name       -anchor w -background LightGray \
    -foreground white -justify left
pack $Name       -anchor nw -fill none -side left

set Name $Parent.main.top.buttons.status
label $Name       -anchor w -background LightGray \
    -foreground white -justify left
pack $Name       -anchor nw -fill none -side left

# ──────────────────────────────────────────────
# The Exit button
# ──────────────────────────────────────────────

set Name $Parent.main.top.buttons.exit
button $Name       -activebackground lavender \
    -background gray40   -command exit \
    -foreground white
```

```
        -highlightbackground LightGray -text Exit
pack $Name -anchor nw -side right


set Name $Parent.main.top.ubar
frame $Name      -background LightGray
pack $Name       -anchor nw -expand 1 \
   -fill x -side top


# ─────────────────────────────────────────────
# The URL label to the left of the URL entry widget
# ─────────────────────────────────────────────

set Name $Parent.main.top.ubar.l13
label $Name       -background LightGray \
   -foreground black -text URL:
pack $Name       -anchor w -side left


# ─────────────────────────────────────────────
# The URL entry widget
# ─────────────────────────────────────────────

set Name $Parent.main.top.ubar.url
entry $Name       -background white \
   -highlightbackground LightGray \
  -highlightcolor cyan -selectbackground skyblue \
  -width 0

pack $Name -anchor nw -expand yes -fill x -side left
set Name $Parent.main.txt
frame $Name       -background LightGray \
   -borderwidth 2 \
   -highlightbackground lightgray \
   -relief raised
pack $Name       -anchor nw -expand 1 \
      -fill both -side top
```

```
# ─────────────────────────────────────────────
# The text widget that displays the Web document
# ─────────────────────────────────────────────

set Name $Parent.main.txt.win
text $Name      -background white \
  -cursor arrow \
  -foreground black -height 100 \
  -highlightbackground lightgray \
  -insertbackground black \
  -selectbackground LightGray \
  -selectforeground black \
  -takefocus 0 -width 20 \
  -yscrollcommand \
          "$Parent.main.txt.scroll set"
$Name insert end {


}
pack $Name      -anchor nw -expand 1 \
      -fill both -padx 2 -pady 2 \
      -side left

set Name $Parent.main.txt.scroll
scrollbar $Name      -activebackground plum \
  -activerelief sunken \
  -background LightGray \
  -command "$Parent.main.txt.win yview" \
  -highlightbackground LightGray \
  -troughcolor gray40 -width 16
pack $Name      -anchor center -fill y \
      -padx 2 -pady 2 -side right


# ─────────────────────────────────────────────
# The _url array variables
# ─────────────────────────────────────────────
```

```
set win $Parent.main.txt.win
global _url
set base .rouser.main

set _url($win~~statuslabel) "$base.top.buttons.status"
set _url($win~~entrywidget) "$base.top.ubar.url"
set _url($win~~backbut)     "$base.top.buttons.back"
set _url($win~~forwardbut)  "$base.top.buttons.forward"
set _url($win~~homebut)     "$base.top.buttons.home"
set _url($win~~gobut)       "$base.top.buttons.go"
set _url($win~~stopbut)     "$base.top.buttons.stop"


# ─────────────────────────────────────────────────
# Load HTML into the browser text widget
# ─────────────────────────────────────────────────

proc LoadHTML {w url} {
    global _url

if {$url != ""} {
    $_url($w~~entrywidget) configure -text $url
    update
    set urllist [HB_resolve_url $w $url]
    HB_load_url $w [lindex $urllist 0] [lindex $url-
list 1] 1
    if {[lindex $urllist 1] != ""} {HMgoto [lindex
$urllist 1]}
    }
}

# ─────────────────────────────────────────────────
# Post browser text widget
# ─────────────────────────────────────────────────

if {!$BUTFLAG(1)} {
    pack forget .rouser.main.top
```

```
} else {
    pack .rouser.main.top \
      -before .rouser.main.txt -anchor nw \
      -expand 1 -fill x -side top
}
if {!$SCROLFLAG(1)} {
    pack forget .rouser.main.txt.scroll
} else {
    pack .rouser.main.txt.scroll \
      -after .rouser.main.txt.win \
      -anchor center -expand 0 -fill y \
      -padx 2 -pady 2 -side right
}
.rouser.main configure -borderwidth $BORDWID(1)
.rouser.main.txt configure -background $FRMBG(1)
.rouser.main.txt.win configure -background $BG(1)
if {$FILLAREA(1)} {
    place .rouser.f1 -x 0 -y 0 -width 0 \
      -height 0 -relx 0 -rely 0 -relwidth 1.0 \
      -relheight 1.0 -anchor nw
}
update
if {$ROUSERURL(1) != ""} {
    LoadHTML .rouser.main.txt.win "$ROUSERURL(1)"
}
#
#————————————————————————————————
```

Enhancing the Rouser

The basic Rouser includes a simple GUI and several predetermined options. You can enhance this interface and allow options to be set by the user through menubuttons.

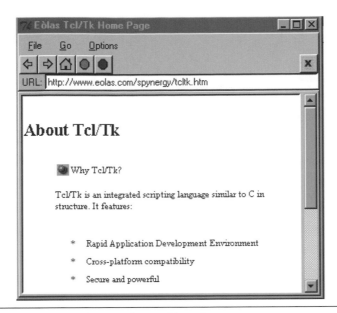

Figure 11.2 A Rouser with menubar and icon buttons

For example, we have built the basic Rouser so you can add icons to the buttons and a menubar that lets you change the colors of the frame and background, set the default URL, hide the button bar, or go directly to a particular URL.

Creating a menubar for the Rouser

You can create a menubar for the Rouser as we do for the Ed Tcl Code Editor in Appendix A. To create a menubar, we include the procedures `construct_menu` and `add_items_to_menu` described in Appendix A in the source code for the Rouser, and then add the following code to the GUI section of the Rouser application.

```
# ────────────────────────────────────────────
# The variable that keeps track of menu names
# ────────────────────────────────────────────

set menucount 1
```

```
# ─────────────────────────────────────────
# Frame for the menubar. It is packed on top
# of the button bar.
# ─────────────────────────────────────────

set Name $Parent.main.top.menu
frame $Name       -background LightGray
pack $Name        -anchor nw -expand 1 \
      -fill both -side top


# ─────────────────────────────────────────
# The file menu
# ─────────────────────────────────────────

set Name $Parent.main.top.menu.file
set Menu_string($Name) {
  {{command} {Open File} {-command "rouse_open_file" \
      -accelerator "Ctrl+F" -underline 0}}
  {{command} {Exit} {-command "exit" \
      -accelerator "Ctrl+X" -underline 1}}
      }

construct_menu $Name File $Menu_string($Name)
pack $Name -side left


# ─────────────────────────────────────────
# The Go menu. Each command calls the command
# already defined in the Spynergy Toolkit.
# ─────────────────────────────────────────

set Name $Parent.main.top.menu.go
set Menu_string($Name) {
  {{command} {Back} {\
      -command "HB_back
.rouser.main.top.buttons.back" \
      -accelerator "Ctrl+B" -underline 0}}
  {{command} {Forward} {-command \
```

```
        "HB_forward .rouser.main.top.buttons.forward" \
        -accelerator "Ctrl+F" -underline 0}}
{{command} {Home} {-command \
        "HB_home .rouser.main.top.buttons.home" \
        -accelerator "Ctrl+H" -underline 0}}
{{command}  {Go} {-command \
        "HB_go_form .rouser.main.top.buttons.go" \
        -accelerator "Ctrl+G" -underline 0}}
{{command}  {Stop} {-command \
        "HB_Stop .rouser.main.top.buttons.stop" \
        -accelerator "Ctrl+P" -underline 0}}
        }


construct_menu $Name Go $Menu_string($Name)
pack $Name -side left


# ————————————————————————————————————————————————
# The Options menu. A user can set the default
# URL, change colors and hide the button bar.
# ————————————————————————————————————————————————


set Name $Parent.main.top.menu.options
set Menu_string($Name) {
 {{command} {Set Home URL} {-command \
        "rouse_set_url" \
        -accelerator "Ctrl+U" -underline 0}}
 {{command} {Colors} {-command \
        "rouse_set_color" \
        -accelerator "Ctrl+C" -underline 2}}
 {{command} {Hide Buttons} {-command \
        "rouse_change_buttons" \
        -accelerator "Ctrl+S" -underline 0}}
        }
```

```
construct_menu $Name Options $Menu_string($Name)
pack $Name -side left
```

Each of the commands on the Option menu open a dialog box for the user to configure the particular option. These options are explained in the following sections.

Setting the default URL

The rouse_set_url command, called when the Set Home URL is selected, creates a dialog box that accepts a string. The ROUSEURL(1) variable is set to the value of this string. This dialog box is similar to the Get URL dialog box constructed for the Ed Tcl Editor in Appendix A.

```
proc rouse_set_url { } {

global ROUSERURL(1)

catch "destroy .url"

toplevel .url
wm title .url "Set URL"


set Parent .url

set Name $Parent.f1
frame $Name -background lightgray
pack $Name -anchor nw -fill x -side top -padx 5

#————————————————————————————————————————
# Create an entry field for the user to enter a URL
#————————————————————————————————————————

set Name $Parent.f1.e1
entry $Name   -background aliceblue \
              -highlightbackground LightGray \
```

```
                        -selectbackground blue \
                        -selectforeground white -width 30
pack $Name -anchor nw -side right

bind .url.f1.e1 <Delete> {
        if [%W selection present] {
                %W delete sel.first sel.last
        } else {
                %W delete insert
        }
        }

bind .url.f1.e1 <Return> {
        set ROUSERURL(1) [.url.f1.e1 get]
         destroy .url
         LoadHTML .rouser.main.txt.win "$ROUSERURL(1)"
         }

$Name delete 0 end
set Name $Parent.mainwin
frame $Name -background lightgray
pack $Name -anchor nw -side top -fill x \
        -padx 5 -pady 5

# ─────────────────────────────────────────────
# Set the entered string to the URL variable and load
# it into the text widget. Create a cancel button.
# ─────────────────────────────────────────────

set Name $Parent.mainwin.b1
button $Name  -activebackground lavender \
        -background navy \
        -command {
        set ROUSERURL(1)[.url.f1.e1 get]
        destroy .url
         LoadHTML .rouser.main.txt.win "$ROUSERURL(1)"
```

```
            }   \
        -foreground white \
        -highlightbackground LightGray \
        -text {Set Home URL}
pack $Name -anchor nw -side left

set Name $Parent.mainwin.b2
button $Name  -activebackground Lavender \
        -background navy \
        -command {destroy .url} -foreground white \
            -highlightbackground LightGray -text Cancel
pack $Name -anchor nw -side right


# ───────────────────────────────────────────
# Geometry for the dialog box
# ───────────────────────────────────────────

set x [expr [winfo rootx .rouser] + 300]
set y [expr [winfo rooty .rouser] + \
        [winfo height .rouser] - 300]
wm geometry .url +$x+$y
wm deiconify .url

raise .url
update
wm minsize .url [winfo width .url] \
                    [winfo height .url]
wm maxsize .url [winfo width .url] \
                    [winfo height .url]
}
```

Figure 11.3 The dialog box to set the home URL

Changing colors

The Colors option on the Option menu also creates a dialog box. This dialog box offers a set of color choices to the user that will change the background or frame color of the application. When a user selects a color, the color changes immediately. Selecting OK will change the background or frame color permanently for that session. Selecting Cancel will return the colors to the default colors defined by the BG(1) and FRMBG(1) variables.

```
proc rouse_set_color { } {

# ─────────────────────────────────────────
# Create the toplevel
# ─────────────────────────────────────────

catch "destroy .colorf"
toplevel .colorf
wm title .colorf "Change colors"
set Parent .colorf

# ─────────────────────────────────────────
# Create frames for the radio buttons
# ─────────────────────────────────────────

set Name $Parent.radios
frame $Name -background lightgray
pack $Name -side top -pady 5 -padx 5

set Name $Parent.radios.mainwin1
frame $Name -background lightgray
pack $Name -anchor nw -side left \
      -fill x -padx 5 -pady 5

set Name $Parent.radios.mainwin2
frame $Name -background lightgray
pack $Name -anchor nw -side left \
      -fill x -padx 5 -pady 5
```

```
# ─────────────────────────────────────────
# Create label and list of radio buttons for
# the background color, using the variable bgcolor.
# ─────────────────────────────────────────

set Name $Parent.radios.mainwin1.label
label $Name -background lightgray \
            -text Background
pack $Name -anchor nw -side top

set Name $Parent.radios.mainwin1.rb1
radiobutton $Name  -background lightgray \
      -text White \
      -variable bgcolor -value white
pack $Name -side top -anchor nw

set Name $Parent.radios.mainwin1.rb2
radiobutton $Name  -background lightgray \
      -text Blue \
      -variable bgcolor -value lightblue
pack $Name -side top     -anchor nw

set Name $Parent.radios.mainwin1.rb3
radiobutton $Name  -background lightgray \
      -text Gray \
      -variable bgcolor -value lightgray
pack $Name -side top -anchor nw

set Name $Parent.radios.mainwin1.rb4
radiobutton $Name  -background lightgray \
      -text Yellow \
      -variable bgcolor -value yellow
pack $Name -side top -anchor nw

set Name $Parent.radios.mainwin1.rb5
radiobutton $Name  -background lightgray \
```

```
                -text Pink -variable bgcolor -value pink
pack $Name -side top -anchor nw

set Name $Parent.radios.mainwin1.rb6
radiobutton $Name  -background lightgray \
        -text Lavender \
        -variable bgcolor -value lavender
pack $Name -side top -anchor nw


# ─────────────────────────────────────────────
# Create the button for the background color
# selection.
# ─────────────────────────────────────────────


set Name $Parent.radios.mainwin1.b1
button $Name  -activebackground lavender \
        -background navy \
        -command {
          .rouser.main.txt.win configure \
                    -background $bgcolor
              } \
        -foreground white \
        -highlightbackground LightGray \
        -text {Select background}
        pack $Name -anchor sw -side left


# ─────────────────────────────────────────────
# Create the label and list of radio buttons
# for the frame color, using the variable frmcolor.
# ─────────────────────────────────────────────


set Name $Parent.radios.mainwin2.label
label $Name -background lightgray -text Frame
pack $Name -anchor nw -side top
```

```
set Name $Parent.radios.mainwin2.rb1
radiobutton $Name  -background lightgray -text White \
                  -variable frmcolor -value white
pack $Name -side top -anchor nw

set Name $Parent.radios.mainwin2.rb2
radiobutton $Name  -background lightgray -text Blue \
                  -variable frmcolor -value lightblue
pack $Name -side top -anchor nw

set Name $Parent.radios.mainwin2.rb3
radiobutton $Name  -background lightgray -text Gray \
                  -variable frmcolor -value lightgray
pack $Name -side top -anchor nw

set Name $Parent.radios.mainwin2.rb4
radiobutton $Name  -background lightgray -text Yellow \
                  -variable frmcolor -value yellow
pack $Name -side top -anchor nw

set Name $Parent.radios.mainwin2.rb5
radiobutton $Name  -background lightgray -text Pink \
                  -variable frmcolor -value pink
pack $Name -side top -anchor nw

set Name $Parent.radios.mainwin2.rb6
radiobutton $Name  -background lightgray
                  -text Lavender \
                  -variable frmcolor -value lavender
pack $Name -side top -anchor nw

# ─────────────────────────────────────────────────────────
# Create the button to set the frame color
# ─────────────────────────────────────────────────────────


set Name $Parent.radios.mainwin2.b1
```

```
button $Name  -activebackground lavender \
          -background navy \
          -command {
                 .rouser.main.txt configure \
                -background $frmcolor
                } \
          -foreground white \
          -highlightbackground LightGray \
          -text {Select frame}
pack $Name -anchor sw -side left


#—————————————————————————————————————————
# Create the OK and Cancel buttons
#—————————————————————————————————————————

set Name $Parent.buttons
frame $Name -background lightgray
pack $Name -side bottom \
      -pady 5 -expand 1 -fill x


set Name $Parent.buttons.b3
button $Name  -activebackground Lavender \
      -background navy \
      -command {
            destroy .colorf
            } \
      -foreground white \
       -highlightbackground LightGray \
      -text OK
pack $Name -anchor center -side left

set Name $Parent.buttons.b2
button $Name  -activebackground Lavender \
      -background navy \
```

```
               -command {
               .rouser.main.txt configure -background $FRMBG(1)
               .rouser.main.txt.win configure -background $BG(1)
               destroy .colorf
               } \
               -foreground white \
                -highlightbackground LightGray \
               -text Cancel
     pack $Name -anchor center -side right

     # ─────────────────────────────────────────────────
     # Geometry for the toplevel
     # ─────────────────────────────────────────────────

     set x [expr [winfo rootx .rouser] + 300]
     set y [expr [winfo rooty .rouser] + \
                 [winfo height .rouser] - 300]
     wm geometry .colorf "+$x+$y"
     wm deiconify .colorf
     raise .colorf
     update
     wm minsize .colorf [winfo width .colorf] \
                        [winfo height .colorf]
     wm maxsize .url [winfo width .colorf] \
                     [winfo height .colorf] \
     }
```

Hiding buttons

The final option on the Options menu lets a user hide or show the button bar. When the Hide Buttons option is selected, the entry on the menu turns to Show Buttons. The procedure simply packs or unpacks the button bar.

Figure 11.4 The dialog box to select colors

```
proc change_buttons { } {
global BUTFLAG

if {!$BUTFLAG(1)} {

# ————————————————————————————————————
# Pack the button bar
# ————————————————————————————————————

pack .rouser.main.top.buttons \
      -before .rouser.main.top.ubar \
      -anchor nw -expand 1 -fill x -side top

# ————————————————————————————————————
# Configure the label on the menu and set the
# BUTFLAG to true.
# ————————————————————————————————————

      .rouser.main.top.menu.options.m4 \
            entryconfigure 3 \
            -label "Hide Buttons"
      set BUTFLAG(1) 1
            } else {
```

```
# ─────────────────────────────────────────────
# Unpack the button bar
# ─────────────────────────────────────────────

pack forget .rouser.main.top.buttons

# ─────────────────────────────────────────────
# Configure the label on the menu and set the
# BUTFLAG to 0.
# ─────────────────────────────────────────────

        .rouser.main.top.menu.options.m4
                entryconfigure 3 \
                -label "Show Buttons"
        set BUTFLAG(1) 0
        }
}
```

Adding icons

In addition to creating a menubar, we added icons to the buttons in the same manner that we did for the Ed Tcl Code Editor. Each button is created with the `construct_button` procedure described in Appendix A, using BASE64 data that is included in the source code for the application. A file attribute is also provided to the `construct_button` procedure.

The BASE64 data is encoded image data that we obtained using an image conversion tool. See Chapter 5 for specifics on working with encoded image data.

```
construct_button $Parent.main.top.buttons.back \
        $back back.ppm \
        "HB_back $Parent.main.top.buttons.back"

construct_button $Parent.main.top.buttons.forward \
        $forward forward.ppm    \
        "HB_forward $Parent.main.top.buttons.forward"
```

```
construct_button $Parent.main.top.buttons.home \
    $home home.ppm \
    "HB_home $Parent.main.top.buttons.home"

construct_button $Parent.main.top.buttons.go \
    $go go.ppm \
    "HB_go_form $Parent.main.top.buttons.go"

construct_button $Parent.main.top.buttons.stop \
    $stop stop.ppm \
    "HB_Stop $Parent.main.top.buttons.stop"
```

Other enhancements

These are just a few enhancements that you can make to the Rouser. Other enhancements could include online help, GUI hints, or more options available to user control. You could add a file browsing system similar to the one included in the Ed Tcl Code Editor that lets you browse your hard drive.

You could also enable the Rouser to remember the user's choices when default values are changed, so that the user can set the home URL or background color as permanent changes and not for just one session. Depending on your use for this application, you could add more variables to let a user change not only background color but also other colors and characteristics as well.

Integrating the Rouser into an Existing Application: Creating Online Help

The Rouser program can also be useful when integrated into another application. For example, we can create an online HTML-based help system for the Ed Tcl Code Editor described in Appendix A by adding a button that sources the file that creates Rouser and then loads an appropriate HTML file.

We only need to make a few modifications to the Rouser code, create a procedure for the Ed Tcl Code Editor to source the file, and create a button for the user to press.

Step 1: Modifying the Rouser

Because the Rouser application will be called from another application, it will use a slave interpreter. The Exit button needs to become a Close button that will destroy the help window but not destroy the parent Tcl application.

The Rouser Exit button is modified as follows, replacing the command `exit` with the command `wm withdraw.rouser` and labeling the button as Close.

```
# ───────────────────────────────────────────
# The Close button
# ───────────────────────────────────────────

set Name $Parent.main.top.buttons.close
button $Name       -activebackground lavender \
     -background LightGray \
     -command {wm withdraw .rouser} \
     -foreground black \
     -highlightbackground LightGray \
     -text Close

pack $Name -anchor nw -side right
```

Each button is also modified with appropriate foreground and background colors to look like the rest of the Ed Tcl Editor application. The background color is LightGray, the foreground color is black.

In this example, we rename the modified file `rouser.tcl` to `help.tcl` and we specify the default URL as `help/index.html`. This loads the file `index.html` from a help directory that we created in the same directory as the Editor. You will need to create a help directory and `index.html` for your version of the Editor.

```
set ROUSERURL(1)  "[pwd]/edhelp.htm"
```

Step 2: Adding a procedure to Ed

We need to add a procedure to Ed that creates a slave interpreter and sources help.tcl. This procedure will be called from the Help button or menu. It creates a slave interpreter in the same way as Ed creates a slave interpreter to text Tcl code. The interpreter sources help.tcl.

```
proc ed_loadhelp {
    if {[lsearch [interp slaves] webhelp] == -1} {
        interp create webhelp
        webhelp eval {load {} Tk}
        webhelp eval {wm withdraw .}
        webhelp eval {catch "source help.tcl"}
    } else {
        webhelp eval {catch "wm deiconify .rouser"}
        webhelp eval {catch "raise .rouser"}
    }
}
```

Step 3: Creating a menubutton for help

We can now add a menubutton for the user to select help.

```
set Name $Parent.menuframe.help
    set Menu_string($Name) {
        {{command}  {Help} {-command "ed_loadhelp" \
            -accelerator "Ctrl+H" \
            -underline 0}}
        {{tearoff}  {no} {}}
        }
```

The procedure construct_menu creates a menubutton and packs it with the other buttons. We repack the button to the right.

```
construct_menu $Name Help $Menu_string($Name)
pack $Name -side right
```

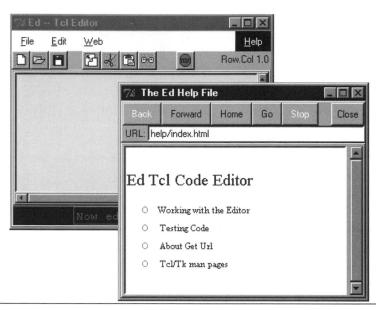

Figure 11.5 The Ed Tcl Editor with a help window

We now have an HTML-based help system for Ed. You can build your own HTML tree of Web pages of help and quick-reference materials for your Tcl applications using the Rouser as an online help tool. See Appendix A for a full discussion on how to construct the Ed Tcl Code Editor.

Embedding the Rouser into a Web Page: Creating an Applet

In addition to running the Rouser as a stand-alone application, you can embed a version of the Rouser into a Web page with only a few modifications.

The embedded Rouser can operate using either the Spynergy security policy under the Tcl 2.0 Plug-in, or the Spynergy Plug-in available from Eòlas Technologies at www.eolas.com.

The embedded Rouser also needs the Spynergy Toolkit. You can provide the Spynergy Toolkit to your users and source the file, as we do for the stand-alone versions of the Rouser. The Spynergy security policy and the Plug-in will look for the file in the SPYN_LIBRARY directory of the computer. This means that the

SPYN_LIBRARY environment variable needs to be set on the user's computer. The applet will search for the spynergy.tcl file in the directory named by the SPYN_LIBRARY environment variable.

If you don't want to distribute the Toolkit and provide instructions on setting the user's environment variable, then an alternative way of using the Spynergy Toolkit on the Web is simply to copy the relevant procedures of the Toolkit into the source code with the rest of the applet code. The Spynergy procedures that the Rouser uses are not only those procedures that it explicitly calls, but also internal procedures that are called by other Spynergy procedures. The only problem with this method is that it will make your applet code excessively large. When you design a applet using the Rouser, you can freely distribute the Spynergy security policy and the Spynergy Toolkit to your users so they can use the applet.

Step 1: Requiring the Spynergy Toolkit and security policy

The first two lines of the application specify the Spynergy security policy and source the Spynergy Toolkit. If you plan to use the Spynergy Plug-in rather than the Spynergy security policy, then you do not need to specify the security policy.

```
# _____
# Use only if you need the security policy.
# Under the Spynergy Plug-in, you do not need
# this command.
# _____

catch "policy Spynergy"

# _____
# Use if you are sourcing the Toolkit rather
# than copying the procedures into your source
# code. If you source the toolkit, then you
# need to distribute it to your users and instruct
# them to set the SPYN_LIBRARY environment variable.
# _____

source $env(SPYN_LIBRARY)/spynergy.tcl
```

Step 2: Turning a toplevel into a frame

Because the applet will be embedded into the Web page, we need to delete the `toplevel` command that creates an independent window. Otherwise, when you run the applet, the Rouser will appear outside the Web page in its own window.

We can easily turn the toplevel `.rouser` window into a frame by substituting the `frame` command for the `toplevel` command and deleting the `wm` commands. We also need to set a specific height and width for the frame, and add a `pack` command.

```
set Name .rouser
frame $Name      -background LightGray -height 300 \
     -width 300
pack $Name

#wm title $Name "Rouser, the Tcl Web browser"
#wm geometry $Name 624x447
#wm geometry $Name +20+20

set Parent .rouser
```

The parent widget is now a frame rather than a toplevel. The rest of the GUI remains the same.

Step 3: Determining embed tag parameters and setting Rouser defaults

The Spynergy Plug-in and Spynergy security policy that operates with the Tcl Plug-in allow for certain parameters in the EMBED tag when you place the Rouser on a Web page. You can set the default URL, the color of the background, and whether or not the rouser has buttons or a scrollbar.

For example, this code on your Web page creates a Rouser that loads www.eolas.com and uses no buttons:

```
<EMBED SRC="rouser.tcl" HEIGHT=200 WIDTH=300
BUTTONS=0 ROUSERURL="http://www.eolas.com" FILLAREA=1>
```

The FILLAREA attribute insures that the rouser will expand to fill the amount of area alloted for it on the Web page.

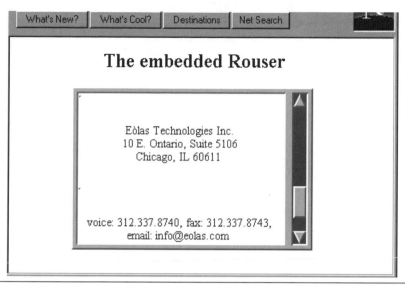

Figure 11.6 The Rouser applet with no buttons, creating a nested frame on the Web page

Table 11.2 Options to use with the embed tag

Option	Description
ROUSERURL *url*	Home URL. Must be a complete path, not relative
BUTTONS *boolean*	Packs or unpacks buttons and URL field
BORDERWDTH *num*	Width of border
BACKGROUND *color*	Color of page background
FRAMEBACKGROUND *color*	Color of frame border
SCROLLBAR *boolean*	Packs or unpacks the scrollbar
FILLAREA *boolean*	Fills the available area if 1

To work with these options, we add the following code to the Rouser tclet to override Rouser defaults when these parameters are specified in the EMBED tag.

```
# ─────────────────────────────────────────
# The variable embed_arg is a list of the embed
# parameters.
# ─────────────────────────────────────────

global embed_args

if {[info exists embed_args]} {

# ─────────────────────────────────────────
# Set each argument to upper case
# ─────────────────────────────────────────

foreach key [array names embed_args] {
        set embed_args([string toupper $key]) \
            $embed_args($key)
    }
# ─────────────────────────────────────────
# If the URL parameter is specified, set the URL
# to the Rouser variable.
# ─────────────────────────────────────────

foreach em_url [array names embed_args ROUSERURL*] {
        if {$em_url == "ROUSERURL"} {
            set ROUSERURL(1) "$embed_args($em_url)"
        } else {
                set i [string range $em_url 12 end]
                set ROUSERURL($i) "$embed_args($em_url)"
            }
        }
        catch "unset em_url"

# ─────────────────────────────────────────
# Set the buttons variable if specified
# ─────────────────────────────────────────

foreach em_butf [array names embed_args BUTTONS*] {
```

```
            if {$em_butf == "BUTTONS"} {
                set BUTFLAG(1) "$embed_args($em_butf)"
            } else {
                set i [string range $em_butf 7 end]
                set BUTFLAG($i) "$embed_args($em_butf)"
            }
        }
        catch "unset em_butf"


#  ————————————————————————————————————————————————
# Set the borderwidth variable if specified
#  ————————————————————————————————————————————————


foreach em_bord [array names embed_args BORDERWIDTH*]
{
            if {$em_bord == "BORDERWIDTH"} {
                set BORDWID(1) "$embed_args($em_bord)"
            } else {
                set i [string range $em_bord 11 end]
                set BORDWID($i) "$embed_args($em_bord)"
            }
        }
        catch "unset em_bord"


#  ————————————————————————————————————————————————
# Set the background variable if specified
#  ————————————————————————————————————————————————


foreach em_bg [array names embed_args BACKGROUND*] {
            if {$em_bg == "BACKGROUND"} {
                set BG(1) "$embed_args($em_bg)"
            } else {
                set i [string range $em_bg 10 end]
                set BG($i) "$embed_args($em_bg)"
```

```
        }
    }
      catch "unset em_bg"

# ─────────────────────────────────────────────
# Set the frame background variable if specified
# ─────────────────────────────────────────────


foreach em_frmbg [array names embed_args FRAMEBACKGROUND*] {
        if {$em_frmbg == "FRAMEBACKGROUND"} {
            set FRMBG(1) "$embed_args($em_frmbg)"
        } else {
            set i [string range $em_frmbg 15 end]
            set FRMBG($i) "$embed_args($em_frmbg)"
        }
    }
    catch "unset em_frmbg"


# ─────────────────────────────────────────────
# Set the scrollbar variable that packs or unpacks
# the scrollbar.
# ─────────────────────────────────────────────


    foreach em_srf [array names embed_args SCROLLBARS*] {
        if {$em_srf == "SCROLLBARS"} {
            set SCROLFLAG(1) "$embed_args($em_srf)"
        } else {
            set i [string range $em_srf 3 end]
            set SCROLFLAG($i) "$embed_args($em_srf)"
        }
    }
      catch "unset em_srf"
```

```
# ─────────────────────────────────────────────
# Set the fillarea variable
# ─────────────────────────────────────────────


    foreach em_fill [array names embed_args FILLAREA*] {
        if {$em_fill == "FILLAREA"} {
            set FILLAREA(1) "$embed_args($em_fill)"
        } else {
            set i [string range $em_fill 8 end]
            set FILLAREA($i) "$embed_args($em_fill)"
        }
    }
    catch "unset em_fill"
}
```

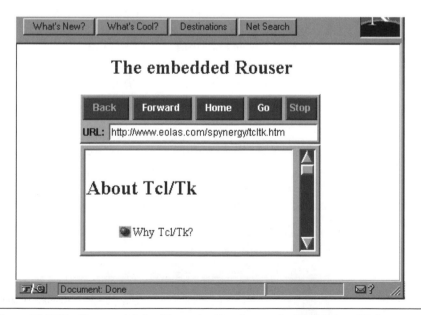

Figure 11.7 The Rouser tclet with navigation bar embedded into a Web page

Step 4: Changing the file extension, if necessary

If you use the Spynergy Plug-in to run this applet rather than the Tcl Plug-in with the Spynergy security policy, then you need to change your file extension to `.app` from `.tcl` so that the file can be recognized by the Spynergy Plug-in.

```
rouser.tcl --> rouser.app
```

Rouser and the Stockticker: Srouser

In this section, we integrate the stockticker applet to enhance the Rouser application that we introduced in the last chapter.

Because the Rouser already uses the Spynergy Toolkit, we don't need to rely on the HTTP package. We can use the Spynergy `fetchURL` procedure rather than the `::http::geturl` procedure to retrieve the data from the Web. This enables the Srouser to run under all Tcl/Tk versions 7.5/4.1 through 8.0, not limited to Tcl 8.0. To use `fetchURL`, which does not have and does not require a command option, we need to modify the code for the stockticker.

The `doticker` procedure remains the same, as well as the `formatTable` procedure that simply returns an organized list of data. But the modified `format_data` procedure absorbs the `get_data` procedure to create one procedure called `readstock` that fetches, formats, and calls the `doticker` procedure.

```
proc readstock {symbol} {
global messages debug formatstr

# ----------------------------------------------------------
# Convert the symbol to upper case for later comparisons
# ----------------------------------------------------------


     set upsym [string toupper $symbol]


# ----------------------------------------------------------
# Get the page of data from newsalert.com
# ----------------------------------------------------------
```

```
set data [geturl \
http://www.newsalert.com/free/stocknews?Symbol=$symbol \
    -initialtimeout 45 -timeout 15]

if {[string first "$upsym not found" $data] != -1} {
    return "";
    }

# ─────────────────────────────────────────────────────
# Extract the table with the stock values from the output.
# This is the portion of the data between Symbol=XXX and
# the end of the table.
# ─────────────────────────────────────────────────────

    set st1 [string first "Symbol=$symbol" $data]
    set st2 [string first "</TABLE>" $data]
    incr st1
    set data [string range $data $st1 $st2]

# ─────────────────────────────────────────────────────
# Skip the first two rows in the table
# ─────────────────────────────────────────────────────

    set st1 [string first "</TR" $data]
    incr st1
    set data [string range $data $st1 end]

    set st2 [string first "</TR" $data]
    set data [string range $data 0 $st2]

# ─────────────────────────────────────────────────────
# Convert this to a list for ease in further processing.
# ─────────────────────────────────────────────────────

    set lst [split $data "\n"]

# ─────────────────────────────────────────────────────
# Reformat the original list into a list with each list
# entry being a separate column in the table.
# ─────────────────────────────────────────────────────

    set tdlst [reform_table $lst]
  if {[llength $tdlst] < 2} {"
    return ""
    }

# ─────────────────────────────────────────────────────
# The table columns are:
# symbol Name last change percentChange open high low
```

```
# Examine these columns one at a time, and extract the
# value.
# ─────────────────────────────────────────────────────


    set line [lindex $tdlst 2]

    set st1 [string first "$upsym>" $line]
    set line [string range $line $st1 end]
    set st1 [string first ">" $line]
    set st2 [string first "<" $line]
    incr st1
    incr st2 -1

    #  puts "st1: $st1 st2: $st2 line: $line"
    set company [string range $line $st1 $st2]"

# ─────────────────────────────────────────────────────
# The numeric values are extracted using a regular
# expression that looks for a string of numbers
# between a ">", and a "<".
# ─────────────────────────────────────────────────────

set last [extract_number [lindex $tdlst 3]]
set chg  [extract_number [lindex $tdlst 4]]
set pct  [extract_number [lindex $tdlst 5]]
set open [extract_number [lindex $tdlst 7]]
set high [extract_number [lindex $tdlst 8]]
set low  [extract_number [lindex $tdlst 9]]

set stockinfo [format $formatstr \
 $upsym [string range $company 0 11] $last $chg $pct \
                   $open $high $low]

   return $stockinfo
}
```

We also modify the `display_stocks` procedure, so that status messages are displayed in the border of the Srouser application.

```
proc display_stocks {stock_list win} {
  global messages header index debug
  wm title .rouser "Srouser: Fetching stock quotes"

  foreach symbol $stock_list {
    set x [readstock $symbol]
    if {$x != ""} {
```

```
            set in  [expr [lsearch -exact $stock_list $symbol]]
            set messages($in) "$x"

            doticker $win 1500 "  ******  " 250
            }
        }
    }
wm title .rouser "Srouser"
after 900000 "display_stocks [list $stock_list] $win"
}
```

The init_ticker, doticker, reform_table, and extract_number procedures remain the same, included in the Rouser code.

Add GUI to Rouser

We can also give the user the option of showing or hiding the stockticker on the Rouser application. The following code creates a button that will display or hide the ticker when pressed.

The button is named with the Rouser naming scheme to be packed into the Rouser button bar. The show_tick variable determines if the command of the button is to hide the ticker or show the ticker. The text of the button is also configured appropriately.

```
set show_tick 1
set Name $Parent.main.top.buttons.ticker
button $Name      -activebackground gray40 \
    -activeforeground green \
    -background gray40 \
    -command  {

# ─────────────────────────────────────────────
# If the show_tick flag is 1, then pack the stockticker
# and configure the text on the button. Set the flag to 0.
# ─────────────────────────────────────────────


if {$show_tick} {
        pack .rouser.main.txt.ticker.t -expand 1 -fill x
        pack .rouser.main.txt.ticker -anchor nw -side bottom \
                -expand 1 -fill x -before
.rouser.main.txt.win
        .rouser.main.top.buttons.ticker configure \
            -text "Hide Ticker"
```

```
      set show_tick 0
} else {

#  ———————————————————————————————————————————————
# If the show_tick flag is 0, unpack the
# stockticker and configure the button.
# Set the flag to 1.
#  ———————————————————————————————————————————————

        pack forget .rouser.main.txt.ticker
        .rouser.main.top.buttons.ticker configure \
             -text "Show Ticker"
        set show_tick 1
              }}   \
-disabledforeground LightGray \
-foreground White -highlightbackground LightGray \
-highlightcolor LightGray \
-padx 5 -pady 1 -text "Show Ticker"

pack $Name       -anchor nw -fill none -side left
```

Figure 11.8 The Srouser Button Bar

The Weather Button and Wrouser

The stockticker is one example of a browser-pull application, because the program automatically requests and fetches data from the Internet to your browser. Another example of the browser-pull technique is a Weather button we can add to Rouser. The weather button fetches a Doppler radar image of a geographical area and displays it using a toplevel Tk window. A button that will show or hide this toplevel window is packed into the button bar. The radar image is refreshed every 15 minutes.

The Rouser application includes the fetchURL Spynergy Toolkit procedure with the outfile option, fetching the image into a file for use in the application. Tk currently only supports GIF images, so you cannot use this code to fetch a JPEG image.

We only need to add two procedures to the Rouser: one that refreshes the weather image and one that displays the current time on the toplevel window. We also create the toplevel for the weather image, and create Hide and Show Weather buttons for the Rouser GUI.

The `fetch_map` procedure accomplishes these tasks:

- Fetches the weather image from the URL and places it in an file, overwriting any previous versions
- Deletes the image created by a previous version of the file
- Creates an image using the current version of the file
- Places the image on the toplevel weather window

```
proc fetch_map {} {
        global weather fetcherr

# ————————————————————————————————————————————————
# Configure the title of the application to display status
# ————————————————————————————————————————————————


wm title .rouser "Wrouser: Fetching weather map

# ————————————————————————————————————————————————
# Fetches the image and places it in the outfile
# ————————————————————————————————————————————————


catch "fetchURL -url \

http://www.weatherpoint.com/wximages/jotrad.gif \
        -outfile "weathermap.gif""

# ————————————————————————————————————————————————
# Deletes the previous version of the image and
# creates the image and places it on the window.
# ————————————————————————————————————————————————

if {[info exists $weather]} {image delete $weather}
  catch "set weather \
        [image create photo -file "weathermap.gif" \
        -gamma 1 -height 484 -width 756 -palette 5/5/4]"

.rouser.main.top.buttons.show_weather.win.label \
        configure -image $weather
```

```
# ─────────────────────────────────────────
# Configures the title of the application to the
# original title.
# ─────────────────────────────────────────

wm title .rouser "Wrouser"

# ─────────────────────────────────────────
# After 15 minutes, calls itself to fetch the
# updated image.
# ─────────────────────────────────────────

    after 900000 fetch_map
}
```

The show_time procedure updates the time on the weather window every second.

```
proc show_time {} {

wm title .win "Doppler Radar: Illinois — Updates every 15
minutes — [clock format [clock seconds]]"
after 1000 show_time

}
```

The Weather button for Wrouser

This code creates a Weather button to add to the Rouser button bar. The Show Weather button is displayed when the application is run. When the user presses it, it displays the Tk window with the Weather image, then changes to the Hide Weather button.

```
set Name $Parent.main.top.buttons.show_weather

set show_weather 1
set weather ""
button $Name      -activebackground gray40 \
    -activeforeground green -background gray40 \
    -command   {

# ─────────────────────────────────────────
```

```
# If the show_weather flag is 1, then display the
# weather window and configure the text on the button.
# Set the flag to 0.
# ─────────────────────────────────────────────────────

if {$show_weather} {
        wm deiconify \
.rouser.main.top.buttons.show_weather.win
        raise .rouser.main.top.buttons.show_weather.win
        .rouser.main.top.buttons.show_weather configure \
                    -text "Hide Weather"
        set show_weather 0
        } else {

# ─────────────────────────────────────────────────────
# If the show_weather flag is 0, withdraw the
# weather window and configure the text on the button.
# Set the flag to 1.
# ─────────────────────────────────────────────────────

        wm withdraw \
.rouser.main.top.buttons.show_weather.win
        .rouser.main.top.buttons.show_weather configure \
        -text "Show Weather"
        set show_weather 1
        }
        } \
    -disabledforeground LightGray \
    -foreground White -highlightbackground LightGray \
    -highlightcolor LightGray  -padx 5 -pady 1 \
    -text "Show Weather"

set Name $Parent.main.top.buttons.hide_weather
```

This inline code creates the toplevel window that displays the weather image. It then withdraws the toplevel; the Show Weather button will deiconify the window. The show_time procedure displays the time.

The code also creates two buttons: one that will withdraw the window, and another that will refresh the image on the Tk window.

```
# ─────────────────────────────────────────────────────
# Create a toplevel, title  and withdraw it
```

```
# ─────────────────────────────────────────
toplevel $Name.win        -background LightGray
wm title $Name.win \
      "Rouser Doppler Radar — Updates every 15 minutes"
wm withdraw $Name.win

# ─────────────────────────────────────────
# Call the show time procedure and create the label
# that will display the image.
# ─────────────────────────────────────────

show_time
label $Name.win.label -border 0
pack $Name.win.label
$Name.win.label configure -image $weather

# ─────────────────────────────────────────
# Create a close button that will withdraw the
# window and change the Weather button.
# ─────────────────────────────────────────

button $Name.win.closebut -text Close -command {
wm withdraw .rouser.main.top.buttons.show_weather.win
pack forget .rouser.main.top.buttons.hide_weather
pack .rouser.main.top.buttons.show_weather -anchor nw \
       -fill none  -side left \
       -before .rouser.main.top.buttons.stop
       }
pack $Name.win.closebut -side right -anchor e

# ─────────────────────────────────────────
# Create a button on the weather toplevel that
# refreshes the image by fetching it using fetchURL.
# ─────────────────────────────────────────

button $Name.win.refresh -text "Refresh Now" -command {
       fetchURL -url \
http://www.weatherpoint.com/wximages/jotrad.gif \
             -outfile weathermap.gif
image delete $weather
set weather [image create photo -file \
       "weathermap.gif" -gamma 1 -height 484 \
       -width 756 -palette 5/5/4]
.rouser.main.top.buttons.show_weather.win.label configure \
       -image $weather
             }
pack $Name.win.refresh -side left -anchor e
```

Figure 11.9 The Wrouser button bar

The last line that we need to include in Wrouser fetches the image from the Internet source for the first time and writes it to a file to display on the Tk window.

```
fetch_map
```

zMap Client and Zrouser

Another way that we can enhance the Rouser application is the addition of an animated image map. This demo uses the zMap server available from Eòlas Technologies at http://www.eolas.com. The spinning globe that we use as a demo is available to use in your Web applications.

In addition to using the zMap server, this demo shows you how easy it is to create animated images in Tcl/Tk applications. We simply create frames of an animation using a paint program, convert it to BASE64 data, and use two simple procedures to cycle through the frames of the animation.

Specifying the Image Data

To create this animated image map, the largest addition to the Rouser code is the data that specify the strip of frames for the animated image. For brevity, we will not repeat that code here.

```
set strip {

. . . . . . . . .

}
```

Figure 11.10 The first five frames of the strip

The zMap Procedures

The animated image uses two procedures, the first of which creates the image on a label. The second procedure initiates the loop that cycles through the frames of the image, creating the animation.

```
proc zMap_setup {} {

global strip which nFrames delayInterval \
        zwin oldurl zMap_url _url

    # ───────────────────────────────────────────
    # Set the width of the animation frame to 50, and the
    # which variable (the frame number of the animation) to 0.
    # ───────────────────────────────────────────

    set width 50
        set which 0

    # ───────────────────────────────────────────
    # Creates the image from the data and the label that
    # displays the image.
    # ───────────────────────────────────────────

    image create photo strip -data $strip
        label $zwin.l -border 0; pack $zwin.l


    # ───────────────────────────────────────────
    # Determines the number of frames using the desired
    # width of the image
    # ───────────────────────────────────────────

    set nFrames [expr [image width strip] / $width]

    # ───────────────────────────────────────────
    # Creates  a photo image for each frame of the strip
    # ───────────────────────────────────────────

    for {set i 0} {$i < $nFrames} {incr i} {
        image create photo p$i
        p$i copy strip -from [expr $i * $width] 0\
                    [expr ($i + 1) * $width] 50
        }
    }
```

This procedure cycles through the frames of the animated strip.

```
proc zMap_playnext {} {
    global nFrames which delayInterval zwin

    incr which
    if {$which >= $nFrames} {set which 0}
    $zwin.l configure -image p$which
      after $delayInterval zMap_playnext
}
```

The zMap Bindings

We also include in the inline code bindings for the image that enable it to interact with the zMap server. The bindings use the _url global variable of the Spynergy Toolkit. It also uses the HTML procedures that the Rouser uses to manipulate and load HTML:

Table 11.3 The Spynergy HTML procedures

Procedure	Function
HB_init win	Sets up a group of variables that allow GUI widgets to be attached to the various URL navigational functions in the Spynergy library. The win argument is the name of the text window that displays the Web page
HB_resolve_url win url	Transforms relative URL pathnames into absolute pathnames that the HTML library functions can handle. The URL argument is the relative URL. The procedure returns the absolute URL as a string
HB_load_url win url	Loads the given URL into the text widget defined by win

This code creates a set of bindings for the label that displays the image. It enables the user to interact with the zMap server by clicking on the image.

When the user enters the animated image with the mouse, the URL of the image is displayed in the URL entry widget. The previous URL of the entry widget is preserved by setting the oldurl variable.

```
bind $zwin.1 <Enter> {set oldurl \
      [.rouser.main.top.ubar.url get]
      .rouser.main.top.ubar.url delete 0 end
      .rouser.main.top.ubar.url insert end "$zMap_url"
      }
```

When the user moves the mouse inside the animated image, the URL in the entry field displays the position of the mouse.

```
bind $zwin.1 <Motion> {
            set zMap_x [winfo pointerx $zwin.1]
            set zMap_y [winfo pointery $zwin.1]
            .rouser.main.top.ubar.url delete 61 end
            .rouser.main.top.ubar.url insert end "%x,%y,"
            }
```

When the user clicks on the image, the application initiates the _url variables and loads the URL into the text window. It constructs the query URL by appending the x,y and z (frame number) coordinates to the zmap_url variable and displays it in the URL entry field. Clicking on the image causes the three-dimensional image map query to be issued to the server specified by the zmap_url with those coordinates.

```
bind $zwin.1 <Button-1> {
      .rouser.main.top.ubar.url delete 61 end
      .rouser.main.top.ubar.url insert end "%x,%y,$which"
      HB_init $win
      set _url($win~~histidx) -1
      set _url($win~~lasturl) "*"
      set urllist [HB_resolve_url $win          \
                        [$_url($win~~entrywidget) get]]
      set turl "[lindex $urllist 0][lindex $urllist 2]"
            HB_load_url $win $turl [lindex $urllist 1]
      .rouser.main.top.ubar.url delete 0 end
      .rouser.main.top.ubar.url insert end "$zMap_url"
      }
```

Clicking mouse button 3 will load the zMap information page into the text window using the Rouser LoadHTML procedure, so the user can get more information about zMap technology.

```
bind $zwin.l <Button-3> {
             LoadHTML .rouser.main.txt.win \
                  "http://www.eolas.com/metamap"
          }
```

When a user leaves the animated image with the mouse, the previous URL specified by the variable `oldurl` is placed in the URL entry widget.

```
bind $zwin.l <Leave> {
      .rouser.main.top.ubar.url delete 0 end
      .rouser.main.top.ubar.url insert end "$oldurl"
}
```

The zMap Global Variables

We add these global variables to the Rouser configuration section. The `zmap_url` is the URL of the server that the image requests data from when the user clicks on it. The `delayInterval` is the speed at which the animation frames appear on the label widget.

```
global zmap_url zwin which oldurl delayInterval
set zmap_url \
"http://www.eolas.com/cgidos/mapper.cmd/demo@world@world.tif?"
set delayInterval 100
```

The final code that we add to Rouser creates and packs the frame to hold the animated image, and calls the two procedures.

```
set Name .zMap
frame $Name    -background LightGray
pack $Name     -anchor w -expand 0 -fill x -side right
set zwin $Name
zMap_setup
zMap_playnext
```

This is a demo that uses the zMap Server. To create your own animated image maps, you can obtain the zMap system available from Eòlas Technologies at `http://www.eolas.com`.

Tcaster: The Tcl Global Information Agent

As a final example of the sophistication you can acheive with a completely Tcl/Tk application, we have combined these enhancements to Rouser into one application. This application is available on the CD. It is a complete Web browser that includes the stock-ticker applet, a weather button that fetches a Doppler radar image, and the zMap animated image map demo.

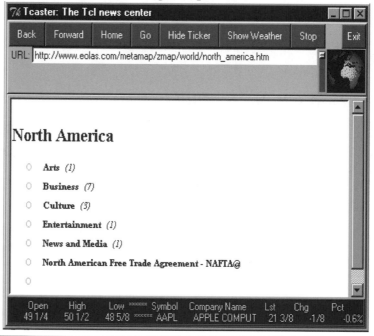

Figure 9.4 The Tcaster application

Conclusion

In this book, we have attempted to demystify many of the catch-phrases of today's Internet jargon -- terms such as browser pull, distributed computing, client/server, agent technology, and server push applications. We have shown you how you can use Tcl/Tk and the Spynergy Toolkit to build your own sophisticated cross-platform applications that exploit these technologies for your own purposes. The ease with which these programs were designed illustrates the power of the Tcl/Tk language. You are now armed to go out and conquer the majority of Internet application problems that may come your way. Enjoy!

Appendices

A. Ed, the Tcl Code Editor

B. About the Spynergy Web Developer

C. PGP and Tcl/Tk Resources

D. CD Resources

Ed, the Tcl Code Editor

In this appendix, we put together some of the concepts that we have covered and build a complete programmer's text editor that you can use to develop your own Tcl projects. We also introduce concepts of independent graphical applications. With graphical applications designed for use on one computer, you can use all the Tcl/Tk commands that you can not easily use on the Web. You can open, read, modify, and save files, as well as create toplevel windows and manipulate them using a window manager.

We introduced Ed in Chapter 3 for you to use as you work with the examples in this book. As you know, this application is not only a text editor but a testing environment that you can use to test your Tcl code merely by clicking a button. By showing you how this application is put together using both new code that we'll develop in this appendix as well as the Spynergy Toolkit, we introduce you to concepts that you can use to develop your own advanced Tcl/Tk applications.

Let's go through the features that we want in Ed. It should have the look and feel that most people generally expect from a text editor, as well as a few bonus features.

Features of Ed:

- A standard menubar including a File menu for creating, opening, and saving files, and an Edit menu for copying, cutting, pasting, and searching through text

- A button bar with GUI hints for managing files, text, and testing code
- A graphical tool to browse through directories on the hard disk and to open and save files
- A mechanism for showing the user the position of the cursor by row and column

Bonus features:

- Ability to fetch text or applet code over the Internet into the Ed editor, from any standard Web server, using the Spynergy `fetchURL` procedure
- A code test utility that uses a slave Tcl interpreter to execute any text that is in the editor window

The first part of this appendix explains how to build the user interface. Then we will build procedures to manage text and files. Finally, we will examine how Ed tests code and retrieves files from the Internet. The source code of the Ed Tcl Code Editor is on the CD included with this book.

The Ed GUI

The first step in the development process is usually to design the graphical user interface. The `ed_start_gui` procedure creates the user interface.

ed_start_gui

The `ed_start_gui` procedure creates a toplevel window, a menubar, a button bar, and a frame to hold the text editor. It calls the procedure `ed_edit`, which creates a text widget and two scrollbars. We will discuss `ed_edit` in the next section.

This procedure is called once when the Ed Tcl Editor application begins.

Step 1: Initialize global variables, create main window

First, we do a little housekeeping by initializing some global variables and configuring the toplevel window that will contain the rest of the application.

The global variables introduced here include the array _ED. The _ED array holds environment and status variables that are too numerous to declare individually. We will set the initial values of these variables at the conclusion of the application, when we "start it all up".

The global variable ed_main_frame is the name of the top-level window; the variable tcl_platform is an environment variable that describes the operating system of the computer that the application is running on. The remaining global variables represent the data that we use to create images for the buttons on the button bar.

```
proc ed_start_gui {} {
    global _ED ed_main_frame tcl_platform \
                    new open save copy \
                    cut paste search test
    toplevel .ed_main_frame -background lightgray
    wm withdraw .ed_main_frame
    wm title .ed_main_frame {Ed — Tcl Editor}
    wm geometry .ed_main_frame \
            +[winfo screenwidth .]+0
```

We create the main window using the toplevel and wm commands. The command toplevel creates a toplevel window, that acts as a "base" for the window application. This command is not available for Web applications, but is essential for independent window applications.

The toplevel command has the form:

```
toplevel windowname options
```

The options available to the toplevel command are similar to the options available to a typical widget command, such as background and foreground color.

You can control the geometry and behavior of a toplevel window using the wm command. The wm command stands for window manager. It has several options. The three options used in this procedure are geometry, title, and withdraw. The option geometry determines the size of the window relative to the screen height and width. Title specifies the title that appears in the application title bar. The withdraw option causes the window to become unmapped and to disappear from the screen.

We do this so we can build all of the elements into the window before displaying the finished GUI to the user. This prevents the sometimes distracting effect of having the various parts of the GUI pop up in sequence. When all the elements are built, the window will be displayed.

Like the toplevel command, wm is not available for Web applications, although it is useful for independent applications. For more information on both of these Tk commands, see the online reference documentation.

Step 2: Create frames to organize the GUI

Now we set up the various frames that organize the GUI. We give the frames names that will make them easy to recognize in other code, such as menuframe.

In this code, we use a convention of setting the name of a widget to a manageable variable to use with the various widget commands. First, we set the toplevel window to the variable Parent. All the widgets built on the toplevel window have this variable in their names.

```
#————————————————————————————————————
# Setting the parent variable
#————————————————————————————————————

set Parent .ed_main_frame

#————————————————————————————————————
# Creates the frame to hold the menu bar
#————————————————————————————————————

set Name $Parent.menuframe
frame $Name   -background white
pack $Name -anchor nw -expand 0 -fill x \
       -ipadx 0 -ipady 0 \
        -padx 0 -pady 0 -side top
```

```
#————————————————————————————————————————————
# Creates the frame to hold the button bar
#————————————————————————————————————————————

set Name $Parent.buttons
frame $Name -background LightGray
pack $Name -anchor nw -side top \
            -expand 0 -fill x \
            -ipadx 0 -ipady 0 \
            -padx 0 -pady 0
```

Step 3: Create the menubar

We create the File, Edit, and Web menu in the frame
`.ed_main_frame.menuframe`. You can create each menu with
the following steps.

- Create a menubutton widget with a unique name. The
  menubutton widget is not available for Web applets, but a
  standard component of independent applications. For a
  complete description of the menubutton widget, see the
  online documentation.
- Next, set a variable to a list of definitions for each menu
  item. The general syntax for a menu item definition is

  ```
  {{command}{item_name}{-command proc_name \
      -accelerator "key" -underline number}}
  ```

  The item_name is the name that appears on the menu, such
  as New File or Save. The proc_name defines the Tcl command or procedure invoked when the user selects that
  menu item. The -accelerator option defines the "hot key"
  combination that will invoke the menu command, such as
  Ctrl-N. The number following the -underline option
  determines which letter of the item's name will be under-
  lined and will select the item when combined with the
  keystroke "Alt."
- Using the string of definitions, evaluate the con-
  struct_menu procedure, described in the next section, to
  create the menu.
- Pack the complete menubutton into the GUI.

For an example of this process, let's look at the code that creates the File menu.

```
#————————————————————————————————————————
# Creates the File menu named by
# .ed_main_frame.menuframe.file. The file menu has
# four selections New, Open, Save, and Exit.
# Each executes a specific procedure. Notice that
# the seperator element is also defined as a string
# that will be evaluated by construct_menu. Instead
# of "command" it is defined as "separator".
#————————————————————————————————————————
    set Name $Parent.menuframe.file
    set Menu_string($Name) {
      {{command} {New}  {-command ed_edit_clear \
            -accelerator "ctrl+N" -underline 0}}
      {{command} {Open} {-command ed_file_load \
            -accelerator "ctrl+O" -underline 0}}
      {{command} {Save} {-command ed_file_save \
            -accelerator "ctrl+S" -underline 0}}
      {{separator} {} {}}
      {{command} {Exit} {-command ed_stop_gui \
            -underline 1}}
    }
    construct_menu $Name File $Menu_string($Name)
```

The procedure construct_menu is explained in the next section.

The two other menus in this application are created in a similar fashion, creating menubuttons named as .ed_main_frame. menuframe.edit and .ed_main_frame.menuframe.web.

```
    set Name $Parent.menuframe.edit
    set Menu_string($Name) {
      {{command} {Copy} {-command "ed_edit_copy" \
            -accelerator "Ctrl+C" -underline 0}}
      {{command} {Cut} {-command "ed_edit_cut" \
            -accelerator "Ctrl+X" -underline 2}}
```

```
    {{command} {Paste} {-command "ed_edit_paste" \
        -accelerator "Ctrl+V" -underline 0}}
    {{separator} {} {}}
    {{command}  {Search} {-command "ed_edit_searchf" \
        -accelerator "Ctrl+R" -underline 0}}
    {{separator} {} {}}
    {{command } {Test} {-command "ed_run_package" \
        -accelerator "Ctrl+T" -underline 0}}
    }
construct_menu $Name Edit $Menu_string($Name)
#—————————————————————————————————————————————————
set Name $Parent.menuframe.web
set Menu_string($Name) {
    {{command}  {Get URL} {-command "ed_get_url" \
        -accelerator "Ctrl+G" -underline 0}}
    {{tearoff}  {no} {}}
    }
construct_menu $Name Web $Menu_string($Name)
```

Step 4: Create a button bar

Now we create a button bar for the application in frame
`.ed_main_frame.buttons` created in Step 2. This is just a row
of buttons that are bound to actions that invoke the most important of the commands from the menus: `new`, `open`, `save`,
`copy`, `cut`, `paste`, `search` and `test`.

Because all the buttons are constructed in a similar fashion, we
use a procedure `construct_button` with arguments that specify the name of the button, the image data and image file, the command of the button, and the help message that is displayed when
a user selects the button. This procedure is explained later in this
appendix.

This code creates the New button. It creates a button using the
image data defined by the variable `new`, or using the image data
contained in the file `new.ppm`.

```
construct_button $Parent.buttons.clear \
```

```
$new new.ppm "ed_edit_clear" \
   "Clear the screen and edit a new file"
```

The rest of the buttons are built in a similar fashion. Note that three spacers are inserted to create separation between the File buttons, the Editing buttons, the Search button, and the Test button, This helps prevent accidental clicking of the wrong button. This is accomplished by merely packing a label containing empty text to create each spacer. Each of the buttons calls a procedure that we will explain later in this appendix.

```
#————————————————————————————————————
   construct_button $Parent.buttons.load \
      $open "ed_file_load" \
         "Open an existing file"
#————————————————————————————————————
   construct_button $Parent.buttons.save \
      $save "ed_file_save" \
         "Save current file"
#————————————————————————————————————
   set Name $Parent.buttons.18
   label $Name -background LightGray \
      -text "      "
   pack $Name -anchor nw -side left \
      -expand 0   -fill x
#————————————————————————————————————
   construct_button $Parent.buttons.copy \
      $copy "ed_edit_copy"\
         "Copy selected object or text"
#————————————————————————————————————
   construct_button $Parent.buttons.cut \
      $cut "ed_edit_cut"   \
         "Cut selected object or text"
#————————————————————————————————————
   construct_button $Parent.buttons.paste \
      $paste "ed_edit_paste" \
         "Paste selected object or text"
```

```
#————————————————————————————————————————
    construct_button $Parent.buttons.search \
        $search "ed_edit_searchf" \
        "Search for string in text"
#————————————————————————————————————————
    set Name $Parent.buttons.115
    label $Name -background LightGray \
        -text "            "
    pack $Name -anchor nw -side left \
        -expand 0   -fill x
#————————————————————————————————————————
    construct_button $Parent.buttons.test \
        $test "ed_run_package" \
        "Test current Tcl code"
```

Step 5: Create frames for the text widget

Now we proceed to create the frames that will hold the text widget, .ed_main_frame.mainwin, which is the main editing area of the program, and the status line, .ed_main_frame.mainwin.statusframe.currentstatus, which provides GUI hints, current file, and other status and error messages to the user.

```
#————————————————————————————————————————
    set Name $Parent.mainwin
    frame $Name -background white \
            -borderwidth 2  -relief ridge
    pack $Name -anchor sw -side left \
            -expand 1 -fill both
#————————————————————————————————————————
    set Name $Parent.mainwin.statusframe
    frame $Name   -background black \
            -borderwidth 0 -relief flat
    pack $Name -anchor nw -side bottom \
            -fill x -expand 0
#————————————————————————————————————————
    set Name $Parent.mainwin.statusframe.currentstatus
```

```
set _ED(status_widget) $Name
label $Name  -background black \
      -font $_ED(courierfont) -foreground green \
         -justify left -textvariable _ED(status) \
         -relief ridge
pack $Name -anchor center
```

Step 6: Display the cursor position

Any programmer's editor should have a capability to show the user the location of the text cursor. This allows the programmer to refer to specific line numbers when communicating with others about code. It is remarkably easy to add this capability to our editor. We add a label to display the starting position of 0.0.

```
#─────────────────────────────────────────────────────
set Name $Parent.buttons.117
label $Name -background LightGray \
            -text "0.0"
pack $Name -anchor nw -side right \
            -expand 0  -fill x
set Name $Parent.buttons.116
label $Name -background LightGray \
            -text "             Row.Col: "
pack $Name -anchor nw -side right \
            -expand 0  -fill x
```

We create two bindings for the text editing window in the procedure `ed_edit` explained later in this appendix. These bindings identify the location of the cursor and change the label. See the section on `ed_edit` for more explanation.

Step 7: Display the user interface

The last step of `ed_start_gui` is to display the completed interface to the user. This is accomplished with the `wm deiconify`

`.ed_main_frame` command. This option of the wm command displays windows that are iconified or not yet mapped. See the online documentation for more information about the wm command.

Notice that the procedure `ed_edit` is also called. This procedure will create scrollbars and the text widget for the text editor. We will go into depth about this procedure.

```tcl
#

    wm geometry .ed_main_frame 640x480+30+30
    if {$tcl_platform(platform) == "windows"} \
            {set y 0}
    wm minsize ed_main_frame 320 240
    ed_edit
    wm deiconify ed_main_frame
    update
}
```

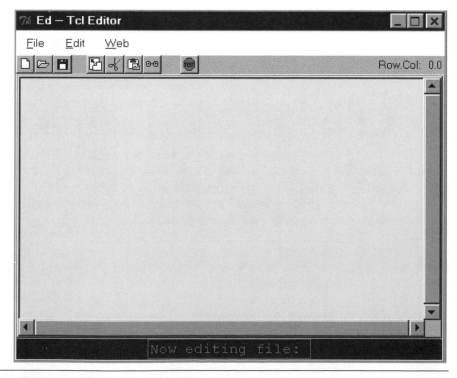

Figure A.1 The finished Ed GUI

Creating menus

The `ed_start_gui` calls several procedures to help build the GUI. One of these builds the menubuttons, `construct_menu`.

This procedure requires the name of the menubutton, the label that appears on the menubutton, and the list of elements that create the menu. In the `ed_start_gui` procedure, a list of menu elements were defined using list of strings in this form:

```
{{command}{item_name}{-command proc_name \
     -accelerator "key" -underline number}}
```

This procedure uses these strings to create a menu.

```
proc construct_menu {Name label cmd_list} {
    global _ED
#————————————————————————————————————————————————
# Create the menubutton with the specified
# Name and label.
#————————————————————————————————————————————————
    menubutton $Name  -activebackground navy \
        -activeforeground white -background white \
        -foreground black -relief flat -text $label \
        -underline 0
#————————————————————————————————————————————————
# Increase the global variable that identifies
# the current menu. Determine the name of the
# menu with this variable. This results in a
# unique identifiable name for each menu that is
# constructed using this procedure.
#————————————————————————————————————————————————
    incr _ED(menuCount);
    set newmenu $Name.m$_ED(menuCount)
    $Name configure -menu $newmenu
#————————————————————————————————————————————————
# Delete any old window that may be around from
# previous runs.
#————————————————————————————————————————————————
```

```
    catch "destroy $newmenu"
#—————————————————————————————————————————
# Create the new menu
#—————————————————————————————————————————
    eval "menu $newmenu"
#—————————————————————————————————————————
# Call the command to examine and add each item
# to the menu definition.
#—————————————————————————————————————————
    eval [list add_items_to_menu $newmenu $cmd_list]
#—————————————————————————————————————————
# Configure the menu and pack it
#—————————————————————————————————————————
    $newmenu configure -activebackground navy \
        -activeforeground white \
        -background white -foreground black
    pack $Name -anchor nw -expand 0 -ipadx 4 \
            -ipady 0 -padx 0 \
            -pady 0 -side left
    }
```

The add_items_to_menu command adds items that are listed in the element list provided. It determines if the item is a separator, a command, a tearoff, or a cascade (another menu).

```
proc add_items_to_menu {menubutton cmdList} {
    global _ED

#—————————————————————————————————————————
# Evaluate each line in the list of menu elements.
# Use the switch command, if the item is a
# separator or a tearoff, create a separator or
# configure the tearoff attribute.
#—————————————————————————————————————————

    foreach cmd $cmdList {
```

```
    switch [lindex $cmd 0] {
       "separator" {
          set doit "$menubutton add separator \
                  [lindex $cmd 2]"
       eval $doit
          }
       "tearoff"  {
          if {[string match [lindex $cmd 2] "no"]} {
          $menubutton configure -tearoff no
          }
          }

#─────────────────────────────────────────────────
# If the menu item is a command, add the label
# to the menu.
#─────────────────────────────────────────────────

       "command"  {
          set doit "$menubutton add \
                  [lindex $cmd 0] -label \
                  {[lindex $cmd 1]} \
                  [lindex $cmd 2]"
       eval $doit
          }


#─────────────────────────────────────────────────
# If the menu item is a cascade, create a new menu
# and call this procedure to add items to it.
#─────────────────────────────────────────────────

       "cascade"  {
           incr _ED(menuCount);
       set newmenu $menubutton.m$_ED(menuCount)
         set doit "$menubutton add cascade \
             -label {[lindex $cmd 1]} \
```

```
                  -menu $newmenu"
        eval $doit
        menu $newmenu
        add_items_to_menu $newmenu [lindex $cmd 2]
            }
        }
    }
}
```

Creating buttons

The command `construct_button` is called by `ed_start_gui` to build the button bar.

The buttons have small icon images instead of text. To place an image on the face of a button, we first create the image using the `image create photo` command that we discussed in Chapter 5. We can either load the icon images from a file, or we can include them inline in the code. The code presented here includes the images inline as well as resourcing files.

The data option for the `image create photo` command works only under Spynergy Tcl/Tk, Tcl/Tk 8.0, or the Tcl Plug-in. In Chapter 5, we were able to use the data option because we were creating applications for the Web under the Plug-in. But if you are not using Spynergy Tcl/Tk or Tcl 8.0 to run Ed, then you cannot use the data option. Instead, you must specify image data in a file using the `file` attribute.

If you specify image data using both the `file` and `data` attributes, then the file attribute will take precedence. However, it is preferable to use the data attribute if possible. The procedure determines what version of Tcl that Ed is running under, then uses the appropriate attribute.

The `<Enter>` and `<Leave>` bindings provide GUI hints for the user in the status line at the bottom of the window, to help the user remember what the various buttons do. This is like the "balloon help" feature found in most Windows programs, but is much easier to implement. The help message that the user will see is defined by the `-help` parameter of the `ed_status_message` procedure (this procedure is explained later.)

By binding the help message to the <Enter> event, and the default message to the <Leave> event, the user will see a help message at the bottom of the screen when the mouse cursor is over a button, and the message will revert back to showing the current filename, when the mouse moves off of the button.

```
proc construct_button {Name data file cmd helpmsg} {

    #───────────────────────────────────────────
    # Use the data or file to create the image,
    # depending on the version of tcl.
    #───────────────────────────────────────────

    global tcl_version

    if {[info exists tcl_version] == 0 \
                || $tcl_version < 8.0} {
     set im [image create photo -file $file \
            -gamma 1 -height 16   \
            -width 16 -palette 5/5/4]
     } else {
       set im [image create photo -data $data \
            -gamma 1 -height 16 \
            -width 16 -palette 5/5/4]
     }
    #───────────────────────────────────────────
    # Create the button using the image and
    # specified command.
    #───────────────────────────────────────────

    button $Name -background LightGray \
            -foreground black \
            -activebackground white -image $im \
            -relief raised -command "$cmd"
    pack $Name -anchor nw -side left \
            -expand 0   -fill x
```

```
#
# Create bindings for help messages.
#

bind $Name <Enter> [list ed_status_message \
        -help $helpmsg]
bind $Name <Leave> {ed_status_message -perm}
}
```

The text editor

The key part of the Ed Tcl Editor consists of a text widget with procedures to add cut, copy, paste, and search capabilities to the widget. These procedures are the commands called by the menu items and buttons of the GUI that we built previously.

ed_edit

The ed_edit procedure creates a text widget with accompanying scrollbars and loads a file, if selected, into the text widget. Unlike the ed_start_gui procedure that is called only once, ed_edit is called whenever a file is opened. It accomplishes these tasks:

- Declares global variables and destroys any widgets created previously by ed_edit
- Sets up container frames, a horizontal scrollbar, and a vertical scrollbar
- Creates a text widget and prepares it for text editing

First we declare global variables and set up the editing window's container frames. If the frames that we will create with this procedure exist when this procedure is called, then those frames are destroyed with the destroy command.

```
proc ed_edit {} {

    #
    # Declare global variables
    #
```

```
global _ED
global Menu_string

#────────────────────────────────────────────
# Destroy any existing frames we intend to
# create. Use the catch command so if the
# destroy command returns an error, the
# script will continue unhindered.
#────────────────────────────────────────────

catch "destroy .ed_mainFrame.mainwin.mainwin"
catch "destroy .ed_mainFrame.mainwin.buttons"
catch "destroy .ed_mainFrame.mainwin.f1"
catch "destroy .ed_mainFrame.mainwin.textFrame"

#────────────────────────────────────────────
# Set the frame created in ed_start_gui to
# hold the text assembly to the global Parent
# variable.
#────────────────────────────────────────────

set Parent .ed_mainFrame.mainwin

set Name $Parent.mainwin
frame .ed_mainFrame.mainwin.mainwin \
      -background lightgray
pack .ed_mainFrame.mainwin.mainwin \
      -anchor nw -side bottom -fill x

set Name $Parent.textFrame
frame $Name  -background LightGray \
      -borderwidth 2 \
      -highlightbackground LightGray \
      -relief raised
 pack $Name -anchor sw -expand 1 \
            -fill both -side bottom
```

We construct horizontal and vertical scrollbars for moving around large documents. This is just a matter of defining and packing the scrollbars, then adding bindings to the text widget that "attach" each scrollbar to the widget. First we put the horizontal scrollbar in a frame of its own. Note the `-orient horizontal` parameter to the scrollbar command. This will create a horizontal bar. If no `-orient` parameter is given, the default orientation is vertical.

```
set Name $Parent.textFrame.right
frame $Name  -background LightGray -height 10 \
        -highlightbackground LightGray -width 15
pack $Name -anchor sw -expand 0 -fill x \
        -ipadx 0 -ipady 0 -padx 0 \
        -pady 0 -side bottom


set Name $Parent.textFrame.right.vertScrollbar
    scrollbar $Name  -activebackground plum \
        -activerelief sunken \
        -background LightGray \
        -command "$Parent.textFrame.left.text xview"
        -highlightbackground LightGray \
        -orient horizontal -troughcolor gray40 \
        -elementborderwidth 1 -width 12
    pack $Name -anchor center -expand 1 \
        -fill x -ipadx 0 -ipady 0 \
        -padx 0 -pady 0 -side left


#────────────────────────────────────────────────────
# This frame creates a space between the
# corners of the horizontal and vertical scrollbars.
#────────────────────────────────────────────────────

set Name $Parent.textFrame.right.buttons0
    frame $Name  -background LightGray -height 10 \
        -highlightbackground LightGray -width 15
    pack $Name -anchor se -expand 0 -fill x \
```

```
        -ipadx 0 -ipady 0 -padx 2 \
        -pady 2 -side bottom
```

```
#─────────────────────────────────────────────
# Frame for the horizontal scrollbar
#─────────────────────────────────────────────

    set Name $Parent.textFrame.left
    frame $Name  -background LightGray  \
            -highlightbackground LightGray
    pack $Name -anchor center -expand 1 \
        -fill both -ipadx 0 -ipady 0 \
        -padx 0 -pady 0 -side top
```

```
#─────────────────────────────────────────────
# The horizontal scrollbar
#─────────────────────────────────────────────

    set Name $Parent.textFrame.left.horizScrollbar
    scrollbar $Name  -activebackground plum \
        -activerelief sunken \
        -background LightGray \
        -command "$Parent.textFrame.left.text yview" \
        -highlightbackground LightGray \
        -troughcolor gray40 -width 12 \
        -elementborderwidth 1
    pack $Name -anchor center -expand 0 \
        -fill y -ipadx 0 -ipady 0 \
        -padx 0 -pady 0 -side right
```

Finally, we create the text widget where code can be entered and edited. Notice the `-xscrollcommand` and `-yscrollcommand` attributes that bind the text widget to the scrollbars.

```
set Name $Parent.textFrame.left.text
text $Name -background AliceBlue -borderwidth 2 \
```

```
                -foreground black -highlightbackground LightGray \
                -insertbackground black \
                -selectbackground lightblue \
                -selectforeground black -wrap none \
                -xscrollcommand \
                "$Parent.textFrame.right.vertScrollbar set" \
                -yscrollcommand \
                "$Parent.textFrame.left.horizScrollbar set"
$Name insert end {

}

pack $Name -anchor center -expand 1 \
        -fill both -ipadx 0 -ipady 0 \
        -padx 0 -pady 0 -side top
```

Then we just add two bindings to the text widget that update the cursor position label at each button press or key press after the key is released with the current cursor position. These bindings use the `index insert` command to identify the cursor position. They change the label that displays the cursor position, `.ed_main_frame.buttons.117`. This label is built by `ed_start_gui`.

```
bind $Parent.textFrame.left.text <Any-ButtonRelease> \
        {.ed_main_frame.buttons.117 configure -text \
        [.ed_main_frame.mainwin.textFrame.left.text \
            index insert]}
bind $Parent.textFrame.left.text <Any-KeyRelease> \
        {.ed_main_frame.buttons.117 configure -text \
        [.ed_main_frame.mainwin.textFrame.left.text \
            index insert]}
```

```
#─────────────────────────────────────────
# To prepare the text widget for a file,
# all text is deleted.
#─────────────────────────────────────────
```

```
$Name delete 1.0 end

#————————————————————————————————————————

# The value assigned to the variable _ED
# temppackage) is inserted into the text
# widget. This variable is assigned when the
# user selects Open from the File menu and
# the ed_file_load procedure is executed.

#————————————————————————————————————————

$Name insert end $_ED(temppackage)

#————————————————————————————————————————

# The ed_edit_commit procedure is explained
# later this chapter. It copies the contents
# of the text widget to the _ED(package)
# global variable.

#————————————————————————————————————————

ed_edit_commit

#————————————————————————————————————————

# The tcl command update "cleans up" the
# application.

#————————————————————————————————————————

update
}
```

Working with text: cut, copy, and paste

The cut, copy, and paste text procedures work with the use of the Tk commands clipboard and selection. The command clipboard enables you to manage the TK clipboard that stores data temporarily. It necessarily works with selection, which identifies and manipulates selected items. Selected items include what has been selected by the user - for example, text that has been highlighted with the mouse. For more information about these commands, see the online reference documentation.

Table A.1 The process for selecting and copying text

Command	Function
selection own	Determines that the selection is owned by the text widget
clipboard clear	Clears the contents of the clipboard contents
selection get	Retrieves the selection from the text widget
clipboard append	Places the selection in the clipboard

To cut text, the `delete sel.first sel.last` command deletes the selection from the text widget. Pasting text is accomplished simply by inserting the contents of the clipboard into the text widget.

We will go over these three procedures in the following sections.

ed_edit_cut

This procedure determines if the selection is in the text widget. It then simply clears the clipboard and copies the data to it. It then deletes the selection from the text widget.

```
proc ed_edit_cut {} {

    #─────────────────────────────────────────────
    # If the thing that is selected is
    # within the text widget, continue.
    #─────────────────────────────────────────────

    if {[selection own -displayof \
      .ed_main_frame.mainwin.textFrame.left.text "] \
      =="..ed_main_frame.mainwin.textFrame.left.text "} {

        #─────────────────────────────────────────
        # Clear the clipboard
        #─────────────────────────────────────────
```

```
clipboard clear -displayof \

.ed_mainFrame.mainwin.textFrame.left.text

    #————————————————————————————————————
    # Add the selected text to the clipboard
    #————————————————————————————————————

       catch {
      clipboard append -displayof
        .ed_mainFrame.mainwin.textFrame.left.text \
      [selection get -displayof \
        .ed_mainFrame.mainwin.textFrame.left.text]

    #————————————————————————————————————
    # Delete the selection from the text widget
    #————————————————————————————————————

       .ed_mainFrame.mainwin.textFrame.left.text delete \
           sel.first sel.last
           }
         }
   }
```

ed_edit_copy

The ed_edit_copy procedure is very similar to the cut procedure above, but without the final delete sel.first sel.last
command.

```
proc ed_edit_copy {} {

    #————————————————————————————————————
    # If the thing that is selected is within the text
    # widget, continue.
    #————————————————————————————————————
```

```
if {[selection own -displayof     \
   .ed_mainFrame.mainwin.textFrame.left.text] \
  == ".ed_mainFrame.mainwin.textFrame.left.text "} {

    #—————————————————————————————
    # Clear the clipboard
    #—————————————————————————————

clipboard clear -displayof     \
    .ed_mainFrame.mainwin.textFrame.left.text

    #—————————————————————————————
    # Add the selected text to the clipboard
    #—————————————————————————————

  catch {
   clipboard append -displayof     \
     .ed_mainFrame.mainwin.textFrame.left.text \
   [selection get -displayof
     .ed_mainFrame.mainwin.textFrame.left.text]
    }
  }
}
```

ed_edit_paste

The ed_edit_paste procedure first deletes the text widget selection, then inserts the contents of the clipboard at the location of the insertion cursor.

```
proc ed_edit_paste {} {

  catch {

    #—————————————————————————————
    # Deletes any selected text
    #—————————————————————————————
```

```
    .ed_mainFrame.mainwin.textFrame.left.text \
        delete sel.first sel.last


    #————————————————————————————————————————————

    # Inserts the contents of the clipboard

    #————————————————————————————————————————————


    .ed_mainFrame.mainwin.textFrame.left.text \
            insert insert \
        [selection get -displayof    \
            .ed_mainFrame.mainwin.textFrame.left.text \
            -selection CLIPBOARD]
        }
    }
```

Alternative cut, copy, and paste

We have built the cut, copy, and paste commands to demonstrate the use of the clipboard and selection commands. But
there are also built-in Tk commands that enable you to cut, copy,
and paste text. You can use these three commands for the cut,
paste, and copy commands of Ed.

```
proc ed_edit_cut {} {
    tk_textCut .ed_mainFrame.mainwin.textFrame.left.text
}

proc ed_edit_copy {} {
    tk_textCopy .ed_mainFrame.mainwin.textFrame.left.text
}

proc ed_edit_paste {} {

    tk_textPaste .ed_mainFrame.mainwin.textFrame.left.text
}
```

Text search

A search utility is an essential component of any programming editor. We need two procedures to create a search utility: one that creates the user interface for the search form, and one that performs the actual search.

First we will design the search form interface, which will be a simple dialog box with an entry field and buttons. When a user selects Search from the Edit menu or the Search button, the procedure ed_edit_searchf is called. This procedure creates the dialog box where a user can enter a search string.

The procedure ed_edit_search is called when the user enters a search string and selects Search or presses Enter.

The search form interface includes a Replace button. This button simply inserts a string into the text and replaces the current selection. This string is entered by the user in an entry field.

ed_edit_searchf

This procedure accomplishes these tasks:

- Declares global variables and destroys the search dialog box if it currently exists
- Creates entry fields for the user search string and replace string
- Creates a list of bindings for the entry fields to manage text and activate the search
- Creates a Search button that will set the contents of the entry field to global variables that allow the procedure ed_edit_search to search through the contents of the text widget
- Creates a Replace button that deletes the current selection and inserts a string
- Creates a Cancel button that destroys the dialog box

```
proc ed_edit_searchf {} {

    #————————————————————————————————————
    # Declare global variables
    #————————————————————————————————————
```

```tcl
global _ED

#—————————————————————————————————————————
# Destroy the search form if it currently exists
#—————————————————————————————————————————

catch "destroy .ed_edit_searchf"

#—————————————————————————————————————————
# Create a toplevel for the base of the search
# window dialog.
#—————————————————————————————————————————

toplevel .ed_edit_searchf  \
    -background LightGray
wm withdraw .ed_edit_searchf
wm title .ed_edit_searchf {Search}

#—————————————————————————————————————————
# Set the toplevel name to the Parent variable
# to use in the rest of the procedure.
#—————————————————————————————————————————

set Parent .ed_edit_searchf

#—————————————————————————————————————————
# Create a frame to hold the entry field, and
# a label.
#—————————————————————————————————————————

set Name $Parent.f1
frame $Name -background lightgray
pack $Name -anchor nw -fill x \
            -side top -padx 5

set Name $Parent.f1.l1
label $Name -text "Search for " -background lightgray
pack $Name -anchor nw -fill x -side left -padx 5
```

```
#------------------------------------------------
# Create an entry field for the search string
#------------------------------------------------

set Name $Parent.f1.e1
entry $Name  -background aliceblue \
    -font $_ED(courierfont) \
    -highlightbackground LightGray  \
    -selectbackground blue \
    -selectforeground white -width 30
pack $Name -anchor nw -side right


#------------------------------------------------
# Creates bindings to keyboard events for the
# entry field.
#------------------------------------------------

bind .ed_edit_searchf.f1.e1 <Delete> {
if [%W selection present] {
        %W delete sel.first sel.last
} else {
        %W delete insert
        }
}
bind .ed_edit_searchf.f1.e1 <Return> \
        {tk_focusNext %W}
$Name delete 0 end


#------------------------------------------------
# Create a frame to hold the replace entry
# field, and a label.
#------------------------------------------------


set Name $Parent.replace
frame $Name -background lightgray
```

```tcl
pack $Name -anchor nw -side top -fill x -padx 5 -pady 5

set Name $Parent.replace.l1
label $Name -text "Replace with" -background lightgray
pack $Name -anchor nw -fill x -side left -padx 5


#─────────────────────────────────────────────
# Create an entry field with bindings for the
# replace string.
#─────────────────────────────────────────────


set Name $Parent.replace.e1
entry $Name  -background aliceblue \
        -font $_ED(courierfont) \
        -highlightbackground LightGray \
        -selectbackground blue \
        -selectforeground white -width 30
pack $Name -anchor nw -side left
bind .ed_edit_searchf.replace.e1 <BackSpace> \
        {tkEntryBackspace %W}
bind .ed_edit_searchf.replace.e1 <Delete> {
        if [%W selection present] {
                %W delete sel.first sel.last
        } else {
                %W delete insert
        }
}
bind .ed_edit_searchf.replace.e1 <Return> \
        {tk_focusNext %W}
$Name delete 0 end


#─────────────────────────────────────────────
# Creates a frame that holds the search,
# replace, and cancel buttons.
#─────────────────────────────────────────────

set Name $Parent.mainwin
```

```
frame $Name -background lightgray
pack $Name -anchor nw -side top -fill x -padx 5 -pady 5
```

The code below creates the Search button. The command of the Search button sets the _ED(srch_new) variable to the contents of the text field. If it is different from the _ED(srch_old) variable, then the search starts over at the beginning of the document. If not, it continues to search from the cursor's position in the document. It then sets the contents of the search field to the _ED(srch_old) variable for the next iteration of the search.

The command also returns focus to the text widget so that the words that are found will be highlighted. It then raises the search dialog to the top of the display list so the dialog appears in front.

```
set Name $Parent.mainwin.b1
button $Name  -activebackground lavender \
   -background navy \
   -command {
      set _ED(srch_new) [.ed_edit_searchf.f1.e1 get]
      if {$_ED(srch_new) != $_ED(srch_old)}\
                        {set _ED(editcursor)1.0}
      ed_edit_search \
          .ed_mainFrame.mainwin.textFrame.left.text \
              $_ED(srch_new)
      focus   .ed_mainFrame.mainwin.textFrame.left.text
      raise .ed_edit_searchf
      set _ED(srch_old) [.ed_edit_searchf.f1.e1 get]
      } \
   -foreground white -highlightbackground LightGray \
   -text {Search}
pack $Name -anchor nw -side left
```

```
#------------------------------------------------------------
# Creates the Replace button that sets the string of
# the entry field to a variable and inserts it into
# the text at the selection position, replacing the
# selected text.
#------------------------------------------------------------
```

```
set Name $Parent.mainwin.b2
button $Name  -activebackground lavender \
    -background gray40 \
    -command {
      if {[.ed_mainFrame.mainwin.textFrame.left.text \
                  get sel.first sel.last] != ""} {
      set _ED(rplc_term) \
                  [.ed_edit_searchf.replace.e1 get]
      .ed_mainFrame.mainwin.textFrame.left.text insert
                  $_ED(editcursor) $_ED(rplc_term)
      .ed_mainFrame.mainwin.textFrame.left.text \
                  delete sel.first sel.last
        }
    }  \
                  -foreground white \
                  -highlightbackground LightGray \
                  -text {Replace}
pack $Name -anchor nw -side left


#————————————————————————————————————
# Creates the Cancel button that destroys the
# search form.
#————————————————————————————————————


set Name $Parent.mainwin.b3
button $Name  -activebackground Lavender \
    -background navy \
    -command {destroy .ed_edit_searchf}       \
    -foreground white \
    -highlightbackground LightGray -text Cancel
pack $Name -anchor nw -side right


#————————————————————————————————————
```

```
    # Creates the size and geometry of the search
    # form.
    #—————————————————————————————

set x [expr [winfo rootx .ed_mainFrame] + 300]
 set y [expr [winfo rooty .ed_mainFrame] \
          + [winfo height .ed_mainFrame] - 300]
wm geometry .ed_edit_searchf +$x+$y
 wm deiconify .ed_edit_searchf
 raise .ed_edit_searchf
 update
 wm minsize .ed_edit_searchf \
      [winfo width .ed_edit_searchf] \
      [winfo height .ed_edit_searchf]
 wm maxsize .ed_edit_searchf \
      [winfo width .ed_edit_searchf] \
      [winfo height .ed_edit_searchf]

}
```

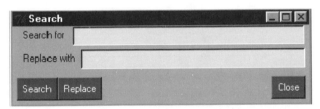

Figure A.2 The search and replace dialog box

The search procedure recursively cycles as the entire document is examined. Keeping track of the srch_old and srch_new variables is critical to tracking these comparisons and determining when the end of the document is reached. These variables are used in the ed_edit_search procedure, which is called when the user either presses Return or clicks on the Search button.

ed_edit_search

The code necessary to search for an entered text string is even less complicated than the code for defining the search dialog box. It

uses the Tcl search command to search from the position of the
cursor towards the end of the text. Each match moves the cursor
down the text. If there is no match, then the cursor won't move
away from 1.0, and the message, "No match for string" is displayed to the user. If the new cursor position is not 1.0, but does-
n't change from the previous cursor position, then the end of the
text must have been reached with no matches, causing the "End of
search" message to be displayed. If a match is found, then the cursor is moved to that location and the matching string is selected
and highlighted.

The procedure requires the name of the text widget and the search
string that the user typed into the entry box. It is called when the
user selects Search.

```
proc ed_edit_search {textwin srch_string} {

    #———————————————————————————————————————
    # Declare global variables, the _ED array
    #———————————————————————————————————————


    global _ED

    #———————————————————————————————————————
    # If the string is empty, then return and place
    # the cursor at the beginning of the text widget.
    #———————————————————————————————————————

    if {$srch_string == ""} {
         set _ED(editcursor) 1.0; return}

    #———————————————————————————————————————
    # Set the fail flag to any errors
    #———————————————————————————————————————

    set fail [catch {\
        $textwin search -regexp \
       -count length $srch_string \
```

```
        $_ED(editcursor) end} _ED(editcursor) ]

#—————————————————————————————————————————————
# If the length is not 0 and there are no errors,
# then tag the location of the cursor and expose
# the location of the cursor to the user.
#—————————————————————————————————————————————

if { ($length != 0) && (!$fail) } {
    $textwin tag add sel $_ED(editcursor) \
        "$_ED(editcursor) + $length char"
    set _ED(editcursor) [$textwin index \
        "$_ED(editcursor) + $length char"]
    $textwin see $_ED(editcursor)

#—————————————————————————————————————————————
# Else set the cursor to the beginning of file
#—————————————————————————————————————————————

} else {set _ED(editcursor) 1.0}

#—————————————————————————————————————————————
# If the location of the cursor is at the
# beginning of the file, then issue a message
# and return.
#—————————————————————————————————————————————

if {$_ED(editcursor) == 1.0} {
    ed_error "No match for string"; return}

#—————————————————————————————————————————————
# If the location of the cursor is the same
# as the previous location, issue a message.
#—————————————————————————————————————————————

if {$_ED(editcursor) == $_ED(editcurold)} {
    ed_error  "End of search"}
```

```
#--------------------------------------------------
# Set the old location of the cursor to the
# current location
#--------------------------------------------------

    set _ED(editcurold) $_ED(editcursor)

}
```

Directory browser

One of the most complex parts of this program is the directory browser. It uses the list widget and relatively intricate management of string concatenation to provide the user with a point-and-click interface for browsing around directories and for selecting files to open and save.

We present the directory browser code for educational purposes. We could replace some of the code you see here with the Tcl commands tk_getOpenFile and tk_getSaveFile. See the online documentation for details of these commands.

ed_file_load

The ed_file_load procedure is called when you select Open from the File menu. It is a "wrapper" procedure, calling other procedures to complete specific tasks:

- Retrieves the filename with ed_loadsave, and sets the _ED(file) global variable
- Opens the file and copies it to the _ED(package) and the _ED(temppackage) global variables. This variable is used in other procedures
- Issues various status messages
- Calls the ed_edit procedure to load the file into the text widget

```
proc ed_file_load {} {

    #--------------------------------------------------
    # Declare global _ED
    #--------------------------------------------------
```

```
global _ED

    #————————————————————————————————————————————————
    # Evaluate ed_loadsave and set the return
    # value to the _ED(file) variable.
    #————————————————————————————————————————————————

    set _ED(file) [ed_loadsave load]

    #————————————————————————————————————————————————
    # If the the file does not exist, return;
    # if the file is not readable, issue an error
    # message and return.
    #————————————————————————————————————————————————
if {$_ED(file) == ""} {return}
if {![file readable $_ED(file)]} {
    ed_error "File \[$_ED(file)\] is not readable."
    return
}

    #————————————————————————————————————————————————
    # Wait until all is clear, then continue
    #————————————————————————————————————————————————

ed_wait_if_blocked

    #————————————————————————————————————————————————
    # Display a message that the file is loading,
    # update application.
    #————————————————————————————————————————————————

set _ED(blockflag) 1
ed_status_message \
        -show "loading file:  \"$_ED(file)\" ..."
update

    #————————————————————————————————————————————————
    # If there's an error opening the file,
```

```
    # display a message and return.
    #─────────────────────────────────────────


if {[catch "open $_ED(file) r" fd]} {
    ed_error \
          "Error while opening $_ED(file): \[$fd\]"
    ed_status_message -perm
    set _ED(blockflag) 0
    return
}



    #─────────────────────────────────────────
    # Set the variable _ED(package) to the
    # contents of the file. Then close the channel
    # to the file.
    #─────────────────────────────────────────

set _ED(package) "[read $fd]"
close $fd



    #─────────────────────────────────────────
    # Set _ED(temppackage) to the contents
    # of the file.
    #─────────────────────────────────────────

    set _ED(temppackage) $_ED(package)


    #─────────────────────────────────────────
    # Set the name of the file to
    # _ED(packagekeyname).
    #─────────────────────────────────────────

    set _ED(packagekeyname) [file tail $_ED(file)]
    if {$_ED(packagekeyname) == ""} \
          {set _ED(packagekeyname)          \
          $_ED(file)}
```

```
if {$_ED(packagekeyname) == ""} \
    {set _ED(packagekeyname)  \
    "UNKNOWN"}

#————————————————————————————————————
# Execute the ed_edit procedure and
# ed_status_message to issue the regular
# status message.
#————————————————————————————————————


ed_edit
ed_status_message -perm
update
set _ED(blockflag) 0
}
```

ed_file_save

This procedure, like ed_file_load, is a wrapper procedure. It is called when a user selects Save from the File menu or presses the Save button. It calls other procedures to complete its tasks:

- Retrieves the filename with ed_loadsave, and sets the _ED(file) global variable
- Copies the contents of the text widget to the _ED(package) and the _ED(temppackage) global variables. This variable is used in other procedures
- Issues various status messages
- Opens the selected file and writes the contents of the text widget, then closes the file

```
proc ed_file_save {} {

    #————————————————————————————————————
    # Declares global variable _ED
    #————————————————————————————————————

    global _ED
```

```
#————————————————————————————————————————
# Waits until all is clear
#————————————————————————————————————————


ed_wait_if_blocked

   #————————————————————————————————————————
   # Sets the _ED(package) variable to the
   # contents of the text widget.
   #————————————————————————————————————————
set _ED(blockflag) 1
set _ED(package)   \
   "[.ed_mainFrame.mainwin.textFrame.left.text   \
                    get 1.0 end]"
set _ED(blockflag) 0

   #————————————————————————————————————————
   # Calls the ed_loadsave procedure and sets
   # its returned value to the _ED(file) variable.
   #————————————————————————————————————————

set $_ED(file) [ed_loadsave save]

   #————————————————————————————————————————
   # If the text widget is empty, return;
   # if the contents are not writable,
   # issue an error message and return.
   #————————————————————————————————————————


if {$_ED(file) == ""} {return}
if {[file exists $_ED(file)]} {
   if {![file writable $_ED(file)]} {
     ed_error "File \[$_ED(file)\] is not writable."
         return
     }
}
```

```
#————————————————————————————————————————
# Wait until all is clear
#————————————————————————————————————————

ed_wait_if_blocked

#————————————————————————————————————————
# Issue status message and update application
#————————————————————————————————————————
set _ED(blockflag) 1
ed_status_message \
        -show "saving file:  \"$_ED(file)\" ..."
update

#————————————————————————————————————————
# Open the file.
# If there's an error opening the file,
# issue an error message, then issue the
# regular status message and return.
#————————————————————————————————————————

if {[catch "open $_ED(file) w" fd]} {
        ed_error \
                "Error opening $_ED(file):  \[$fd\]"
        ed_status_message -perm
        update
        set _ED(blockflag) 0
        return
}

#————————————————————————————————————————
# Place the value of _ED(package) (the con
# tents of the text widget) into the file.
# Close the file. Issue the regular status
# message and update the application, unblock
# the application.
#————————————————————————————————————————
```

```
      puts $fd "$_ED(package)"
         close $fd
         ed_status_message -perm
         update
         set _ED(blockflag) 0
   }
```

Directory browser GUI

These procedures create the interface for the directory browser. This will consist of entry fields for specifying or displaying the directory name, file type, and the filename, as well as a scrolling listbox to display the files in the current directory.

ed_loadsave

This procedure is called by both `ed_save_file` and `ed_load_file`. It uses an argument specified by either Save or Load to produce a dialog box that either saves or opens a file. If the argument is Save, the procedure creates a Save dialog box. If the argument is Load, the procedure creates an Open dialog box. The two types of dialog boxes are so similar that it is easier to write one procedure that will create both.

This procedure accomplishes these tasks:

- Creates a dialog box to display the contents of a directory in a listbox, and filename and type in entry fields
- Creates bindings for the listbox to behave as a standard directory browser
- Destroys the dialog box when a file is chosen
- Returns the pathname of the file selected to be opened or saved to disk

The first part of the procedure sets variables used in the procedure. The `ed_loadsave(pwd)` variable is initially set to the current working directory. This appears in the directory entry field when the user initially opens the Open/Save dialog box.

```
proc ed_loadsave {loadflag} {
```

```
#————————————————————————————————————
# Declare and set variables that will be used
# in this procedure. The ed_loadsave(pwd)
# variable is set to the current working
# directory using the Tcl command pwd.
#————————————————————————————————————

global ed_loadsave _ED
if {![info exists ed_loadsave(pwd)]} {
        set ed_loadsave(pwd) [pwd]
        set ed_loadsave(filter) "*"
        set ed_loadsave(file) ""
}
set ed_loadsave(loadflag) $loadflag
set ed_loadsave(path) ""
set ed_loadsave(done) 0
```

This code creates the user interface for the Open/Save dialog box.

```
#————————————————————————————————————
# Create a toplevel for the dialog file
# selection box. Withdraw it until the rest
# of the GUI is built. Title the window
# appropriately.
#————————————————————————————————————

toplevel .ed_loadsave  -background LightGray
wm withdraw .ed_loadsave
if {[string match $loadflag "load"]} {
        wm title .ed_loadsave "Open File"
} else {
        wm title .ed_loadsave "Save File"
}

wm geometry .ed_loadsave +[expr \
        ([winfo screenwidth .]/2) \
        - 173]+[expr ([winfo screenheight .]/2) \
```

```
    - 148]


#
# Set the variable Parent to the name of the
# toplevel.
#


set Parent .ed_loadsave


#
# Create a frame to hold the entry field
#
```

```
set Name $Parent.dir
frame $Name -background lightgray
pack $Name -anchor nw -side top
```

This entry field that displays the current directory. The text variable is the value of the variable ed_loadsave(pwd), the current working directory.

```
set Name $Parent.dir.e3
entry $Name  -background aliceblue \
      -foreground black \
      -highlightbackground LightGray -width 35 \
      -textvariable ed_loadsave(pwd)
pack $Name -side right -anchor nw -padx 5


#
# Create bindings that  will let you delete
# text and call the ed_loadsavegetentries
# procedure by pressing the Return key.
#


bind $Name <Return> {ed_loadsavegetentries}
bind $Name <Delete> {
      if [%W selection present] {
```

```
                    %W delete sel.first sel.last
            } else {
                    %W delete insert
            }
    }
    #─────────────────────────────────────────────
    # Create a label for the directory entry field
    #─────────────────────────────────────────────

    set Name $Parent.dir.ll
    label $Name  -background LightGray  \
                -text "Directory: "
    pack $Name -side right -anchor nw


    #─────────────────────────────────────────────
    # Create a frame to hold the entry field that
    # will display type of file.
    #─────────────────────────────────────────────

    set Name $Parent.type
    frame $Name -background lightgray
    pack $Name -anchor nw -side top -fill x
```

This code creates an entry field that will display the type of file that is being saved or opened. The value of the text variable is the ed_loadsave(filter). Its initial value is an empty string.

```
    set Name $Parent.type.e7
    entry $Name  -background aliceblue \
                -foreground black \
                -highlightbackground LightGray \
                -width 35 \
                -textvariable ed_loadsave(filter)
    pack $Name -side right -anchor nw -padx 5


    #─────────────────────────────────────────────
    # Create bindings that  will let you delete
```

```
# text and call the ed_loadsavegetentries
# procedure by pressing the Return key.
#────────────────────────────────────────────────

bind $Name <Return> {ed_loadsavegetentries}
bind $Name <Delete> {
     if [%W selection present] {
          %W delete sel.first sel.last
     } else {
          %W delete insert
     }
}


#────────────────────────────────────────────────
# Create a label for the entry field that
# displays the file type.
#────────────────────────────────────────────────

set Name $Parent.type.15
label $Name  -background LightGray \
     -text "File Type: "
pack $Name -side right -anchor nw

#────────────────────────────────────────────────
# Create a frame to hold the entry field that
# will display the file name that will be
# saved or opened.
#────────────────────────────────────────────────


set Name $Parent.file
frame $Name -background lightgray
pack $Name -anchor nw -side top -fill x
```

This code creates an entry field that displays the filename. The text variable is ed_loadsave(file). This variable will be assigned a value when a user selects a file from the directory browser or enters a name into the field.

```tcl
set Name $Parent.file.e11

entry $Name  -background aliceblue \
            -foreground black \
            -highlightbackground LightGray \
            -width 35 \

            -textvariable ed_loadsave(file)

pack $Name -side right -anchor nw -padx 5


#────────────────────────────────────────────
# Insert the value of _ED(packagekeyname)
# into the entry field, if it has a value.
# Create bindings that let you delete text,
# and that invoke the procedures to open
# or save a file (the OK button).
#────────────────────────────────────────────


.ed_loadsave.file.e11 delete 0 end

.ed_loadsave.file.e11 insert 0 \
    $_ED(packagekeyname)

bind $Name <Delete> {

    if [%W selection present] {

        %W delete sel.first sel.last

    } else {

        %W delete insert

    }

}

bind $Name <Return> \

    {if {[ed_loadsavevalentry]} {set    \
        ed_loadsave(done) 1}}



#────────────────────────────────────────────
# Create a label for the entry widget that
# displays the file name.
#────────────────────────────────────────────


set Name $Parent.file.19

label $Name  -background LightGray \
```

```
                    -text "File: "
pack $Name -side right -anchor nw


#──────────────────────────────────────────────
# Create a frame to hold the listbox
#──────────────────────────────────────────────
set Name $Parent.list
frame $Name  -background LightGray \
        -borderwidth 2 -height 50 \
        -highlightbackground LightGray \
        -relief raised  \
        -width 50
pack $Name -side top -anchor nw \
        -expand yes -fill both


#──────────────────────────────────────────────
# Create a listbox to display the
# directory listing.
#──────────────────────────────────────────────


set Name $Parent.list.lb1
listbox $Name  -background aliceblue \
        -font $_ED(courierfont) \
        -foreground black \
        -highlightbackground LightGray    \
        -selectbackground LightBlue \
        -selectforeground black \
        -yscrollcommand "$Parent.list.sb2 set"
        -selectmode browse
pack $Name -anchor center -expand 1 \
        -fill both -ipadx 0 -ipady 0 \
        -padx 2 -pady 2 -side left
```

This code creates bindings for the listbox. The bindings are essential in order to replicate the kind of directory browsing interaction popularized by the Windows interface. The idea is to divide up the various types of selection events. Selecting a file from the list with a single click causes that filename to be displayed in the file entry box once a file is selected, then the user should be able to either click the OK button, or press Return to cause the file to be either loaded or saved. Double clicking on a file in the listbox is equivalent to selecting a file and then hitting OK or Return. The procedures that these events are bound to are explained later in this appendix.

```tcl
bind $Name <Any-ButtonPress> \
        {ed_loadsaveselbegin %W %y}
bind $Name <Any-ButtonRelease> \
        {ed_loadsaveselbegin2 %W}
bind $Name <Any-Double-ButtonPress> \
        {ed_loadsaveselbegin %W %y}
bind $Name <Any-Double-ButtonRelease> \
        {set _ED(packagekeyname) $seld_file; \
        ed_loadsaveselend %W %y}
bind $Name <Any-Triple-ButtonPress> {break}
bind $Name <Any-Triple-ButtonRelease> {break}
bind $Name <Return> {ed_loadsaveselend %W %y}
bind $Name <Up> {
        tkCancelRepeat
        tkListboxBeginSelect %W [%W index active]
        %W activate [%W index active]
}
bind $Name <Down> {
        tkCancelRepeat
        tkListboxBeginSelect %W [%W index active]
        %W activate [%W index active]
}

#————————————————————————————————————
# Create a vertical scrollbar for the listbox
# widget.
#————————————————————————————————————
```

```
set Name $Parent.list.sb2
scrollbar $Name  -activebackground plum \
               -activerelief sunken \
               -background LightGray     \
               -command "$Parent.list.lb1 yview" \
               -highlightbackground LightGray \
               -troughcolor gray40
pack $Name -anchor center -expand 0 -fill y \
               -ipadx 0 -ipady 0 \
               -padx 2 -pady 2 -side left

#————————————————————————————————————————
# Create a frame to hold the buttons
#————————————————————————————————————————


set Name $Parent.buttons
frame $Name -background lightgray
pack $Name -side top -anchor nw -fill x
```

This code creates the OK button. The command sets the name of the file to the contents of the entry field. If the procedure ed_loadsavevalentry returns True, then it sets the done flag to 1. This procedure is explained later in this appendix.

```
set Name $Parent.buttons.ok
button $Name  -activebackground lavender
               -background navy \
               -foreground white \
               -highlightbackground LightGray  \
               -text OK \
               -command {set _ED(packagekeyname) \
               [.ed_loadsave.file.e11 get];
               if {[ed_loadsavevalentry]} {
               set ed_loadsave(done) 1}}
pack $Name -side left -anchor nw -padx 3 -pady 3
```

```tcl
#————————————————————————————————————
# Create the Cancel button. The command simply
# destroys the dialog box.
#————————————————————————————————————
set Name $Parent.buttons.cancel
button $Name  -activebackground lavender \
       -background navy \
       -foreground white \
       -highlightbackground LightGray  \
       -text Cancel \
       -command {destroy .ed_loadsave}
pack $Name -side right -anchor nw -padx 3 \
       -pady 3


#————————————————————————————————————
# Calls ed_loadsavegetentries. This
# procedure is explained later in this appendix.
#————————————————————————————————————


ed_loadsavegetentries


#————————————————————————————————————
# Display the complete GUI
#————————————————————————————————————


wm deiconify .ed_loadsave
```

This code causes the application to wait until ed_load-save(done) is set to 1. When it is, then the window is destroyed. The command vwait is not available for Web applications under the current Tcl Plug-in. See the online documentation for specifics.

```tcl
vwait ed_loadsave(done)
destroy .ed_loadsave


#————————————————————————————————————
# If the value of ed_loadsave(path)is a
# directory, then the variable is set to an
```

```
# empty string.
#————————————————————————————
if {[[file isdirectory $ed_loadsave(path)]} {
                set ed_loadsave(path) ""}
```

Finally, the path of the filename is returned. This is the value given
to the procedures `ed_load_file` and `ed_save_file`.

```
        return $ed_loadsave(path)
}
```

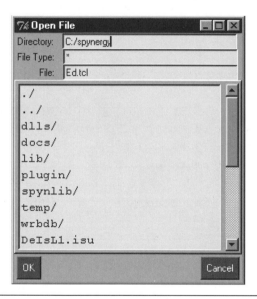

Figure A.3 The directory browser interface

These two procedures are bound to keyboard events for the listbox. When you select a file displayed in the listbox, the `ed_load-
saveselbegin` procedure is called. It selects the file nearest to
your mouse. When you release your key, the `ed_loadsavesel-
begin2` procedure is called. It sets the name of the file that you
selected to the `_Ed(packagekeyname)` variable. This variable is
used in the following procedures that do the real work of this
directory browsing and file selection.

```
proc ed_loadsaveselbegin {win ypos} {
        $win select anchor [$win nearest $ypos]
```

```
}

proc ed_loadsaveselbegin2 {win} {
    global seld_file
    set seld_file \
        [$win get [$win curselection]]
    .ed_loadsave.file.e11 delete 0 end
    .ed_loadsave.file.e11 insert 0 $seld_file
    set _ED(packagekeyname) $seld_file

}
```

Directory browser internal procedures

The code in the next four procedures is complex beyond the scope of this discussion, but it is given here so that you can incorporate it into any of your applications that require a directory browser utility. This code will allow you to create utilities that will be backward-compatible with earlier versions of the interpreter.

The system needs to distinguish between a user selecting a filename, a directory name, or "../" entry that causes everything to move up one directory. As the user clicks on these items, these procedures assemble the result and eventually return a final pathname through ed_loadsave, which gives it to either ed_file_open or ed_file_save, the original "wrapping" procedures that are called when the user selects Open or Save.

ed_loadsaveselend

The procedure ed_loadsaveselend gets things ready to open or save a file. It is called when you double-click on the name of the file or when you select a file and press the return key.

It accomplishes these tasks:

- Retrieves the string at the y position of the listbox.
- Sets the ed_loadsave array variables for filename and path, appending the filename with the directory pathname

previously in the entry fields before the user selected the
file or directory

• Calls the ed_loadsavegetentries procedure

```
proc ed_loadsaveselend {win ypos} {
    global ed_loadsave
    $win select set anchor [$win nearest $ypos]
    set fil [.ed_loadsave.list.lb1 get \
            [lindex [$win curselection] 0]]
    if {-1 == [string last "/" $fil]} {
        set ed_loadsave(file) $fil
        set ed_loadsave(path) \
                [eval file join $ed_loadsave(pwd) \
                $ed_loadsave(file)]
        set ed_loadsave(done) 1
            return ""
    }
    set ed_loadsave(pwd) \
        [ed_loadsavemergepaths \
        $ed_loadsave(pwd) [string trimright $fil "/"]]
    ed_loadsavegetentries
    return ""

}
```

ed_loadsavegetentries

This procedure simply displays the current file directory in the
listbox. Unfortunately, there's nothing simple about it! Each time
it is called, which is every time you enter a new file name or directory name, it examines the contents of the directory and displays
only those files that are specified by the file type.

This procedure is called in the ed_loadsave procedure when
the dialog box is first created. It is called whenever you press
Return while the dialog box is open, whether you have selected a
file or not. It is also called by the ed_loadsavevalentry procedure, which is called when you enter a filename or directory,
and press the OK button or the Return key.

```tcl
proc ed_loadsavegetentries {} {

    global ed_loadsave tcl_version

    set e 0


    #————————————————————————————
    # If the path is not a directory, issue error
    # and set e variable to 1.
    #————————————————————————————

    if {![file isdirectory $ed_loadsave(pwd)]} {
        gui_error "\"$ed_loadsave(pwd)\" \
                is not a valid directory"
        .ed_loadsave configure -cursor {}
        set e 1
    }


    #————————————————————————————
    # Configure the cursor in the dialog box to
    # the watch icon, indicating that the
    # application is processing, and update the
    # application.
    #————————————————————————————

    .ed_loadsave configure -cursor watch
    update


    #————————————————————————————
    # Set the sort mode to -dictionary. This mode
    # ignores case and treats integers as integers
    # and not numbers. This option is only sup-
    # ported under Tcl 8.0 and higher, so the
    # program checks the tcl version and sets the
    # mode to -ascii if the version is less than 8.0.
    #————————————————————————————

    set sort_mode "-dictionary"
    if {[info exists tcl_version] == 0 || \
```

```tcl
        $tcl_version < 8.0} {
     set sort_mode "-ascii"
}


#————————————————————————————————————————————————
# If there is no specific file type, set the
# file type to a wildcard character, *.
#————————————————————————————————————————————————

if {$ed_loadsave(filter) == ""} {
     set ed_loadsave(filter) "*"
     }

#————————————————————————————————————————————————
# Sort files in directory using the specified
# sort mode.
#————————————————————————————————————————————————

set files [lsort $sort_mode "[glob -nocomplain \
          $ed_loadsave(pwd)/.*] \
     [glob -nocomplain $ed_loadsave(pwd)/*]"]

#————————————————————————————————————————————————
# Delete the contents of the listbox
#————————————————————————————————————————————————

.ed_loadsave.list.lb1 delete 0 end

#————————————————————————————————————————————————
# If the e variable is 1, then return and do
# no more. The e variable is set to 1 only
# when the directory is not valid.
#————————————————————————————————————————————————

     if {$e} {
     .ed_loadsave configure -cursor {}
     update
```

```
        return
}
#———————————————————————————————
# Set initial values of the list of directories
# "d" and the list of files, "fils". These
# lists will be augmented in the following
# code.
#———————————————————————————————

set d "./ ../"
set fils ""


#———————————————————————————————
# Examine each object in the directory. If it
# is a directory, append its name with "/" and
# add it to the "d" list. If it is a
# file, then add it to the "fils" list only
# if it matches the filtering variable, i.e.
# the file type.
#———————————————————————————————

foreach f $files {
        set ff [file tail $f]
        if {$ff != "." && $ff != ".."} {
                if {[file isdirectory $f]} {
                        lappend d "$ff/"
                } else {
                        if {[string match \
                          $ed_loadsave(filter) $ff]} {
                          lappend fils "$ff"
                          }
                }
        }
}


#———————————————————————————————
# Set the list of files to the d variable,
```

```
# which is the list of directories created
# in the above foreach loop, and the
# fils variable, which is the list of files
# created in the above foreach loop.
#————————————————————————————————————————


set files "$d $fils"


#————————————————————————————————————————
# List each object of the "files" list in
# the listbox.
#————————————————————————————————————————


foreach f $files {
        .ed_loadsave.list.lb1 insert end $f
}


#————————————————————————————————————————
# Configure the cursor to its normal state
# and update the application.
#————————————————————————————————————————


.ed_loadsave configure -cursor {}
update
}
```

ed_loadsavevalentry

This procedure uses the Tcl command `file` that manipulates file-names and attributes. The command `file` has many options: You can examine the name, the extension, who owns the file, the size, if you can read it or write to it, and so on. See the online documentation included on the CD for all the options available for the `file` command. This command is not available for use on the Web under Sun's Tcl Plug-in.

This procedure is called by the `ed_loadsave` procedure when you enter a filename into the entry box labeled "File," and then press the OK button or the Return key. It examines the file that you entered and determines if it can be opened or written to. It returns 1 or 0.

When it returns 1, then the global variable ed_loadsave(done) is set to 1. Remember that the ed_load-save procedure waits until this variable is set to 1. Then it destroys the window and continues with ed_file_load or ed_file_save, working with the file that is indicated by the _ED(file) global variable, which is set in this procedure.

```
proc ed_loadsavevalentry {} {
    global ed_loadsave _ED

    if {"." != [file dirname $ed_loadsave(file)]} {

        #------------------------------------------------
        # If the file selected is not the directory,
        # then set its path to the merge of the
        # directory and the file name.
        #------------------------------------------------

            set path [ed_loadsavemergepaths \
                    $ed_loadsave(pwd) \
                    $ed_loadsave(file)]

        #------------------------------------------------
        # Set the working directory variable to the
        # path.
        #------------------------------------------------

            set ed_loadsave(pwd) [file dirname $path]

        #------------------------------------------------
        # If the file has an extension, set the file
        # type variable to the file's extension. Else
        # set the file type variable to the wildcard
        # character.
        #------------------------------------------------

            if {[file extension $path] != ""} {
```

```
              set ed_loadsave(filter) \
                    "*[file extension $path]"
        } else {
              set ed_loadsave(filter) "*"
        }
```

```
#————————————————————————————————————————
# Set the current file variable to the
# selected file name.
#————————————————————————————————————————
```

```
        set ed_loadsave(file) [file tail $path]
```

```
#————————————————————————————————————————
# Call the ed_loadsavegetentries procedure,
# refreshing the directory display.
#————————————————————————————————————————
```

```
        ed_loadsavegetentries
        return 0
}
```

```
set fil [ed_loadsavemergepaths ed_loadsave(pwd) \
            $ed_loadsave(file)]
```

```
#————————————————————————————————————————
# If the file is being opened (the loadflag is
# 1), then continue, else skip to the "else"
# clause.
#————————————————————————————————————————
```

```
if {$ed_loadsave(loadflag) == 1} {
```

```
#————————————————————————————————————————
# If the file does not exist or it isn't read-
# able, issue an error and return 0. Set the
# path to an empty string.
#————————————————————————————————————————
```

```
if {(![file exists $fil]) || (![file readable \
    $fil])} {
    gui_error "\"$fil\" cannot be loaded."
    set ed_loadsave(path) ""
    return 0
} else {


#————————————————————————————————
# If file is readable, set the _ED(file)
# global variable  (the file being
# manipulated) to the actual file, and return 1.
#————————————————————————————————

            set ed_loadsave(path) $fil
            set _ED(file) $fil
            set ed_loadsave(done) 1
            return 1

    }


#————————————————————————————————
# If the selected file is being saved, then
# continue.
#————————————————————————————————

} else {


#————————————————————————————————
# If the file is not writable, issue an error
# and return 0.
#————————————————————————————————


set d [file dirname $fil]
if {![file writable $d]} {
    gui_error \
        "\"$d\" directory cannot be written to."
    set ed_loadsave(path) ""
    set _ED(file) ""
```

```
                    return 0
                    }


          #————————————————————————————————————————————

          # If the file exists and is not writable,
          # issue an error and return 0.

          #————————————————————————————————————————————

          if {[file exists $fil] && (![file writable $fil])} {
                    gui_error "\"$file\" cannot be written to."
                    set ed_loadsave(path) ""
                    set _ED(file) ""
                    return 0
          }


          #————————————————————————————————————————————

          # If there is no error, then set the global
          # variable _ED(file) to the actual file, and
          # return 1.

          #————————————————————————————————————————————

                    set ed_loadsave(path) $fil
                    set ed_loadsave(done) 1
                    set _ED(file) $fil
                    return 1

          }

}
```

ed_loadsavemergepaths

This procedure is called in the `ed_loadsaveselend` and `ed_loadsavevalentry` procedures. It simply merges two paths, the current directory and the current filename, into one unit to use with these procedures.

It returns a complete pathname to the selected file.

```
proc ed_loadsavemergepaths {patha pathb} {
```

```
#────────────────────────────────────────
# Split the pathnames up into a list of
# components.
#────────────────────────────────────────

set pa [file split $patha]
set pb [file split $pathb]


#────────────────────────────────────────
# If the  first element of the second path is
# not ":", then  return the joined filename.
# Else, continue with modifications.
#────────────────────────────────────────


if {[string first ":" [lindex $pb 0]] != -1} {
        return  [eval file join $pb]}


#────────────────────────────────────────
# If the  first element of the second path is
# "/", then return the joined filename.
#────────────────────────────────────────

if {[lindex $pb 0] == "/"} {
        return [eval file join $pb]
        }


#────────────────────────────────────────
# Examine each item in the second pathname. If
# it indicates to go up a directory "..", then
# delete the last element of the first
# pathname. Else append the item to the first
# pathname.
#────────────────────────────────────────


set i [expr [llength $pa] - 1]
foreach item $pb {
        if {$item == ".."} {
```

```
            incr i -1
            set pa [lrange $pa 0 $i]
        } elseif {$item == "."} {
            # - do nothing
        } else {
            lappend pa $item
        }
    }


    #————————————————————————————————————
    # Return the completed file name
    #————————————————————————————————————


    return [eval file join $pa]
}
```

This is a small procedure to notify the user that an error has occured in one of these directory browser procedures.

```
proc gui_error {message} {
    catch "destroy .xxx"
    bell
    tk_dialog .xxx "Error" "$message" warning 0 Close
}
```

Tcl code testing utility

As we stated earlier in this appendix, we would like to create a utility that will allow users to test Tcl code easily without leaving the Ed editor.

One way that we could provide this feature is by creating a utility that simply copies the contents of the text widget to a variable and then uses the Tcl eval command to execute that code. However, the problem with this method is that erroneous user-written code could potentially cause the Ed Tcl application to hang or crash if it is executed in the same interpreter as the one executing the master code that creates Ed.

The Tcl interp command allows us to add a test utility that will isolate the executing code from the Ed program. The Ed application is executing in the *master* interpreter, while the code being tested is executed by a *slave* intepreter. This will drastically reduce the possibility that problematic user-written code can crash the editor.

ed_run_package

The ed_run_package procedure tests code from the text editor safely and cleanly. It accomplishes these tasks:

- Examines the value of the _ED(package) variable
- Stops any running applications with ed_kill_apps
- Makes interface moifications, including issuing status messages and turning the Test button into a Stop button
- Creates a slave Tcl interpreter, and creates a window for the application
- Runs the code through the slave interpreter, displaying any errors

```
proc ed_run_package {} {
    global _ED ed_loadsave argv argv0 argc \
            embed_args env

        #-------------------------------------------------
        # If _ED(package) is an empty string, issue an
        # error message, and return.
        #-------------------------------------------------

        if {"$_ED(package)" == ""} {
            ed_status_message \
                -alert "No code currently in run buffer."
            update
            return
        }
```

We want to kill any code that is already running to prevent conflicts by calling the ed_kill_apps procedure.

```
ed_kill_apps
```

Next, we want to make sure that the latest changes in the code will be executed, by replacing the contents of _ED(package) with the contents of the text widget. This is accomplished by calling the ed_edit_commit procedure.

```
ed_edit_commit

#─────────────────────────────────────────────
# Configure the cursor to be a watch icon,
# indicating that the application is
# processing. Display status message.
#─────────────────────────────────────────────

.ed_main_frame configure -cursor watch
ed_status_message \
        -show "running package:   \
        $_ED(packagekeyname)"
update

#─────────────────────────────────────────────
# Call the ed_stop_button procedure, which
# changes the test  button into a stop button,
# including the icon and command associated
# with the button.
#─────────────────────────────────────────────


ed_stop_button
```

This code creates a slave Tk interpreter that will run the code in _ED(package). This is done by using the Tcl interp command to create a slave interpreter, called runslave, and then loading Tk into it. Command execution in the slave interpreter is invoked by preceding the commands with the runslave name.

In order to prevent an exit command in user-written code from killing the Ed master interpreter, we also redefine the exit command, so that it calls the ed_kill_apps procedure (see below), which provides a safe mechanism for killing code running in the slave. For more information about the interp and alias commands, see the online documentation.

```
set _ED(runslave) [interp create runslave]


#————————————————————————————————
# Load Tk into slave interpreter
#————————————————————————————————

runslave eval {load {} Tk}


#————————————————————————————————
# Create a toplevel and geometry for the code
# being tested.
#————————————————————————————————

set cmd "wm geometry . +100+100"
runslave eval $cmd
set cmd          \
"wm title . \
    [list "Main Window for $_ED(packagekeyname)"]"
runslave eval $cmd


#————————————————————————————————
# Redefines the exit command as ed_kill_apps
#————————————————————————————————

runslave alias exit ed_kill_apps


#————————————————————————————————
# Wait until all is clear
#————————————————————————————————

ed_wait_if_blocked
```

Now comes the section that actually runs the code contained in _ED(package). The catch command traps any errors in the user's code and flashes an alert message at the bottom of the screen if an error is encountered by the slave interpreter.

```
if {[catch "$_ED(runslave) eval [list $_ED(package)]"
result]} {

    ed_status_message -alert "Error occured while
running        \                        $_ED(packagekey-
name)"

        update
        bgerror $result

}


    #————————————————————————————————————
    # Set status message to regular status and
    # cursor to normal state. Update application.
    # Set the blockflag to 0.
    #————————————————————————————————————

    ed_status_message -perm
    .ed_main_frame configure -cursor {}
      update
    set _ED(blockflag) 0

}
```

ed_kill_apps

The ed_kill_apps procedure destroys Tk windows, procedures, and variables through the slave interpreter. When called from the slave interpreter, it kills the slave interpreter without interfering with the master interpreter.

```
proc ed_kill_apps {args} {
    global _ED ed_mainf


    #————————————————————————————————————
    # If there is no slave interpreter, then
    # return.
    #————————————————————————————————————
```

```
            if {$_ED(runslave) == ""} {return}

    #————————————————————————————————
    # Configure the cursor to the watch icon,
    # indicating the application is processing.
    #————————————————————————————————

.ed_main_frame configure -cursor watch

    #————————————————————————————————
    # Display status message and update application
    #————————————————————————————————

ed_status_message -show         \
   "... closing down active GUI applications ..."
update

    #————————————————————————————————
    # Wait until all is clear, then delete the
    # slave interpreter. Configure all interface
    # items and variables to normal status,
    # including cursor, status message, and test
    # button.
    #————————————————————————————————

    ed_wait_if_blocked
    set _ED(blockflag) 1
      catch "interp delete $_ED(runslave)"
      set _ED(blockflag) 0
      set _ED(runslave) ""
      .ed_main_frame configure -cursor {}
      ed_status_message -perm
    ed_test_button
    update
}
```

ed_stop_button and ed_test_button

The `ed_stop_button` changes the Test button to a Stop button by changing its image and associated command. It is called in the `ed_test_package` procedure. When you click on the Test button to test your code, it changes into a Stop button until you click on it again.

When you click on it again to stop testing your code, then the button calls the `ed_kill_apps` procedure, which destroys the slave interpreter and also calls `ed_test_button`, changing the button back to the Test button.

```
proc ed_stop_button {} {
    global _ED stop tcl_version

    #-----------------------------------------------
    # Set Name to the name of the button
    #-----------------------------------------------

    set Name .ed_main_frame.f3.b3

    #-----------------------------------------------
    # Create an image using image data or a file
    #-----------------------------------------------

    if {[info exists tcl_version] == 0 || \
                $tcl_version < 8.0} {
      set im [image create photo -file stop.ppm \
         -gamma 1 -height 16 -width 16 -palette 5/5/4]
    } else {
      set im [image create photo -data $stop \
         -gamma 1 -height 16 -width 16 -palette 5/5/4]
    }


    #-----------------------------------------------
    # Change the icon on the button and the
    # button's command.
    #-----------------------------------------------
```

```
    $Name config -image $im -command "ed_kill_apps"

    #----------------------------------------------------------------
    # Bind a help status message
    #----------------------------------------------------------------

    bind .ed_main_frame.f3.b3 <Enter> \
        {ed_status_message -help \
            "Stop running code"}
}


proc ed_test_button {} {
    global _ED test tcl_version
    set Name .ed_main_frame.f3.b3

    #----------------------------------------------------------------
    # Create an image with the test image data
    # or from a file.
    #----------------------------------------------------------------

    if {[info exists tcl_version] == 0 || \
        $tcl_version < 8.0} {
      set im [image create photo -file test.ppm \
        -gamma 1 -height 16 \
        -width 16 -palette 5/5/4]
      } else {
      set im [image create photo -data $test \
        -gamma 1 -height 16 \
        -width 16 -palette 5/5/4]
      }


    #----------------------------------------------------------------
    # Change the icon and button command,
    # and help message.
    #----------------------------------------------------------------
```

```
$Name config -image $im -command "ed_run_package"
     bind .ed_main_frame.f3.b3 <Enter>        \
     {ed_status_message -help "Test current code"}
}
```

Figure A.4 The Test and Stop buttons

Accessing the web

With the Spynergy Toolkit, you can easily give your Tcl applications the ability to access the Web.

In Chapter 5, we looked at a demo that used the Tcl 8.0 HTTP package to retrieve files over the Internet. The Spynergy `fetchURL` procedure is very similar to the HTTP package, but one important difference is that Tcl applications do not need to be running under Tcl 8.0 to use the Spynergy Toolkit, while the HTTP package is exclusive to Tcl 8.0. We wanted to develop Ed so that it can run under Tcl 7.6/Tk 4.2, as well as Tcl/Tk 8.0, so we use the Spynergy `fetchURL` procedure instead of the HTTP package.

fetchURL

The syntax of `fetchURL` is:

```
fetchURL -url   url -outfile filename -timeout secs \
     -initialtimeout secs
```

The only required option is the URL.

The `ed_get_url` procedure integrates the functionality of `spynergy.tcl` that includes the `fetchURL` procedure into the Ed program. Similar to the search utility, a simple dialog box allows you to input any network-accessible URL. The Get URL button calls the `fetchURL` function with the string that you enter in the entry field.

Table A.2 FetchURL options

Option	Function
`-url` *url*	URL to retrieve
`-outfile` *filename*	Place output in named file rather than returning it from this procedure
`-timeout` *secs*	Timeout between I/O buffers before assuming a connection closure (default 5 seconds)
`-initialtimeout` *secs*	Timeout to wait for initial connection establishment and 1st buffer retrieval (default 30 seconds)

ed_get_url

```
proc ed_get_url {} {
    global _ED

    #─────────────────────────────────
    # Destroys any existing Get URL dialog box
    #─────────────────────────────────

    catch "destroy .ed_get_urlf"

    #─────────────────────────────────
    # Creates toplevel and geometry for
    # Get URL form.
    #─────────────────────────────────

    toplevel .ed_get_urlf -background LightGray
    wm withdraw .ed_get_urlf
    wm title .ed_get_urlf {Get URL }

    #─────────────────────────────────
    # Set toplevel name to Parent variable
    #─────────────────────────────────
```

```
set Parent .ed_get_urlf

#───────────────────────────────────────────
# Create a frame to hold the entry widget
#───────────────────────────────────────────

set Name $Parent.f1
frame $Name -background lightgray
pack $Name -anchor nw -fill x -side top -padx 5

#───────────────────────────────────────────
# Create an entry field for the user to
# enter a URL.
#───────────────────────────────────────────

set Name $Parent.f1.e1
entry $Name -background aliceblue \
            -font $_ED(courierfont) \
            -highlightbackground LightGray \
            -selectbackground blue \
            -selectforeground white -width 30
pack $Name -anchor nw -side right

#───────────────────────────────────────────
# Create a list of bindings to let user
# delete text.
#───────────────────────────────────────────

bind .ed_get_urlf.f1.e1 <Delete> {
    if [%W selection present] {
        %W delete sel.first sel.last
    } else {
        %W delete insert
    }
}
```

```
#————————————————————————————
# Bind the Return key to the same commands
# as the Get URL button.
#————————————————————————————

bind .ed_get_urlf.f1.e1 <Return> {
        set url_string [.ed_get_urlf.f1.e1 get]
        ed_edit_clear
        set _ED(package) [fetchURL $url_string]
        .ed_main_frame.f5.f4.f17.t3 insert end\
                              $_ED(package)
        destroy .ed_get_urlf
             }


#————————————————————————————
# Delete any text in the entry field
#————————————————————————————

$Name delete 0 end

#————————————————————————————
# Create a frame that holds the buttons
#————————————————————————————
set Name $Parent.mainwin
frame $Name -background lightgray
pack $Name -anchor nw -side top \
      -fill x -padx 5 -pady 5
```

This code creates the Get URL button. It sets the contents of the entry field to a variable, clears the text widget, calls the fetchURL procedure with the variable, and inserts the results in the text editor. It then destroys the Get URL dialog box.

```
set Name $Parent.mainwin.b1
button $Name  -activebackground lavender \
      -background navy \
      -command {
```

```
            set url_string [.ed_get_urlf.f1.e1 get]
            ed_edit_clear
            set _ED(package) [fetchURL $url_string]
            .ed_main_frame.mainwin.textFrame.left.text \
                    insert end $_ED(package)
            destroy .ed_get_urlf
                    } \
        -foreground white \
        -highlightbackground LightGray \
        -text {Get URL}
pack $Name -anchor nw -side left


#————————————————————————————————
# Creates Cancel button that destroys the
# dialog box.
#————————————————————————————————

set Name $Parent.mainwin.b2
button $Name  -activebackground Lavender \
            -background navy \
            -command {destroy .ed_get_urlf} \
            -foreground white \
            -highlightbackground LightGray \
            -text Cancel
pack $Name -anchor nw -side right


#————————————————————————————————
# Creates the geometry for the Get URL window
#————————————————————————————————
set x [expr [winfo rootx .ed_main_frame] + 300]
set y [expr [winfo rooty .ed_main_frame] + \
            [winfo height .ed_main_frame] - 300]
wm geometry .ed_get_urlf +$x+$y
wm deiconify .ed_get_urlf
```

```
#—————————————————————————————————
# Raises the Get URL window to appear in
# front of the other windows.
#—————————————————————————————————

raise .ed_get_urlf
update
wm minsize \
        .ed_get_urlf [winfo width .ed_get_urlf] \
                [winfo height .ed_get_urlf]
wm maxsize \
        .ed_get_urlf [winfo width .ed_get_urlf] \
                [winfo height .ed_get_urlf]
}
```

Figure A.5 The Get URL dialog box

Utility procedures

There are several housekeeping procedures that are used in most Ed procedures perform simple but necessary tasks.

Any changes made to text in the editing window need to be saved before testing the code or before saving the text to a file. We need a couple of utility routines to clear the text widget and to commit the latest changes to the text before saving or testing the code.

ed_edit_commit

The `ed_edit_commit` procedure copies the contents of the text widget to the `_ED(package)` global variable, which is used for testing and saving code text.

This procedure is called from the procedures that test or save the code.

```
proc ed_edit_commit {} {

    global _ED

    #————————————————————————————————————
    # Wait until all is clear
    #————————————————————————————————————

    ed_wait_if_blocked

    #————————————————————————————————————
    # Set _ED(package) variable to the contents
    # of the text widget.
    #————————————————————————————————————

    set _ED(blockflag) 1
    set _ED(package) \
      "[.ed_main_frame.mainwin.textFrame.left.text \
          get 1.0 end]"
    set _ED(blockflag) 0
    #————————————————————————————————————
    # Update the application
    #————————————————————————————————————

    update
}
```

ed_edit_clear

The ed_edit_clear procedure clears the text widget when the user opens a new file by selecting New from the File menu.

```
proc ed_edit_clear {} {

  global _ED
```

```
#─────────────────────────────────────
# Wait until all is clear
#─────────────────────────────────────

ed_wait_if_blocked

#─────────────────────────────────────
# Clear the temporary buffer. If something
# exists in the text widget, delete it.
# Clear the file buffer.
#─────────────────────────────────────

set _ED(blockflag) 1
set _ED(temppackage) ""
set _ED(blockflag) 0
if {[info commands .ed_main_frame.f5.f1] != ""} {
  .ed_main_frame. mainwin.textFrame.left.text delete 1.0 end
        }
set _ED(package) ""

#─────────────────────────────────────
# Load the new or empty file by calling ed_edit
#─────────────────────────────────────

ed_edit

}
```

ed_status_message

The ed_status_message procedure defines a number of switch-es such as -temp, -show, and -alert. The switches allow for messages to be presented in different fonts, or background or fore-ground color, or wait different time periods and allow for multiple messages.

```
proc ed_status_message {option {message ""}} {
  global _ED
```

```
            set _ED(status) "Now editing file: $_ED(packagekeyname)"

        switch -glob — $option {
                -setperm {
                        set _ED(permstatus) "$message"
                        set _ED(status) "$message"
                }
                -temp {
                        set _ED(status) "$message"
                        if {$_ED(permstatus) != ""} {
                                after 1000 "set _ED(status) \
                                [list $_ED(permstatus)]"
                        }
                }

            -show {
                        set _ED(status) "$message"
                    }
            -help {
                set _ED(status) "$message"
                    }
            -perm {
                        set _ED(status) "$_ED(permstatus)"
                }
             -alert {
                        bell; bell
                        set _ED(status) "$message"
                        catch "$_ED(status_widget) configure \
                                    -foreground white"
                        catch "$_ED(status_widget) configure \
                                    -background red"
                        update
                        after 2000
                        catch "$_ED(status_widget) configure \
                                    -foreground green"
```

```
                catch "$_ED(status_widget) configure \
                        -background black"
                if {$_ED(permstatus) != ""} {
                    set _ED(status) "$_ED(permstatus)"
                }
                update
        }
        default {ed_status_message -temp "$message"}
    }
}
```

ed_wait_if_blocked

This procedure is used in many of the Ed procedures. It sets the
_ED(blockflag) variable to 0 and waits up to 20 seconds until
all processes that are running are complete.

```
proc ed_wait_if_blocked {} {
    global _ED

    set i 0
    while {$_ED(blockflag)} {
        incr i

        #————————————————————————————————————
        # Allow a maximum of 20 seconds of blockage
        #————————————————————————————————————
        if {$i > 20} {
            set _ED(blockflag) 0
        return
        }

        after 500
    }
}
```

ed_error

The procedure ed_error displays an error by using the tk_dia-log command.

```
proc ed_error {message} {
        bell
        bell

    #————————————————————————————————
    # After 100 milliseconds
    #————————————————————————————————

    after 100 {
        grab -global .xxx
    }
        tk_dialog .xxx "Weblet Developer    \
            - Alert" "$message" warning 0 Close

    #————————————————————————————————
    # Release the window
    #————————————————————————————————

    grab release .xxx
}
```

ed_stop_gui

The ed_stop_gui procedure simply checks to see if any block-ing operations are going on, such as a file being written, and then issues the exit command if the coast is clear. This command is called when the user selects Exit from the File menu.

The exit command is a standard Tcl command.

```
proc ed_stop_gui {} {
    ed_wait_if_blocked
        exit
}
```

Initialize the code

Now we need to start it all up. The code below isn't contained within a procedure, unlike all of the other code that falls within various procedure definitions. The code below will execute immediately when the application runs.

To start it all up:

- Declare the inline image data.
- Determine if the user has a release of Tcl and Tk that will support the application.
- Declare the initial values of global variables
- Destroy the application if it is already running
- Source the spynergy.tcl file to give the Editor access to the fetchURL command.
- Call ed_start_gui.

Step 1: Declare image data

You can include BASE64 image data for each of the icons on the buttons. We describe how to work with image data in Chapter 5. To include the data in the source code, you simply set the string of data to a variable. We have used these variables in the procedures to create the buttons of this application: New, Open, Save, Copy, Cut, Paste, Search, Test, Stop.

These are the data for the New button.

```
set new {

R0lGOD1hEAAQAPcAAAAAAMbGxv/////////////////////////////////////
///////////////////////////////////////////////////////////////
///////////////////////////////////////////////////////////////
///////////////////////////////////////////////////////////////
///////////////////////////////////////////////////////////////
///////////////////////////////////////////////////////////////
///////////////////////////////////////////////////////////////
///////////////////////////////////////////////////////////////
///////////////////////////////////////////////////////////////
///////////////////////////////////////////////////////////////
///////////////////////////////////////////////////////////////
///////////////////////////////////////////////////////////////
///////////////////////////////////////////////////////////////
///////////////////////////////////////////////////////////////
```

```
/////////////////////////////////////////////////////////////////
////////////////////////////////////////yH5BAEAAAIALAAAAAAQABAAAAhJAAMI
HEiwIEEACBMiNCgQwL+HEBcadAjxoUMAEytaTFiQokaLHT9GDCnyH8aDJU2SFHlyoMe
PLRumjBngpUaaCnNKZMizJ8+AAAA7
```

```
}
```

You can convert GIF images to BASE64 image data with the image conversion tool included on the CD.

Step 2: Determine Tcl and Tk version compatibility

We need to make sure that the user has a current release of Tcl and Tk. Although most of the program uses plain-vanilla Tcl, some key features that we've added towards the end of this appendix, such as the slave interpreter code, require at least Tcl version 7.6 and Tk version 4.2.

The `tcl_version` and `tk_version` variables provide an easy way to check what versions of Tcl and Tk interpreters are being used to run the program.

First we set up two global variables to hold the returned value from the commands:

```
global tcl_version  tk_version
```

Next we test for the version numbers using two `if` statements, and issue an error if either the Tcl or Tk version is not new enough to run our program.

```
if {[info exists tcl_version] == 0 || \
            $tcl_version < 7.6} {
    error "Error — Tcl Editor:\
        This program requires Tcl 7.6\
        or higher"
}


if {[info exists tk_version] == 0 || \
        $tk_version < 4.2} {
    error "Error–– Tcl Editor:\
```

```
                     This program requires Tk 4.2 or higher"
}
```

Step 3: Set global variables

We set up and initialize the various global variables that are referenced by the Ed procedures.

```
#————————————————————————————————————
# Clears previous global variables
#————————————————————————————————————

    foreach globalvar [info globals *ED*] {
    global $globalvar
    catch "unset $globalvar" dummy
}
foreach globalvar [info globals *ed*] {
    global $globalvar
    catch "unset $globalvar" dummy
}


#————————————————————————————————————
# Initialize session global variables
#————————————————————————————————————

set _ED(menuCount) 0;
set _ED(pwd) [pwd]
set _ED(editcursor) ""
set _ED(editcurold) ""
set _ED(srch_old) ""
set _ED(srch_new) ""
set _ED(file) ""
set _ED(runslave) ""
set _ED(package) ""
set _ED(temppackage) ""
```

```
        set _ED(packagekeyname) ""
        set _ED(status) "Now editing file: $_ED(file)"
        set _ED(permstatus) "Now editing file: $_ED(file)"
        set _ED(blockflag) 0


#————————————————————————————————————————————
# If the operating system is Windows,
# set a windows font.
#————————————————————————————————————————————
if {$tcl_platform(platform) == "windows"} {
        set _ED(courierfont) \
            {{Courier New} 11 {normal}}
    } else {
        set _ED(courierfont) \
        "-*-Helvetica-Medium-R-Normal—12-*-*-*-*-*-*-*"
    }
```

Step 4: Destroy the application if it is already running

This simple command insures that there will not be copies of the Ed editor window.

```
catch "destroy .ed_main_frame"
```

Step 5: Source spynergy.tcl

The Tcl command source simply takes the contents of the file specified by its argument and makes it available, or integrates it, with the current code. If the file is not in the same directory as the source of the application, then you can specify the complete path-name to the file.

This command assumes that the spynergy.tcl file is in the same directory as ed.tcl.

```
source spynergy.tcl
```

Table A.3 Summary of procedures of Ed.tcl

Procedure	Function	Pg #
`ed_start_gui`	Creates the GUI of the main application	494
`ed_edit`	Creates text box and loads a file	509
`ed_edit_cut`	Cuts selected text	515
`ed_edit_copy`	Copies selected text	516
`ed_edit_paste`	Paste selected text	517
`ed_edit_searchf`	Creates the search dialog box	519
`ed_edit_search`	Searches the text box with a string entered in the search dialog	525
`ed_edit_commit`	Saves the text into a variable for testing or saving to a file	569
`ed_edit_clear`	Clears the text box of all text	570
`ed_file_load`	Opens a file, calls `ed_loadsave`	528
`ed_file_save`	Saves a file, calls `ed_loadsave`	531
`ed_loadsave`	Creates the GUI to open or save files	534
`ed_loadsaveselbegin`	Selects an object from the directory list	544
`ed_loadsaveselbegin2`	Sets the selected object to a variable	545
`ed_loadsaveselend`	Prepares the variables	545
`ed_loadsavegetentries`	Displays the contents of a directory	546
`ed_loadsavevalentry`	Evaluates the selected file	530
`ed_loadsavemergepaths`	Merges the directory and filename into one path	554
`ed_run_package`	Creates a slave interpreter and test the code in the text box	557
`ed_kill_apps`	Destroys all applications through the slave interpreter	560
`ed_stop_button`	Changes the Test button to the Stop button	562
`ed_test_button`	Changes the Stop button to the Test button	562
`ed_get_url`	Invokes Spynergy FetchURL to retrieve a file over the Internet	560
`ed_status_message`	Displays a status message in the status field	571
`ed_wait_if_blocked`	Waits and sets the block flag to 0	573
`ed_error`	Displays an error	574
`gui_error`	Displays an error when opening or saving a file	556

Step 6: Call ed_start_gui

This procedure creates the GUI, as we saw at the beginning of this appendix. No other procedures are explicitly called, but they automatically initiate each other in sequence.

```
ed_start_gui
```

This command completes the Ed Tcl editor. The full source code can be found on the CD; the file is named `ed.tcl`.

You can use this program for many of your Tcl programming tasks. Feel free to enhance this code to add any new features that you might think of. Some useful enhancements might include an integrated debug console for the code testing tool.

B

About the Spynergy Web Developer

The Spynergy Toolkit gives you the resources to create advanced applications such as the ones presented in this book. Developed by Eòlas Technologies and freely available, the Spynergy Toolkit makes it easy to create Internet applications that interact with remote servers and databases.

Also available from Eòlas Technologies is the Spynergy Web Developer, a companion to the Spynergy Toolkit. The Spynergy Web Developer is a sophisticated rapid application development (RAD) environment featuring a drag-and-drop GUIbuilder and automatic code generator. Since it is based upon Tcl/Tk, using the Spynergy Web Developer is easier than other similar tools such as those based on Java, OLE (ActiveX), CORBA, and OpenDoc. It includes built-in composite widgets such as the WebRouser widget, as well as support for all standard Tk widgets. You can even build and store your own library of composite widgets that you can drag and drop into your own applications.

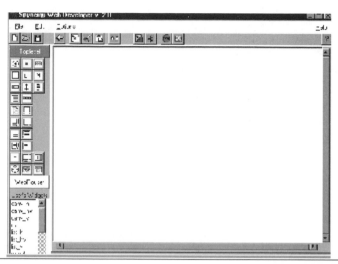

Figure B.1 The Spynergy Web Developer interface

Using the Spynergy Web Developer

Build a Tcl/Tk applets quickly: Just click on the Toplevel button to create a toplevel, and then drag and drop widgets. Each widget that you create has its own menu, from which you can configure the color, relief, and size of the widgets, and add associated commands.

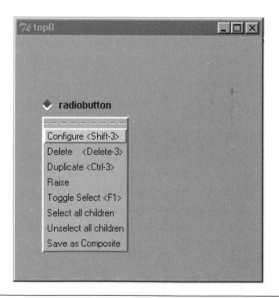

Figure B.2 A radiobutton widget with a menu

Each Tk widget is available for you to drag and drop onto the toplevel, configurable through drop-down menus. The Web Developer also offers composite widgets, including the WebRouser widget, a fully embeddable Web browser widget.

When you have finished designing your applet, you can generate the complete Tcl/Tk code by simply clicking a button on the button bar.

Figure B.3 Generate Code button

When you click this button, all the code for your applet appears in a powerful text editor. You can then modify and search through your code, or test it by clicking on the Test button. You can build on the applet by dragging and dropping more GUI elements, or by directly editing the Tcl/Tk code in the text editor.

You debug your code efficiently with the Developer's interpretive development environment, informative error messages, and search and replace utility. The Spynergy Web Developer helps you develop your Tcl/Tk applets in less than half the time that it would take you to write code by hand.

Downloading the Spynergy Web Developer

The Spynergy Web Developer is written entirely in Tcl/Tk and runs on Windows, UNIX, and Macintosh platforms. You can download the Spynergy Web Developer for free using the coupon included at the back of this book - an $80 value! Just go to the Eòlas Technologies Web site at `http://www.eolas.com/`. You will find full instructions for downloading and installing the developer onto your computer. The Spynergy Web Developer also includes full reference documentation and a tutorial for developing applets.

PGP and Tcl/Tk Resources

Pretty Good Privacy is available on the Web at the Pretty Good Privacy, Inc Web site at `http://www.pgp.com`, and on the MIT distribution site at `http:///www.mit.edu/network/pgp`. The MIT distribution site only offers freeware versions for noncommercial use.

PGP was originally released as freeware. It is now in use by millions of users worldwide for commercial as well as personal applications. PGP Version 5.0 is available in professional and freeware versions. Version 5.0 provides a graphical user interface that lets you manage your PGP keyrings and integrates with your e-mail programs and your operating system. With the previous version, PGP 2.6.2, you need to use the DOS command prompt to encrypt, sign, and decrypt messages, and manage keys.

PGP offers the most powerful cryptography available in the world. Using PGP is simple. You generate a pair of keys. One key is your public key, which you distribute to others and which people use to encrypt messages to send to you. The other key in your key pair is your private key. This private key is kept only by you. You use it to decrypt messages you receive. You can sign messages with your private key, which other people can verify using your public key. To encrypt a message to someone else, or to verify a digital signature form someone, you need that person's public key. You keep public and secret keyrings, which contain all of your public and private keys. With PGP Version 5.0, you have a graphical interface to manage these keyrings.

PGP is cryptographic software, and therefore is classified by the U.S. State Department as export-controlled "munitions" by the U.S. Department of Commerce. To purchase and download PGP, you must be a US or Canadian citizen, or have permanent alien resident status.

For the most up-to-date information on the features of the current versions of PGP, see the PGP Web site at `http://www.pgp.com` and the MIT distribution site at `http://www.mit.edu/network/pgp`. You can download the freeware version of PGP, Version 5.0 and PGP 2.6.2 for noncommercial use at MIT. For commercial use, you can purchase the professional version of PGP from the PGP Inc Web site for $49.00.

Books about PGP

The Official PGP User's Guide by Phil Zimmermann, MIT Press, 1995, ISBN:0-262-74017-6, 216 pages

PGP: Source Code and Internals by Phil Zimmermann, MIT Press, 1995, ISBN: 0-262-24039-4, 900 pages

PGP: Pretty Good Privacy by Simson Garfinkel, O'Reilly & Associates, 1994, ISBN: 1-56592-098-8

Protect Your Privacy - A Guide for PGP Users by William Stallings. Prentice-Hall, 1994, ISBN 0-13-185596-4

Tcl/Tk resources

Tcl/Tk books

Tcl and the Tk Toolkit by John Ousterhout. Addison-Wesley, 1994. Written by the creator of Tcl/Tk. Provides extensive information about C programming and Tcl extensions

Practical Programming in Tcl and Tk, Second Edition by Brent Welch. Prentice Hall, 1997. An up-to-date and detailed book covering all aspects of the Tcl/Tk language

Graphical Applications with Tcl &Tk by Eric Johnson. M&T Press, 1996. Focus on graphical applications on the Windows operating system

Exploring Expect by Don Libes. O'Reilly & Associates, 1995. Detailed book about a powerful Tcl/Tk extension, Expect, that lets you automate interactive programs

Tcl/Tk Tools by Mark Harrison. O'Reilly & Associates, Inc, 1997. Covers many Tcl/Tk extensions

Effective Tcl/Tk Programming by Micheal Mclennan and Mark Harrison. Addison Wesley, 1997

CGI Developers Resource, Web Programming with Tcl and Perl by John Ivler. Prentice Hall, 1997

On-line resources

Tcl/Tk Frequently-Asked Questions (FAQ): `http://www.ter-aform.com/~/virden/tcl-faq/`

Official Tcl/Tk Contributed Sources Archive: `http://www.NeoSoft.com/tcl/`

Sun Microsystems' Tcl/Tk home page: `http://sunscript.sun.com`

Lucent Technologies' Tcl/Tk home page: `http://www.tcltk.com`

SCO's Tcl/Tk resources page: `http://www.sco.com/Technology/tcl/Tcl.html`

Tcl/Tk Consortium: `http://www.tcltk.com/consortium`

CD Resources

The CD-Rom that accompanies this book includes everything you need to get started building Tcl/Tk applications for the Web. You will find Tcl/Tk for all platforms, Tcl/Tk development tools like the Ed Tcl Code Editor, all the example applications from this book, and Tcl/Tk freeware and extensions. We include an HTML interface to make it easy to find all the resources using your Web browser, with links to Tcl/Tk resources on the Web. The following pages outline these resources in depth.

Accessing the CD Resources

You can access the resources on the CD directly or through the HTML interface that we provide. To go to the main HTML page on the CD, just start your Web browser application and select "Open File" from the File menu. Browse your CD-Rom drive or type in:

```
D:/index.htm
```

where "D" is the letter that represents your CD-Rom drive. This HTML page will direct you to all the resources included on the CD.

589

All the CD resources are also located on the Eòlas Technologies Tcl Web at `http://www.eolas.com/tcl`. This Web site contains updated information and Tcl/Tk resources, as well as all the latest versions of the examples from this book.

Tcl/Tk Distributions

- **Tcl/Tk 8.0**
  This is the version that you should probably use for any development of Tcl/Tk applications, unless you are interested in maintaining the same look and feel for your applications on Windows and UNIX platforms. See the Sun Microsystems' Tcl Web site at `http://sunscript.sun.com` for more information on the differences between Tcl/Tk 8.0 and earlier versions.

- **Tcl 7.6 Tk 4.2, Tcl 7.5 Tk 4.1, Tcl/Tk for DOS version 7.5/4.0**

- **The Spynergy Toolkit**
  Works with any version of Tcl/Tk from 7.5/4.1 through 8.0 and Spynergy Tcl/Tk (an enhanced version of 7.6/4.2). This set of pure-Tcl procedures allows you to easily add powerful capabilities to your Tcl/Tk programs, such as distributed processing, URL retrieval, HTML rendering, database management, and platform-independent file manipulation.

- **The Spynergy Web Browser Plug-in**
  Compatible with Tcl/Tk 7.6/4.2 and supporting PGP-signed Tcl/Tk applets.

Tcl/Tk Development Applications

Ed, the Tcl Editor

Use this Tcl-based editor and code testing environment to write your own Tcl programs and to try out and modify the book's example applications.

Image Conversion Tool

This tool will allow you to easily convert your GIF images to BASE64 text format and copy it to the desktop clipboard, so that you can include the images as inline images in your Tcl 8.0, Tcl Plug-in, or Spynergy Tcl/Tk programs. For Windows systems, you will also need the `gifto64.exe` DOS executable to be in the same directory that you launch the conversion tool's Tcl script from. For UNIX or Mac systems, you can compile your own `gifto64` executable using the C source code.

To use the image conversion tool, run the Tcl program by sourcing it in the Tcl console. Select "Load and Convert File." You can then select a GIF file from your hard drive. The application will convert the file and display the data. You can view the resulting image, and copy the data directly to the window clipboard to paste into your Tcl code programs.

Book Examples

You should check at the Eòlas Technologies Tcl Web site for the latest versions of the software included with this book. You can also download a ZIP file of just the book's example code from this site.

Chapter 3

Tk demo - This demo uses almost all the Tk widgets and shows how widgets can interact. We build this demo step-by-step as a tutorial in Chapter 3.

Chapter 4

Ticker tape - Text moves across a text widget, imitating a ticker tape.

Typewriter - A text widget mimics a typewriter display by printing out a predefined message.

An entry Tcl/Tk typwriter - The typewriter text widget with an entry field for a user to enter any message.

Text slider - Text "slides" across a text widget to form a predefined message.

Nervous text - Each letter of a message moves independently on a canvas widget for "nervous" text.

Bubbles - Oval objects replace the text objects of the nervous text demo to create bubbles.

Canvas slider - Text objects slide across a canvas widget.

Chapter 5

DragText - A canvas widget demo that enables the user to move text objects with the mouse.

Puppy - An interactive animation on the canvas widget.

Drawing ovals - Drawing oval objects on a canvas widget with the mouse button.

Drawing lines - Drawing line objects on a canvas widget with the mouse button.

Embed - Example of embedded objects of a canvas widget.

Wordsearch - A complete wordsearch game written in Tcl/Tk.

Fish - A Tcl/Tk 8.0 canvas animation using BASE64 inline image data. Fish move across the screen and blow bubbles.

Calculator - A Tcl/Tk calculator with keyboard entry.

Crossword - A complete crossword game written in Tcl/Tk.

Notecards - A Tcl/Tk 8.0 Web applet using the Safesock security policy, the Tcl 2.0 Plug-in, and the HTTP package. The application accesses text files across the Internet.

Chapter 6

Sample HTML pages.

Chapter 7

Rolodex: The Tcl personal information database - Demonstrates how to use the Spynergy Toolkit's pure-Tcl Web Fusion database engine to build your own fully functional personal information database application.

Internet Rolodex: A client/server database - Demonstrates how to use the Spynergy Toolkit's remote procedure call (RPC) facility to easily convert the Rolodex application into a client/server system.

Roloclnt - Runs on any client machine and provides access to a centralized Rolodex database running on a remotely networked server.

Roloserv - Runs on an Internet server and allows a remote client to access and manage the Rolodex database.

Chapter 8

A Tcl Web server

Chapter 9

File Push: A true server push system - This system demonstrates how to use the Spynergy Toolkit's RPC facility to create a server - push and server-client application.

PushServ - Runs on an Internet server in the root directory and pushes selected files to specified clients.

PushClnt - Runs on any client machine and accepts files from a specified server.

Chapter 10

Stockticker - This program demonstrates how to build an applet that periodically downloads Web pages for a list of companies from a stock quoting service and then parses those pages to extract the relevant stock information. It then formats the stock quotes into an animated ticker tape for display in the Web page.

Stockticker as an autonomous agent - This demo shows how to turn the Stockticker app into an autonomous agent that examines stock quotes as they come in and automatically sends an e-mail alert if certain stock prices move either higher or lower than predetermined ranges.

Chapter 11

Browser-pull applications - These programs demonstrate how to build Web-based applications that periodically and automatically fetch information from the Web and display it through the Web browser.

Srouser - Rouser combined with Stockticker. Fetches stock quotes every 15 minutes and displays them in a moving ticker tape at the bottom of the browser window. The user can show or hide the ticker display by clicking a button on the button bar.

Wrouser - Rouser with a weather radar display. Pulls down a Doppler radar image for the Midwest U.S. every 15 minutes.

Zrouser - Rouser with an embedded animated imagemap (a zMap). Just click on the globe animation and pull up an associated hot link for that region.

Tcaster - The Tcl online information center. This puts it all together — a Web browser with periodic automatic downloading of weather and stock information, as well as an easy point-and-click interface to news and other information about various regions of the globe.

Rouser: The Tcl-based Web Browser - A versatile Tcl/Tk application that accesses the Web and renders HTML.

Rouser with GUI enhancements.

The Rouser as online help - The Rouser integrated into the Ed Tcl Code Editor application.

Appendix A

Ed, the Tcl code editor - A complete Tcl/Tk code editor and testing environment.

Online Documentation

We provide all the online documentation for the Tcl/Tk language, plus all the reference documentation for the Spynergy Toolkit in HTML. The Spynergy Toolkit reference documentation is also available in a Windows help file.

Tcl-based Freeware Applications

Tcl Tutor - Created by Clif Flynt, this UNIX and Windows application teaches Tcl step-by-step.

Juice - Created by Ioi Lam, this is a pure-Tcl/Tk script debugger.

Sun's Tcl Web server - A very powerful and feature-full pure-Tcl Web server.

SpecTcl - A drag-and-drop GUI builder.

Extensions

IncrTcl - Adds object-oriented capabilities to Tcl/Tk.

Tix - A very popular collection of enhanced widgets.

ODBCTcl and TclODBC - Allows your Tcl programs to transparently access and manage ODBC databases.

OraTcl and SybTcl - Allows Tcl programs to access and manage Oracle and Sybase databases.

Tcl-DP - Provides powerful distributed processing and messaging capabilities to your Tcl scripts.

OpenGL - Uses Tcl to control high-end 3D modeling and rendering applications.

The Visualization Toolkit - A set of Tcl-based tools for 3D data visualization, VRML and volume imaging.

The main HTML page on the CD also includes other Tcl/Tk related links, including FAQs, Tcl/Tk archives, and Tcl/Tk Web sites.

Index

—G—

—H—

—I—

–Z–